TUCKER TRAILS

through

SOUTHSIDE VIRGINIA

Reprint Edition

Soft Cover Print Format

Edited
by
Royal S. Tucker

First Edition
Compiled
by
B. DeRoy Beale

Reprint Edition

Soft Cover Print Format

ISBN: 978-0-9968423-0-3

Library of Congress Control Number: 2015915549

Published by: Royal S. Tucker, LLC
Richmond, Virginia
United States of America

First Edition, Copyright © 1986 by B. DeRoy Beale

Table of Contents

PREFACE to the Reprint Edition

After being out of print for many years, the First Edition of "Tucker Trails through Southside Virginia", compiled by B. DeRoy Beale, is available again in this Reprint Edition. This valuable reference has been a standard for Tucker and early Virginia family research for many years.

In preparing this Reprint Edition, the book has been completely reformatted. The available content source was a .PDF format digital image file of the First Edition book. Working files were produced by scanning the digital file using Optical Character Recognition (OCR) software and then producing a basic text file of the whole book. The individual chapters were separated into chapter files; editing was done while all new formatting was added that replicated the original book. Most of the editing was done using the LibreOffice open source software program.

The OCR software used is accurate, but not totally accurate. Even after concerted efforts to correct inaccuracies, some persistently repeated and difficult to search out errors may not have been corrected; such as: 'h' for 'b', 'an' for 'm', etc.

Very few editing changes have been made in the original content information. Changes in the presentation of the information have been made. The most noticeable presentation change may be in the type font; the Times New Roman font replaces the original typewriter style font. The presentation of tabular content has generally been changed.

The numerous original record citations paraphrase and replicate those original documents, including their spelling and punctuation; spelling or punctuation updates for these citations have generally not been added.

Chapter titles now have the original Tucker Trails chapter number and the name of the subject male descendant. A short chapter discussing the scope of the book and the chapter numbering method has been added.

The TABLE of CONTENTS and the 'lastname, firstname' INDEX were produced by the editing software.

The PREFACE to the First Edition is included in this Reprint Edition. The original contributors acknowledged there, and elsewhere in the First Edition, are again gratefully acknowledged and thanked for their original contributions. I thank them for the re-use of their contributions in the Reprint Edition. Efforts to locate the original cover artist, Frederick M. Powell, or his descendants, have been unsuccessful; special thanks for re-use of the art are hereby offered.

* * *

DeRoy and I first met at a social event in 1985, shortly before he completed the manuscript for the First Edition of Tucker Trails. I had some information about our Tucker line that DeRoy did not have, and some potential interview sources for other information; I gladly shared.

We soon realized that many of the Tucker ancestors being documented in his book were my ancestors. He included all of my family line in the book and concluded that we were distant cousins.

My documented male line is:

Capt. Robert Tucker, Sr. (born about 1677 – died 1750),

Robert Tucker, Jr, (born about 1706 – died 1769.),

William Tucker (born 1733 – died 1806),

Nelson Tucker (born about 1768 – died 1843),

John Tucker (born about 1792 -died after 1860),

William Henry Tucker (born 1839 – died 1920),

John William Tucker (born 1877 – died 1943),

Royal Stevens Tucker (born 1905 – died 1950),

Royal Stevens Tucker, Jr. (born 1938 -)

* * *

DeRoy Beale died in 2007. The rights to the "Tucker Trails through Southside Virginia" original work, the First Edition book, and to the Copyright © for the work, were transferred from his legal heir to Royal S. Tucker by a written agreement in 2014. The transfer was registered with the United States Copyright Office.

Roy Tucker, 2015

BOOK SCOPE and CHAPTER CODING

SCOPE OF THE BOOK

In the PREFACE to the First Edition chapter, as a part of his discussion of a prior Beale family book and research into his Tucker family, DeRoy Beale says that he: "recorded that my grandmother Beale, great-grandmother Beale and great-great-grandmother Beale were all Tucker women".

He then says: "The purpose of this book is to document all the Tucker data resulting from my research. It begins primarily with the Tucker families who patented land in Prince George County, Virginia, early in the 18th century, and traces them through those counties lying south of the Appomattox River, including Prince George, Amelia, Nottoway, Prince Edward, Dinwiddie, Lunenburg, Mecklenburg, Halifax and Pittsylvania Counties.

My approach for this book was to research all patents, grants, parish records, deeds, wills, marriage records, land tax records, tithable records, personal tax records, court orders, and references from other published sources and personal interviews, for all the Tuckers, and to identify each document with the correct Tucker male."

The book scope is discussed again in THE TUCKER NAME chapter with the following: "This book will document the history of one Capt Robert Tucker Sr., (died 1750 in Amelia Co.), and his descendants, as they migrated through the counties of Prince George, Amelia, Nottoway, Prince Edward, Lunenburg, Mecklenburg, Halifax and Pittsylvania Counties. While this compiler was unable to identify, with certainty, the parents and brothers and sisters of the subject Capt Robert Tucker Sr and his wife Martha, my research revealed the Tucker Families to be among the early settlers of the Virginia Colony, particularly in the counties of southside Virginia."

The sorting and analyzing of the numerous Tucker families of the time in the area is done in the chapters EARLY TUCKERS, CHARLES CITY COUNTY TUCKERS, and PRINCE GEORGE COUNTY TUCKERS.

Near the end of PRINCE GEORGE COUNTY TUCKERS, he again outlines the scope of the book as follows: "This book identifies the descendants of Capt Robert Tucker Sr, from about 1700 to 1850, documented with citations from land patents, deeds, wills, marriages, births, tithables, personal tax, and land tax, as they migrated through the Virginia counties of Charles City, Prince George, Amelia, Nottoway, Prince Edward, Lunenburg, Mecklenburg, Halifax and Pittsylvania."

The first of the descendants chapters, <u>TR100000 - CAPT. ROBERT TUCKER SR.</u>, follows <u>PRINCE GEORGE COUNTY TUCKERS</u>.

In the First Edition, these chapters used only the numeric code, described below, as the chapter title. In the Reprint Edition, the name of the subject male descendant is also included in the chapter title.

CHAPTER CODING METHOD

From near the end of the <u>PRINCE GEORGE COUNTY TUCKERS</u> chapter in the First Edition: "The coding pattern for the family chapters consists of two parts:

The first four characters identify the family line of one of the sons of Capt Robert Tucker Sr (who is TR10), from whom all others are descended. (e.g. TG13 = the family line of George Tucker who is third son of Capt Robert Tucker Sr.)

The remaining numbers represent the successive father-son relationship in that family line. (e.g. TG1361 = the 1st son of the 6th son of the 3rd son of Capt Robert Tucker Sr.

Trailing zeros of the 8-digit code are reserved for identification of additional generations, which were not researched beyond 1850, except for some in my own family line."

PREFACE to the First Edition

by B. DeRoy Beale

In my 1978 publication of "The Beale Family of Halifax County, Virginia", I recorded that my grandmother Beale, great-grandmother Beale and great-great-grandmother Beale were all Tucker women. This triple relation to the Tucker family led me to further research my Tucker ancestors, and in the process, some errors in assumptions made in the "Beale" book were revealed.

The purpose of this book is to document all the Tucker data resulting from my research. It begins primarily with the Tucker families who patented land in Prince George County, Virginia early in the 18th century, and traces them through those counties lying south of the Appomattox River, including Prince George, Amelia, Nottoway, Prince Edward, Dinwiddie, Lunenhurg, Mecklenburg, Halifax and Pittsylvania Counties. Unfortunately, only fragmented records remain for the present Prince George and Dinwiddie Counties, and information on the families who lived in these areas is lost. Other researchers, as well as myself, have made erroneous assumptions in trying to establish relations with these early Tucker families.

My approach for this book was to research all patents, grants, parish records, deeds, wills, marriage records, land tax records, tithable records, personal tax records, court orders, and references from other published sources and personal interviews, for all the Tuckers, and to identify each document with the correct Tucker male. Insofar as practical, the data was arranged in chronological order to provide a history of that person. Special notes call attention to given documents which establish a relationship, or an approximate birth, marriage or death date, not otherwise revealed. In many instances, the relationship was established only by tracing the passage of land.

Special appreciation is expressed to the following:

Mrs. Marian Chiarito, from Halifax Co., Va. for her encouragement in the Tucker research, and for her publications of the 1850 census of Halifax Co, Va., and marriage records of Halifax and Pittsylvania Counties in Va.

Mrs. Faye Tuck, formerly from Richmond, Va. and now Halifax Co , Va., who was most helpful in unscrambling the George Tucker Sr. family, from whom she and I are descended, and in providing some of the Tucker data in her line.

Mrs. Mary McCampbell Bell, who provided data on the family lines of James Tucker Jr, Herbert Tucker, Bartlett Tucker and Godfrey Tucker.

Mrs. Martha Tucker Bass who provided descendant charts for the Joseph Tucker line, which were prepared by her aunt Josephine Tucker, former dean of students at Westhampton College. Miss Annie Waller, Miss Nina Waller, Mr. Richard Green Tucker Jr, and Mr. Wayne Tucker who provided information on the James Tucker family of Halifax Co, Va.

Mrs. Berta Yeatts Faust, Mr. Royal Stevens Tucker Jr, and Mr. Thomas Tucker who provided information on the Nelson Tucker family of Pittsylvania Co, Va.

To my commercial artist friend, Frederick M. Powell, who designed the book cover depicting the trails through Virginia revealed in the Tucker Family Tree.

And to my sister Blanche Beale Booker, who was such a good listener during all the years of my research.

Data for this book was keyed and stored onto magnetic diskettes, in a KAYPRO II personal computer, using the PERFECT WRITER word processing program. Working drafts were printed by an OKIDATA 92 dot matrix printer, but the final draft was printed by a BROTHER HR-10 letter quality printer, with a PRESTIGE 1012 daisywheel. The final camera-ready 8.5x11 sheets were then reduced 82% for the 6x9 hook.

REPETITIVE CODES USED

a - acres
ac - acres
adj- adjacent
b - born
bo - bounds
b.s. - both sides
bro - brother
c - others
ca - circa
d - died
dau - daughter
e.s. - east side
fr - from
incr - increase
l.s. - left side
m - married
md - married
n.s. - north side
rec - recorded
s.s. - south side
u.s. - upper side

Co. - County
Cr. - Creek
DB - Deed Book
Ex. - Executor
Exor. - Executor
Extrx. - Executrix
G - Grant
Jr., Jun., Junr. - Junior
L - English Pounds
MB - Marriage Book
OB - Order Book
P - Patent
Ri. - River
Rd. - Road
S/ - Signed
Sr., Sen., Senr. - Senior
WB - Will Book
Wit. - Witness
wd - will dated
wf - wife
wp - will probated

THE TUCKER NAME

The name "TUCKER" is an English occupation name, meaning "one who cleaned and thickened cloth". [1]

A more elaborate description is provided by Reaney. [2] "The weaver is represented by a variety of names: Webb, Webber, Webster, Weaver. The raw cloth had to be fulled, ie., scoured and thickened by beating it in water, a process known as 'walking', because originally done by men trampling upon it in a trough. Hence 'Walker', 'Fuller', and 'Tucker'. 'Tucker' from Old English 'tucian', originally 'to torment', later 'to tuck'." Fuller, Walker and Tucker are identical in meaning found in different parts of the country. 'Fuller' is southern and eastern. The common term in the west and north is 'Walker', corresponding in the south-west, especially in Somerset, to 'Tucker'."

This book will document the history of one Capt Robert Tucker Sr., (died 1750 in Amelia Co.), and his descendants, as they migrated through the counties of Prince George, Amelia, Nottoway, Prince Edward, Lunenburg, Mecklenburg, Halifax and Pittsylvania Counties. While this compiler was unable to identify, with certainty, the parents and brothers and sisters of the subject Capt Robert Tucker Sr and his wife Martha, my research revealed the Tucker Families to be among the early settlers of the Virginia Colony, particularly in the counties of southside Virginia.

* * *

1. Smith, Elsdon C., "New Dictionary of American Family Names", 1956.

2. Reaney, P. H., "The Origin of English Surnames", 1967.

EARLY COUNTIES

In 1634 the Virginia Colony was divided into 7 shires, which were to be governed as shires in England. The designation of shires was soon discontinued and thereafter the sub-divisions were known as counties. The names of the original shires, later counties, were: James City, Henrico, Charles City, Elizabeth City, Warwick River, Warrosquyoake, Charles River and Accowmack.

From Elizabeth City County were formed the counties of Nansemond, Norfolk and Princess Anne.

From Warrosquyoake County were formed the counties of Isle of Wight and Southampton.

From James City County were formed the counties of Surry and Sussex.

Charles City County, at its creation in 1634, included lands on both sides of the James River, on the south side from Upper Chippokes Creek to Appomattox River, and on the north side from Sandy Point to Turkey Island Creek. Charles City County was divided by an act passed in 1702. That part on the north side of the James retained the name of Charles City County. That part on the south side of the James was named Prince George County. [3]

Prince George County was subdivided to form the counties of Brunswick (1732), Amelia (1735) and Dinwiddie (1752). Brunswick County was subdivided to form the counties of Lunenhurg (1746), and Greenville (1781). Lunenhurg County was subdivided to form the counties of Halifax (1752), Bedford (1754), Charlotte (1765) and Mecklenburg (1765). Amelia County was subdivided to form the counties of Prince Edward (1754) and Nottoway (1789). Halifax County was subdivided to form Pittsylvania in 1767.

The Tucker families were among the early settlers of these Southside Virginia counties. Unfortunately, only a few records remain for Charles City, Prince George and Dinwiddie counties, and some have been destroyed for Nottoway and Prince Edward. Generally, records are well preserved for Amelia, Lunenhurg, Mecklenburg, Halifax and Pittsylvania counties.

* * *

3. Bell, Landon Covington, "Old Free State", a history of Lunenhurg County Virginia, William Byrd Press, Inc., Richmond, Va.,, Volume 1, 1927.

EARLY TUCKERS

The Land Patent books housed in the Virginia State Library provide a valuable source of information about early settlements. Early Tucker families who patented land in the Southside Virginia counties included Capt William Tucker, Thomas Tucker and Robert Tucker.

CAPT WILLIAM TUCKER & WIFE FRANCES

P 1-29 20 Sep 1624, Capt William Tucker, Elizabeth City Co, 150 ac, w/i corporation of Elizabeth City west of land of Richard Boulton.

P 1-122, 1 Jun , Capt William Tucker, Elizabeth City Co, 100 ac Back Ri w/i precincts of Elizabeth City.

P 1-231, 14 Jul 1635, Capt William Tucker, (county not shown), 200 ac, n.s. of Westernmost Br of Elizabeth Ri, beg at Allington's Cr.

P 1-410, 9 Feb 1636, William Tucker & others, Charles City Co, 8,000 ac, commonly called "Barckley Hundred".

P 1-864, 6 Jan 1642, William Tucker, Upper Norfolk Co, 250 am, w.s. Southward Br. of Nansumund Ri.

Will of William Tucker, Member of the House of Burgesses from Elizabeth City County 1619-1625 [4], William Tucker of the City of London Esq, now bound for the Kingdom of Ireland. 12 Oct 1642. Proved 17 Feb 1643-44. - names: wife Frances, three children, viz sonne William, sonne Thomas and daughter Mary Tucker, brother Thomas Tucker.

Researchers of Tucker families like to claim descendency from this prominent William Tucker. This compiler makes no claim of any evidence to link any of the other Tucker families in this book with this William Tucker. He is shown here as the first Tucker to patent land in Virginia.

THOMAS TUCKER

P 9-228, 26 Oct 1699, Thomas Tucker, Norfolk Co, 640 ac, w.s. Southern Br of Elizabeth Ri, n.s. Deep Cr.

NOTE: This Thomas Tucker may have been the son of Capt William Tucker, but this compiler has no information to suggest this relationship.

ROBERT TUCKER

P 6-242, 22 Apr 1669, Robert Tucker, (location not given) 100 ac. on western br of Elizabeth Ri. adj land of the widdow Jennings & Jno Elliott &c. Transp. 2 persons: Richard Murfee & Nath. Dibble.

P 7-424, 21 Oct 1684, <u>Robert Tucker</u>, Lower Norfolk Co, 50 ac n.e. side of main run of Deep Cr. beg at Old Slough's & young Slough's cor. Trans. of Walter Drove.

P 10-453, 11 Dec 1719, <u>Robert Tucker</u>, Norfolk Co, 81 ac in Norfolk Co, & 3 lots of 1/2 ac in Town of Norfolk. Escheat land formerly belonging to Rosamund Tabor of about 100 ac, upon a survey found to contain but 81 ac.

P 18-99, 12 Sep 1738, <u>Robert Tucker</u>, Norfolk Co, 1 1/2 ac. escheat land near Norfolk Town btwn Edward Portlock & John Munds decd.

P 23-921, 10 Jul 1745, <u>Robert Tucker</u>, Norfolk Co, 3 ac, 60 sq. po., in Borough of Norfolk, adj his lott where he now liveth.

NOTE: The above Robert Tucker is probably not the same Robert Tucker who patented land in Charles City Co in 1680. No relation is determined or implied by this compiler. See next chapter.

Under the headright system, many other colonists were imported, and the person paying the transportation cost was granted 50 acres of land for each person imported (known as a headright). Other Tuckers, who came to the southern counties of the colony as headrights, included the following: [5]

1635	Alex. Tucker	Warrasquioake Co.
1638	Allen Tucker	Charles City Co.
1639	Barthol. Tucker	Upper Norfolk Co.
1649	Alice Tucker	James City Co.
1650	William Tucker	Charles City Co.
1666	William Tucker	Isle of Wight Co.
1673	Eliz. Tucker	Isle of Wight Co.
1680	John Tucker	Charles City Co.
1683	John Tucker	Charles City Co.
1688	Samll Tucker	Lower Norfolk Co.
1688	Tho. Tucker	Isle of Wight Co.

These colonists may or may not have settled in the same area as the person who paid their transportation, and they were not further researched by this compiler.

* * *

4. Virginia Historical Magazine, Vol. 22, pg 267.

5. Nugent, Nell Marion, "Cavaliers and Pioneers", Vol I, 1934, Vol II, 1937.

CHARLES CITY COUNTY TUCKERS

ROBERT TUCKER & WIFE ELIZABETH

NOTE: A close but undefined relationship existed between Robert and Francis Tucker and the Coleman families.

PATENTS [6]

P 5-166, 18 Mar 1662. John Coleman, Chas. City Co, 813 ac, s.s. Appomattox Ri adj Mr. Tounstall.

P 5-519, 20 Oct 1665, Robert Coleman Jr., Chas. City Co, 450 ac, s.s. Appomatox Ri, beg at Robert Coleman Sr's head line.

P 6-181, 25 Sep 1667, Robert Coleman, Isle of Wight Co, 634 ac, beg Cyprus Br.

P 6-189, 29 Oct 1668, Robert Coleman Sr, Chas. City Co, 283 ac, s.s. Appamattox Ri, btwn Henry Leadbeater & sd Coleman, thence to head line of the Island patent.

P 8-422, 21 Apr 1695, Robert Coleman, Isle of Wight Co, 80 ac, in lower marsh adj Thomas Jordan & Giles Driver.

P 9-109, 28 Oct 1697, Robert Coleman, Nansemond Co, 450 ac. near Wickham swamp, adj Thomas & John Milner.

P 7-29, 20 Apr 1680, Robert Tucker, Charles City Co, 172 ac, n.s. Blackwater, adj Wm. Jones, Jordan's path, Edward Bircherd, the Reedy Br, Baynes' path & c. Transp 4 persons. Jno Tucker, 3 times, Sar. Twill.

NOTE: if Robert Tucker was at least age 21 when he patented land in 1680, then he was b before 1659.

Patent (Nugent p 303), 30 Oct 1686, Mr. Edward Birchett, Chas. City Co., 230 ac. in Bristol Parish on n.s. Main Blackwater, adj. Mr. Robert Tucker. Transp 5 persons.

NOTE: The above land became Prince George Co. in 1703.

CHARLES CITY CO, VA [7]

p 180, 18 Dec 1688. John, orphan of Robert Coleman, chooses his brother Robert Coleman, his guardian.

NOTE: Robert Coleman (Sr.) d 1688, leaving son Robert Coleman (Jr.) & minor son John Coleman.

p 180, 18 Dec 1688. Robert Coleman granted administration of Warner Coleman's estate.

NOTE: Warner Coleman d 1688. Was he also a son of Robert Coleman Sr?

p 181, 18 Dec 1688. If witnesses to <u>Robert Coleman</u>'s will do not appear at next court to prove same, they will be fined.

p 202, 3 Apr 1689, Administration granted Hon. Wm. Byrd, Esq, on est of <u>Jno. Coleman decd</u>, the widow assenting. Mr. Jno Mays, Ja. Hall & Edward Birchett to inventory est. Capt. Hen. Batte & Mr. Robert Bolling to swear them.

NOTE: John Coleman d 1689. Was he a brother of Robert Coleman Sr? Notice the name Edward Birchett, who owned land adj to Robert Tucker on n.s. the Blackwater (Patent 7-29)

p 242, 16 Sep 1689. Administration granted <u>Fra. Tucker</u> on estate of <u>Warner Coleman</u>, dec'd; and Jarvis Dix and <u>Francis Coleman</u> give bond.

NOTE: Francis Tucker replaced Robert Coleman (Jr) as admr of Warner Coleman. Was Francis Tucker a son-in-law of Robert Coleman Sr? Was Francis Coleman also a son of Robert Coleman Sr?

p 242, 16 Sep 1689. Ordered that estate of <u>Warner and John Coleman, dec'd</u> be delivered to <u>Francis Tucker, Adm'r., of Warner Coleman</u>. <u>Robert Coleman</u>, who is possessed with those estates, submits to this order in court.

p 242, 16 Sep 1689. Estate of <u>Robert Coleman</u> in hands of <u>Robert Tucker</u> to be inventoried and Capt. Henry Batte to assign and swear appraisers and take secuity for delivery of legacies.

NOTE: Was Robert Tucker a son-in-law of Robert Coleman Sr?

p 426, 3 Oct 1692. Judgement granted <u>Robert Tucker agst Francis Tucker</u> for 1717 lbs tobacco.

P - 482, 1693. Persons assigned court surveyors of the highways - included Mr James Thewat & Mr. <u>Robert Tucker</u> for Apamatox.

p 555, 4 Feb 1694. Deed of land by <u>Robert Coleman</u> and <u>Robert Tucker and Elizabeth his wife</u>, by her attorney Richard Bland, to Francis Hobson is proved by John Heath and Solomon Crook.

NOTE: Was Elizabeth Tucker a dau of Robert Coleman Sr? And did Robert Coleman (Jr) & Robert Tucker (in right of his wife Elizabeth) sell land inherited from Robert Coleman Sr?

p 555, 4 Feb 1694. Lease of 50 acres of land by Abraham Coulston to Daniel Sandburne ano 1675 and a lease of same 50 acres by said Sandburne to <u>Robert Tucker</u> ano 1676 and both endorsed with assignment of <u>Robert Tucker and Elizabeth his wife</u> to John Butler, and acknowledged by Tucker and his wife by Richard Bland her attorney, and recorded.

6

NOTE: The above item is most confusing, in that the transactions which occurred in 1675-76 were not recorded until 18 years later in 1694. If the dates are correct, then that Robert Tucker would have been born before 1655, and would have married Elizabeth before 1675. See Patent 7-29, 1680.

NOTE: While there is no direct evidence, this compiler believes the records above suggest that Robert Tucker's wife Elizabeth, and Francis Tucker's wife (later identified as Mary) were each a Coleman. There are no salvaged records for Charles City Co. and Prince George Co for the period 1695-1712. No will was found for Robert Tucker, but he may have died before 1704, for Elizabeth Tucker held 212 ac in the Prince George Quit Rents of 1704. [8]

JOHN TUCKER

CHARLES CITY CO, VA [9]

NOTE: Notice in Robert Tucker's Patent 7-29, 1680, cited above, that Robert Tucker transported John Tucker three times. No patents were found for this John Tucker.

p 571, 3 Jun 1695. John Tucker of Martins Brandon Parish, exhibits a certificate from the vestry of his inability to labor and is discharged from parish levy and is discharged from county and public levy's.

PRINCE GEORGE CO, VA. 1713-1728 [10]

p 133, 18 Aug 1716, rec 13 Nov 1716, will of John Tucker of Martins Brandon Parish, Pr. Geo. Co., names: widow Ann Jackson, executor, God-dau Elizabeth Jackson, Mary Thornhill, Thomas Daniell, James Cragg, William Smith, widow Blayton. Wit: Thomas Daniel, Eliza. x Jackson.

NOTE: John Tucker d 1716, apparently without issue.

FRANCIS TUCKER

NOTE: See section on Robert Tucker above for transactions involving both Robert Tucker and Francis Tucker in Charles City Co.

PATENTS [11]

P 10-339, 15 Jul 1717, Francis Tucker, Pr Geo Co, 289 ac, b.s. Mawhipponock Cr, adj Herbert's land.

p 663, 12 Dec 1722, rec 10 Dec 1723, <u>will of Francis Tucker</u>
names: <u>wife Mary</u>;
son <u>Francis</u> - land e.s. Mawhipponoak Cr at lower end;
son <u>John</u> - land on n.s. same cr adj Henry Mayes;
son <u>Henry</u> - land btwn sons Francis & John, incl plantation where I live;
son <u>Abram</u> - land on n.s Mawhipponoak Cr adj son Henry & Thomas Mitchell;
son <u>Mathew</u>, land adj Thomas Mitchell
Wit: Mathew Mayes, Henry Mayes, John Powell.

NOTE: Francis Tucker did not patent any land in the original Charles City Co. The 289 ac which he patented in Prince George Co. in 1717, and willed to his sons in 1723, lay in the area which became Dinwiddie Co. in 1752.

NOTE: Research revealed that the descendants of Francis Tucker perpetuated the given names Francis, John, Henry, Abram & Mathew. This contrasts significantly with the descendants of Robert Tucker who perpetuated the given names Robert, James, George, John, William, Joseph & Daniel. Except for the name John, each family rarely used the given names of the other . They seemed to have become completely separate family lines. This compiler researched the Francis Tucker line primarily to distinguish between the several John Tuckers in both family lines. Research material on the Francis Tucker family line is not included in this book, so that it can be kept within a reasonable number of pages. Apparently the Francis Tucker line has already been researched by others, as evidenced by a group of family charts made available to me.

NOTE: Salvaged Prince George Co. records include land surveys and other references for the next generation of Tuckers.

* * *

6. Card File of Land Patents and Grants, Virginia State Library Archives.

7. Weisiger, Benjamin B. III, "Charles City County, Virginia Court Orders 1687-1695", reprinted 1984.

8. Boddie, John B., "Historical Southern Families", Vol 5.

9. Weisiger, Benjamin B. III, "Charles City County, Virginia Court Orders 1687-1695", reprinted 1984.

10. Weisiger, Benjamin B. III, "Prince George County, Virginia Wills & Deeds 1713-1728", 1973.

11. Card File of Land Patents and Grants, Virginia State Library Archives.

12. Weisiger, Benjamin B. III, "Prince George County, Virginia Wills & Deeds 1713-1728", 1973.

PRINCE GEORGE COUNTY TUCKERS

As pointed out in a previous chapter, that part of Charles City County which lay south of the James River became Prince George County in 1703. Generally it encompassed the area south of the James and Appomattox Rivers, and in a southwestward direction to the North Carolina border. From Prince George were formed the counties of Brunswick (1732), Amelia (1735) and Dinwiddie (1752).

Most of Prince George County records were destroyed during the civil war. There are no records for this area from 1696-1712. Salvaged Deed and Will Books 1713-1728 and some court records 1733-1792 have been extracted by Weisiger, and are cited throughout this book.

These salvaged records include lists of land surveys made by surveyor Robert Bolling during the period 1710-1725, and many other references to Tucker Families, including Francis, John, Matthew, Robert, William, Joseph, Daniel, and James Tucker.

Research information for Francis Tucker identified his sons John and Matthew (above), and Francis, Henry and Abram. (See previous chapter). The Francis Tucker family is not included in the remainder of this book.

Robert, William, Joseph and Daniel Tucker were probably brothers and may have been sons of the Robert Tucker & wf Elizabeth (?Coleman) of Charles City Co, cited in the previous chapter. See citations following.

WILLIAM TUCKER

PATENTS [13]

P 10-446, 11 Jul 1719, William Tucker, Pr Geo Co, 143 ac, n.s. Stony Cr.

P 11-337, 20 Feb 1723, William Tucker, Pr Geo Co, 300 ac, b.s. Turkey Egg Cr, n.s. Nottoway Ri.

P 12-508, 7 Jul 1726, William Tucker, Brunswick Co, 361 ac, sm br of Cocke Cr, n.s. Roanoke Ri.

P 14-19, 28 Sep 1730, William Tucker, Pr Geo Co, 200 ac, l.s. Beaverpond Cr, adj Matthew Sturdivant & Robert Wynne.

PRINCE GEORGE CO, VA. [14]

p 749, Survey, 20 May 1712, William Tucker, 100 ac, w.s. Numosseen Cr.

NOTE: If this William Tucker was at least age 21 when he surveyed land in 1712, then he was b before 1691. However, no patent was found for this 100 ac.

p 753, Survey, 20 Oct 1715, William Tucker, 143 ac, n.s. Stony Cr. (See Patent 10-446)

p 818, Survey, 1 Feb 1724, William Tucker, 200 ac, l.s. Beaver Pond Cr, adj his own land. (See Patent 14-19)

p 745, 13 Oct 1724, William Tucker & wf Elizabeth to William Mallone, son of Nathaniel Mallone of Surry Co, 143 ac on n.s. Stony Cr in Pr Geo Co. Wit: George Hamilton Jr, Michael Wallis, Litt. Hardyman. (See Patent 10-446)

NOTE: Notice that William Tucker's wife was also named Elizabeth.

p 994, 13 Oct 1726, rec 13 Jun 1727. Francis Bressie of Pr Geo Co to William Tucker of Elizabeth City Co, for L10, 200 ac on Stony Cr, Pr Geo, being part of a tract granted to Francis Bressie by patent in 1726. Bo. by sd Tucker, John Manson, Henry Maynard, Chamberlains Bedd, Stony Cr. Wit: William Tucker, William Bressie, Randolph Snowden, Ellyson Armistead, Thomas Smith.

NOTE: Could this William Tucker, 1726 of Elizabeth City Co, be a descendant of the Capt. William Tucker who patented land 100 years earlier, 1624-35 in Elizabeth City Co? Notice also that another William Tucker witnessed this deed.

BRISTOL PARISH VESTRY BOOK [15]

The Bristol Parish Vestry Book includes an entry pertaining to the continuing relationship between the Coleman and Tucker families:

17 Sep 1721. Upon the petition of Wm. Tucker sheweth that Robt Coleman lys at his house in a very weak helpless condition & has been so these six months past, which grows very changeable & troubelesome to the sd Tucker. Tis ord that Wm. Tucker take care of the foresd Robt Coleman & find him such necessaries as is convenient and at the next levie, the sd Tucker to bring his account to the vestry & what is thought just to be allowed from the parish. Tis further ordered that the church wardens enquire how the foresd Robt Coleman gave his estate to Robert Tucker Senr & upon what terms.

BRISTOL PARISH REGISTER [16]

Susanna dau of Wm & Eliz:Tucker born 19th of April 1721 bap 14th feb 1722-3.

Geo S: of Wm & Eliz: Tucker born 4th Septr 1723 bapt 11th octobr 1724.

Daniel Son of William and Eliza Tucker born 29th Janr 1725.

The land which William Tucker surveyed, patented and bought in Pr Geo Co, lay in the area which became Dinwiddie Co in 1752, and no further information on this family was available to this compiler.

SUMMARY: This William Tucker, b before 1691, m before 1721, Elizabeth ____, & had issue:

Susanna Tucker b 19 Apr 1721.

George Tucker b 4 Sep 1723.

Daniel Tucker b 29 Jan 1725.

JOSEPH TUCKER

PATENTS [17]

P-10-402, 14 Jul 1718, Joseph Tucker 403 ac, Pr Geo Co, b.s. Stony Cr.

P 11-117, 22 Jun 1722, Joseph Tucker, 180 ac, Pr Geo Co, head of Reedy Br of Sappone Cr, adj. Geo Tillman, Harry's Swamp.

NOTE: Notice also that Robert Tucker owned land in 1719 adj John Tillman, on Monks Neck Cr.

P 13-462, 28 Sep 1730, Joseph Tucker 150 ac, Pr Geo Co, s.s. Stony Cr, adj his old land.

P 14-23, 28 Sep 1730, Joseph Tucker, 302 ac, Pr Geo Co, l.s. Beaverpond Cr, adj Robt Wynn. (Note: See comment below)

P 18-679, 10 Jun 1740, Joseph Tucker, 739 ac, Pr Geo Co, l.s. Beaverpond .Br, ____ Ri, adj & including his old (?line).

P 19-687, 10 Jun 1740, Joseph Tucker, 400 ac, Pr Geo Co, l.s. Reedy Br of Stony Cr.

P 26-426, 5 Apr 1748, Joseph Tucker, 138 ac, Pr Geo Co, head of Mirey Br of Beaverpond Cr, adj Peter Thomas & Jackson's lines.

P 31-622, 10 Sep 1755, Joseph Tucker & Stephen Evans, Dinwiddie Co, 430 ac, n.s. Sapone Cr.

P 22-457, 20 Aug 1745, Joseph Tucker Jr, 286 ac, Pr Geo Co, u.s. Plat Br of Stony Cr.

NOTE: If Joseph Tucker Jr was at least age 21 when he patented land in 1745, then he was b before 1724.

P 22-538, 20 Sep 1745, Joseph Tucker Jr, 400 ac, Pr Geo Co, btn Stony & Sappone Cr, adj Richd Harrison, Joseph Tucker & c.

P 33-232, 16 Aug 1756, Joseph Tucker Jr, 46 ac, Pr Geo Co, n.s. Stony Cr, adj Melone, Wingfield

PRINCE GEORGE CO, VA. [18]

p 16, 17 Jun 1714, rec 13 Jul 1714. Indenture btwn John Coleman & Robert Munford, for 10 ac in Bristol Parish, Pr Geo Co, next to Coleman & Munford on the river, for 1400 lbs tobacco & 10 shillings. Wit: Charles Roberts, Joseph Tucker

p 750, Survey, 19 Hay 1712, Joseph Tucker, 100 ac, w.s. Numisseen Cr, adj above survey (of William Coleman Sr.)

NOTE: If Joseph Tucker was at least age 21 when he surveyed land in 1712, then he was b before 1691. However, no patent was found for this 100 ac. p 752, Survey, 20 Oct 1715, Joseph Tucker, 403 ac, b.s. Stony Cr. (See Patent 10-402)

NOTE: Also on p 752, Survey, 20 Oct 1715, Joseph Wynne, 153 ac, b.s. Stony Cr. See comment below.

p 756, Survey, 24 Nov 1719, Joseph Tucker, 180 ac, on head of Reedy Br of Sapponee. (See Patent 11-117)

BRISTOL PARISH REGISTER [19]

Robt son of Joss: & Martha Tucker born 3d of Octobr Last bapt May 28th 1721.

David Son of Joseph and Martha Tucker Born 24th Dcember 1729 Bapt 31th May 1730.

Lucretia D of Joseph & Lucretia Tucker Born 15th august 1731 Bapt 10th octber.

Mary D. of Joseph & Lucretia Tuckers born Aprile 3d & hapd May 26th 1745.

NOTE: Boddie [20] states that "Joseph Tucker, son of Robert & Martha, was b about 1710 -- married Lucretia, daughter of Maj Robert Wynne -- , & names children born beginning in 1731 --", This cannot be correct, since Joseph son of Robert & Martha was not born until 22 Jun 1722. (See chapter for Capt Robert Tucker Sr) The Joseph Tucker who m Lucretia Wynne was most probably the subject Joseph Tucker who was b before 1691, who surveyed land in 1712, & who patented land 1730 adj Robert Wynn (Patent 14-23). Also, Boddie's account of the children of Joseph & Lucretia was inconsistent with the Bristol Parish Register.

NOTE: The lands which Joseph Tucker and Joseph Tucker Jr surveyed and patented in Pr Geo Co, lay in the area which became Dinwiddie Co in 1752, and no further information on this family was available to this compiler.

SUMMARY: Joseph Tucker, b before 1691, m 1st before 1720 Martha ____, m 2nd before 17.31 Lucretia ____ & had issue:

Tucker Jr b before 1724.

David Tucker b 24 Dec 1729.

Lucretia Tucker b 15 Aug 1Robert Tucker b 3 Oct 1720.

Joseph 731.

Mary Tucker b 3 Apr 1745.

DANIEL TUCKER

PRINCE GEORGE CO, VA. [21]

p 761, Survey, 18 Dec 1722 Daniel Tucker, 129 ac, w.s. Reedy Br. Sapponnee. (See Patent 12-229)

NOTE: If this Daniel Tucker was at least age 21 when he surveyed land in 1722, then he was b before 1701.

PATENTS [22]

P 12-229, 22 Feb 1724, Daniel Tucker, Pr Geo Co, 129 ac, u.s. Reedy Br btwn his brother Jos. Tucker & Maj Robert Munford.

NOTE: This is another indication that Daniel and Joseph Tucker were brothers.

BRISTOL PARISH REGISTER [23]

Nevil Son of Daniel & Eliza Tucker Born 25th aprill 1730.

PRINCE GEORGE CO., VA.[24]

p 384, 12 Feb 1739, Will of Daniel Tucker exhibited in court by Elizabeth Tucker , his relict & executrix. Will was proved by oaths of Joseph Tucker, William Tucker, & Robert Whitehall, witnesses, and probate granted.

NOTE: The above is further indication that Daniel, Joseph and William Tucker were brothers, and probably sons of the earlier Robert Tucker & wf Elizabeth (?Coleman) of Charles City Co. Furthermore, Capt Robert Tucker Sr was also probably their brother, because he named his last three sons William, Joseph and Daniel. (See next chapter).

The land which Daniel Tucker surveyed and patented in Prince George Co lay in the area which became Dinwiddie Co in 1752, and no further information was available to this compiler.

SUMMARY: Daniel Tucker b before 1701, d 1739 Pr Geo Co, m before 1730 Elizabeth ____, & had issue:

Nevil Tucker b 25 Apr 1730.

ROBERT TUCKER

As stated earlier in this chapter, this compiler has a conviction that William Tucker, Joseph Tucker, Daniel Tucker and Robert Tucker of Prince George Co, were probably brothers, and probably sons of an earlier Robert Tucker & wife Elizabeth (?Coleman) of Charles City Co (circa 1676). There is ample evidence that the Tucker and Coleman families migrated together, owned adjacent lands, and participated together in legal matters.

BRISTOL PARISH VESTRY BOOK [25]

The Bristol Parish Vestry Book includes an entry pertaining to the relationship between the Coleman and Tucker families:

17 Sep 1721. Upon the petition of <u>Wm. Tucker</u> sheweth that <u>Robt Coleman</u> lys at his house in a very weak helpless condition & has been so these six months past, which grows very changeable & troublesome to the sd Tucker. Tis ord that <u>Wm. Tucker</u> take care of the foresd <u>Robt Coleman</u> & find him such necessaries as is convenient and at the laying of the next levie, the sd Tucker to bring his account to the vestry & what is thought just to be allowed from the parish. Tis further ord that the church wardens enquire how the foresd <u>Robt Coleman gave his estate to Robt Tucker Senr</u> & upon what terms.

NOTE; The above Robert Tucker Sr seems to be the same Capt Robert Tucker Sr who d Amelia Co, 1750, but different from the Robert Tucker named in Charles City Co. Court Order p 242, 16 Sep 1689 (32 years earlier) in which a Robert Coleman's estate was in hands of a Robert Tucker.

There is evidence that the subject Robert Tucker owned land on s.s. Appomattox Ri in Prince George Co before 1714.

PRINCE GEORGE CO, VA, [26]

p 43, 7 Feb 1714/15 Deed. Matthew Anderson Jr of Bristol Parish, Pr Geo Co, to Robert Munford of same, 100 ac, <u>next to</u> Math Mayse, John Mayse, "Haycocks", <u>Robert Tucker</u>, Capt John Coleman, & sd Munford, formerly belonging to William Byrd, Esq.

p 44, 8 Feb 1714/15. Mathew Anderson Jr of Bristol Parish, Pr Geo Co, to Robert Munford of same, 100 ac, bo Mathew Mayse, John Mayse, sd Mundford's land "Haycocks", <u>Robert Tinker (Tucker?)</u> & Capt John Coleman, & sd Munford's land which formerly belonged to Wm Byrd, Esq, & John Mayse.

NOTE: If this Robert Tucker was at least age 21, when he owned land in 1714, then he was b before 1693.

p 160, 14 May 1717, <u>Robert Tucker</u> of Bristol Parish, Pr Geo Co, to

David Crawley of same, <u>200 ac</u>, bo Appomattox Ri, Maj Robert Bolling, John Coleman, Maj Robert Munford.

NOTE: Since no patent was found, it can be assumed that Robert Tucker either bought the above 200 ac. or inherited it. See previous chapter for a discussion of an earlier Robert Tucker & wf Elizabeth (circa 1676), and patents of Robert Coleman & John Coleman on s.s. Appomattox Ri in Charles City Co.

NOTE: There is evidence also that the subject Robert Tucker owned land in the area of Monks Neck Cr (spelled variously) in Pr Geo Co, and that he was closely associated with the Parham and Tillman families.

p 364, 12 Oct 1719, rec 13 Oct 1719. <u>John Tillman</u> of Pr Geo Co to Richard Cooke of York Co, 100 ac on <u>n.s. Monksneck Cr</u> on mouth of Russell Br, on <u>Robert Tucker's line</u>.

NOTE: Since no patent was found for Robert Tucker's land on Monks Neck Cr, it is assumed he either bought or inherited it. It lay in the area of Pr Geo Co which became Dinwiddie Co in 1752. An old map of Dinwiddie Co. in the Archives of Virginia State Library, shows Monks Neck Rd going east from Dinwiddie Courthouse (roughly present county road 605), and crossing Monks Neck Cr, flowing south (now the northernmost part of Rowanty Cr).

NOTE: Early patents include: Roger Tilman, Patent 7-107, 20 Apr 1689, Charles City Co, 1,060 ac, s.s. Appomattox Ri, at a place known as <u>Moncus-a-Neak</u>. Also Thomas Parham & Henry King, Patent 8-76, 21 Apr 1690, Charles City Co, 824 ac, at or near <u>Moncosaneak</u>, beg land of <u>late Roger Tyllman</u> on the side of the great branch. Roger Tillman probably was b long before 1668, & d before 1690. Thomas Parham probably was b before 1669.

p 144, 19 Nov 1716, rec 12 Mar 1716 (?1717). <u>Will of Susannah Tillman</u>, aged 69. To <u>son Thomas Parram</u>, son George Tillman, son John Tillman, dau Jane Robinson, dau Christian Abernathy, grandau Mary Bethell all miscellaneous items. To grandson Robert Abernathy - all remainder of est & to be exor.

NOTE: Susannah ____ was b ca 1647, m 1st after 1663 (after age 16), ____ Parham, & had issue Thomas Parham, b before 1669. Susannah m 2nd after 1669 Roger Tillman (d ca 1690) & had issue George, John, Jane, & Christian Tillman. George Tillman, who surveyed land Mar 1711, probably was b btwn 1670-1690.

p 168, 5 Feb 1716, rec 14 May 1717. <u>Will of Thomas Parram</u>. To Nicholas Robyson - 100 ac <u>btwn Monck's Neck & Cattail Run</u>, which did formerly belong to George Tillman, & after to William Hulm. To John Tillman - 50 ac on <u>n.s. Monks Neck Cr</u>. To my son Thomas Parram - several items. To son William Parram - plantation I now live on, 100 ac. To dau Amy Jones - a cow. To <u>dau Eliza.Tucker</u> - cow & steer. To dau Feebe several items. To dau Susannah - cow & calf. To dau Jane - cow & calf. To loving <u>wife Eliza</u> - all remainder of est & to be exec. Wit. Geo. Tillman, Robert Abernathy, John Patteson. Brought in by Elizabeth Parram, exec.

NOTE: Thomas Parham (b before 1669, d 1716/17) was son of Susannah Parham Tillman (1647-1717) whose first husband was Parham, and whose second husband was Roger Tillman. Thomas Parham's half brothers & sisters were George Tillman, John Tillman, Jane Robinson, and Christian Abernathy. Thomas Parham md Elizabeth ____, and they had issue: Thomas Parham, William Parham, Amy Jones, <u>Elizabeth Tucker</u>, & Feebe, Susannah & Jane Parham. These references suggest also that Thomas Parham's dau Elizabeth Tucker may have been the wife of Robert Tucker who owned land near Tillman and Parham on Monks Neck Creek.

Boddie [27] suggests that the earlier Robert Tucker d before 1704, was m to Elizabeth Parham dau of Thomas Parham, and they were the parents of Robert Tucker who m Martha, and settled in Amelia Co.

The earlier Robert Tucker, whose wife was Elizabeth as early as 1676, was b probably before 1655. If Elizabeth was at least age 15 when m to Robert Tucker in 1676, she probably was b before 1660, and would have been at least age 56 in 1716 when Thomas Parham died. She would have been older than Thomas Parham, and could not have been his daughter. Thus the earlier Elizabeth Tucker wife of Robert Tucker was not the same Elizabeth Tucker dau of Thomas Parham.

If Thomas Parham was b before 1669, and m before 1690, then his dau Elizabeth was b probably before 1691, & m ____ Tucker before 1707, and would have been at least age 25 in 1716 when her father died. All these dates could be earlier.

If Susannah Tillman was age 69 when she wrote her will in 1716, she was b ca 1647. If Susannah m Parham after age 16 in 1663, then her son Thomas Parham was b after 1663 and before 1669, was m after 1684. Therefore Thomas Parham's dau Elizabeth Tucker was b after 1684, m after 1700, and could not be the same "Elizabeth wf of Robert Tucker" shown in Charles City Co. reference p 555 in 1676-1694.

The subject Robert Tucker was b before 1693 (perhaps as early as 1676), and may have been the son of the earlier Robert Tucker who was b before 1655 & who was m to Elizabeth (?Coleman). Elizabeth Parham may have m the subject Robert Tucker, but she would have been very young, for the subject Robert Tucker is known to have had a son James b ca 1698.

It should be remembered from previous discussions, however, that (1) William Tucker's, wife was also named Elizabeth as early as 1721, and they had a dau named Susannah, and (2) Daniel Tucker's wife was also named Elizabeth, and they had a son as early as 1730. So - did Thomas Parham's dau Elizabeth Tucker marry Robert Tucker, or William Tucker, or Daniel Tucker? The incomplete salvaged records of Prince George Co do not provide the answers.

This compiler suggests that the earlier Robert Tucker (ca 1655-1704) m Elizabeth (?Coleman), and their sons were Robert, William, Joseph & Daniel. Their son the subject Robert Tucker (ca 1676-1750) m 1st ca 1698 Elizabeth Parham (ca 1684-1719), and m 2nd before 1720, Martha ____. I should like to suggest further that this subject Robert Tucker was the same Capt Robert Tucker Sr who d 1750 in Amelia Co, who is the subject of the next chapter, and who was the ancestor of the Tuckers in the remaining chapters of this book.

The coding pattern for the remaining chapters consists of two parts. The first four characters identify the family line of one of the sons of Capt Robert Tucker Sr (who is TR10), from whom all others are descended. (e.g. TG13 = the family line of George Tucker who is third son of Capt Robert Tucker Sr.) The remaining numbers represent the successive father-son relationship in that family line. (e.g. TG1361 = the 1st son of the 6th son of the 3rd son of Capt Robert Tucker Sr. Trailing zeros of the 8-digit code are reserved for identification of additional generations, which were not researched beyond 1850, except for some in my own family line.

This book identifies the descendants of Capt Robert Tucker Sr, from about 1700 to 1850, documented with citations from land patents, deeds, wills, marriages, births, tithables, personal tax, and land tax, as they migrated through the Virginia counties of Charles City, Prince George, Amelia, Nottoway, Prince Edward, Lunenburg, Mecklenburg, Halifax and Pittsylvania.

* * *

13. Card File of Land Patents and Grants, Virginia State Library Archives.

14 Weisiger, Benjamin B., III, "Prince George County, Virginia, Wills &

Deeds 1713-1728", 1973.

15. Bristol Parish Vestry Book, Virginia State Library.

16. Boddie, John B., "Births 1720-1792 from the Bristol Parish Register of Henrico, Prince George and Dinwiddie".

17. Card File of Land Patents and Grants, Virginia State Library Archives.

18. Weisiger, Benjamin B., III, "Prince George County, Virginia, Wills & Deeds 1713-1728", 1973.

19. Boddie, John B., "Births 1720-1792 from the Bristol Parish Register of Henrico, Prince George and Dinwiddie".

20. Boddie, John B., "Historical Southern Families", Vol 5, p 296.

21. Weisiger, Benjamin B., III, "Prince George County, Virginia, Wills & Deeds 1713-1728", 1973.

22. Card File of Land Patents and Grants, Virginia State Library Archives.

23. Boddie, John B., "Births 1720-1792 from the Bristol Parish Register of Henrico, Prince George and Dinwiddie".

24. Weisiger, Benjamin B., III, "Prince George County, Virginia Records 1733-1792", 1975.25. Bristol Parish Vestry Book, Virginia State Library.

26. Weisiger, Benjamin B., III, "Prince George County, Virginia, Wills & Deeds 1713-1728", 1973.

27. Boddie, John B., "Historical Southern Families", Vol 5, p 296.

TR100000 - CAPT. ROBERT TUCKER SR

MD MARTHA
POSSIBLY SON OF ROBERT TUCKER
MD ELIZABETH (?COLEMAN)

In the previous chapter, this compiler made several conjectures about the subject Capt Robert Tucker Sr:

(1) that he probably was the son of an earlier Robert Tucker of Charles City Co who may have m Elizabeth Coleman.

(2) that his brothers probably were William Tucker, Joseph Tucker and Daniel Tucker.

(3) that he probably m 1st before 1698 Elizabeth Parham, dau of Thomas Parham & wf Elizabeth, and m 2nd before 1720 Martha. The incomplete records of Charles City and Prince George Counties do not provide complete answers.

This chapter includes the more complete and documented information about Capt Robert Tucker Sr, recorded in Amelia Co which was formed from Prince George Co in 1735.

NOTE: Boddie [1] conjectured that Robert Tucker's wife Martha may have been an 'Epes', based upon the adjoining lands of Robert Tucker and Col. Francis Eppes. But Robert Tucker had many other adjacent neighbors, including Wm. Coleman Sr., Thomas Clay, John Coleman, David Crawley, Maj. Robt Bolling, Maj. Robt Munford, Drury Bolling, as indicated in surveys, patents and deeds.

PRINCE GEORGE CO. VA. [2]

NOTE: Refer to previous chapter for evidence that Robert Tucker owned and sold land on Appomattox Ri., and owned land on Monks Neck Cr., in the part of Pr Geo Co. which became Dinwidie Co. The following transactions involve land in the part of Pr Geo Co. which became Amelia Co.

p 750, Survey, 8 May 1712, Robert Tucker, Pr. Geo. Co., 141 ac. w.s. Numiseen Cr. (See Patent 10-340)

p 753, Survey, 7 Dec 1715, Thomas Clay, Pr. Geo. Co., 223 ac. on w.s. Tuckers Br, of Numisseen Cr.

p 756, Survey, 19 Dec 1719, Capt. Drury Bolling, on w.s. of Tuckers Br, on u.s. of Mims Cr., 972 ac.

p 756, Survey, 9 Feb 1720, Robert Tucker, Pr. Geo Co., 331 ac, l.s. Wintocomake Cr. (See Patent 13-270, & Amelia Co DB 1-341, & DB 1-344) p 762, Survey, 19 Mar 1722, <u>Robert Tucker</u>, Pr. Geo. Co. <u>200 ac</u>. u.s. Middle Cr. on s.s. Appomattox Ri. (See Patent-13-271, & Amelia Co DB 1-343).

p 319, Survey, 19 Mar 1724, Col. Francis Epes, Pr. Geo. Co., <u>750 ac.</u> on s.s. Appomattox Ri, on l.s. of Winticomoke Cr. (See Patent, Nugent p 295)

p 834, Deed, 8 May 1725, rec. 10 Aug 1725, John Coleman & wf Mary of Pr. Geo. Co. to Robert Munford of same, <u>208 ac.</u> in Bristol Par. on s.s. of Appamattox Ri, now or late in the tenure of John Coleman, bo. by Robert Munford, the Ridge Bottom; <u>12 ac. was deeded to Coleman by Robert Tucker 3 Mar 1701</u>. The residue thereof is part of a tract gr. to Robert Coleman decd, father of John Coleman by patent 9 Sep 1668. S/ John Coleman, Mary x Coleman. Wit: Charles Roberts, John Mayes, Isham Epes.

p 843, Will, 10 Sep 1725, Pr. Geo. Co. Inv. of Daniel Magee by John (I) Tally, adm'r. <u>Appr.</u> by: William x Coleman, <u>Robert Tucker</u>, John Curdle, L10.12.9.

Will p 935, 16 Jun 1726, Rec. 8 Nov 1726, Pr. Geo. Co. <u>Will of Thomas Clay</u>, names: Son Charles - land my brother Richard Munny now lives on & Indian slave, items; Son James - land & plantation I live on, - land adj. Edw. Broadway & items; <u>Son John</u> - my entry of 250 ac. on s.s. of Deep Cr. "Wolf Pitt Point", L10. at his coming of age, various items, & what Maj. Munford owes me; Dau. Dorothy Clay - items & L5. credit at Col. Bolling's store. Daus. Phebe & Hannah, L30. each; To all children, remainder of est. equally divided; To John Fitzgerrald, my son John Clay until he is 21 during Fitzgerrald's life.(?); Son Charles - 2 shares of crop growing on my plantation, the rest to son James; My brother Henry Clay to be sole executor. <u>Wit</u>: James Powell, <u>Robert Tucker</u>, John Cordle. S/ Thomas (C) Clay.

NOTE: Robert Tucker was a witness, in 1726, to the will of Thomas Clay, whose son John Clay and Sarah Tucker, dau of Robert Tucker. See Amelia Co. WB 1-63 and WB 1-73, in 1750, and WB 3-201 in 1782 below.

p 1016, Inventory of John Tucker, Value L27.16.1/2, by John (I) Tally, Adm'r, Appraised by John Cordle, <u>Robert Tucker</u>, William (WC) Coleman. Recorded 13 Jun 1727.

PATENTS [3]

Patent 10-340, 15 Jul 1717, <u>Robert Tucker</u>, Pr. Geo. Co., <u>141 ac</u>. w.s. Namusend Cr. & w.s. Gr. Br.

NOTE: No disposition was found for the 141 ac. He may have sold it or given it to his oldest son before 1735, e.i., before this area became Amelia Co.

Patent 13-270, 13 Oct 1727, Robert Tucker, Pr. Geo. Co., 331 ac. l.s. Wintocomatck Cr. (See Amelia Co. DB 1-341 71-7 1PT-1-344)

Patent 13-271, 13 Oct 1727, Robert Tucker, Pr. Geo. Co., 200 ac, u.s. Middle Cr., s.s. Appomattox. (See Amelia Co. DB 1-343).

Patent 23-775, 30 Aug 1744, Robert Tucker, Amelia Co., 176 ac. fork of Tucker's Br. of Namazeen Cr.

NOTE: See Amelia Co. WB 1-63 in which Robert Tucker willed the above 176 ac to his wf for life then to son Daniel. See also Amelia DB 10-67 for sale by Daniel Tucker.

OTHER PATENTS [4]

Patent p 236, 22 Jun 1722, Drury Bolling Gent, NL Pr. Geo. Co., 972 ac. s.s. Tucker's Br. of Nummiseen Cr. adj. Robert Tucker & Thomas Clay, L5.

Patent p 270, 9 Jul 1724, William Coleman Sr, NL Pr. Geo Co., 154 ac. on s.s. Nummisseen Cr. adj. his own land of Thos. Clay, next to Robert Tucker. 15 Sh.

Patent p 295, 24 Mar 1725, Pr. Geo. Co., Col. Francis Epes Gent of Henrico Co, 759 ac. NL beg. Richard Chambers cor. to Robert Tucker's line down Winticomick. L3.14.

Patent p 359, 27 Sep 1729, Richard Cook, Pr. Geo. Co. 350 ac. OL & NL n.s. Moccosoneck Cr. whereon he lives, beg. Russell's Br. div, sd Cooke & Robert Tucker on James Pittillo's line to John Tillman. 25 Sh.

Patent p 406, 25 Aug 1731, John Eggleston, Pr. Geo. Co., 222 ac. lapsed Land on u.s. Nummisseen Cr., adj Thomas Clay's land whereon he lives, Tally's path, Coldwater run, Drury Bollings, down Robert Tucker's br., Cow br. Gr. to Allin Howard 5 Sep 1723 who conveyed to Joseph Turner, who failed to seat. Gr. to Jos. Eggleston who assigned to his son sd John. 25 Sh.

Patent p 419, 28 Sep 1732, Robert Munns of Pr. Geo. Co. 47 ac NL on Tucker's Br. of Nummissheen Cr., on b.s. Deep Cr. Rd. bet. Chas. Clay & Robert Tucker.

AMELIA CO. VA.

1735 Amelia Co. was formed from Pr. Geo. Co., west of Numisseen Cr.

DB 1-341. 10 Oct 1741, rec. 16 Oct 1741. Robert Tucker Sr to John Tucker for L100 - 165 1/2 ac. l.s. Wintocomake Cr. bo. in pt. by sd John Tucker's spring br. & the rd to John Tucker's sp. br. Wit: John Powell, Robert Coleman & Robert Tucker Jr. (See Patent 13-270).

DB 1-343, 10 Oct 1741, rec 16 Oct 1741, Robert Tucker Sr to George Tucker for L70. - 200 ac. s.s. Appomattox Ri. & on u.s. Middle Cr. Wit: John Powell, Robert Coleman & Robert Tucker Jr. (See Patent 13-271),

DB 1-344, 10 Oct 1741, rec 16 Oct 1741, Robert Tucker Sr to Robert Tucker Jr for L100. - 165 1/2 ac. l.s. Wintocomake Cr., bo. in pt. by the Gr. Br. against the Great Beaver Pond, the road & John Tucker's spring Br. Wit: John Powell, Robert Coleman & John Tucker. (See Patent 13-270).

NOTE: The above three simultaneous deeds indicate that Robert Tucker Sr was father to John Tucker, George Tucker and Robert Tucker Jr. Other evidence follows. They probably were sons by a 1st wf, who probably was Elizabeth Parham, dau of Thomas Parham.

WB 1-72, 19 May 1746. James Clarke, Est. I&A, further Est. 6 Jun 1746. Apprs: Robert x Tucker Sr, Robert Causens, Robert x Tucker Jr. Adm. Hugh Miller.

LIST OF TITHABLES

1736	4	Capt Robert Tucker, William Tucker	Joe, Lacy
1737	4	Robt Tucker, William Tucker	Joe, Sarah
1738	4	Robert Tucker, William Tucker	Joe, Sarah
1739	4	Robert Tucker Snr, Joseph Tucker	Joe, Sarah
1740	4	Capt Robert Tucker, Joseph	Jo. Surry
1741	5	Capt Robert Tucker, Jos. Tucker, Daniel Tucker	Joseph, Sarah
1743	5	Robt Tucker Sen, Joseph Tucker, Daniel Tucker, ___	Sarah
1744	3	Robt Tucker Sen, Danl Tucker	Joe
1747	2	Robt Tucker Sen	Joe
1749	1	Robt Tucker Snr	Joe

(See WB 1-63, 1750, Robert Tucker).

From the above tithe records we see that our subject was referred to variously as Robert Tucker, Capt Robert Tucker and Robert Tucker Sen. In order to distinguish him from other Robert Tuckers in this book, he will be addressed as Capt Robert Tucker Sr. Note also that other sons of Capt Robert Tucker Sr were William Tucker, Joseph Tucker and Daniel Tucker.

WB 1-63, d 26 Sep 1744, p 13 May 1750, will of Robert Tucker.
Wit: John Cordle Jr, Henry x Hasten, John Powell.
Exr. son Robert.
Wife Martha - land & plant. where I live for life, then to son Daniel.
Son Joseph.
Dau. Sarah Clay.
Son Robert.
Rest of personal est to be equally div btwn my children.
No appraisement to be made. Slaves: Negro man Joe to wife then to Joseph. Negro man Dick to wife then to Daniel. Negro girl Sal.

WB 1-73, 15 Mar 1750. Capt, Robert Tucker Est. Inv. ret by Exr. Robert (R) Tucker. Mentions certain furniture at John Clay's. (John Clay md Sarah Tucker, dau. of Capt. Robert Tucker Sr.)

Capt Robert Tucker Sr did not name all his children in his will, but named only one daughter Sarah Clay and three sons Robert, Daniel and Joseph. However there is evidence that he also had a daughter Anne and sons James, George, John, and William.

BRISTOL PARISH REGISTER [5]

Anne, dau: of Robt & Martha Tucker born Aug 29 last, bapt Octobr 9th 1720.

Joseph son of Robt & Martha Tucker born 22th June last bapt 15th April 1723. (i.e. b 22 Jun 1722)

Dan: of Robt & Martha Tucker born Janr last bapt Nay 10th 1725.

COMPILER'S COMMENTS

By DB 1-341, DB 1-343 and DB 1-344 above, Robert Tucker Sr simultaneously deeded land to John Tucker, George Tucker and Robert Tucker Jr on 10 Oct 1741, so we can conclude they are his sons. Since he had already deeded land to them, there was no need to include them in his will, but he did name son Robert as executor. Although Martha was the wife of Robert (Sr) as early as 1720, and was named in his will, she probably was not the mother of. Robert Jr, John and George. They most probably were sons by their father's 1st wf, who most probably was Elizabeth Parham.

Robert Tucker Jr, in 1731 (Patent 14-341) had already patented 400 ac., adj. land whereon he lives, at which time he must have been at least age 21. And since he and his wf Frances recorded the birth of their daughter Martha in the Bristol Parish Register in 1727, he must have been age 21 at that time and must have been born by 1706. (See chapter on Robert Tucker Jr.)

John Tucker, in 1735 (Patent 16-67) had already patented 200 ac., at which time he must have been age 21, and must have been born by 1714. (See chapter on John Tucker Sr.)

George Tucker & 1st wf Frances recorded in the Bristol Parish Register the birth of a dau. Ilanna in 1731, at which time he must have been age 21, and must have been born by 1710. (See chapter on George Tucker Sr.)

Now consider the following land patents:

> P 14-341, 17 Sep 1731, <u>Robert Tucker Jr</u> patented 400 ac. on l.s. Wintocomaick Cr. adj. back line & land whereon he lives.

> P 16-67, 26 Jul 1735, <u>John Tucker</u> patented 200 ac. on l.s. Winkomaick Cr..

> P 18-389, 22 Sep 1739, <u>James Tucker</u> patented 400 ac. l.s. Wintocomaick Cr. "between his brothers Robert and John Tucker's lines".

Since James is brother to Robert and John, he is also son of Capt Robert Tucker Sr. This conclusion is supported also by DB 8-250 and DB 8-253, both dated 20 Dec 1763, in which <u>James Tucker and Robert Tucker</u> exchanged 15 ac. on n.s. and 12 ac. on s.s. of the Main Sampson's Br. (See chapter on James Tucker Sr.)

James Tucker, in 1719, had already surveyed 450 ac., which was later patented in 1723 (Patent 11-203). James must have been age 21 at time of survey and must have been born ca 1698. Martha probably was not his mother. James also most probably was a son by his father's 1st marriage to probably Elizabeth Parham.

If James was born ca 1698, his father Capt. Robert Tucker Sr must have been at least age 21 in 1698, and most probably was born ca 1677 in Charles City Co. Va.

The Amelia Co. Tithables List shows <u>William Tucker</u> as a tithable in the household of Capt. Robert Tucker from 1736-1738, so it is concluded that he also is a son of Capt Robert Tucker Sr., born before 1720. This conclusion is supported by DB 10-51, 16 Jul 1768 in which <u>John Tucker Sen sold 200 ac. to "his brother William Tucker"</u>. It is uncertain if Martha was his mother, but she probably was. (See chapter on William Tucker Sr.)

Sarah Tucker, named as daughter Sarah Clay in the will of her father Robert Tucker, married John Clay, son of Thomas Clay. See will of Thomas Clay in Pr. George Co., cited above, and the following will of John Clay Sr recorded in Amelia Co.

WB 3-201, 12 Oct 1782, date recorded not shown, will of <u>John Clay Sr.</u>

son John Clay, Junior - that land which he sold to David Crawley, 150 ac. joining my own land on Deep Cr.; also all the slaves, stock & furniture already given; plus 5 pounds.

dau. Amy Clements - the 2 slaves, cattle & furniture which I some years ago gave to her; plus 10 pounds.

wife Sarah Clay - land & plantation where I now live 250 ac. joining land which my son John has agreed to sell to David Crawley, for life; plus slaves George, James, Sen, Belt, Rachel, Miles, Pegg, Moll, Jesse & Essie; upon death - all my land, slaves, stocks, furniture & other estate to daughters Sarah, Martha, Dorothy & Phebe.

Ex: my friends Peter Jones & Thos Griffin.

Wit: John Taylor, Peter Lambkin Junr, ___ Peachy.

NOTE: Sarah Tucker who married John Clay (Sr) was the mother of Ama Clay, who married William Clemons. William & Ama Clemons' daughter Elizabeth Clemons married Joel Tucker Sr, son of George Tucker Sr who was son of Capt. Robert Tucker Sr. See Chapter on Joel Tucker Sr who md Elizabeth Clemons. William & Ama Clemons' daughter Dolly Clemons married Robert Gabriel Tucker, son of Robert Tucker (the 1st) who was son of George Tucker Sr, who was son of Capt Robert Tucker Sr. See chapter on Robert Gabriel Tucker who md Dolly Clemons.

SUMMARY: Capt. Robert Tucker Sr b ca 1677 probably in Charles City Co., Va., probably md 1st ca 1698 in Charles City Co, probably Elizabeth Parham, dau of Thomas Parham, was married to Martha before 1720 until 1750, surveyed and patented land in Prince George Co. (later. Amelia) as early as 1712, died 1750 in Amelia Co. Va. and had issue:

James Tucker, b ca 1698, md 1st Mary, md 2nd Elizabeth.

Robert Tucker Jr, b ca 1706, md Frances Coleman.

George Tucker, b ca 1710, md 1st Frances, md 2nd Catharine.

John Tucker, b ca 1712, md Sarah Old.

William Tucker b before 1720, md Ann.

Ann Tucker b 1720.

Joseph Tucker b 1722, md Prudence.

Daniel Tucker b 1725, md Elizabeth.

Sarah Tucker, b before 1728, md before 1744 John Clay, d after 1732.

It is significant also that each of the sons became known as Sr, when he became father to a son of the same name known as Jr. Specifically, after Capt Robert Tucker Sr died, his son Robert Tucker Jr designated himself as Robert Tucker Sr, and he fathered a son who became known as Robert Tucker Jr.

See separate chapter for each son.

* * *

1. Boddie, John B., "Historical Southern Families", Vol II, p 259.

2. Weisiger, Benjamin B., III, "Prince George County, Virginia Wills & Deeds 1713-1728" 1973.

3. Card File of Land Patents and Grants, Virginia State Library Archives.

4. Nugent, "Cavaliers & Pioneers (Abstracts of Virginia Land Patents & Grants)", Volume III 1695-1732.

5. Boddie, John B., "Births 1720-1792 From The Bristol Parish Register of Henrico, Prince George and Dinwiddie".

TJ110000 - JAMES TUCKER SR
(THE ELDER)
MD 1ST MARY
MD 2ND ELIZABETH
SON OF CAPT ROBERT TUCKER SR
MD MARTHA

James Tucker Sr (the Elder) is believed to be the oldest son of Capt. Robert Tucker Sr of Pr. Geo. & Amelia Counties, although he is not mentioned in his father's will (WB 1-63, 1750). Other older sons of Capt Robert Tucker Sr not mentioned in his will include George Tucker, John Tucker and William Tucker. Capt Robert Tucker Sr made simultaneous deeds in Amelia Co. to Robert Tucker Jr, George Tucker and John Tucker (DB 1-341,43,44, 1741). It seems apparent that Robert Jr, George and John are brothers and sons of Capt. Robert Tucker Sr. James Tucker is shown to be the brother of Robert and John (Patent 18-389, 1739). John & Robert are shown to be brothers in John's will (Amelia Co. WB 2X-304, 1768). John & William are shown to be brothers in Amelia Co. DB 10-51, 1768. William is shown to he the son of Capt Robert Tucker Sr, as a 16-yr-up tithable in his father's household 1736-38. Capt Robert Tucker Sr may have married twice, and James, Robert Jr, George, John and William may have been sons by his first wife prior to 1720. The Bristol Parish Register records the births to Robert and Martha Tucker beginning in 1720, of dau. Anne 1720, son Joseph 1722 and son Dan (Daniel) 1723. Martha may he the second wife of Capt Robert Tucker Sr, however there is no evidence to support this theory. Named in his will are wife Martha, sons Robert, Joseph and Daniel, and another daughter Sarah Clay.

James Tucker lived in the area of Pr. Geo. Co. which became Dinwiddie Co., and moved to Lunenburg Co., in the area which became Mecklenburg Co. He patented Land in Amelia Co., but gave it to his son James, and did not move there himself. His brother George who lived in Amelia Co, also moved to Lunenburg Co. Both brothers John and William also bought and sold land in Lunenburg Co., but continued to live in Amelia Co.

James Tucker Sr was at least age 21 when he surveyed land in Pr. Geo. Co. in 1719. James Tucker Sr was b probably ca 1598 and married Mary probably ca 1719. His son James Tucker Jr was at least age 21 when he was listed as a separate household tithable in Amelia Co. in 1740, and was born probably ca 1719. The births of three other children of James and Mary Tucker were reported in the Bristol Parish Register between 1721 and 1732. Mary was named as his wife in deeds through 1760. In 1768 deeds, and in his will written in 1770, James Tucker Sr's wife was named as Elizabeth.

THE BRISTOL PARISH REGISTER [1]

Micael son of James & Mary Tucker born llth July 1721 bap 17th October 1722.

Lucretia d. (dau.) of James & Mary Tucker born 5th June 1729.

Warner son of James & Mary Tucker born 15th April 1732 bapt 1st Jun 1732.

PRINCE GEORGE CO. VA.

Survey, 20 Nov 1719, James Tucker, Pr. Geo. Co., 450 ac. l.s. Numisseen Cr. (See Patent 11-203. This area became part of Dinwiddie Co. in 1752).

Patent 11-203, 5 Sep 1723, James Tucker, Pr. Geo. Co. 450 ac. l.s. Numisseen Cr adj, John Ellington,, John Tucker, etal. (See Survey above.) (This area became part of Dinwiddie Co. in 1752).

Patent 13-531, 28 Sep 1730, James Tucker, Pr. Geo. Co., 300 ac. u.s. Wintocomaick Cr. (This area became part of Amelia Co. in 1735. See Amelia Co. DB 3-529)

1735. Amelia Co. was formed from the area of Pr. Geo. Co. on the west side (or upper side) of Numiseen Cr.

1752. Dinwiddie Co. was formed from the area of Pr. Geo. Co. on the east side (or lower side) of Numiseen Cr.

Nothing more is known of the land which James Tucker Sr patented in the area of Pr. Geo. Co. which became Dinwiddie Co., since only fragmented records remain for these counties.

AMELIA CO. VA.

Patent 18-389, 22 Sep 1739, James Tucker, Amelia Co., 400 ac. l.s.Wintocomaick Cr. btwn his brothers Robert & John Tucker's lines. (See DB 3-58 & DB 3-243).

NOTE: The above patent identifies James Tucker as a brother of Robert Tucker and John Tucker. See Robert Tucker Jr md Frances Coleman & Patent 14-341 in 1731 for 400 ac. l.s. Wintocomaick Cr. See John Tucker Sr and Sarah Old & Patent 16-67 in 1735 for 200 ac. l.s. Winkomaick Cr. Since Robert Tucker Jr and John Tucker Sr are sons of Capt Robert Tucker Sr, then it follows that James Tucker (the Elder, or Sr.) is also a son of Capt Robert Tucker Sr. (See also DB 3-58 below).

DB 3-58, 9 Apr 1748, James Tucker the Elder of Pr. Geo. Co. to James Tucker of. Amelia Co., in consideration of natural love he bears for his son, 300 ac. in Amelia Co., bo. Robert Tucker's line Robert Tucker Jun's corner, John Tucker's line, Sampson's Br., Wintocomack (Cr.). Wit: David Ragsdale, Danil Coleman, Edward Tanner. (See Patent 18-389, DB 3-243.)

DB 3-243, 4 Jul 1749, James Tucker Sen of Bath Parish, Pr Geo Co. to James Tucker Jun of RawlehParish, -Amelia Co., Va. For the Petecural Affection which he beareth unto sd James Tucker Jun, 100 ac. l.s. Winticomake Cr. which is part of 400 ac. granted to sd James Tucker Sen by patent, except one ac. adi. to mill reserved for convenience of the mill, the 1/2 of the mill I likewise give to sd James Tucker Jun. Wit: Edward Tanner, William Bevill, William (W) Hudson. S/ James x Tucker Sen. (See Patent 18-389, DB 3-58, DB 3-243. 100 ac. - 1 ac. = 99 ac.)

DB 3-529, 1 Sep 1750, rec 21 Sep 1750, James Tucker of Amelia Co. Va, to Thomas Cowles of Charles City Co. Va., for L65. (1) 300 ac. which sd James Tucker holds by Patent dated 28 Sep 1730, bo as per patent & also (2) 1 ac. with the moiety (share or portion) of a water mill being (that) which the sd James Tucker reserved out of a certain grant made by him to his son James Tucker 14 Jul 1749. Wife Mary relinq. dower. (See Patent 13-531 & DB 3--243. 300 ac. + 1 ac. = 301 ac.)

LUNENBURG CO. VA.

DB 2-270, 1 Jul 1751, rec 1 Oct 1751, John Humphreys to James Tucker Senr of Pr. Geo. Co., for L30., 200 ac. on l.s. Allens Cr. in Lunenburg Co. Wife, Morinirai, relinq. dower right. (See DB 2-418).

DB 2-418, 12 Jan 1752, rec 7 Apr 1752, James Tucker Senr of Pr. Geo. Co. to William Bevill Junr, for L41., 200 ac, on l.s. Allens Cr. in Lunenburg Co., being part of a larger tract which James Tucker bought of John Humphries. S/ James x Tucker. Wit: Pat Mullen, Edward Bevill, Joseph Ragsdale, Joseph Bevill, Christopher Hudson, James Tucker Junr, Warner Tucker. (See DB 2-270). (Note - the words "part of a larger tract" is confusing, since only 200 ac, was bought from Humphries.)

DB 4-47, 4 Oct 1754, rec 4 Feb 1754, James Tucker of Lunenburg Co., to Parmenas Palmer of Amelia Co., for L35., to be-paid April next ensuing, 80 ac., bo. Hudson, Allens Cr., mouth of Little Br. on n.s. of sd cr. Wit: Joseph Gibson, Jacob Coleson, Thomas Draper. S/ James x Tucker. Wf Mary relinq. dower. (Note: This deed is confusing since no deed could be found for the purchase of this 80 ac. by James Tucker. It appears to he part of Patent 33-517 or Patent 33-518, but they were not recorded until 1758.)

DB 4-273, 8 Nov 1755, rec 6 Jul 1756, Abraham Coleson Alias

Rainwater, to James Tucker, for L35., 100 ac., bo. mouth of branch on n.s. Allens Cr., Nicholas Major, Abraham Coleson, Jacob Coleson, Pinkethman Hawkins, being part of 304 ac. patented to Nicholas Majors. Wit: Pink Hawkins, Field Farrar, Robert Coleman, Martha Farrar. S/ Abraham x Coleson. (See DB 5-120).

DB 4-391, 6 Jan 1757, rec. 5 Apr 1757. Jacob Coleson to James Tucker, for L30., 100 ac, on n.s Allens Cr. joining James Tucker, bo Thos Farars, Sarah Clark, Stephen Mallet. Wit: Anthony Hughes, John Coleman, Thomas Chamberlain, James Easter. S/ Jacob Coleson. (See DB 6-182).

DB 5-120, 31 Dec 1757, rec 7 Mar 1758, James Tucker to Robert Coleman, for L40., 100 ac. on l.s. Allens Cr., bo. Pinkethman Hawkins, Jacob Coleson, James Tucker, Robert Coleman, it being the land sd Tucker had of Abraham Coleson, alias Rainwater. Wit: Pink Hawkins, James Coleman, Thomas Farrar. S/ James Tucker. Wf Mary, relinq dower right. (See DB 4-273).

Patent 33-517, 15 Dec 1758, James Tucker, Lunenbur,g Co., 324 ac. on br. of Allen's Cr. & adj. Thomas Loyd.

Patent 33-518, 15 Dec 1758, James Tucker, Lunenburg Co., 940 ac. on ridge btwn Butcher's Cr. & Allen's Cr., adj. land of Hill Mitchell & c.

DB 5-559, 5 Feb 1760, rec. 5 Feb 1760, James Tucker to Solomon Draper, for L45., 274 ac., bo Thomas Loyd, little fork of Allens Cr. Wit: Parmeson Palmer, John Alloway, Hudson (H) Tucker. S/ James x Tucker. Wf Mary relinq dower right. (See Patent 33-517 & DB 6-313).

DB 6-182, 21 Jul 1759, rec 5 Aug 1760, James Tucker & Jacob Coleson, alias Reignwater, to William Farrar, for L30., 100 ac. on n.s. Allens Cr., bo. James Tucker, John Easter, Thomas Farar, the Orphens of Thomas Clark decd. Wit: P. Hawkins, Parrnenas Palmer, Thomas Draper, Wilm. Palmer. S/ Jacob Colson. (See DB 4-391).

DB 6-313, 3 Nov 1760, rec 2 Dec 1760, James Tucker to William Palmer, for L26., 150 ac., bo. John Hyde, Mitchell, Thomas Loyde, Little Fork of Allens Cr. Wit: Robin Hood, Stephen Mallet, John Cardin. S/ James Tucker. (See Patent 33-517 & DB 5-559).

DB 6-326, 2 Dec 1760, rec 2 Dec 1760, James Tucker to John Humphries, for L60. , 450 ac., bo. Wm.Mills, gr. br. of Butcher Cr., William Hill, Ravenscroft, Thomas Sumers. S/ James Tucker. Wf Mary relinq dower right. (See Patent 33-518).

DB 7-252, 26 Dec 1761, rec 1 Jun 1762, James Tucker of Lunenburg Co., to James Tucker of Amelia Co., for L275., 303 ac. on n.s. Allens Cr., bo Permenus Palmer, James Tucker, John Hudson, Ruffin, Delany, John Umphreys, it being a part of two pattens. Wit: Edward Tanner, William Hudson, Isam Tucker, Joseph Freeman, Abraham Burton, Edward Bevill, Elisha Brooks. S/ James x Tucker. (See Patent 33-517 & Patent 33-518).

NOTE: The above deed did not include a wife's relinquishment of dower right, so James Tucker Sr's wife Mary must have died prior to 26 Dec 1761.

MECKLENBURG CO. VA.

1765 - Mecklenburg Co. was formed from Lunenburg Co. The land owned by James Tucker Sr in this area of Lunenburg Co. then fell into Mecklenburg Co.

DB 1-35, 9 Mar 1765, rec 13 May 1765, Joseph Freeman to James Tucker, for L35., 50 ac. on br. of Allens Cr., bo. Jones, Bilbow, Indian Camp Fork, sd Tucker. S/ Joseph Freeman. Wit: Jonathan Patterson Jr, Benja Estes, David Christopher, John Westbrook, Thos Green, Edward Bevill. (See DB 1-393 & DB 3-236).

DB 1-227, 14 Jul 1766, James Tucker Jr of Mecklenburg Co. to James Tucker Sr of same Co., for L90., 300 ac., on branches of Butchers & Allens Cr., bo. Robert Bailey, , Jones, Charles Humphries, Indian Camp Branch, Bilbow, Burwell. S/ James c Tucker. Acknowledged by James Tucker Jr & wf Mary & rec. 14 Jul 1766. (See Lunenburg Co. DB 7-252 & Mecklenburg WB 1-84).

DB 1-345, 7 Jan 1767, rec 9 Feb 1767, James Tucker Jr to James Tucker Sr for L55., 300 ac. on branches of Allens Cr., bo Indian Camp Branch, Edward Bevil, Wm. Murphey. Wit: Spence Waddy, James Tucker, Garner Tucker. S/ James x Tucker. (See DB 1-240 & WB 1-84 in which James Tucker Sr willed this 300 ac. to sons Matthew, Harbud and Bartlett).

DB 1-393, 12 Feb 1767, rec 13 Apr 1767, James Tucker Sr to William Murphey, for L13.2.6., 25 ac., bo. Murphey, Indian Camp Br., being part of tract held by Peter Bilbo. Wit: Spence Waddy, Garner Tucker, James Tucker. S/ James x Tucker. (See DB 1-35 & DB 3-236).

NOTE: The above deed did not include a wife's relinquishment of dower right, so it is assumed that James Tucker Sr was still a widower in 1767.

NOTE: The name of the witness in the above two deeds which appeared to be spelled Garner Tucker, may be Warner Tucker, son of James Sr.

DB 2-43, 9 May 1768, rec 9 May 1768, <u>James Tucker Senr to Robert Burton</u>, for L150., <u>151.5 ac.</u> on Allens Cr., bo. John Hammon, <u>Thomas Hudson, James Tucker Jr, Hudson Tucker, Robert Burton</u>. Wit: Spence Waddy, Hudson x Tucker, S/ James x Tucker. Acknowledged by <u>James Tucker Senr & Elizabeth his wife</u>. (Note: Robert Burton is probably son-in-law of James Tucker, Sr).

DB 2-44, 19 Apr 1768, rec 9 May 1768, <u>James Tucker Senr to son Hudson Tucker</u>, for L151.10., <u>151 ac.</u> on Allens Cr., <u>bo</u> Robert Burton, <u>James Tucker Junr</u>, John Humphries. Wit: Spence Waddy, Robert Burton. S/ James x Tucker. Acknowledged by <u>James Tucker Senr & Elizabeth his wife</u>. (See DB 2-401 for Hudson Tucker).

NOTE: In deeds prior to 1761, James Tucker Sr's wife is named as Mary. The two deeds above indicate that James Tucker Sr had married a second wife Elizabeth prior to May 1768. This compiler, however, has been unable to determine where he obtained these tracts of 151.5 and 151 ac. of land.

DB 3-236, 11 Nov 1771, rec 11 Nov 1771, <u>James Tucker</u> to Elizabeth Hammons, for L8., <u>25 ac.</u>, bo. Boyd, Little Cr., Soloman Draper, John Crowder. S/ James Tucker. (See DB 1-35 & DB 1-393).

DB 3-242, 9 Oct 1771, rec 11 Nov 1771, <u>James Tucker</u>, Holman Freeman, Spence Waddy, John Farley Thompson, & Joseph Southerland to John Overton for L50., <u>103 ac.</u> bo. Wiltons Rd, Burwell, John Wilson's Church Rd. Wit: Saml Whitworth, Fanney Hawkins, Mary Ann Southerland, Richd Easter. Grezzel & Elizabeth, the wives of Joseph Southerland & John Farley Thompson privately examined. (Note: The source of the joint ownership of this 103 ac. is not clear, but possibly it was inherited by James Tucker's 1st wf Mary as joint heirs with other parties named).

WB 1-84, 19 Oct 1770, (date probated not shown) <u>will of James Tucker Sen</u>.
<u>Son Robert - 100 ac.</u> known by name of His Clearing & to extend up to my son James Tucker's line, plus negro man Will.
<u>Son Eliiah - plantation whereon I live with ___ hundred ac.</u> adj Robert to dividing-line btwn them, <u>after death of my wife;</u> plus negro boy Sam.
<u>Son George - 100 ac.</u> on Jones's line, being the last part of the first tract I bought of my son James Tucker; plus negro man Joe after wife's death.
I give the last tract of land I purchased of my son James Tucker & known by name of Bilbors(?), to be <u>equally divided btwn my other three sons:</u>
<u>son Matthew</u> to be laid off on s.s. of branch; plus negro woman after wife's death.
<u>son Harbud's (Herbert)</u> part to be laid off ___ to Murpheys line & to include the clearing & barn; plus negro boy Peter.

son Bartley (or Bartlett) his part btwn Harbud & Elijah; plus negro named ____?.

Wife Elizabeth Tucker - negro man Joe & negro woman Sarah, for life, then Joe to son George Tucker, & Sarah to son Matthew; plus feather bed & furniture & residue of stock, household goods & chattels.

dau Lucyetia (or Lucretia?) Burton - ____? Kittle.

son Myhall (or Micael?) - ____? shillings sterling.

son James Tucker - ten shillings sterling.

son Warner Tucker - ten shillings sterling.

son Hutson (Hudson) Tucker - ten shillings sterling

dau Mary Hudson - ten shillings sterling.

Exor: wife & Benjamin George.

Estate not to he brought to appraisement.

Wit: James Freeman, Holeman Freeman. S/ James x Tucker.

SUMMARY OF LAND TRANSACTIONS:

Year Reference		Plus		Minus	Balance
Prince George - Dinwiddie:		---		---	---
1723 Patent 11-203		450			450
Prince George - Amelia:		---		---	---
1730 Patent 13-531	(b)	300			300
1739 Patent 18-389	(a)	400			700
1748 DB 3-58 to son James Jr			(a)	300	400
1749 DB 3-243 to son James Jr			(a)	99	301
1750 DB 3-529 to Cowles			(b)	301	0
Lunenburg - Mecklenburg:		---		---	---
1751 DB 2-270 fr Humphries	(c)	200			200
1752 DB 2-418 to Bevill			(c)	200	0
1755 DB 4-273 fr A. Coleson	(d)	100			100
1757 DB 4-391 fr J. Coleson	(e)	100			200
1758 DB 5-120 to Coleman			(d)	100	100
1758 Patent 33-517	(f)	324			424
1758 Patent 33-513	(f)	940			1364
1754 DB 4-47 to Palmer			(f)	80	1284
1760 DB 5-559 to Draper			(f)	274	1010
1760 DB 6-182 to J. Coleson			(e)	100	910
1760 DB 6-313 to Palmer			(f)	150	760
1760 DB 6-326 to Humphries			(f)	450	310
1762 DB 7-252 to son James			(f)	303	7
difference			(f)	7	0
Mecklenburg:		---		---	---
1765 DB 1-35 fr Freeman	(g)	50			50
1765 DB 1-227 fr son James Jr	(h)	300			350
1766 DB 1-345 fr son James Jr	(i)	300			650

SUMMARY OF LAND TRANSACTIONS:

Year Reference	Plus		Minus	Balance
1767 DB 1-393 to Murphey		(g)	25	625
1771 DB 3-236 to Hammons		(g)	25	600
1773 WB 1-84 to son Robert		(h)	100	500
1773 WB 1-84 to son Elijah		(h)	100	400
1773 WB 1-84 to son George		(h)	100	300
1773 WB 1-84 to son Matthew		(i)	100	200
1773 WB 1-84 to son Harbud (Herbert)		(i)	100	100
1773 WB 1-84 to son Bartlett		(i)	100	0
1768 DB 2-43 to son-in-law Burton		(1)	151.5	
1768 DB 2-44 to son Hudson		(1)	151	
1771 DB 3-242 to Overton		(1)	103	

(1) unable to determine how these tracts of land were received.

DB 5-15, rec 10 Mar 1777, <u>Elizabeth Tucker to Robert Tucker</u> for L50., the <u>100 ac. I now live on</u>, also one negro man Joe, one wench Sarah, 9 head cattle, all hogs, 4 head of horses. S/ Elizabeth Tucker. Wit: James Brown, Susanna Brown, Edward x Moore.

WB 1-244, wd 5 Sep 1777, wp 10 Nov 1777, <u>will of Matthew Tucker, names mother Elizabeth Tucker & brother Robert Tucker</u>. Refers to his part of land & a negro wench left him by his father. <u>Leaves estate to mother for life and then to go to brother Robert Tucker</u>. Exor: Friend Peter Oliver. Wit: Peter Oliver, Henry Carleton & Edmund Bentley. (See WB 1-84, DB 5-15 & DB 5-480)

NOTE: If Matthew Tucker was age 21 when he wrote his will in 1777, then he would have been born ca 1756. And if Elizabeth was his blood mother, then she would have been married to his father James Sr prior to 1756. And James Sr willed land (which he bought in 1766) to sons Elijah, George, Matthew, Harbud & Bartley "after death of my wife", which might imply they were sons of 2nd wife Elizabeth. On the other hand, Matthew may not been age 21 when he wrote his will, and Elizabeth may have been his step-mother.

George must have been at least age 21 in 1777 when he sold his inherited land, so he would have been horn ca 1756. And Elizabeth must have died ca 1777.

Harbud (Herbert) and Bartley (Bartlett) both must have been at least age 21 in 1784 when they sold their inherited land, so they would have been born before or ca 1763.

Elijah was probably at least age 21 when he married in 1789 in Halifax Co., so he would have been born before or ca 1768, but the 1850 Census of Halifax Co. indicated he was age 84 in 1850, so he would have been born ca 1766.

But James Sr's 1st wife Mary was a party to his deeds as late as 1760. So James Sr must have married Elizabeth between 1760-68. It appears then that certainly Elijah, and possibly Harbud and Bartley were sons of Elizabeth.

DB 5-480, 29 Jun 1779, rec 13 Sep 1779, Robert Tucker to William W. Green, for L800., 100 ac. on s.s. of a br. of Allens Cr., being land willed by my father James Tucker Sr., to my brother Mathew Tucker & by his death it fell to me as heir, including 16 ac. adj. that I purchased of my brother James Tucker, the whole of the above joins Peter Jones & Peter Burton. S/ Robert x Tucker, Wit: Asa Oliver, Edward x Moore, Sarah Oliver. Wf Mary relinq dower. (See WB 1-84, WB 1-244, & DB 5-280.)

WB 1-256, 2 Mar 1778, appraisemant of est. of James Tucker, included no slaves, total value L107.7.9. Appr: William Robertson, Bagzel Wagstaff, John Doggett.

SUMMARY: From the surveys, patents, deeds & parish registers above, the following conclusions are drawn:

James Tucker Sr (the Elder) b ca 1698, the son of Capt. Robert Tucker Sr, who md Martha. While Martha was Robert's wife as early as 1720, she may or may not have been the mother of James. His brothers and sisters were: Sarah md John Clay; Robert Jr md Frances Coleman; George md 1st Frances, md 2nd Catharine; John md Sarah Old; William md Ann; Ann; Joseph md Prudence; Daniel md Elizabeth.

James Tucker Sr most probably lived in the area of Pr. Geo. Co. which became Dinwiddie Co. in 1752, for he is referred to as James Tucker of Pr. Geo. Co. 1748 through April 1752, and James Tucker of Dinwiddie Co. in Jul 1752. Only fragmented records remain for these two counties.

James Tucker Sr. then moved to Lunenburg Co. ca 1754 where he bought and sold extensive lands along both sides of Allens Cr. & on east side of Butchers Cr. & along the ridges between the two creeks. He is referred to as James Tucker of Lunenburg Co. 1754-1764. This area became part of Mecklenburg Co. in 1765. Afterward, he is referred to as James Tucker of Mecklenburg Co. until his death before 1773.

James Tucker Sr b ca 1698, d before 1773, married to wf Mary from ca 1719 to ca 1760. In 1768 he was married to wf Elizabeth who d ca 1777. Most of his children named below were born to 1st wife Mary, except perhaps Elijah, who was born ca 1766, and possibly Harbud and Bartley.

James Tucker Jr b ca 1719, md Mary _____.

Myhall (or Micael) Tucker (son) b 1721.

Lucretia Tucker b 1729, md _____ Burton (probably Robert Burton).

Warner Tucker b 1732.

Mary Tucker md _____ Hudson (probably William Hudson).

Hutson (or Hudson) Tucker, b ca 1747.

Robert Tucker b ca 1752, md Mary _____.

Matthew Tucker b ca 1756, d ca 1777.

George Tucker h ca 1756, md ea 1777 Kezia _____.

Harbud (or Herbert) Tucker b ca 1763.

Bartley (or Bartlett) Tucker b ca 1763.

Elijah Tucker b ca 1766, md 1789 Betsy Barley.

See separate chapter for each son

* * *

1. Boddie, John B., "Births 1720-1792 From The Bristol Parish Register of Henrico, Prince George and Dinwiddie"

TJ111000 - JAMES TUCKER JR

MD MARY
SON OF JAMES TUCKER SR
(THE ELDER)
MD 1ST MARY
MD 2ND ELIZABETH

AMELIA CO. VA.

James Tucker Jr was at least age 21 when his father James Tucker Sr deeded land to him in 1748. He was age 21 when he first appeared as a separate tithable household in Amelia Co. in 1740, so he would have been born by 1719. His birth was not included in the Bristol Parish Register compiled by Boddie, which began in 1720. He is the son of James Tucker Sr. & 1st wf Mary.

DB 3-58, 9 Apr 1748, James Tucker the Elder of Pr. Geo. Co. to James Tucker of Amelia Co. in consideration of natural love he bears for his son, 300 ac. in Amelia Co., bo. Robert Tucker's line, Robert Tucker Jun's corner, John Tucker's line, Sampsons Br., Wintocomack (Cr.). Wit: David Ragsdale, Danil Coleman, Edward Tanner. (See DB 3-533) (See also Patent 3-531 for James Tucker Sr.)

NOTE: In the above deed, Robert Tucker is father of James the Elder, and Robert Tucker Jr & John Tucker are brothers of James the Elder.

DB 3-243, 4 Jul 1749, James Tucker Sen of Bath Parish, Pr Geo Co. to James Tucker Jun of Rawleigh Parish, Amelia Co. Va. for the Petecural Affection which he beareth unto sd James Tucker Jun, 100 ac. l.s. Winticomake Cr. which is part of 400 ac. granted to sd James Tucker Sen by patent, except one ac. adj. to mill reserved for convenience of the mill, the 1/2 of the mill I likewise give to sd James Tucker Jun. Wit: Edward Tanner, William Bevill, William (W) Hudson. S/ James x Tucker Sen. (99 ac. transferred.) (100 ac. - 1 ac. = 99 ac. See DB 3-533).

DB 3-533, 1 Sep 1750, James Tucker (Jun) of Amelia Co., to Thomas Cowles of Charles City Co., for L60., 399 ac. & one moiety of a water mill adj., which land James Tucker conveyed to sd James Tucker his son by several deeds of gift, bo. as by Patent granted to James Tucker the father 24 Sep 1739. S/ James Tucker Jun. (See DB 3-53 and DB 3-243 above).

DB 4-440, 14 Jul 1752, rec. 27 Aug 1752, Benjamin Ragsdale of Dinwiddie Co. to James Tucker of county aforesaid, for L30., 200 ac. on head of Sampson's Br. of Wintocomake Cr. in Amelia Co., bo. Robert Tucker Jun cor. Wit: Pat Mullin, George Burrus, Rich x George. (See DB 9-200).

DB 7-292, 15 Apr 1760, <u>Worner (or Warner) Tucker of Raleigh Parish to James Tucker for L10., 200 ac.</u> bo. Ragsdale's line, Bowles' line. Wit: William Adams, Francis Drinkard, Sam'l Sandifur. S/ Worner x Tucker. (See DB 9-200)

DB 8-250, 20 Dec 1763, rec. 22 Dec 1763, <u>James Tucker to Robert Tucker</u>, for L7.10, <u>15 ac.</u> on n.s. of the Main Sampson's Br., <u>bo Robert Tuckers line</u>, Sampson's Br. <u>Wit: Daniel Tucker</u>, Edward Tanner, Hezekiah Coleman. S/ James Tucker. (See DB 9-200).

DB 8-253, 20 Dec 1763, rec. 22 Dec 1763, <u>Robert Tucker to James Tucker</u>, for L5, <u>12 ac.</u> on s.s. of the main Sampson's Br. at the mouth of a that comes through sd James Tucker's corn field, up Sampson's Br. to <u>Robert Tucker's line</u>, crosses Sampson's Br. <u>Wit:</u> Edward Tanner, Hezekiah Coleman, <u>Daniel Tucker</u>. S / Robert (R) Tucker. (See DB 9-200),

NOTE: The effect of the above two deeds is that James Tucker (Jr) and his uncle Robert Tucker (Jr) exchanged the small acreage each owned on opposite sides of Sampson's Br. (See DB 4-440 & DB 7-292).

DB 9-200, 28 Feb 1767, rec. 24 Sep 1767, <u>James Tucker of Mecklenberg Co.</u> to Benjamin Patterson of Amelia Co. for LI50., <u>397 ac.</u> bo. Sampson's Br., Bolling's line, John Patterson's line, John Meremoon's line, James Tucker's old line, <u>Robert Tucker's line</u>, small br., Sampsons Br. Wit: John Cousins, <u>William Tucker</u>, John Patterson. S/ James x Tucker. (See DB4-440, DB 7-292, DB 8-250, & DB 8-253. 200 ac. + 200 ac. - 15 ac. + 12 ac. = 397 ac.).

LIST OF TITHES

1740	-	---	James Tucker	
1743	-	---	James Tucker	
1744	-	---	James Tucker	
1748	-	---	James Tucker	
1749	-	---	James Tucker	
1750	-	---	James Tucker, Edward Murfe	Bess
1755	3	---	James Tucker	Joe, Moll
1756	6	---	James Tucker, Hundjon Tucker	Wells, Jo, Sall, Moll
1761		---	James Tucker	
1762	3	---	James Tucker	Willard, Sarah
1763	3	400	James Tucker	____, ____
1765	5	397	James Tucker	Will, Joe, Sara, Moll

NOTE: The "Hundjon" Tucker listed as a 16-yr-up tithable in the household of James Tucker in 1756 is probably his brother Hudson Tucker, who was probably born ca 1740. See Mecklenburg Co. WB 1-84 below.

NOTE: At this point, James Tucker Jr had sold all his land in Amelia Co. and moved to Lunenhurg Co.

LUNENBURG CO., VA.

DB 2-167, 1 Oct. 1750, rec 2 Oct 1750, John, William, Thomas & Charles Humphrys to James Tucker of Amelia Co., for one shilling, 183 ac. on b.s. Allens Cr. in Co. of Lunenhurg. Wit: Christopher Hudson, William White, John Mayse. S/ John, William, Thomas, & Charles Humphrys. (See Release in DB 2-168).

DB 2-168, 2 Oct 1750, rec 2 Oct 1750, John, William, Thomas & Charles Humphrys to James Tucker of Amelia Co., for L96., 183 ac. on b.s. Allens Cr in Lunenhurg Co. (This appears to be a release of the above deed DB 2-167.)

DB 6-5, 5 Mar 1760, rec 4 Mar 1760, John Humphrey to James Tucker Jr., for L30., 250 ac. on n.s Allens Cr. bo. Ruffin, Delany's Courthouse Rd., being part of land left John Humphrey by his father, & being part of land patented by John Ruffin & James Baker. (See DB 7-264 & DB 8-19).

DB 7-252, 26 Dec 1761, rec 1 Jun 1762, James Tucker of Lunenburg Co., to James Tucker of Amelia Co., for L275., 303 ac, on n.s. Allens Cr., bo. Permenus Palmer, James Tucker, John Hudson, Ruffin, Delany, John Umphreys, it being a part of two pattens. Wit: Edward Tanner, William Hudson, Isam Tucker, Joseph Freeman, Abraham Burton, Edward Bevill, Elisha Brooks. S/ James x Tucker. (See Patent 33-517 & Patent 33-513 for James Tucker Sr. See also Mecklenburg Co. DB 1-227 below).

DB 7-264, 23 Feb 1762, rec 1 Jun 1762, James Tucker Jr of St. James Parish, Lunenburg Co., to John Hammon, planter, for L20., 50 ac, on s.s. Allens Cr., bo. Christopher Hudson, being part of greater tract sd James Tucker bought of John Humphries. Wit: Christopher Hudson, William Palmer, James Easter. S/ James x Tucker Junr. (See DB 6-5 & DB 8-19).

DB 7-311, 7 May 1762, rec 6 Jul 1762, Lewis Burwell of James City Co to James Tucker of Lunenhurg Co., for L210., 832 ac. on n.s. Butchers Cr., being part of larger tract granted to sd Lewis Burwell, bo. Twitty's Branch, Jones. Wit: Richard Witton, Jos. Williams, Jno. Speed Jr, Sarnl Comer. S/ Lewis Burwell. (See Lunenburg DB 8-15 & Mecklenburg DB 2-530 & DB 5-366).

DB 7-347, 6 Feb 1762, rec 7 Sep 1762, James Tucker Junr to John Glasscock, planter, for L50., 130 ac. & plantation thereon, on b.s. Little Fork of Allens Cr., bo. Christopher Hudson, James Tucker Junr, Solomon Draper, being part of greater patent to James Tucker Junr. Wit: Cary x Hudson, William Palmer, John x Hammond. S/ James x Tucker. (See DB 2-167-163 for 183 ac.).

DB 8-15, 12 Apr 1764, rec 12 Apr 1764, James Tucker & wf Mary to Robert Bailey, for L125., 200 ac. being part of tract sd Tucker purchased of Coll. Lewis Burwell on Butchers Cr., bo. Jones, Twitty's Branch, Butchers Cr. S/ James x Tucker. Wf Mary relinq dower right. (See DB 7-311).

DB 3-19, 10 Apr 1764, rec 12 Apr 1764, James Tucker to John Hammons, for L60., 200 ac. bo. Jon Medis, Little Fork of Allens Cr., Glasscock's Spring Branch, Thomson, Richard Stith. S/ James x Tucker. (See DB 6-5 & DB 7-264).

MECKLENBURG CO. VA.

1765, Mecklenburg Co. was formed from Lunenburg Co. All the land which James Tucker Jr owned in Lunenburg Co. now fell in Mecklenburg Co.

DB 1-227, 14 Jul 1766, James Tucker Jr of Mecklenburg Co _to James Tucker Sr of same Co., for L90., 300 ac., on branches of Butchers & Allens Cr., bo. Robert Bailey, Jones, Charles Humphries, Indian Camp Branch, Bilbow, Burwell. S/ James x Tucker. Acknowledged by James Tucker Jr & wf Mary & rec. 14 Jul 1766. (See Lunenburg Co. DB 7-252 & Mecklenburg WE 1-84).

NOTE: From above deed in 1766, James Tucker Jr's wife is identified as Mary ____. Although he was a 21-yr-old tithable in 1740 in Amelia Co., and had lived in Lunenburg Co beginning in 1762, a wife is mentioned for the first time in the above deed. James Tucker Sr's 1st wife, and mother of James Tucker Jr, was named Mary also, and it was most difficult to identify transactions to the right person. But James Tucker Sr's 2nd wife, beginning in 1766 was named Elizabeth.

DB 1-240, 11 Aug 1766, rec 11 Aug 1766, Peter Bilbors of Goochland Co. to James Tucker for L55., 300 ac., on branches of Allens Cr. , bo Edward Bevil, Wm. Murphey, Indian Camp Br., Whitworth. Wit: Robert Bailey, Jonathan Patterson Jr. S/ Peter Bilbo. (See DB 1-345).

DB 1-345, 7 Jan 1767, rec 9 Feb 1767, James Tucker Jr to James Tucker Sr for L55., 300 ac. on branches of Allens Cr., bo. Indian Camp Branch, Edward Bevil, Wm. Murphey. Wit: Spence Waddy, James Tucker, Garner Tucker. S/ James x Tucker. (See DB 1-240 & WB 1-84).

DB 1-377, 13 Apr 1767, rec 13 Apr 1767, Richard Booker of Lunenburg Co. to James Tucker Junr of Mecklenburg Co., for L123., 196 ac, on n.s. Butchers Cr., bo. Burwell, Wittons Rd., Baley, Bukhorn(?) Cr. Wit: Garner Tucker, John Murphey Jun. S/ Richard Booker. Wf Frances relinq dower.

Patent 38-621, 6 Apr 1769, James Tucker, Mecklenburg Co., 16 ac. on br. of Allens Cr. adj. land of Bilbo, Jones, etal.

DB 2-401, 14 May 1770, rec 14 May 1770, Hudson Tucker to James Tucker Jr, for L150.10., 151 ac. on Allens Cr. at mouth of a spring branch, bo. Robert Burton, James Tucker, Thomas Whitworth, Edwards. Wit: Spence Waddy, Robt Blake, Saml Whitworth. S/ Hudson x Tucker. (See DB 2-44 where James Tucker Sr sold this 151 ac. to his son Hudson Tucker, who now sells it to his brother James Tucker Jr). (See DB 5-58)

DB 2-530, 10 Dec 1770, rec 10 Dec 1770, James Tucker & wf Mary, to Peter Oliver of Granville Co. N.C., for. L200., 400 ac., bo Church Rd, Murray(?), Jones, Twittys Br. S/ James (J) Tucker, Mary (M) Tucker. (See Lunenburg DB 7-311)

Patent 42-469, 15 Jun 1773, James Tucker, Mecklenburg Co. 800 ac. on br. of Allen's Cr. adj. Hutson, Bevel, Ruffin & Baker.

WB 1-84, 19 Oct 1770, (date probated not shown) will of James Tucker Sen. - names: Son Robert - Son Elijah - Son George- son Matthew - son Harbud - son Bartley - Wife Elizabeth Tucker - dau Lucyetia Burton - son Myhall Tucker -son James Tucker - ten shillings sterling. - son Warner Tucker - son Hutson Tucker - dau Mary ; Hudson -

WB 1-256, 2 Mar 1778, appraisemant of est. of James Tucker, included no slaves, total value L107.7.9. Appr: William Robertson, Bagzel Wagstaff, John Doggett.

DB 5-58, 7 Jan 1777, rec 12 May 1777, James Tucker Sr, to Hudson Tucker, for L52., 200 ac., bo. Old Courthouse Rd., James Brown, old Ordinary Spring Br., Allens Cr., Robert Burton, John Hudson. S/ James Tucker. Wit: Peter Oliver, Thomas Berry, Garner Tucker. (See DB 2-401).

NOTE: Following the death of James Tucker Sr btwn 1771-1773, his son James Tucker Jr then sometimes assumed the title of James Tucker Sr. Whereas James Tucker Sr's 1st wf was named Mary, James Tucker Jr's wife was also named Mary.

DB 5-80, 13 Apr 1777, rec 11 Aug 1777, <u>George Tucker to James Tucker Jr</u> for L44., <u>97 ac. being left to sd George Tucker by his father James Tucker</u> & adj. Capt Peter Jones. S/ George Tucker. Wit: Thomas Berry, Edward x Moore, James x Tucker Senr. Acknowledged by George Tucker & wf. Keziah relinq dower.

NOTE: The above deed is most difficult to understand. George Tucker sold his inheritance from his father James Tucker Sr, to a James Tucker Jr. But a James Tucker Sr is witness to the deed. Is the witness actually George's brother James Tucker Jr now become Sr? And is the buyer actually George's nephew, a younger James Tucker Jr, son of James Tucker Jr now Sr?

DB 5-88, 11 Aug 1777, rec 11 Aug 1777, <u>James Tucker & wf Mary</u> to William Farrar for L77.3., <u>381 ac</u>, bo. John Easter, sd Farrar, John Johns, Thomas Stone, William Hunt. S/ James x Tucker, Mary x Tucker. Wit: Claul.(?) Clausel, trignal(?) Jones Jr.

DB 5-163, 12 Jan 1778, John Murray Exor. of James Murray decd of Bristol Parish in Pr. Geo. Co., to <u>James Tucker</u> of St. James Parish of Mecklenburg Co., <u>395 ac.,</u> bo. Jones. S/ John Murray. (See DB 6-269 for 389 ac.).

DB 5-178, 13 Jan 1778 rec 9 Feb 1778, <u>James Tucker</u> to Wm. Hudson, for L93.6., <u>311 ac.</u> bo. Farrar. S/ James x Tucker. Wit: Ben Whitehead. Wf Mary relinq dower.

DB 5-187, 28 Jan 1778, rec 9 Feb 1778, <u>James Tucker</u> to David Crowder for L50., <u>100 ac.,</u> bo. Hudson Tucker, William Hudson, David Crowder, Felps, Francis Ruffin, James Brown. S/ James x Tucker. Wit: James Brown, Edward Colley, John Johns.

DB 5-280, 20 Apr 1778, rec 13 Jul 1778, <u>James Tucker to Robert Tucker</u> for L16., <u>16 ac</u>, on br. of Allens Cr. bo. Bilbow, Jones, Stith. S/ James Tucker. (See Patent 36-121. (See DB 5--480 for Robert Tucker).

DB 5-366, 9 Nov 1778, rec 8 Feb 1779, <u>James Tucker</u> to William Wills Green, for L800., <u>200 ac,,</u> the greatest part on the east side of Butchers Cr., bo. Hightower, Jones, Twitty, sd Green, Wilson's Rd., Booker's Rd. S/ James x Tucker. Wit: Benjamin Whitehead, John Archer, John Bevill. <u>Wf Mary</u> relinq dower. (See DB 7-311)

DB 6-269, 26 Mar. 1733, rec 9 Jun 1783, <u>James Tucker of Surry Co, N.C.,</u> to Thomas Burton for L100., <u>385 ac.,</u> bo. Edward Bevil, Abraham Burton, Joseph Goode, William Green, William Wills, Thomas Whitworth. S/ James x Tucker. Wit: Robert Evans, Edward Bevil, John Keeton, Abraham Burton. (See DB 5-15.3 for 395 ac.).

NOTE: From the several deeds above, it appears James Tucker Jr. sold all his land in Mecklenburg Co. Va. and moved to Surry Co., N.C.

SUMMARY OF LAND TRANSACTIONS:

Year Transaction		Plus	Minus	Bal.
Amelia Co.		---	---	---
1748 DB 3-58 fr father James Sr		300		300
1749 DB 3-243 fr father James Sr		99		399
1750 DB 3-533 to Cowles			399	0
1752 DB 4-440 fr Ragsdale		200		200
1760 DB 7-212 fr bro. Warner		200		400
1763 DB 3-250 to uncle Robert			15	385
1763 DB 8-253 fr uncle Robert		12		397
1767 DS 9-200 to Patterson			397	0
Lunenburg Co.		---	---	---
1750 DB 2-167 fr Humphries	(a)	183		183
1760 DB 6-5 fr Humphries	(b)	250		433
1762 DB 7-252 fr father James Sr	(c)	303		736
1762 DB 7-264 to Hammon	(b)		50	686
1762 DB 7-311 fr Burwell		832		1518
1762 DB 7-347 to Glascock	(a)		150	1338
adj	(a)		3	1335
1764 DB 8-15 to Bailey			200	1135
1764 DB 9-19 to Hammons	(b)		200	935
Mecklenburg Co.		---	---	---
1766 DB 1-227 to father James Sr	(c)		300	635
adj	(c)		3	632
1766 DB 1-240 fr Bilbors	(d)	300		932
1767 DB 1-345 to Father James Sr	(d)		300	632
1767 DB 1-377 fr Booker		196		828
1769 Patent 38-621	(e)	16		844
1770 DB 2-401 fr bro Hudson		151		995
1770 DB 2-530 to Oliver			400	595
1773 Patent 42-469		800		1395
1777 DB 5-58 to bro Hudson			200	1195
1777 DB .5-80 fr bro George		97		1292
1777 DB 5-88 to Farrar			381	911
1778 DB 5-163 fr Murray	(f)	395		1306
1778 DB 5-178 to Wm. Hudson			311	995
1778 DS 5-187 to Crowder			100	895
1778 DS 5-280 to bro Robert	(e)		16	879
1778 DB 5-366 to Green			200	679
1783 DB 6-269 to Burton	(f)		385	294
adj	(f)		10	284

(Unable to reconcile items not coded.)

MONONGALIA CO. VA. (NOW W.V.)

Grant N-31, 15 Jun 1784, James Tucker, Mongalia Co., 380 ac. west fork of Ten Mile Cr. incl. his settlement made thereon in 1773.

NOTE: Whether the above James Tucker is our subject James Tucker Jr who moved from Mecklenburg Co, Va. to Surry Co. N.C. in 1783 is not determined by this compiler.

SUMMARY: From the deeds, patents, tithe records & will above, the following conclusions are drawn:

James Tucker Jr b ca 1719 in Pr. Geo. Co., son of James Tucker Sr (the Elder) & 1st wf Mary. James Tucker Jr's wife was also named Mary.

James Tucker Jr was given land by his father & bought & sold land in Amelia Co 1748-67, & was included in the list of tithes of Amelia Co. from 1740-50 & 1753-65. He was not included 1751-54, nor after 1765. He was referred to as James Tucker of Dinwiddie in 1752. He was given land by his father & bought & sold land along Allens Cr. in Lunenburg Co. 1750-64, which area became Mecklenburg Co. in 1765.

James Tucker Jr. sold most of his land in Mecklenburg Co. by 1783, and was living in Surry Co., N.C. in 1783.

This compiler did not further research this James Tucker Jr in Surry Co., N.C.

NOTE: The following information was graciously provided by Mary McCamphell Bell, C.G.R.S., who is a descendant of Bartley Tucker, brother of James Jr. Her proof notes are indicated in parenthesis ().

James Tucker Jr b ca 1726?, probably Pr Geo Co, Va, d aft 24 Feb 1797 (6) Surry Co, NC. (6), son of James Tucker Sr b 1700? & wf Mary (2), m ca 1747? Mary (2), d 1767? (no longer in deeds), & had issue:

1. Gardiner Tucker b 1748 (3), liv. Surry Co 1800-over 45 yrs.

2. John Tucker (4,6).

3. James P. Tucker?, (conj), d 1778 Mecklenburg Co, Va, m 14 Dec 1772 (5) Mecklenburg Co, Va,

4. Branch Tucker (6), d inven. Nov 1832 Surry Co, NC, m Lucy (7).

5. William Tucker (6).

6. Archer Tucker? (8).

PROOF NOTES of Mary McCampbell Bell:

(1) will of James Tucker Sr.

(2) Meck. Co, Va deeds

(3) listed as a tith under James Tucker 1764 Lunenburg Co

(4) Meck. DB 5-366

(5) Meck. Co, Va marriages

(6) Surry Co, NC DB G-24, 24 Feb 1797

(7) Branch Tucker estate paper NC state Archives - WB 4-42 Surry Co, NC.

(8) conj.-wit. all deeds

TJ112000 - WARNER TUCKER

SON OF JAMES TUCKER SR
(THE ELDER)
MD 1ST MARY
MD 2ND ELIZABETH

BRISTOL PARISH REGISTER [1]

Warner son of James & Mary Tucker born 15th April 1732 bapt 1st Jun 1732.

NOTE: If 1732 is the correct year of birth of Warner Tucker, then he would have been age 21 in 1753. However, when he bought land in Lunenhurg Co. in 1751 he should have been age 21, and if so, then he would have been born in 1730.

LUNENBURG CO., VA.

DB 2-300, 1 Jul 1751, rec 1 Jul 1751, John Humphreys to Warner Tucker of Pr. Geo. Co., for L75., 168 ac. on u.s. Allins Cr. in Lunenburg Co., being part of a tract granted to Benjamin Garner of Brunswick Co. & afterwards acknowledged to John Humphreys. (See DB 2-432).

DB 2-432, 6 Apr 1752, rec 7 Apr 1752, Warner Tucker of Lunenburg Co. to Thomas Hawkins of same co. for L37.12.6, 168 ac. on Allens Cr. at mouth of a great branch, being part of land patented to Benjamin Lanier (or Garner?) 5 Apr 1748, that part on u.s. of Allens Cr. Wit: James Tucker, Nicholas Major, William Bevill. S/ Warner Tucker. (See 03 2-300).

DB 5-181, 9 Oct 1752, rec 1 May 1753, William Bevill & Warner Tucker, of Cumberland Parish, to Thomas Hawkins, for L83., 368 ac. along Allens Cr. Wit: Nicholas Major, Abraham Coleson, Jacob Coleson, Mary Major, S/ William Bevill, Warner x Tucker.

NOTE: How William Bevill & Warner Tucker came into joint possession of this 368 ac. is not clear.

AMELIA CO. VA.

DB 6-99, 13 Aug 1757, William Coleman & wf Frances to Warner Tucker, for L32.17., 438 ac., bo. Ragsdale, Bom___, Bolling, Bevil, Tucker. Wit: Abra'm Green, M. Wills, David Greenhill, ___ Wills, Edm. Booker Jr. S/ William Coleman, Frances x Coleman. (See DB 7-292 & DB 7-297).

DB 7-292, 1.5 Apr 1760, Warner Tucker of Raleigh Parish to James Tucker for L10., 200 ac. bo. Ragsdale, Bowles. Wit: William Adams, Francis Drinkard, Sam'l Sandifur. S/ Warner x Tucker. (See DB 6-99 & DB 7-297)

DB 7-297, 15 Apr 1760, <u>Warner Tucker of Raleigh Parish</u>, to Richard Newman of Bath Parish in Dinwiddie Co., for L10., <u>238 ac. bo.</u> Bolling, Bevil, <u>Robert Tucker</u>. Wit: William Adams, Samil Sandifur, Francis Drinkard. Proved 24 Jul 1760 and 20 Aug 1760, & rec. 20 Aug 1760. S/ Warner x Tucker. (See DB 6-99 & DB 7-292)

NOTE: The above two deeds had the same witnesses as DB 7-295 for Isham Tucker. It is not clear if there was a relationship between Warner Tucker & Isham Tucker. Isham Tucker is most probably the Isham Tucker b 1 Feb 1732, son of John & Mary Tucker. [2]

MECKLENBURG CO. VA.

WB 1-84, 19 Oct 1770, (date probated not shown) <u>will of James Tucker Sen</u>. - names: Son Robert - Son Elijah - Son George - son Matthew - son Harbud - son Bartley - Wife Elizabeth Tucker - dad Lucyetia Burton - son Myhall Tucker - son James Tucker - son <u>Warner Tucker</u> - <u>ten shillings sterling</u>, son Hutson Tucker - dau Mary Hudson -

SUMMARY:

Warner Tucker was b 1732 in Pr. Geo. Co., Va. and was among the older sons of James Tucker Sr (the Elder) and his 1st wf Mary. He lived in Pr. Geo. Co. 1751, in Lunenburg Co. 1752 & in Amelia Co. 1757-60. The Lists of Tithables for Amelia Co. are incomplete 1757-60, but he is not found on the records of Amelia, Lunenburg or Mecklenburg Counties 1760-99.

What happened to him after 1760 is not clear. However, he is named In the will of his father. James Tucker, Sr in Mecklenburg Co. Va. written in 1770.

* * *

1. Boddie, John B., "Births 1720-1792 From The Bristol Parish Register of Henrico, Prince George and Dinwiddie"

2. Boddie, John B., "Births 1720-1792 From The Bristol Parish Register of Henrico, Prince George and Dinwiddie"

TJ113000 - HUDSON TUCKER

SON OF JAMES TUCKER SR
(THE ELDER)
MD 1ST MARY
MD 2ND ELIZABETH

MECKLENBURG CO. VA.

DB 2-44, 19 Apr 1768, rec 9 May 1768, James Tucker Senr to son Hudson Tucker, for L151.10., 151 ac. on Allens Cr., bo Robert Burton, James Tucker Junr, John Humphries. Wit: Spence Waddy, Robert Burton. S/ James x Tucker. Acknowledged by James Tucker Senr & Elizabeth his wife. (See DB 2-401)

DB 2-401, 14 May 1770, rec 14 May 1770, Hudson Tucker to James Tucker Jr. for L150.10., 151 ac. on Allens Cr. at mouth of a spring branch, bo. Robert Burton, James Tucker, Thomas Whitworth, Edwards. Wit: Spence Waddy, Robt Blake, Saml Whitworth. S/ Hudson x Tucker. (See DB 2-44)

WB 1-84, 19 Oct 1770, (date probated not shown) will of James Tucker Sen. - names: Son Robert - Son Elijah - Son George - son Matthew - son Harbud - son Bartley - Wife Elizabeth Tucker - dan Lucyetia Burton - son Myhall Tucker- son James Tucker - son Warner Tucker - son Hutson (Hudson) Tucker - ten shillings sterling - dau Mary Hudson,

DB 5-58, 7 Jan 1777, rec 12 May 1777, James Tucker Sr. to Hudson Tucker, for L52., 200 ac., bo. Old Courthouse Rd., James Brown, old Ordinary Spring Br., Allens Cr., Robert Burton, John Hudson. S/ James Tucker. Wit: Peter Oliver, Thomas Berry, Garner Tucker. (See DB 6-506).

NOTE: Since Hudson Tucker's father James Tucker Sr had already died, the James Tucker Sr (formerly Jr) was Hudson's brother.

DB 6-506, 12 Sep 1785, rec 12 Sep 1785, Hudson Tucker to Robert Burton, for L200., 200 ac. on n.s. Allens Cr., bo Thomas Stone, William Green, William Hudson, David Crowder, James Brown, John Edwards, sd Burton. S/ Hudson Tucker, Wit: Robert Burton, Archer Burton, William Coleman. (See DB 5-58).

DB 8-227, 19 Nov 1792, rec 10 Dec 1792, Catharine Tucker appoint my well beloved friend Robert Burton as lawful attorney -- to make lawful conveyance of any lands. -- S/ Catharine x Tucker, Wit: Hudson x Tucker, Zachariah Shackleford.

DB 8-227, 1 Nov 1792, rec 10 Dec 1792, <u>Hudson Tucker appoint my beloved friend Robert Burton as lawful attorney -- to make lawful conveyance of any lands</u> --. S / Hudson x Tucker, Wit: Thomas Crowder, Archer Wilson.

NOTE: Robert Burton in the above deeds is brother-in-law to Hudson Tucker.

SUMMARY: Hudson Tucker was at least age 21 when his father deeded land to him in 1768, in Mecklenburg Co. Va. He was born by 1747 or earlier, most probably in Pr. Geo. Co. Va., son of James Tucker Sr (the Elder) & 1st wf Mary.

He lived in Mecklenburg Co. from ca 1768. In 1785, he sold all his land to his brother-in-law Robert Burton, husband of his sister Lucretia, whom he also appointed power of attorney in 1792, and probably moved to another county or state.

TJ114000 - ROBERT TUCKER

MD MARY
SON OF JAMES TUCKER SR
(THE ELDER)
MD 1ST MARY
MD 2ND ELIZABETH

MECKLENBURG CO. VA.

WB 1-84, 19 Oct 1770, (date probated not shown) will of James Tucker Sen. - names: Son Robert -100 ac. known by name of His Clearing & to extend up to my son James Tucker's line plus negro man Will. - Son Elijah - Son George – son Matthew - son Harbud - son Bartley - Wife Elizabeth Tucker - dau Lucyetia Burton - son Myhall Tucker - son James Tucker - son Warner Tucker - son Hutson Tucker - dau Mary Hudson.

DB 4-17, 14 Jan 1773, rec 12 Apr 1773, Robert Tucker of Mecklenburg Co. to Mathew Marable, for L23.16.1., which sd Tucker is indebted to Mathew Marable & desires to secure & pay, & further consideration of 5 shillings pd to Robert Tucker by Mathew Marable, 100 ac. being same given to sd Robert by his father's will; also-one negro man slave Will, given to sd Robert by his father's will. S/ Robert x Tucker. Wit: Edward Finch, Daniel Thweatt, James x Tucker Senr. (See DB 4-519)

DB 4-519, 16 Mar 1776, rec 13 May 1776, whereas Robert Tucker having fully complied with payment of L23.16.1. & all costs & interest thereon, it is agreed by both parties that title to property shall revert to sd Robert Tucker. S/ Mat Marable. Wit: Dionysius Oliver, George Tucker, Ransone Foster.

NOTE: (Property referred to was 100 ac. & negro man Will). (Ref DB 4-17 above & DB 4-522 below)

DB 4-522, 13 May 1776, rec 13 May 1776, Robert Tucker to Peter Oliver, for L50., 100 ac. on br. of Butchers Cr., bo. Jones, Oliver, Tucker, Murray, being land given to Robert Tucker by his father's will. S/ Robert x Tucker, Wit: Dionysius Oliver, Ransone Foster, George Tucker. On 13 Sep 1779 Mary Tucker, wife of Robert Tucker relinq dower. (See WB 1-84)

DB 5-15, rec 10 Mar 1777, Elizabeth Tucker to Robert Tucker for L50., the 100 ac. I now live on, also one negro man Joe, one wench Sarah, 9 head cattle, all hogs, 4 head of horses. S/ Elizabeth Tucker. Wit: James Brown, Susanna Brown, Edward x Moore. (See WB 1-244 & DB 5-480)

WB 1-244, wd 5 Sep 1777, wp 1(1 Nov 1777, <u>will of Matthew Tucker names mother Elizabeth Tucker & brother Robert Tucker</u>.- Refers to his part of land & a negro wench left him by his father. <u>Leaves estate to mother for life and then to go to brother Robert Tucker</u>. Exor: Friend Peter Oliver. Wit: Peter Oliver, Henry Carleton & Edmund Bentley. (See WB 1-84, DB 5-15 & DB 5-480)

DB 5-280, 20 Apr 1778, rec 13 Jul 1778, <u>James Tucker to Robert Tucker</u> for L16., <u>16 ac.</u> on br. of Allens Cr. bo. Bilbow, Jones, Stith. S/ James Tucker. (See DB 5-480)

DB 5-480, 29 Jun 1779, rec 13 Sep 1779, <u>Robert Tucker</u> to William W. Green, for L800., <u>100 ac.</u> on s.s. of a br. of Allens Cr., <u>being land willed by my father James Tucker Sr., to my brother Mathew Tucker & by his death it fell to me as heir, including 16 ac. adj. that I purchased of my brother James Tucker</u>, the whole of the above joins Peter Jones & Peter Burton. S/ Robert x Tucker, Wit: Asa Oliver, Edward x Moore, Sarah Oliver. <u>Wf Mary. relinq dower</u>. (See WE 1-84, WE 1-244, DB 5-15 & DB 5-280)

NOTE: The above deed identifies Robert Tucker's wife as Mary. This compiler could find no record of this marriage in either Mecklenburg Co. or Lunenhurg Co.

Robert Tucker was at least age 21 in 1773 when he pledged the 100 ac. inherited from his father to secure a debt, so he was born ca 1752, the son of James Tucker Sr & 1st wife Mary.

His younger brother Matthew died in 1777, leaving his inheritance of 100 ac. & a wench to his mother for life, then to brother Robert. It appears that DB 5-15 above refers to this 100 ac. which James Tucker Sr had willed (WB 1-84) to son Matthew after wife's death, & which Matthew willed (WE 1-244) to mother Elizabeth for Life, then to brother Robert, and upon Matthew's death, Elizabeth deeded the 100 ac. to Robert.

In 1779, Robert Tucker & wf Mary sold their land in Mecklenburg Co. and probably moved to Halifax Co., Va..

HALIFAX CO., VA.

DB 12-18, 18 May 1780, rec 18 May 1780, James Bailey of Halifax Co. to <u>Robert Tucker of Mecklenburg Co.</u>, for. L300, <u>150 ac.</u> on-the bold branch of Banister Ri., it being part of 250 ac. formerly surveyed For John Howell. (See DB 13-179).

DB 12-368, 3 Sep 1783, rec 16 Oct 1783, Jeffery Barksdale of state of N.C., to Robert Tucker of Halifax Co., Va., 185 ac. on b.s. Bradley Cr. S/ Jeffrey x Barksdale. Wit: Reuben Ragsdale, Sam'l Bentley, Reuben Ragsdale, Jr. (See DB 12-369).

NOTE: Robert Tucker's younger brother Elijah Tucker also sold his inheritance in Mecklenburg Co. and bought land in Halifax Co. on Bradley Cr. beginning in 1796.

DB 12-369, 16 Oct 1783, rec 16 Oct 1783, Robert Tucker of Halifax Co. to Henry Baird of Buckingham Co., for L80., 185 ac. on b.s. Bradley Cr. S/ Robert (R) Tucker. Wf Mary relinq dower right. (See 12-368).

DB 12-426, 28 Feb 1784, rec 18 Mar 1784, John Milam Jr to Robert Tucker for L75., 100 ac. btwn Bradley Cr. & Foulouse's Br., which sd Milam purchased fr Nathaniel Hall. S/ John Milam, Nancy x (his wife). Wit: Nath'l Hall, Frederick Farmer, Daniel Easley. (See DB 13-309).

DB 13-179, 19 May 1785, rec 19 May 1735, Robert Tucker to John Murphy, for L150., 150 ac., bo. - Haskins, Smith & Richard Cox. S/Robert Tucker. (See DB 12-18).

DB 13-309, 20 Oct 1785, rec 20 Oct 1785, Robert Tucker & wf Mary to Isaac Easely, for L105., 100 ac. on Bradley Cr., bo. Francis Petty, Sarah Dejarnett, William Pearman, Daniel Easely, Thomas Boyce. S/ Robert x Tucker, Mary x Tucker. Wit: Reuben Ragland, Nipper Adams, John Butler. (See DB 12-426).

DB 14-179, 18 Oct 1787, rec 18 Oct 1787, Fenton Hall to Robert Tucker, for L115., 100 ac. on s.s. Banister Ri, including plantation where sd Fenton Hall now lives, bo. King, Follesses, Murphy, Gill. S/ Fenton Hall. Wit: James W. Cran Jr., Joseph Collins, Thomas Vaughan Nance. (See DB 15-76).

DB 14-263, 18 Oct 1787, rec 23 Jun 1788, Robert Tucker to Benjamin Abbott, for for L100., negro fellow Tom, negro woman Sarah, 5 head cattle, 2 feather beds, one bay mare. S/ Robert (R) Tucker. Wit: James Stevens, Benjamin Hall, Nimrod Ferguson.

DB 15-76, 28 May 1790, rec 28 Feb 1791, Robert Tucker to Richard Walne, for L75., 100 ac. on s.s. Banister Ri, bo. John Gilles & Samuel. Murphey, James Fowlass(?), Robert Wooding, Henry King. S/ Robert Tucker. Wit: William Phelps, John M. Allister, Like Milner, Ni____ Adams, Bartly Tucker. Wf Mary relinq dower right. (See DB 14-179)

NOTE: Bartly Tucker who witnesses the above deed, was also a brother of the subject Robert Tucker.

SUMMARY OF LAND TRANSACTIONS IN HALIFAX CO.:

Year	Reference	Transaction		Plus		Minus	Bal
1780	DB 12-18	fr Bailey	(a)	150			150
1783	DB 12-368	fr Barksdale	(b)	185			335
1783	DB 12-369	to Baird			(b)	185	150
1784	DB 12-426	fr Milam	(c)	100			250
1785	DB 13-179	to Murphy			(a)	150	100
1785	DB 13-309	to Easely			(c)	100	0
1787	DB 14-179	fr Hall	(d)	100			100
1790	DB 15-76	to Walne			(d)	100	0

LAND TAX RECORDS

1782   Robert Tucker 150 ac.
1784   Robert Tucker 100 ac. fr John Milam.
1788   Robert Tucker 100 ac. fr Fenton Hall
1789   Robert Tucker 100 ac.
1790   Robert Tucker 100 ac.

NOTE: Robert Tucker's brothers also appeared on the personal tax records of Halifax Co, Va, beginning in 1785: Harbert in 1785-86-87-88; Bartlett 1786-87-88-90; George 1788 only, and Elijah 1789-1856. There is no evidence that Harbert, Bartlett or George owned any land there. Elijah owned land on Bradley Cr where he resided until his death in 1856.

NOTE: Robert Tucker did not appear on the land tax records of Halifax Co., Va. after 1790. This compiler has not further researched this Robert Tucker & wf Mary.

SUMMARY: Robert Tucker son of James Tucker & 1st wf Mary, b 1752 in Lunenburg Co., md Mary ____, lived in Mecklenburg Co. until 1779 & lived in Halifax Co, Va. until 1790.

TJ115000 - MATTHEW TUCKER

SON OF JAMES TUCKER SR
(THE ELDER)
MD 1ST MARY
MD 2ND ELIZABETH

MECKLENBURG CO. VA.

WB 1-84, 19 Oct 1770, (date probated not shown) will of James Tucker Sen. - names: - Son Robert - Son Elijah - Son George -. I give the last tract of land I purchased of my son James Tucker & known by name of Bilbors(?), to be equally divided btwn my other three sons: son Matthew to be laid off on s.s. of branch; plus negro woman after wife's death. son Harbud's part to be laid off _____ to Murpheys line & to include the clearing & barn; plus negro boy Peter. son Bartley (or Bartlett) his part btwn Harbud & Elijah; plus negro named ___?. - Wife Elizabeth Tucker - dau Lucyetia Burton - son Myhall Tucker - son James Tucker - son Warner Tucker - son Hutson Tucker -dau Mary Hudson.

WB 1-244, wd 5 Sep 1777, wp 10 Nov 1777, will of Matthew Tucker names mother Elizabeth Tucker & brother Robert Tucker. Refers to his part of land & a negro wench left him by his father. Leaves estate to mother for life and then to go to brother Robert Tucker. Exor: Friend Peter Oliver. Wit: Peter Oliver, Henry Carleton & Edmund Bentley. (See WB 1-84, DB 5-15 & DB 5-480)

DB 5-15, rec 10 Mar 1777, Elizabeth Tucker to Robert Tucker for L50., the 100 ac. I now live on, also one negro man Joe, one wench Sarah, 9 head cattle, all hogs, 4head of horses. S/ Elizabeth Tucker. Wit: James Brown, Susanna Brown, Edward x Moore.

DB 5-480, 29 Jun 1779, rec 13 Sep 1779, Robert Tucker to William W. Green, for L800., 100 ac. on s.s. of a br. of Allens Gr., being land willed by my father James Tucker Sr., to my brother Mathew Tucker & by his death it fell to me as heir, including 16 ac. adj. that I purchased of my brother James Tucker, the whole of the above joins Peter Jones & Peter Burton. S/ Robert x Tucker, Wit: Asa Oliver, Edward x Moore, Sarah Oliver. Wf Mary relinq dower. (See WB 1-84, WE 1-244, & DB 5-280.)

SUMMARY: Matthew Tucker must have been at least age 21 when he wrote his will in 1777, so he would have been born ca 1756. He died in 1777 without issue.

TJ116000 - GEORGE TUCKER

MD KEZIA
SON OF JAMES TUCKER SR
(THE ELDER)
MD 1ST MARY
MD 2ND ELIZABETH

MECKLENBURG CO. VA.

WB 1-84, 19 Oct 1770, (date probated not shown) <u>will of James Tucker Sen.</u> - names: - Son Robert - Son Elijah - <u>Son George - 100 ac. on Jones's line, being the last part of the first tract I bought of my son James Tucker-plus negro man Joe after wife's death</u>.- son Matthew son Harbud - son Bartley - Wife Elizabeth Tucker - negro man Joe - for life, then <u>Joe to son George Tucker</u>. Dau Lucyetia Burton - son Tucker - son James Tucker - son Warner Tucker - son Hutson Tucker - dau Mary Hudson.

DB 5-80, 13 Apr 1777, rec 11 Aug 1777, <u>George Tucker to James Tucker Jr.</u> for L44., <u>97 ac., being left to sd George Tucker by his father James Tucker</u> & adj. Capt Peter Jones. S/ George Tucker. Wit: Thomas Berry, Edward x Moore, James x Tucker Senr. Acknowledged by <u>George Tucker & wf. Keziah</u> relinq dower.

HALIFAX CO., VA

NOTE: George Tucker and his brothers appeared on the personal tax records of Halifax Co, Va, beginning in 1782: Robert 1782-89, Harbert in 1785-86-87-88; Bartlett 1786-87-88-90; George 1788 only with his brother Harbert, and Elijah 1789-1856. There is no evidence that Harbert, Bartlett or George owned any land there. Robert owned land on Bradley Cr & Banister Ri 1780-90. Elijah owned land on Bradley Cr beginning in 1796 where he resided until his death in 1556.

This compiler has not further researched the subject George Tucker.

SUMMARY: George Tucker, son of James Tucker Sr & 1st wf Mary, b ca 1756, was married to Kezia ____ in 1777 when he sold land inherited from his father, in Mecklenburg Co., Va. and probably moved to another county or state.

TJ117000 - HERBERT TUCKER

MD 1ST FRANCES DEJARNETTE
MD 2ND HELENA VARNAN
SON OF JAMES TUCKER SR
(THE ELDER)
MD 1ST MARY
MD 2ND ELIZABETH

MECKLENBURG CO. VA.

WB 1-84, 19 Oct 1770, (date probated not shown) will of James Tucker Sen. - names: - Son Robert - Son Elijah - Son George -. I give the last tract of land I purchased of my son James Tucker & known by name of Bilbors(?), to be equally divided btwn my other three sons: son Matthew to be laid off on s.s. of branch; plus negro woman after wife's death. son Harbud's (or Herbert) part to be laid off _?_ to Murpheys line & to include the clearing & barn; plus negro boy Peter. - son Bartley - Wife Elizabeth Tucker - dau Lucyetia Burton - son Myhall Tucker - son James Tucker - son Warner Tucker - son Hutson Tucker - dau Mary Hudson.

DB 6-397, 21 Aug 1784, rec 13 Sep 1784, Herbert Tucker to John Hyde Sr., for L120., 98 3/4 ac. (as of late survey), being willed to sd Herbert by his father, bo. Joel Bevil, Edward Bevil. S/ Herbert Tucker. Wit: Robt Hyde, Erwin Hyde, Thomas Whitworth. (See WB1-84)

NOTE: Herbert Tucker must have been at least age 21 in 1784 in Mecklenburg Co, Va, when he sold his inheritance and moved to Halifax Co, Va, so he was probably b ca 1763.

HALIFAX CO., VA.

NOTE: Herbert Tucker and his brothers appeared on the personal tax records of Halifax Co, Va, beginning in 1782: Robert 1732-89, Herbert in 1785-86-87-88; Bartlett 1786-87-88-90; George 1788 only, and Elijah 1789-1856. There is no evidence that Herbert, Bartlett or George owned any land there. Robert owned land on Bradley Cr & Banister Ri 1782-90. Elijah owned land on Bradley Cr beginning in 1796 where he resided until his death in 1856.

SUMMARY: Herbert (Harbud) Tucker b ca 1763 in Lunenburg Go, Va, son of James Tucker Sr, & probably his 2nd wife Elizabeth.

This compiler did not further research the subject Herbert Tucker.

NOTE: The following information was graciously provided by Mary McCampbell Bell, C.G.R.S., who is a descendant of Bartlett Tucker, brother of Herbert. Her proof notes are indicated in parentheses ().

Harbert Tucker b 1760 (1) in Amelia Co Va, (1) d either 1835 Abbeville Co, SC (12) or 1843 Madison Co, GA (3), m 1st 22 May 1785 (13) Halifax Co, Va, (3) Frances DeJarnette (2,13) b 1768 (3,12) Halifax Co, Va, d 9 Feb 1805 (2,12) Anderson Co, SC, dau of. Elias DeJarnet (9) d 1783 (9) Halifax Co, Va, & wf Sarah Hall. (9) , and had issue:

1. Sally Tucker (2,12,13) b 10 Dec 1786 (13) d 1834 (3) md John Griggs Hall.

2. Elizabeth Tucker (2,13) b 2 Dec 1788 (13).

3. Henry C. Tucker (1,13) b 17 Apr 1792, alive 1854 (1).

4. Degarnet Tucker (2,13) b 13 Jun 1794 (13), d 29 Dec 1877 (15), m 1st Lucy Hall (1794-16 Oct 1836) (15) m 2nd Sarah Tucker (1793-1883) (dau of Bartley).

5. Nancy Tucker (2,13) b 23 Jun 1796 (2,13), d 1 Aug 1877, m 1312 (12) William Shaw.

6. Frances Tucker (2,13) b 30 Jun 1798 (13), d 3 Sep 1883, m 11 Oct 1815 (12) William Pruitt (12) (28 Dec 1790-1855).

7. Herbert Tucker (2,13) b 9 Jan 1800 (13), d 1836 (6) Anderson Co, SC.

8. James Tucker (13) b 28 May 1802 (2,13), m Rhoda Hall (?) Frances Hall (12), out of state 1832 (10).

Harbert Tucker m 2nd 22 May 1806 (3,11) Abbeville Co, SC, (11), or 1800 (13), Helena Varnan, & had issue:

9. Williama G. Tucker (13) b 28 Sep 1807 (13), m 17 May 1827 (13) Emily L. Haley.

10. Louisa Tucker (13), b 9 Aug 1809 (13), m 22 May 1831 (13) Joshua K. Erwin.

11. Permelia Tucker (13) b 15 Jul 1811 (13).

12. Thomas Jefferson Tucker (13) h 17 Dec 1313 (13).

13. Eleanor Tucker (13), b 14 Nov 1816 (13).

14. Elmina Earle Tucker (13), b 26 Nov 1820 (13), m 25 Nov 1841 (13) Henry D. Paton.

15. Elizabeth Katherine Tucker (13), b 2 Sep 1824 (13) d prior 1840?.

PROOF NOTES of Mary McCampbell Bell.

1) Harbert's pension application

2) Bible belonging to B.S. Mitchel

3) DeJarnette & Allied Families

4) estate settlement 1836 And. Co.

5) Fenton Hall will 1817 And. Co.

6) heirs of Harbert Jr 1836

7) S.C. marriages DAR

8) James Tucker will-Mecklen. Co.

9) Elias DeJarnette-Halifax Co.

10) Fenton Hall estate-Abbe.

11) LDS computer file index

12) Pruitt Family by A.B. Pruitt

13) Harbert Tucker Bible

14) Mecklenburg Co Fidiciary Bk

15) Book of the Dead

TJ118000 - BARTLETT (BARTLEY) TUCKER

MD 1ST HANNAH DEJARNETTE
MD 2ND NANCY LEVERETT

SON OF JAMES TUCKER SR
(THE ELDER)

MD 1ST MARY
MD 2ND ELIZABETH

MECKLENBURG CO. VA.

WB 1-84, 19 Oct 1770, (date probated not shown) <u>will of James Tucker Sen</u>. - names - Son Robert - Son Elijah - Son George. I give the last tract of land I purchased of my on James Tucker & known by name of Bilbors(?), to be equally divided btwn my other three sons: son Matthew to be laid off on s.s. of branch; plus negro woman after wife's death. son Harbud's part to be laid off ___ to Murpheys line & to include the clearing & barn; plus negro boy Peter. <u>son Bartley (or Bartlett) his part btwn Harbud & Elijah; plus negro named ___</u>?. - Wife Elizabeth Tucker - dau Lucyetia Burton - son James Tucker - son Warner Tucker - son Hutson Tucker - dau Mary Hudson.

DB 6-407, 26 Oct 1784, rec 8 Nov 1784, <u>Bartlett Tucker</u> to Erwin Hyde, for L60., <u>98 3/4 ac. by recent survey being land left to him by will of his father</u>, bo. Edward Bevil, John Keeton. S/ Bartlett Tucker. Wit: John Keeton, John Keeton Jr, Peter Burton, Hudson x Tucker.

NOTE: Bartlett Tucker must have been at least age 21 in 1784 in Mecklenburg Co, Va, when he sold his inheritance and moved to Halifax Co, Va, so he was probably b ca 1763. However, see conflicting dates following.

HALIFAX CO., VA

NOTE: Bartlett Tucker and his brothers appeared on the personal tax records of Halifax Co, Va, beginning in 1782: Robert 1782-89, Harbert in 1785-86-87-88; Bartlett 1786-87-88-90; George 1788 only, and Elijah 1789-1856. In 1786 Bartlett was listed as not having attained age 21; in 1787 he was listed as age 16-21; and in 1788 he was listed as age over 21. This would indicate he was b ca 1766. His cemetery record (see below) shows him b 1760. His mother's name and his place of birth depend upon which birth date is correct. His parents lived in Lunenburg Co 1754-64, in Mecklenburg Co 1765-73. His father's 1st wf was named Mary, his 2nd wf Elizabeth.

There is no evidence that Harbert, Bartlett or George owned any land in Halifax Co. Robert owned land on Bradley Cr & Banister Ri 1780-90. Elijah owned land on Bradley Cr beginning in 1796, where he resided until his death in 1856.

SUMMARY: Bartlett (Bartley) Tucker b ca 1760/66 most probably in Lunenburg Co., the son of James Tucker Sr & most probably his 2nd wife Elizabeth. This compiler did not further research Bartlett Tucker, but see the following.

NOTE: The following information was graciously provided by Mary McCampbell Bell, C.G.R.S., who is a descendant of Bartley Tucker. Her proof notes are indicated by numbers (_) for Bartley Tucker and (R_) for Reuben Tucker, which follow this summary.

Bartley Tucker b ca 1760 (18) in Amelia Co Va, son of James Tucker & wf Elizabeth Jackson (can't prove this at all - MMB), d 10 Mar 1841 (18) at Anderson Co SC (2), buried First Creek Cemetery, Anderson Co. SC (2,18), denomination Baptist, md 1st ca 1785 Halifax Co VA, (6) Hannah (18) DeJarnette (9), md 2nd Nancy Leverett, dau of Stephen.

Hannah DeJarnette b ca 1769 (2,18) Prince Edward Co. VA (9), dau of Elias DeJarnette (9,10) & wf Sarah Hall , d 5 Jun 1835 (2,18) Anderson Co. SC, buried First Creek Cemetery Anderson Co. SC, denomination Baptist.

Bartley Tucker & 1st wf Hannah DeJarnette had issue:

1. William Tucker (17) b ca 1786-7 (4) probably Halifax Co. VA, d 1872 wd 17 Jan 1870, wp 1872 (12) Anderson Co. SC, md 1st Alcanza Milford (9), md 2nd Eunice Plunkett (9), md 3rd Sarah Purdy Boyd (9,12).

2. Reuben DeJarnette Tucker (17) b ca 1789(?) probably Halifax Co. VA, d 30 Mar 1857 Cobb Co. GA (14), md 3 Jun 1824 (13) probab. Abbeville Go. SC, Mary H. Hall, dau of probably William A. Hall (son of Fenton) of Halifax. Reuben DeJarnette Tucker & wf Mary had issue:

2.1 Robert A. Tucker b 15 Apr 1825 (R1) Anderson Co. SC, md 9 Oct 1848 Mary Burton (R9) Anderson Co. SC.

2.2 Etherlinder E. Tucker b 21 Feb 1827 (R1) Anderson Co. SC, d .5 Dec 1898 (R10) Cobb Co. GA, md 29 Aug 1861 James Burton, (R10) Anderson Co SC.

2.3 Hannah B. Tucker (Brown?) b 26 Aug 1829 (R1) Anderson Co. SC, d 6 May 1916 (R4) Cobb Co. GA, md 29 Aug 1861 Jackson Delk, (R1) Cobb Co. GA.

2.4 Rhoda Ann Tucker b 12 Feb 1832 (R1), md ca 1853

Benjamin F. Bishop (R11).

2.5 Jency Emaline Tucker b 9 Jun 1834 (R1) Anderson Co. SC, md ca 1860 Fletcher M. Simpson (R11).

2.6 Mary Massanine Tucker b 13 Dec 1836 (R1) Anderson Co. SC, md 4 Oct 1868 William Roberts (R12) Cobb Co. GA.

2.7 Nancy Sabina Tucker b 13 Jul 1840 (R1) Anderson Co. SC, d 13 Oct 1914 (R2) Cobb Co. GA., md ca 1360-63 Jact D. Roberts, Cobb Co. GA.

2.8 Rebecca Dallis Tucker b 7 Dec 1844 (R1) Anderson Co. SC, d 22 Jul 1933 (R15) Calhoun Co. MS, md 3 Nov 1868 Haston Dunn (R12).

3. Elizabeth Tucker (17) b 27 Apr 1791 (2) Pendleton Dist, SC, d 15 Jun 1876 (2) Anderson Go. SC, md ca 1825 Alexander D. Gray (13).

4. John C. (1,3) [Cleo?](2) Tucker b ca 1793? (2) Pendleton Dist, d 1864 (2) Anderson Co. SC, md Vanner Brown? (2).

5. Sarah Tucker (17) b 1795 (2,18) Pendleton Dist, d 1 Nov 1883 (2,18) Anderson Co. SC, md (1st) ca 1820 Absolem Hall (he died 1824), md (2nd) 1st cousin DeJarnette Tucker (he died 1877).

6. Mary Tucker (17) b ca 1800 Pendleton Dist, md Fenton Hall Jr (he died 1848 Abbeville Co. SC).

7. Jane (Jincy) Tucker (17) b ca 1803 (11) Pendleton Dist, d 1859 (2) Anderson Co. SC, md ca 1819 William Newell (13).

8. Frances Tucker (17) b ca 1803 (11) Pendleton Dist, d 1859 (2) Anderson Co. SC., md ca 1828 Eziekiel Hall (9,17).

9. James Tucker (17) b ca 1807 (11) Pendleton Dist. md 1st Priscilla Davis (9) (she d 1836)(9), md 2nd ca 1844 Fannie Hall (9).

10. Nancy Tucker (17) b ca 1810 (11) Pendleton Dist, living in 1883 (17) Gwinnett Co. GA, md ca 1828 Robert D. Gray (13).

* * *

PROOF NOTES OF MARY MCCAMPBELL BELL:

(1) Reuben C. Tucker est. paper 1872, Anderson Co. SC.

(2) "Book of the Dead" by Smith (Anderson Co. cemetery).

(3) "Abstracts of 96" by Young.

(4) 1850 census Abbeville Co., SC.

(5) Harbert Tucker Rev War Pension application.

(6) Personal property tax records show him in Halifax.

(7) James Tucker will Mecklenberg Co. VA. (Bk 1, p 88).

(8) Meck. D.B.1

(9) "DeJarnette & Allied families" by Frost.

(10) Elias DeJarnett will - Hal

(11) 1850 census Anderson Co. SG

(12) Wm Tucker will 1870-Anderson Co. SC.

(13) Bartley Tucker account book in possession of Lucille Burton, Marietta, Cobb Co. GA.

(14) Sardis Baptist Church cemetery, Marietta, Cobb Co.GA.

(15) Abbeville Co. SC - Equity case Davis vs Hall.

(16) Jackson Delk Bible gives birth dates of Reuben Tucker's children.

(17) Bartley Tucker will and estate papers - Anderson Co. SC.

(18) First Creek Baptist Church cemetery, Anderson Co. SC (Abbeville Co. line).

(19) 1830 Abbeville Co. SC census p 78.

(20) Abington Parish Register, Gloucester Co. VA.

(21) DAR #214524 - Essie R. Cook Bryson, grandfather of Rebecca & Abner Clinkscales.

(R1) Bartley Tucker account bk, Delk family Bible.

(R2) Sardis Baptist Church, Marietta, Cobb Co. GA.

(R4) First Creek Baptist Church Cemetery, Anderson Co. SC.

(R9) Tucker Bible - Mrs. Mary White, Anderson, SC.

(R10) Burton Bible-Lucille Reece, Marietta, GA.

(R11) Mary Hall Tucker est papers, Cobb Co. GA.

(R12) Not shown on Bell papers.

(R15) Not shown on Bell papers.

TJ119000 - ELIJAH TUCKER

MD 1ST BETSY (ELIZABETH) BARLEY
MD 2ND SALLY BAINES

SON OF JAMES TUCKER SR
(THE ELDER)
MD 1ST MARY
MD 2ND ELIZABETH

MECKLENBURG CO. VA.

WB 1-84, 19 Oct 1770, (date probated not shown) will of James Tucker Sen. - names: - Son Robert - Son Elijah plantation whereon I live with ? _ hundred ac. adj Robert to dividing line btwn them., after death of my wife; plus negro boy Sam. - Son George - son Matthew - son Harbud - son Bartley - Wife Elizabeth Tucker - dau Lucyetia Burton - son Myhall Tucker - son James Tucker son Warner Tucker - son Hutson Tucker - dau Mary Hudson.

DB 8-40. 2 feb 1791, rec 13 Jun 1791, Elijah Tucker of Halifax Co., (Va) to Richard Walne, for L50., 100 ac., being land given me by my father, joining Robert Tucker, Caty Tucker, Peter Jones, John Keeton, Irvin Hyde & John Bevil. S/ Elijah x Tucker. Wit: Thomas Carr, Josiah Clay, John McAlister, William Harry Bass, John Philps.

NOTE: The identity of Caty Tucker is unknown to this compiler. Elijah Tucker sold his inheritance in Mecklenburg Co. and moved to Halifax Co., Va.

HALIFAX CO., VA.

MARRIAGE BOOK 1-17. 3 Dec 1789, Elijah Tucker md Betsy Bailey (or Barley), Bondsman: John Bailey (or Barley), Witness: James Thompson.

NOTE: The John Bailey & Betsy Bailey in the above marriage record are most likely John Barley, & his sister Betsy (or Elizabeth) Barley who married Elijah Tucker, they being children of Elizabeth Barley who died 1815. (See below).

WB 10-164, wd 13 Apr 1815, wp 24 Apr 1815, will of Elizabeth Barley. to granddaughter Elizabeth Barley - 1 feather bed. to daughter Elizabeth Tucker - one woman saddle & one chair. to son John Barley & Elizabeth Tucker - negro boy Ransome, equally divided btwn them. to grandson Stephen Barley - 1 pine chest. to two grandchildren David B. Wiatt(sic) & Lacey Wyatt(sic) $100.00 to be equally divided btwn them to be put out on interest until they become of age. to granddaughter Polly Witt (sic) – one ____. to son William Barley – 32 pounds, 10 shillings, which he is owing me. <u>All other proper to son John Barley & dau, Elizabeth Tucker, equally divided btwn them</u>. Ex: John Barley. Wit: Mary H. Phelps, Mildred T. Phelps, Wm. Royster.

NOTE: Elijah Tucker's older brothers appeared on the personal tax records of Halifax Co, Va, beginning in 1782: Robert 1782-89, Harbert in 1785-86-87-88; Bartlett 1786-87-88-90; George 1788 only. There is no evidence that Harbert, Bartlett or George owned any land there. Robert owned land on Bradley Cr & Banister Ri 1780-90. Elijah owned land on Bradley Cr beginning in 1796, where he resided until his death in 1856.

DB 16-583, 15 Jun 1796, rec 27 Jun 1796, William Steel & wf Polly, to <u>Elijah Tucker</u> for L50., <u>50 ac.</u> on Bradley Cr., bo. Robert Weakley Sr, Henry Baird.

DB 22-66, 27 Mar 1809, <u>Elijah Tucker & wf Betsy to John Barley Jr</u>, for L27., <u>43 ac.</u> on By Cr., bo. Charles Thompson. (Note: This 43 ac. was most probably inherited by Betsy Tucker from her father John Barley Sr.)

DB 24-25, 28 Sep 1812, rec 28 Sep 1812, John Woosley, for L47., to <u>Elijah Tucker</u> <u>57 1/4 ac.</u> on Bradley Cr., bo. sd Tucker, William Carr. S/ John x Woosley. Wit: Peter Rives, Wm. T. Rives.

DB 25-40, 1 Feb 1814, rec 22 Aug 1814, Thomas Carr for $52.00, to <u>Elijah Tucker</u>, 13 ac. on Bradley Cr., being part of land on which Thomas Carr now lives, bo. Sd Tucker, sd Carr. S/ Thomas Carr. Wit: Peter Rives, William T. Rives, Charles Rives.

DB 25-41, 30 Jun 1814, John Woosley for $100., to <u>Elijah Tucker</u>, <u>57 ac.</u> on Bradley Cr., bo Barnett Freeman, Peter Rives, Charles Rives & sd Elijah Tucker. Jeriah Woosley, wf of John Woosley, gave her acknowledgment. S/ John x Woosley, Jeriah x Woosley. Wit: Peter Rives, Dudley Glass, James Old.

DB 26-340, 31 Dec 1816, rec 27 Jan 1817, <u>John Barley & Elijah Tucker</u> for $12.50, to John Wimbish, <u>10 ac.</u> being. <u>the land inherited by the late</u> Elizabeth Barley decd at the death of her son <u>David Barley & devised to</u> <u>sd John Barley & Elijah Tucker by the late will of sd Elizabeth</u>, & adj. land assigned to her as her dower of the est. of John Barley decd. S/ John Barley, Elijah x Tucker. Wit: Armistd Barksdale, John Light, Samuel Lacy. (See WB 10-164)

DB 27-151, 7 Dec 1817, rec 11 Dec 1817, Susanna Hodges, Miles Hodges & wf Nancy, Fielding Hodges & wf Catharine, Elijah Hodges & wf Frances to <u>Elijah Tucker</u>, for L300., <u>200 ac.</u> on Bradley Cr., bo. Barnett Farmer, William C. Tucker, Bush Hodges, Joshua Clay & William Carr.

NOTE: Catharine, wf of Fielding Hodges, was dau. of Elijah Tucker.

William C. Tucker, son of Joel Tucker Sr & wf. Elizabeth Clemons, was 1st cousin of Elijah Tucker.

DB 32-229, 8 Apr 1824, rec 12 Apr 1824, Joseph Bass to secure debt to George Rives for $280., to Elijah Tucker, negro woman Mary, Thomas & Armistead. S/ Joseph Bass, Elijah x Tucker, George Rives. Wit: Wm. T. Rives, William Tucker, J. T. Farmer, James Tucker. (See DB 33-131)

NOTE: William Tucker and James Tucker were most probably sons of Elijah Tucker. Joseph Bass may be related to Sarah Bass who married James Tucker.

DB 33-131 30 Dec 1824, Joseph Bass & Elijah Tucker to Henry Turner, negro woman Mary, boy Thomas & boy Armistead. (See DB 32-229)

DB 34-63, 1 Jan 1826, 10 Jun 1826 William Pringle & wf Alice, for $972., to Elijah Tucker, 162 ac. on Bradley Cr., bo. sd Tucker, Thomas Carr. S/ William Pringle, Alice Pringle.

DB 44-399, 28 Oct 1837, rec 2 Dec 1837, Elijah Tucker for $660., to John Tucker, 165 ac., being part of tract on which Elijah Tucker now lives, bo. Richard Thornton, Thomas Carr. S/ Elijah Tucker, Elizabeth Tucker. Acknowledged by Elizabeth Tucker, wf of Eliiah Tucker.

NOTE: John Tucker is most probably son of Elijah & Elizabeth (Betsy) Tucker. See WB 25-262 below.

DB 44-406, 28 Oct 1837, John F. Farmer & wf Elizabeth, to Elijah Tucker, for $415., 100 ac. on Runaway Cr., bo. sd Elljah Tucker, Joel W. Tucker.

NOTE: Joel W. Tucker was son of Joel Tucker Sr & wf Elizabeth Clemons, Joel Sr being 1st cousin of Elijah.

DB 52-540, 2 Jun 1843, rec 20 Jun 1848, Elilah Tucker to Alexander L. Peters for $135., 90 ac. bo. sd Tucker, Talbalt, Ferrell. S/ Elijah Tucker.

NOTE: Elijah Tucker's first wife Betsy (Elizabeth) Tucker had most probably died before 1848, since she was not a party to the above deed.

MB 1-197, 15 Mar 1851, Elijah Tucker md Sally Baines, signed by bride & minister.

NOTE: Elijah Tucker was shown in the 1850 Census of Halifax Co. as age 84, and living in the same household with Ann Epperson age 40, and Thomas Tucker, overseer, age 20. Ann Epperson was most probably his dau Nancy Epperson. The identity of Thomas Tucker is uncertain. Elijah Tucker was age 85 when he md Sally Baines in 1851, and the marriage record did not further identity her. She was probably the Sarah Bain age 24 in the household of Matthew & Ann Bain, in the 1850 census. Elijah Tucker deeded 50 ac. of his estate to his new wife, Sally, which was later confirmed by commissioners after his death in 1857. As Sally Tucker, she was still holding that 50 ac. in the land tax records 1858-1865.

DB 57-35, 25 Feb 1854, rec 21 Apr 1857, <u>Elijah Tucker to his wf Nancy Bays</u>, for $20., a tract of land (no. ac. not shown) adj. the lands of sd Elijah Tucker. S/ Elijah Tucker.

NOTE: The meaning of above deed is not clear, since Elijah Tucker had married Sally Bains in 1851, unless what this compiler read as "Nancy Bays" was actually "Sally Bains".

WB 25-262, wd 29 Feb 1856, wp 23 Feb 1857, <u>will of Elijah Tucker</u>.
<u>wife Sally Tucker - mansion house & 50 ac. attached</u>.
<u>sons John, James, William, David, daus. Catherine wf of Fielding Hodges, Elizabeth wf of Jack Barber, Nancy Epperson</u>, - $5.00 each.
<u>dau. Martha Bryant</u> - $50.00.
Remainder of est. equally divided btwn son <u>Samuel Tucker, Polly Craddock wife of Daniel Craddock & Sally Epperson wife of Samuel R. Eepperson</u>.
That portion to Sally Epperson to be held in trust by executor for her benefit during her life, and then to be disposed of by her as she may think proper. That portion for son Samuel, & Polly Craddock to be held likewise in trust by executor for their benefit during their lives & then to be equally divided between their children.
Ex: friend Logan P. Anderson. S/ Elijah Tucker. Wit: Peyton Bradshaw, John A. Pringe.

At Dec Court 1856, will of Elijah Tucker presented in court by Logan P. Anderson, executor, & thereupon William, John, & James Tucker and Elizabeth Barber made themselves parties defendants to contest the will.

At court held 23 Feb 1857, defendants appeared & approved the proof of & will was ordered to be recorded & certificate granted to executor to probate the will.

NOTE: It is unusual that Elijah Tucker did not deed any land to his sons John, James, William and David, nor appoint any of them executor, but left remainder of est to son Samuel Tucker, and Polly Craddock and Sally Epperson, who apparently were his daughters. After the will was contested by William, John, James & Elizabeth, it was finally proved, and distribution of his estate was made by Executor Logan P. Anderson.

The birth years of some of the Elijah Tucker family are calculated from ages shown in the 1850 Census: [1]

Household	Name	Age	Calculated Birthyear	
161	Robert R. Adams	30	ca 1820	Overseer
	Sarah A	24	ca 1826	
	John W.	3	ca 1847	
	Robert F.	2	ca 1848	
	Mary A.	1	ca 1849	
162	John Tucker	59	ca 1791	
	Scina	50	ca 1800	
	Mary	20	ca 1830	
	Perlina F.	17	ca 1833	
163	Elijah Tucker	84	ca 1766	
	Ann Epperson	40	ca 1810	
	Thomas Tucker	20	ca 1830	
164	Ann Tucker	60	ca 1790	
	Mary	57	ca 1793	
	Martha	40	ca 1810	
	Sarah	27	ca 1823	
771	James Tucker	57	ca 1793	
	Sarah	50	ca 1800	
	Wesley	23	ca 1827	
	Elda	17F	ca 1833	
	Adaline	15	ca 1835	
	Julia A.	13	ca 1837	
	Cassanna	8	ca 1842	
	James	6	ca 1844	
	Cain (Coan)	3	ca 1847	
368	Samuel R. Epperson	60	ca 1790	
	Sarah	57	ca 1793	
826	Samuel Tucker	30	(see NOTE)	
	Nancy	30	(see NOTE)	
	Richard T.	14	ca 1836	
	Martha C.	12	ca 1838	
	Robert E.	10	ca 1840	
	Izabella	8	ca 1842	
	Sarah	6	ca 1844	
	Devavous T.	4	ca 1846	
	John T.	2/12	ca 1850	

NOTE: Ages questioned - probably both age 38 & b ca 1812.

The marriages of some of the children of Elijah Tucker are also recorded in Halifax Co., Va.: [2]

16 Dec 1813, John Tucker md Wilmoth Hodges who signs her own consent, Sur Bush Hodges, Wit Bush Hodges & Mills Hodges, P 83.

16 May 1317, Fielding Hodges md Catherine Tucker, Sur Elijah Tucker, p 94.

21 Dec 1824, James Tucker md Sarah Bass who signs her own consent. Sur Wm. Tucker, Wit Wm. Tucker & C. L. Davenport, p 117.

13 Mar 1826, Joel M. Barbour md Elizabeth Tucker who signs her own consent. Wit M. M. Stewart & John Carben. p 121.

25 Dec 1830, Daniel Craddock md Polly Tucker, Sur Jno. Tucker, p 133.

DB 57-80, 21 Apr 1857, rec 25 May 1857, commissioners reviewed the land which Elijah Tucker died seized, & assigned to Sally Tucker widow of sd Tucker, 50 ac on both sides of road leading from Concord to Repuhlican Grove, including the mansion house, according to will of sd Tucker. bo. F. F. Thornton, John Tucker.

DB 58-378, 24 Sep 1859, rec 26 Sep 1859, Logan P. Anderson, a Comr in the case of Polly Craddock & c, vs Elijah Tucker Exs & c, to Christopher H. Jennings for $200.90, 98 ac., being a part of lands of est. of Elijah Tucker decd., adj. F. F. Thornton & c. (See DB 59-99)

NOTE: Polly Craddock was wife of Daniel Craddock & dau of Elijah Tucker, as per WB 25-262, will of Elijah Tucker.

DB 59-99, 25 Feb 1860, rec 31 Aug 1860, Christopher H. Jennings & wf. Elizabeth to Robert E. Tucker, for $200.98, 98 ac., it being a part of land belonging to est. of Elijah Tucker decd., adj. F. F. Thornton & c. (See 58-378)

NOTE: Robert E. Tucker was son of Samuel Tucker & wf Nancy, and grandson of Elijah Tucker.

DB 59-432, 27 Nov 1858, rec 25 Nov 1861, Logan P. Anderson, Comr., under a decree of county court Sep term 1858, in the case of Polly Craddock & c, vs Elijah Tucker exr., to Richard Blanks, for $705.60, 196 ac. adj. Paul Carr & c., being part of lands belonging to est. of Elijah Tucker decd.

NOTE: Polly Craddock was wife of Daniel Craddock & dau of Elijah Tucker, as per WB 25-262, will of. Elijah Tucker.

DB 96-40, 30 Nov 1901, rec 8 Apr 1902, James H. Guthrie spec. comr., W. M. Bates & wf Lola J., Jane Clements, <u>Nannie K. Tucke</u>r, Kate Coates, William Coates, William Reese, Elizabeth Owen wife of W. T. Owen - to - Richard Blanks, for $736.36, 199 1/8 ac., in vicinity of Republican Grove, adj. sd Richard Blanks, Mrs. T. R. Fisher, W.I. Jordan & c., - whereas Richard Blanks acting as spec. comr. of circuit court appointed by decree at April term 1901, in suit of Richard Blanks Sr's administrators & c, vs Joseph Blanks & c, did on 28 Jun 1901 sell by public auction the land in the suit, & sd W.M. Bates was purchaser at $3.70 per ac., – & sd Bates having requested that sd land be conveyed to sd Richard Blanks - & Richard Blanks desiring that the other parties named herein who are heirs at law of sd Richard Blanks Sr, decd, -- and the sd Jane Clements, <u>Nannie K. Tucker</u>, Kate Coates, William Coates, William Reese, and Elizabeth Owen for & in consideration of the paymnent to them by the sd Richard Blanks of the respective sums due them in full of their distributive shares in the proceeds of the sale of sd land due them respectively as heirs at law of sd Richard Blanks Sr decd.

NOTE: The above deed may not be pertinent to the subject Elijah Tucker, but is included by this compiler because (1) it was land formerly in the estate of Elijah Tucker per DB 59-432, (2) Elijah Tucker was my great-great grandfather on my father's side of the family, (3) Richard Blanks was my great-great grandfather on my mother's side of the family, (4) his dau Jane Blanks Clements was my great grandmother, and (5) her sister Elizabeth Blanks Owen was married to William Owen, brother of my grandfather Henry Edmund Owen.

LAND TAX RECORDS

1797-98-99	Tucker, Elijah - 50 ac.
1819	Tucker, Elijah - 13 ac. Bradley Cr. (probably 19 ac.)
1822-23-24	Tucker, Elijah - 50 + 200 + 19 ac. Bradley Cr + 57.5 + 57 ac. (. 383.5 ac.)
--	-----
1856-57	Elijah Tucker, 364.5 ac.
1858-59	Elijah Tucker est, 314.5 ac. (50 ac. to wife Sally)
1860-61	Elijah Tucker est, 216.5 ac. (98 ac. to Jennings)
1862	Elijah Tucker est, 20.5 ac. (196 ac. to Blanks)
1863	Elijah Tucker est no longer appeared on tax records.
1858-1865	Sally Tucker, 50 ac. Bradley Cr. (fr Elijah Tucker est.)

NOTE: This compiler could not reconcile the differences between the land tax records and the summary of land transactions shown below. Neither could he account for the 20.5 ac. remaining in the estate in 1862 on land tax records, or the 40.25 ac. remaining in the summary below.

SUMMARY OF LAND TRANSACTIONS OF
ELIJAH TUCKER IN HALIFAX CO. VA.:

Year	Reference	Plus	Minus	Bal.
1796	DB 16-583 fr William Steel,	50		50
	probably inherited fr John Barley Sr	43		93
1809	DB 22-66 to John Barley Jr		43	50
1812	DB 24-25 fr John Woosley	57.25		107.25
1814	DB 25-40 fr Thomas Carr	13		120.25
1814	DB 25-41 fr John Woosley	57		177.25
	Inherited fr Elizabeth Barley	10		187.25
1816	DB 26-340 to John Wimbish		10	177.25
1817	DB 27-151 fr Hodges est.	200		377.25
1826	DB 34-63 fr William Pringle	162		539.25
1837	DB 44-399 to son John Tucker		165	374.25
1837	DB 44-406 fr John Farmer	100		474.25
1848	DB 52-540 to Alexander Peters		90	384.25
1854	DB 57-35 to wife Sally		50	334.25
1859	DB 58-378 est. to Christopher Jennings		98	236.25
1858	DB 59-432 est. to Richard Blanks		196	40.25

SUMMARY: Elijah Tucker, youngest son of James Tucker Sr & 2nd wf Elizabeth, b ca 1766 in Mecklenburg Co., Va., d 1856 in Halifax Co., Va., md 1st 1789 in Halifax Co. Va., Betsy (Elizabeth) Barley, dau. of John Barley & wf Elizabeth, md 2nd 1851 in Halifax Co. Va., Sally Baines, and had issue by his 1st wf:

John Tucker b ca 1791, md 1813 Wilmoth Hodges.

Sally Tucker b ca 1793, md Samuel R. Epperson b ca 1790.

James Tucker b ca 1793, md 1824 Sarah (Sally) Bass.

William Tucker.

David Tucker.

Catharine Tucker, md 1817 Fielding Hodges.

Elizabeth Tucker, md 1826 Joel M. (Jack) Barber.

Nancy Tucker, md _____ Epperson.

Martha Tucker, md _____ Bryant.

Samuel Tucker b ca 1812, md Nancy O. Clark.

Polly Tucker, md 1830 Daniel Craddock.

* * *

1. Chiarito, Marian Dodson, "1850 Census of Halifax County, Virginia"

2. Chiarito, Marian Dodson and Prendergast, James Hadley, "Marriages of Halifax County, Virginia 1801-1831", 1985

TJ119100 - JOHN TUCKER

MD 1ST WILMOTH HODGES
MD 2ND SEANEY (SCINA) GUTHREY
SON OF ELIJAH TUCKER
MD 1ST BETSY (ELIZABETH) BARLEY
MD 2ND SALLY BAINES

HALIFAX CO. VA.

MB 1-83, 16 Dec 1813, John Tucker md Wilmoth Hodges. Bondsman Bush Hodges; Wit: Bush Hodges & Miles Hodges; Signer Wilmoth Hodges, self.

16 May 1817, Fielding Hodges md Catherine Tucker, Sur Elijah Tucker. p 94.

MB 1-175, 28 Aug 1843, John Tucker md Seaney Guthrey, Bondsman Archibald Rowlett.

DB 27-151, 7 Dec 1817, rec 11 Dec 1817, Susanna Hodges, Miles Hodges & wf Nancy, Fielding Hodges & wf Catharine, Elijah Hodges & wf Frances to Elijah Tucker, for L300., 200 ac, on Bradley Cr., bo. Barnett Farmer, William C. Tucker, Bush Hodges, Joshua Clay & William Carr.

DB 44-399, 28 Oct 1837, rec 2 Dec 1837, Elijah Tucker for $660., to John Tucker, 165 ac., being. part of tract on which Elijah Tucker now lives, bo. Richard Thornton, Thomas Carr. S/ Elijah Tucker, Elizabeth Tucker. Acknowledged by Elizabeth Tucker, wf of Elijah Tucker. (See DB 50-629)

WB 25-262, wd 29 Feb 1856, wp 23 Feb 1857, will of Elijah Tucker. - names: - wife Sally Tucker - sons John, James, William, David, daus. Catherine wf of Fielding Hodges, Elizabeth wf of Jack Barber, Nancy Epperson, - all $5.00 each. - dau. Martha Bryant - son Samuel Tucker - Polly Craddock wife of Daniel. Craddock - Sally Epperson wife of Samuel R. Epperson.

At Dec Court 1856, will of Elijah Tucker presented in court by Logan P. Anderson, executor, & thereupon William, John, & James Tucker and Elizabeth Barber made themselves parties defendants to contest the will.

At court held 23 Feb 1857, defendants appeared & approved the proof of & will was ordered to be recorded & certificate granted to executor to probate the will.

The birthdates of some of the John Tucker family are calculated from ages shown in the 1850 census:

Household	Name	Age	Calculated Birthdate	
161	Robert R. Adams	30	ca 1820	Overseer
	Sarah A.	24	ca 1826	
	John W.	3	ca 1847	
	Robert F.	2	ca 1848	
	Mary A.	1	ca 1849	
162	John Tucker	59	ca 1791	Farmer $1,200
	Scina	50	ca 1800	
	Mary	20	ca 1830	
	Perlina F.	17	ca 1833	
163	Elijah Tucker	84	ca 1766	Farmer $1,000
	Ann Epperson	40	ca 1810	
	Thomas Tucker	20	ca 1830	
164	Ann Tucker	60	ca 1790	
	Mary	57	ca 1793	
	Martha	40	ca 1310	
	Sarah	27	ca 1823	
378	Issac H. High	27	ca 1823	Wheel-right
	Elizabeth	25	ca 1825	
	Maneas D. S.	23	ca 1827	

(Note that the four adjacent households and the fifth household include the children of Elijah Tucker.)

NOTES:

The John Tucker who bought part of land on which Elijah Tucker lived, was most probably son of. Elijah & Elizabeth (Betsy) Tucker.

The John Tucker who lived adjacent to Elijah Tucker, and who was age 59 in the census of 1850, would have been born ca 1791-2. This John & wf "Scina" in the 1850 census is most probably the John Tucker who md "Seany" Guthrie in 1843.

The John Tucker who married Wilmoth Hodges in 1813 was probably age 21 when he married, and would have been born ca 1791-2.

Elijah Tucker's dau Catherine md Fielding Hodges in 1817. Elijah Tucker bought 200 ac. from the Hodges family in 1817 (DB 27-151), and sold part of it to his son John Tucker.

This compiler concludes that the John Tucker who md Wilmoth Hodges in 1813, was the same John Tucker who married Seany Guthrey in 1843, and was the same John Tucker (with wf Scina) age 59 in the 1850 census adjacent to Elijah Tucker, and was the same John Tucker son of Elijah Tucter.

DB 50-629, 5 Sep 1845, rec 5 Sep 1845, John Tucker & wf Senea, to secure several debts, (including debts to Nancy Epperson and to Elijah Tucker), sold to Jesse E. Adams, 282 ac adj Elijah Tucker, Peter Rives, Paul Carr, plus another tract of 110 ac adj Coleman ____, John E. Crews, plus negro man Anthony, woman Aggy, boy Isaac, & girl Lize, plus furniture, plantation tools, plus 1 horse, 5 cows & 15 hogs., but if debts paid by 1 Jan 1826, then this endenture to be void, otherwise to remain in full force. (See DB 44-399 for 165 ac & DB 52-332 for 117 ½ ac. -written in 1844, recorded in 1847- total 282 1/2 ac) (Note: No deed could be found for purchase of the 110 ac, but see DB 52-120 for sale of 110 ac)

DB 52-120, 13 Jan 1847, rec 25 May 1847, John Tucker & wf Seney to Holman H. Woosley, for $300., 110 ac, being land bought of John Crews, bo. Woodley, Joseph Jennings, crossing Bookers Rd, David Tribble, Sarah Ship, Sarah R. Crews, Spraggins entry. (Note: No deed could be found for purchase of 110 ac from John Crews. But see DB 50-269 above)

DB 52-332, 22 Jun 1844, rec 23 Nov 1847, Peter Rives & wf Lucy, for $439., to John Tucker, 117 1/2 ac on both sides of road leading from Concord Mills to Republican Grove, bo Thornton. (Note: Although this deed was written in 1844, it was not recorded until 1847. This land was pledged to secure debt in 1845. See DB 50-629)

DB 54-595, 1 Jan 1853, I John Tucker of Halifax Co, Va. for natural love & affection to Elizabeth High, formerly Elizabeth Tucker, Sarah Adams, formerly Sarah Tucker, Mary High, formerly Mary Tucker, Thomas T. Tucker, William G. Tucker, Perlina F. Owen, formerly Perlina F. Tucker, & in consideration of my future handsome maintenance during my natural life, give to (above named), who are my children, all my lands, possessions, one negro woman Aggy, negro girl Eliza, all my household & kitchen furniture, plantation utensils & stock of every description, who bind themselves to handsomely maintain the aforesaid John Tucker during his natural life. (Note: See 1850 Census, Northern District, Households 162, 163, & 378)

MB 1-200, 27 Oct 1852, Thomas T. Tucker md Margaret Ann Fisher. Signed by minister & parents (not named). (Note: Thomas T. Tucker was son of John Tucker - see DB 54-595. Margaret Ann Fisher was dau of Martha Fisher of Campbell Co. - see MB 3-48)

MB 3-48, 28 Sep 1868, Margaret Ann Tucker, widow, md James T. Guthrey. His parents Richard & Betsy. Her parent Martha Fisher of Campbell Co. (See MB 1-200)

MB ____, 28 Oct 1852, Mark D. High md Mary Tucker

DB 61-136, 17 Jan 1868, rec 27 Apr 1868, Survey & assignment of dower land. Commissioners aptd to go upon the land owned by John T. Tucker at time of his death, & assign 1/3 part in value thereof to Margaret Ann Tucker, widow of John T. Tucker, as will appear on plat. (Note: plat in deed book showed 34 ac., bo Spring Br, Thornton, Carr, Concord Rd.) (See DB 54-595 and DB 62-678) (Note: See MB 1-200, 27 Oct 1852, "Thomas T. Tucker" md "Margaret Ann Fisher" above. Although this deed said "John T. Tucker", it most probably should be "Thomas T. Tucker".)

DB 61-365, 22 Feb 1869, Alfred Owen & wf to John T. Tucker, 1/6 of 300 ac. (Note: Alfred Owen's wf was Perlina F. Tucker, sister of Thomas T. Tucker & dau of John Tucker.) (See 1850 Census #162 & DB 54-595)

DB 61-366, 22 Feb 1869, Wm. J. Tucker & wf to John T. Tucker 1/6 part of tract. (Wm. J. & John T. Tucker were brothers and sons of John Tucker. See DB 54-595)

DB 63-286, 6 Jul 1873, Wm Conner est to John T. Tucker, 30 ac.

DB 62-673, 22 Jan 1870, rec 17 Jul 1870, in consideration of the support & necessarey comfortable clothing to him furnished & agreed to be furnished by R. R. Adams, for & during lifetime of John Tucker, the sd John Tucker conveys all right & title to sd Adams to land formerly owned by sd Tucker & which he some years ago conveyed by deed to his children & by reason of the death of his son ____ T. Tucker (looks like Tho. T. or Jno. T. Tucker), without issue, a part of sd land reverted to sd John Tucker the father, & which he now conveys to sd R. R. Adams in consideration of aforesaid. The above land adjoins the lands of Richard Blanks, Sally Inge, Paul Carr, Tho. A. Carr &c. (See DB 54-495)

NOTE: Although the above five deeds refer to John T. Tucker, this compiler contends that Thomas T. Tucker and John T. Tucker are one and the same son of John Tucker.

SUMMARY: John Tucker son of Elijah Tucker & 1st wf Betsy (Elizabeth) Barley, b ca 1791 in Halifax Co, Va, d after 1870, md 1st 1813 Halifax Co, Wilmoth Hodges, md 2nd 1843 Seaney (Scina) Guthrey, and had issue by 1st wf:

Elizabeth Tucker b ca 1825, md Issac H. High, b ca 1823.

Sarah Tucker b ca 1826, md before 1847 Robert R. Adams. b ca 1820.

Thomas T. Tucker b ca 1830, d ca 1870, md 1852 Margaret Ann Fisher.

William G. Tucker b ?.

Mary Tucker b ca 1830, md 1852 Mark D. High.

Perlina F. Tucker b ca 1833, md Alfred Owen.

* * *

3. Chiarito, Marian Dodson, "1850 Census of Halifax County, Virginia", 1982

TJ119200 - JAMES TUCKER

MD SARAH (SALLY) BASS
SON OF ELIJAH TUCKER
MD 1ST BETSY (ELIZABETH) BARLEY
MD 2ND SALLY BAINES

HALIFAX CO. VA.

NOTE: This compiler, B. DeRoy Beale, in his book "The Beale Family of Halifax County, Virginia", 1979, erroneously concluded that his great-grandfather James Tucker who married Sarah (Sally) Bass, was son of Henry Tucker & wf Elizabeth Green. Further research has revealed that the James Tucker, son of Henry & Elizabeth, married <u>Sarah (Sally) Fuqua</u>, dau. of Joseph H. Fuqua, as per will of Joseph H. Fuqua, 21 Jul 1829 (WB 22-352), and deed of trust for James Tucker in 1841 (DB 48-227). The subject James Tucker who married Sarah (Sally) Bass appears to be the son of Elijah Tucker & 1st wife Betsy (Elizabeth) Barley.

WB 25--262, wd 29 Feb 1856, wp 23 Feb 1857, <u>will of Elijah Tucker</u>. -names: - <u>wife Sally Tucker</u> - <u>sons</u> John, <u>James</u>, William, David, daus. Catherine wf of Fielding Hodges, Elizabeth wf of Jack Barber, Nancy Epperson, - <u>$5.00 each</u>. - dau. Martha Bryant - son Samuel Tucker - Polly Craddock wife of Daniel Craddock - Sally Epperson wife of Samuel R. Epperson.

> At Dec Court 1856, will of Elijah Tucker presented in court by Logan P. Anderson, executor, & thereupon William, John, & <u>James Tucker</u> and Elizabeth Barber made themselves parties defendants to <u>contest the will</u>.

> At court held 23 Feb 1837, defendants appeared & <u>approved</u> the proof of & will was ordered to be recorded & certificate granted to executor to probate the will.

MB 1-117, 21 Dec 1825 <u>James Tucker md Sarah Bass. Bondsman William Tucker</u>; Wit: C. L. Davenport & William Tucker; Signer, Sarah Bass, self.

NOTE: The James Tucker son of Elijah is believed by this compiler to be the same James Tucker who married Sarah (Sally) Bass in 1825, for the following reasons:

> (1) When Elijah Tucker sold his inheritance of 100 ac in Mecklenburg Co, William Harry Bass was a witness to that deed (DB 8-40).

(2) This James Tucker had a brother named William, and William was both bondsman and witness to the marriage of James to Sarah Bass.

(3) Joseph Bass sold slaves to Elijah Tucker in 1824 (See DB 32-229 & DB 33-131), so there was come communication between Tucker and Bass.

(4) Elijah Tucker assigned to his 2nd wife Sally, his mansion house & 50 ac. on both sides of road leading from Concord to Republican Grove, bo. by F. F. Thornton & John Tucker. (See DB 44-399, DB 57-35, WB 25-262 & DB 57-80 for Elijah Tucker).

(5) James Tucker bought land adj. John C. Tucker in 1847 (DB 52-150), and gave land up Concord Rd to his son James H. Tucker in 1877 (See DB 65-329).

NOTE: The parents of Sarah Bass are not known by this compiler, but the Tucker, Bass, Carr, Farmer and Mann families were neighbors on Bradley Cr. and inter-married. The following Bass transactions may provide a reference.

MB 1-206, 29 Nov 1783, John Beal md Rebecca Bass.

MB 1-15, 21 Dec 1789, William Bass md Rachel King. Bondsman Daniel Easley, Witness Isaac Easley, Signed Henry King father.

WB 3-59 William Bass Inquisition. An inquest indented was taken on the body of William Bass deceased on the land of Matthew Bates by James _____ ?, coroner, on 5 Dec 1791 -- James Eastham, William Layne, David Mullins, Richard Mitchell, Gabriel Sibley, Ambrose Hart, William Cox, Frances Cox, John C. McGraw, Jas. Clay, ____? Owen, Robert Sibley, good & lawful men empanneled as juries to this inquest upon their oath do say that William Br____? was casually(?) the death of sd William Bass. Rec. 27 May 1793.

MB 1-26, 5 Mar 1792 Robert Mann md Rebeckah Bass, Bondsman Stith Harrison, Witness & Signer Henry Bass, father.

MB 1-41, 11 Jan 1799, Amos Faris md Patsy Bass, Bondsman, Witness & Signer Henry Bass, father.

MB 1-44, 20 Oct 1800, Peter Bass md Jane Carr, Bondsman Wm. Carr.

MB 1-64, 12 Jan 1807, John Bass md Frances Farmer. Bondsman Matthew Farmer.

MB 1-146, 24 Feb 1834, William Bass md Sarah Talbot. Bondsman Jere Talbert.

MB 1-157, 18 Feb 1837, John A. Holloway md Mary A.W. Bass.

MB 1-161, 19 Nov 1839, Daniel Craddock md Sarah F. Bass.

DB 52-150, 18 Mar 1847, William Collins to James Tucker, 174 1/2 ac, on headwaters of Childrey Cr., bo. John C. Tucker & James Clay.

DB 54-273, 1 May 1857, Commissioner for est. of Sarah Pringle to James Tucker, 72 1/2 ac. known as Tucker Place

DB 59-583, 29 Nov 1862, Henry Stowe to James Tucker, 152 ac. adj. James Tucker. (See DB 64-603)

DB 60-141, 24 Aug 1863, Thomas Barker to James Tucker 63 1/2 ac. btwn Republican Grove & Cody.

DB 64-603, 30 Oct 1875, James Tucker & wf Sally, for $150., & further consideration of affection I have for him my son, sold to Coan Tucker 152 ac., it being land formerly owned by Henry Stowe. (See DB 59-586)

DB 65-329, 21 Feb 1877, James Tucker, for consideration of love & affection for his son James H. Tucker, & for $5., sold to his son James H. Tucker, a tract of land, (no. ac. not shown.) beginning at Coan Tucker's corner in James Tucker's line, up Concord Road to Lynchburg Rd.

> (Note: See DB 57-80, 1857, for Elijah Tucker, in which 50 ac. on both sides of road leading from Concord to Republican Grove was assigned to Sally Tucker, widow of Elijah Tucker. Elijah Tucker had a son named James).

DB 66-334, 19 May 1877, James Tucker gave to Elden Ann Stowe his daughter and her 5 children, the dwelling house in which he now resides, together with 60 ac., adj. Russell Beal, James H. Tucker, Coan Tucker, James Glay and Joel Beal.

DB 67-382, 28 Jan 1880, James H. Guthrie, special commissioner, appointed by Court in suit of James H. Tucker & c, against Eldora A. Stowe & c on one part, and Cowan Tucker of other part, --- James H. Tucker, for $80., grant to Cowan Tucker 80 ac. being, part of lands belonging to James Tucker's estate.

DB 67-385, 22 Jan 1880, James H. Guthrie, special commissioner appointed by Court in suit of James H. Tucker & c., against Eldora A. Stowe & c of one part, and Coan Tucker of other part, --- James H., Tucker, for $36., grant to Eldora A. Stowe 36 ac. being. part of lands of James Tucker's estate.

NOTE: The above deed indicates James Tucker died ca 1879.

SUMMARY OF LAND TRANSACTIONS OF JAMES TUCKER:

Year	Reference	Plus	Minus	Bal.
1847	DB 52-150 fr Wm. Collins	174 1/2		174 1/2
1857	DB 54-273 fr Sarah Pringle est	72 1/2		247
1862	DB 59-583 fr Henry Stowe	152		399
1863	DB 60-141 fr Thomas Barker	63 1/2		462 1/2
1875	DB 64-603 to son Coan Tucker		152	310 1/2
1877	DB 65-329 to son James H. Tucker		?	
1877	DB 66-334 to dau Elden Ann Stowe		60	
1880	DB 67-382 to son Coan Tucker		80	
1880	DB 67-385 to dau Eldora A. Stowe		36	

WB 32-491, 1 Sep 1881, Settlement of est. of James Tucker by N. R. Hobson, Administrator. Distribution was made to:

Mrs. Eldora Stowe (Eldora Tucker Stowe)

James H. Tucker

Charles L. Beale (for Adeline Tucker Beale)

Cowan Tucker

E. W. Waller (for Cassie Tucker Waller)

This compiler could find no evidence that James Tucker deeded or willed any land to his daughters Adeline who married Charles L. Beale, or Cassie who married E. W. Waller.

The marriages of some of the children of James and Sarah (Sally) Tucker are recorded in Halifax Co.

MB 3-55, 23 Dec 1869, Charles L. Beale to Adeline M. Tucker. Parents of groom Joel T & Ann. Parents of bride James & Sallie. (The Joel Thomas Beale Family Bible records the marriage of Charles L. Beale to Adeline M. Tucker on 23 Dec 1869, by Rev. Peter M. Reeves.)

NOTE: The Family Bible of Joel Thomas Beale (1821-1901) was passed down to his son Hinton Richard Beale (1862-1930), who passed it to his son Richard Bunyan Beale (1898-) who showed it to this compiler in 1964. This compiler, B. DeRoy Beale, (1924-) is son of Charlie Joel Beale (1876-1958) (& wf Anna Lee Owen), who was son of Charles Lacy Beale 1846-1885) (& wf Adeline M. Tucker), who was son of Joel Thomas Beale (1821-1901) (& wf Elizabeth Ann Tucker), who was son of Charles Beal (1790-1836) (& wf Elizabeth Tucker). Charles L. Beale & his wf Adeline M. Tucker are buried in unmarked graves in the Joel Thomas Beale family cemetery, which is located just off route 603 west of the community of Republican Grave. My father told me his mother Adeline died when he was only 2 years old (ca 1878) and his father Charles L. died when he was only 9 years old (ca 1885)

MB 3-140, 26 Jan 1885, <u>James Tucker</u> age 40, and Harriett A. Eads, widow. age 26. <u>Father of groom James & Sarah.</u>

Mrs. Mattie Tucker Hodnett, in a letter to this compiler's sister Blanche Beale Booker, wrote:

"the brothers and sisters of your grandmother
Adeline Tucker Beale are:

Coan J. Tucker married Emma Hubbard.

James H. Tucker married Harriett Ann Dalton.

Berry Tucker killed in Confederate War.

Wesley Tucker killed in Confederate War.

Cassie Tucker married Erine Waller.

Eldie Tucker married (John) Stowe."

<u>The birthdates of the James Tucker family
are calculated from ages shown in the 1850 Census:</u> [1]

Household	Name	Age	Calculated Birthyear	
<u>771</u>	James Tucker	57	ca 1793	
	Sarah Tucker	50	ca 1800	
	Wesley Tucker	23	ca 1827	
	Elda Tucker	17	ca 1833	
	Adaline Tucker	15	ca 1835	
	Julia A. Tucker	13	ca 1837	
	Cassanna Tucker	8	ca 1842	
	James Tucker	6	ca 1844	
	Cain (Cowan)	3	ca 1847	(1848)
<u>664</u>	John Stowe	17	ca 1833	
<u>773</u>	Charles L. Beale	4	ca 1846	
<u>817</u>	Evan W. Waller	5	ca 1845	

SUMMARY: James Tucker, b ca 1793, son of Elijah Tucker & 1st wf Betsy (Elizabeth) Barley, d ca 1879, md 1824 Sarah (Sally) Bass b ca 1800 & had issue:

Wesley Tucker b ca 1827, killed in Confederate War.

Berry Tucker b ?, killed in Confederate War.

Eldora A. (Elden Ann) Tucker b ca 1833, md 1854(?) John Stowe b ca 1833, (son of William Stow & wf Obedience (per 1850 census).

Adeline M. Tucker b ca 1835, d ca 1878, md 1869 Charles Lacy Beale b 1846 son of Joel Thomas Beale & wf Elizabeth Ann Tucker (MB 3-55). (See Beale family)

Julia A. Tucker b ca 1837, unmarried.

Cassana (Cassie) Tucker b ca 1842, md Erwin (Evan) W. Waller b ca 1845, (son of Richard Waller & wf Emeline per 1850 census).

James Harrison Tucker b ca 1844, md 1885 Harriett A. Eads, widow, (MB 3-140), nee Harriett Ann Dalton.

Cowan Tucker b 6 May 1848, d 26 Nov 1920, md Emma T. Hubbard, b 29 Jan 1849, d 24 Sep 1898.

* * *

1. Chiarito, Marian Dodson, "1850 Census of Halifax County, Virginia"

TJ119210 - JAMES H. TUCKER

MD HARRIETT A. EADS
SON OF JAMES TUCKER
MD SARAH (SALLY) BASS

HALIFAX CO. VA.

DB 65-329, 21 Feb 1877, <u>James Tucker</u>, for consideration of love & affection for his son James H. Tucker, & for $5., <u>sold to his son James H. Tucker, a tract of land, (no. ac. not shown) beginning at Coan Tucker's corner in James Tuckers line, up Concord Road to Lynchburg Rd.</u>

WB 32-491, 1 Sep 1881, Settlement of <u>est</u>. of <u>James Tucker</u> by N. R. Hobson, Administrator. Distribution was made to:

> Mrs. Eldora Stowe (Eldora Tucker Stowe)
>
> <u>James H. Tucker</u>
>
> Charles L. Beale (for Adeline Tucker Beale)
>
> Cowan Tucker
>
> E. W. Waller (for Cassie Tucker Waller)

MB 3-140, 26 Jan 1885, <u>James Tucker</u> age 40, md Harriett A. Eads, widow. age 26. <u>Father of groom James & Sarah</u>.

SUMMARY: James Harrison Tucker b ca 1844, md 1885 Harriett A. Eads, widow, (MB 3-140), nee Harriett Ann Dalton, and had issue:

> (Information on James Harrison Tucker family provided by Miss Nina Waller, Miss Annie Waller & Mrs. Blanche Booker)

1. Annie Tucker b ca 1896, d 11 Mar 1964 at age 68, md James (Jim) Oliver Edmonds.

2. James (Jim) E. Tucker b 5 Feb 1885 at Republican Grove, Va., d 19 Jan 1978, at Stanley, Va., md 28 Jun 1918 Elva Wolfersberger, was a retired Baptist Minister upon his death at age 91.

3. Buster Tucker, a Baptist Minister.

4. Richard (Dick) Green Tucker Sr b 14 Apr 1893 Halifax Co, Va, d 28 Dec 1972 South Boston, Va, md 1st 22 Jul 1916 Halifax Co, Va, Ethel Ann Starkey b 23 Mar 1896 Halifax Co, Va, d 4 Sep 1985 Annandale Va, dau of William Thomas Starkey & wf Stella Mustain, & had issue by his 1st wf:

> 4.1 Katherine Louise Tucker b 13 Oct 1919, md 1st William Charles Colfelt, md 2nd John Paul Long.
>
> 4.2 Richard Green Tucker Jr b 15 Jul 1924 Halifax Co, Va, md 18 Sep 1948 Franconia, Va, Mabel Esther Hoddinott b 25 Jul 1925

Fayetteville, NC, dau of Robert B. Hoddinott & wf. Ella Mae Black, and had issue:

4.2.1 Richard Green Tucker III b 15 Apr 1953 Alexandria Va, d infant 9 Nov 1954.

4.2.2 Janice Elaine Tucker b 2 Dec 1955 Alexandria Va, md 13 May 1978 Franconia Va, Donald Allan Monayhan

4.2.3 Nora Ellen Tucker b 26 Oct 1959 Alexandria Va, md 20 Jun 1981 Franconia, Va, Richard Lynn Monayhan

4.3 Hurley Starkey Tucker b 6 Aug 1928 Halifax Co, Va, d 31 Jan 1985 Fairfax, Va, md 7 Oct 1950 Washington, DC, Mary Louise Parrish

4. Richard (Dick) Green Tucker Sr md 2nd 13 Nov 1936 Alpha Tanette Farson, b 22 Aug 1917 Pittsylvania, Co, Va, dau of Samuel Thomas Farson & wf Lottie May Smith, and had issue by his 2nd wf:

4.4 Alpha Mourine Tucker b 23 unmarried in 1985.

4.5 Connie Buena Tucker b 25 unmarried in 1985.

4.6 Alvin Levi Tucker b 10 Jan 1943 Pittsylvania Co. md 25 Dec 1963 South Boston, Va (name not provided)

5. Pensy Tucker md ___ Vassar.

(data supplied by Richard Green Tucker)

TJ119220 - COAN TUCKER

MD EMMA T. HUBBARD
SON OF JAMES TUCKER
MD SARAH (SALLY) BASS

HALIFAX CO. VA.

DB 64-603, 30 Oct 1875, James Tucker & wf Sally, for $150., & further consideration of affection I have for him my son, sold to Coan Tucker 152 ac., it being land formerly owned by Henry Stowe. (See DB 59-583)

DB 67-382, 28 Jan 1880, James H. Guthrie, special commissioner, appointed by Court in suit of James H. Tucker & c, against Eldora A. Stowe & c on one part, and Cowan Tucker of other part, --- James H. Tucker, for $80., grant to Cowan Tucker 80 ac. being part of lands belonging to James Tucker's estate.

WB 32-491, 1 Sep 1881, Settlement of est. of James Tucker by N. R. Hobson, Administrator. Distribution was made to:

   Mrs. Eldora Stowe (Eldora Tucker Stowe)

   James H. Tucker

   Charles L. Beale (for Adeline Tucker Beale)

   Cowan Tucker

   E. W. Waller (for Cassie Tucker Waller)

Tombstones at the Cowan Tucker family cemetery, near intersection of roads 603 & 649 at community of North Staunton, include the following inscriptions:

   Cowan Tucker b May 6, 1848, d Nov 26, 1920; wife: Emma T., b Jan 29, 1849, d Sep 24, 1898.

   Mack Tucker b July 9, 1868, d Sep 18, 1919.

   Samuel H. Tucker b Apr 4, 1881, d Feb 24, 1957; wife: Ida Landrum, b May 6, 1878, d July 30, 1961.

Tombstones at cemetery of First Baptist Church of Republican Grove include the following inscriptions:

   Willie O. Tucker b Sep 30, 1870, d July 28, 1916.

   Otis L. Tucker b Nov 2, 1904, d May 21, 1957.

SUMMARY: Cowan Tucker b 6 May 1848, d 26 Nov 1920, md Emma T. Hubbard, b 29 Jan 1849, d 24 Sep 1898, & had issue:

(Information on Cowan Tucker family provided by Miss Nina Waller, Miss Annie Waller & Mrs. Mattie Tucker Hodnett.)

1. Mattie Tucker md Less Hodnett.

2. Gennie Tucker md Ernest Williams.

3. Emma Tucker unmarried.

4. Sallie (Sis) Tucker and Charlie Lewis.

5. Mack Tucker, unmarried, b 9 Jul 1868, d 18 Sep 1919.

6. Willie O. Tucker b 30 Sep 1870, d 28 Jul 1916.

6.1 Otis Linwood Tucker, b 2 Nov 1904, d 21 May 1957 and 16 Jul 1928 Emma Christine Myers (MB 6-62).

7. Coan Jackson Tucker b 29 Mar 1872, d 2 Jun 1962, m Hattie Elizabeth Moon b ca 1877, d 1922 at age 45, and had issue: (information on Coan Jackson Tucker family provided by his grandson Bobby Wayne Tucker)

7.1 Marie Tucker b 1898, d 1927, m Fred Clark, and had issue: Harold Clark , Alene Clart, & Isabelle Clark.

7.2 Mattie Tucker b 1900, m Flugh Layne , & had issue: Ryland Layne, Elizabeth Layne, Geraldine Layne , & Everette Layne.

7.3 William Brace Tucker b 11 Oct 1902, d 4 Jun 1985, m 28 Nov 1921 Elsie Moon b 1 Mar 1904, & had issue: (information provided by Inez Mae Tucker)

7.3.1 Margaret Tucker b 7 Jun 1922, m 10 Jan 1940 Esther L. Davis.

7.3.2 Loda Tucker b 20 Apr 1924, d 23 Sep 1985, m 6 Jul 1959 Willie Lawrence Coffey.

7.3.3 Inez Mae Tucker b 19 Feb 1926.

7.3.4 William Brace (W.B.) Tucker Jr b 24 Oct 1929, d Dec 1981.

7.3.5 Henry Archibald Tucker b 20 Apr 1932, d Jun 1972, Virginia E. ____ .

7.3.6 James (Jim) Anderson Tucker b 17 Aug 1933, Shirley ____ .

7.3.7 Paul Edwin Tucker b 28 May 1936, divorced.

7.3.8 Jeanette Tucker b 16 Oct 1939, m Alton Latane Edwards.

7.3.9 Malcolm Everette Tucker b 15 Jun 1941, m Marie B. Sterne.

7.3.10 Reuben Wayne Tucker b 12 Jun 1943, m Judy Moorefield.

7.4 Theodore Roosevelt Tucker b 1904, d Jan 1979, Virginia ____, & adopted 2 children Ann & Billy.

7.5 Charlie Jackson Tucker b 1907, m Emma Chrystine East b 1911 & had issue:

> 7.5.1 Charlie Ralph Tucker b 7 Aug 1930, m Jean Marie Golladay & had issue:
>
>> 7.5.1.1 Charles Ralph Tucker b May 1957.
>>
>> 7.5.1.2 Diane Marie Tucker b Aug 1962.
>
> 7.5.2 William Marvin Tucker b 7 Mar 1935, m Sue Dickerson & had issue:
>
>> 7.5.2.1 Michael Marvin Tucker b 11 Feb 1956.
>>
>> 7.5.2.2 Cindy Sue Tucker b 24 Apr 1957.
>>
>> 7.5.2.3 Ronnie Lee Tucker b 18 Apr 1958.
>
> 7.5.3 Bobby Wayne Tucker b 20 Mar 1938, m Jacqueline Godfrey b 25 Dec 1943, & had issue:
>
> 7.5.3.1 Brian Wayne Tucker b 21 Jul 1972.
>
> 7.5.4 Charlene Joyce Tucker b 12 Jul 1950.

7.6 Hattie Fleda Tucker b 1908, m Eugene Pugh, & had issue: Ellis Pugh , Lawrence Pugh, Joan Marie Pugh, & Nora Lee Pugh .

7.7 Mamie Elizabeth Tucker, m Dave Layne and had no children.

7.8 Thomas Owen Tucker, m 1st 26 Dec 1936 Ruth Melvin Marr, dau of Hunter J. Marr & wf Kallie Dillard, m 2nd 25 Nov 1972 Pearl Marie Burks Treadway, & had issue by his 1st wf: (information provided by Mr. & Mrs. Thomas Owen Tucker)

> 7.8.1 Melvin Owen Tucker b 9 Jul 1938, d 5 Dec 1940.
>
> 7.8.2 Kallie Jackline Tucker b 31 Oct 1941, m 2 Nov 1962 Ashby Graves.
>
> 7.8.3 Marlene Marie Tucker b 3 Mar 1945, m 7 Aug 1965 John Richard Stallings.
>
> 7.8.4 Larry Dale Tucker b 21 Feb 1949, m 5 Jul 1975 Deborah Garren.
>
> 7.8.5 David Thomas Tucker b 5 Dec 1956, unmarried.

7.9 Janie Wiggington Tucker, m ____ Adkins.

7.10 Robert Barnhardt Tucker never married.

8. Charlie Tucker md Adie Mae Moon.

9. Grover C. Tucker md 6 Mar 1915 Elsie H. Peak. (MB 4-94)

10. Samuel (Sam) H. Tucker b 4 Apr 1881, d 24 Feb 1957, md Ida Landrum b 6 May 1878, d 30 Jul 1961.

    10.1 Ruby Tucker, twin.

    10.2 Annie Tucker, twin.

TJ119300 - WILLIAM TUCKER

MD NANCY FARIS
SON OF ELIJAH TUCKER
MD 1ST BETSY (ELIZABETH) BARLEY
MD 2ND SALLY BAINES

HALIFAX CO. VA.

WB 25-262, wd 29 Feb 1856, wp 23 Feb 1857, <u>will of Elijah Tucker</u>. names: - wife Sally Tucker - <u>sons</u> John, James, <u>William</u>, David, daus. Catherine wf of Fielding Hodges, Elizabeth wf of Jack Barber, Nancy Epperson, - $5.00 each. - dau. Martha Bryant - son Samuel Tucker - Polly Craddock wife of Daniel Craddock - Sally Epperson wife of Samuel R. Epperson.

> At Dec Court 1856, will of Elijah Tucker presented in court by Logan P. Anderson, executor, & thereupon <u>William</u>, John, & James <u>Tucker</u> and Elizabeth Barber made themselves parties defendants to <u>contest the will</u>.

> At court held 23 Feb 1857, defendants appeared & approved the proof of & will was ordered to be recorded & certificate granted to executor to probate the will.

NOTE: It is unusual that Elijah Tucker did not will any land to his sons John, James, William and David, nor appoint any of them executor, but left remainder of est to son Samuel Tucker, and Polly Craddock and Sally Epperson, who apparently were his daughters. After the will was contested by William, John, James & Elizabeth, it was finally proved, and distribution of his estate was made by Executor Logan P. Anderson.

MB 1-117, 21 Dec 1825 James Tucker md Sarah Bass. <u>Bondsman William Tucker</u>; <u>Wit</u>: C. L. Davenport & <u>William Tucker</u>; Signer, Sarah Bass, self.

NOTE: William Tucker is believed by this compiler to be the brother of James Tucker for whose marriage he was bondsman and witness in 1825. William was at least age 21 at this time and would have been born before or ca 1804.

This compiler found no other reference to the subject William Tucker son of Elijah in Halifax Co, Va, and he was not included in the 1850 census of Halifax Co., Va. He apparently moved to Pittsylvania Co.

PITTSYLVANIA CO., VA.

MARRIAGES [1]

26 Oct 1824, Demarcas Lane m Polly B. Faris. Sur James Henderson. John B. Dawson signs certificate. M 28 Oct by Rev. Griffith Dickenson. p 81.

21 Nov 1825, William Tucker m Nancy Faris. Sur Daniel Johns, p 84.

12 Apr 1830, Amos Faris Jr m Jane Faris. Sur James B. Faris. Danl Johns, guardian of Jane, consents. M 15 Apr by Rev. Griffith Dickenson Sr. p 96.

12 Apr 1830, Allen Scruggs m Elizabeth Faris. Danl John, guardian of Elizabeth, consents. Sur James B. Faris. 15 Apr by Griffith Dickenson Sr. p 97.

17 May 1830, James B. Faris m Nancy Scruggs, dau of Drury Scruggs who consents. Sur Daniel Johns. p 96.

MARRIAGES [2]

25 Apr 1838, John Tucker m Sally Faris, who signs her own consent Salley Faris. Sur. Thomas R. Jenkins. M by John W. Rosser. p 118. (Note: See John Tucker son of Nelson)

18 Apr 1861. Creed I. Tucker m Nancy Hodnett, dau of James & Mary Hodnett who consent. Son of William & Nancy E. Tucker, who consent. Married by Asa Hodnett. p 181.

DB 37-211, 2 Jan 1835, rec 19 Jan 1835, Demarcus Lain & wf. Mary B. to James B. Faris, William Tucker, Allen Scruggs, Amos Faris Jr, Mary Faris, Sarah Faris, James Abbott & Samuel D. Faris, all of Pittsylvania Co., for $1,000., 190 ac., on branches of Fly Blow Cr., bo Francis Irby, Doc. Rawley White, Wm. Smith Sr. & others, also the following slaves: Nelly & her 3 children David, Ben & Jordon; Creasy & her 8 children Henry, Dilcy, Dicey, Abram, Mary, Titus, Lucinda & Sam, which slaves Demarcus Lain now holds in right of his sd wife Mary B., who held them as her dower in the estate of her former husband John Faris Sr. decd. Mary B., wf of Demarcus Lain prively acknowledged deed.

DB 37-214, 2 Jan 1835, rec 19 Jan 1835, James B. Faris & wf Nancy, William Tucker & wf Nancy, Allen Scruggs & wf Elizabeth, Amos Faris Jr & wf Jane, Mary Faris, Sarah Faris, James Abbott & wf Susan, Samuel D. Faris, to Demarcus Lain, all of Pittsylvania Co., for $475., 190 ac. on drafts of Flyblow Cr., bo. Francis Irby, Doc. Rawley White, William Smith & others, land formerly belonging to John Faris Sen decd. All wives examined separately & acknowledged deed.

NOTE: The above two deeds identify the children of Mary B. Faris, widow of John Faris Sr, as:

James B. Faris m Nancy Scruggs,

Nancy Faris m William Tucker,

Elizabeth Faris m Allen Scruggs,

Jane Faris m Amos Faris Jr,

Mary Faris,

Sarah (Sally) Faris m John W. Tucker, son of Nelson,

Susan Faris m James Abbott,

Samuel D. Faris

NOTE: Various Pittsylvania Co. Court Orders include guardian accts of Daniel Johns as guardian of Jane, Mary, Eliza, Susan, Sarah, & Samuel Faris, orphans of John Faris Sr, which were settled in Feb 1830. James B. Faris & Nancy Faris most probably had attained majority, since they were not named as orphans.

DB 44-327, 4 Jan 1840, rec 18 Jan 1847, Charles W. Wood & wf Martha to William Tucker, for $1,789., 596 1/2 ac. On b.s. Striat Stone Cr. , bo John, crosses Strait Stone Cr., Coleman, Martin, Hunt.

DB 45-17, 2 Aug 1838, rec 17 May 1841, George W. Coleman & wf Sarah W. to William Tucker, for $2,700., 432 ac. on b.s. of middle fork of Straitstone Cr., being land bought by sd Coleman of Mary, Nancy & Martha E. Hunt & devised to them by will of Col Davis Hunt decd, bo. Dillard, Hunt, Scruggs.

DB 49-180, 22 Feb 1845, rec 17 Mar 1845, Allen Scruggs, to secure debt to William Tucker, for $398.79, in trust, to William L. Pannill, 100 ac. on Straitstone Cr, bo. Win. Waller, Geo. W. Coleman & others, 1 horse, 2 cows, 1 yoke oxen, all crops & other property.

DB 49-300, 21 Jul 1845, rec 21 Jul 1845, Demarkes Lain, to secure debt to William Tucker for $279.07, in trust, to Daniel Johns, 169 ac. on waters of Flyblow Cr., bo. Col. Wm. T. Smith, Dr. Raleigh White & others. It being land where sd Demarkes Lain now lives. If debt paid when due, then this deed void. (See DB 50-469)

DB 50-142, 18 Jul 1840, rec 17 Aug 1840, Jas. B. Faris to secure debts to Vincent Dickenson & others, for some of which William Tucker & others are security, in trust to Wm. H. Waller, 2 negro men Pleasant & William, 1 sorrell horse, 1 work steer, 2 cows & calves, 4 yearling, 30 head of hogs, 10 head of sheep, & bal of household furniture & plantation tools.

DB 50-268, 10 May 1840 (or 1846), rec 21 Dec 1840 (or 1846). Whereas on 21 Jul 1845, Demarcus Laine conveyed to Daniel Johns trustee for securing debts to William Tucker, sold to WilliamTucker, 169 1/2 ac. (See DB 49-300 & DB 57-73)

DB 50-469, 8 Jun 1847, whereas James B. Faris is indebted to William Tucker, & to others with William Tucker as security, to Williama C. Grasty, 1 bay horse, 1 mare's saddle, 1 milch cow & 2 calves, all crops, & all interest in right of his wife in willed by George Dejarnett to Molly Scruggs for life then to her children, his wife being one of the children.

DB 54-525. 10 Apr 1852, rec 28 Aep 1853. William Tucker & wf Nancy E. to Nancy Turner for $340., 85 ac. On Straightstone Cr, bo Stone, Martins Br, Hunt, James East

DB 55-75, 9 Apr 1853, rec 30 Mar 1854, Danl R. Hunt of Campbell Co, Lucy Ann Clement, J. H. Hargrove & wf Ruth, John D. Hunt, J. S. Lewis Exor of C. Alonzo Hunt decd of Pittsylvania Co., to William Tucker of Pittsylvania Co., for $1,912.16, 425 ac. on south prong of Striatstone, bo sd William Tucker, James T. Lewis, John L. Lewis, Dr. Morton Pannill & Martin Templeton

DB 57-73, 16 Jan 1857, rec 16 Feb 1867, William Tucker & wf Nancy E. to Maria Shields widow of Joshua Shields decd, Mary Robin formerly Mary Shields, John Shields, William Shields, Lucy Shields, Joshua Shields, Maria Shields, Samuel Shields, Susan Elizabeth Shields's children & heirs of sd Joshua Shields deced, all of Pittsylvania Co., for $678., 169 1/2 ac. on b.s. Wards Road near Good Hope, bo Dr. Raleigh White, William Smith, Chaney Barksdale, subject to the dower of Polly Layne wife of Mark Lain. (See DB 50-268)

DB 57-202, 14 Apr 1857, rec 19 May 1857, Jamers P. Lewis & William L. Pannill Trustees, for $450., to William Tucker, 100 ac on Striatstone Cr., whereas Allen Scruggs by trust 22 Feb 1845, conveyed to William L. Pannill as Trustee to secure debt due William Tucker.

DB 59-351, 18 Aug 1860, rec 20 Aug 1860, Trust, John W. Tucker & Creed J. Tucker to John W. Lewis, horses, buggies & miscellaneous items to secure debt to William Tucker of $2,500. due by bond on demand dated 18 Aug 1860.

NOTE: Deed Book 60 is the last book on microfilm in State Library Archives. The deed index included many other deeds for William Tucker beginning with Deed Book 63, 1868 & beyond, but these were not researched.

SUMMARY: William Tucker b before 1804 in Halifax Co., Va., son of. Elijah Tucker & 1st wf Betsy (Elizabeth) Barley, m 21 Nov 1825, Nancy Faris, dau of John Faris Sr & wf Mary B., d ?, and had issue, at least one son:

Creed I. Tucker m 18 Apr 1861, Nancy Hodnett, dau of James & Mary Hodnett.

* * *

1. Williams, Kathleen Booth, "Marriages of Pittsylvania County, Virginia, 1806-1830", 1965

2. Chiarito, Marian Dodson, "Marriages of Pittsylvania County, Virginia, 1831-1861", 1982

TJ119400 - DAVID TUCKER
SON OF ELIJAH TUCKER
MD 1ST BETSY (ELIZABETH) BARLEY
MD 2ND SALLY BAINES

HALIFAX CO., VA.

WB 25-262, wd 29 Feb 1856, wp 23 Feb 1857, will of Elijah Tucker. - names: - wife Sally Tucker - sons John, James, William, David, daus. Catherine wf of Fielding Hodges, Elizabeth wf of Jack Barber, Nancy Epperson, - $5.00 each. - dau. Martha Bryant - son Samuel Tucker - Polly Craddock wife of Daniel Craddock - Sally Epperson wife of Samuel R. Epperson.

NOTE: It is unusual that Elijah Tucker did not deed any land to his sons John, James, William and David, nor appoint any of them executor, but left remainder of est to son Samuel Tucker, and Polly Craddock and Sally Epperson, who apparently were his daughters. After the will was contested by William, John, James & Elizabeth, it was finally proved, and distribution of his estate was made by Executor Logan P. Anderson.

SUMMARY: The subject David Tucker was named in the will of his father Elijah Tucker, written in Feb 1856, but was not among those who contested the will in Dec 1856, and he was not included in the 1850 census of. Halifax Co, Va. This compiler has found no other reference to the subject David Tucker.

TJ119500 - SAMUEL TUCKER

MD NANCY O. CLARK
SON OF ELIJAH TUCKER
MD 1ST BETSY (ELIZABETH) BARLEY
MD 2ND SALLY BAINES

HALIFAX CO., VA.

DB 52-211, 4 Aug 1847, rec 9 Aug 1847, Samuel Tucker, to secure debts, sold to John C. Light, negro woman Aggy & her 3 children, Pleasant, Drucilla & Mary, all his household & kitchen furniture, crops, upon trust, nevertheless that sd John C. Light shall permit sd Samuel Tucker to remain in possession of sd property & to take profits therefrom until default be made.

DB 52-356, 29 Nov 1847, rec 2 Dec 1847, Samuel Tucker, to secure debts, sold to Eppa H. Clark the following property: negro woman Aggy & her child Lucinda, 4 bedsteads & furniture, 1 side board, 4 chests, 9 stacks fodder, 75 bbls corn, 1 blk mare, 2 head cattle, 4 sh__, 20 bu. wheat, household & kitchen furniture, plantation tools, upon special trust.

DB 52-461. 29 Mar 1848, rec 3 Apr 1849, Samuel Tucker, to secure debts, sold to Eppy H. Clark, negro woman Aggy, negro girl Drucilla, 1 black mare, 1 cow, all household & kitchen furniture, plantation utensils, 50 bbls corn, 2 foder stacks together with every species of property he may possess at day of sale.

WB 25-262, wd 29 Feb 1856, wp 23 Feb 1857, will of Elijah Tucker. - names: - wife Sally Tucker - sons John, James, William, David - daus. Catherine wf of Fielding Hodges, Elizabeth wf of Jack Barber, Nancy Epperson, - dau. Martha Bryant - Remainder of est. equally divided btwn son Samuel Tucker, Polly Craddock wife of Daniel Craddock & Sally Epperson wife of Samuel R. Epperson. That portion for son Samuel, & Polly Craddock to be held likewise in trust by executor for their benefit during their lives & then to be equally divided between their children.

NOTE: The will of Elijah Tucker, who was ca age 90 when he died in 1856, implied that his son Samuel was married with children. The following marriage records apply to the family of Samuel Tucker son of Elijah. If this Samuel Tucker and Nancy Clark were age 21 in 1833, both would have been born ca 1812.

MB 1-145, 29 Jun 1833, Samuel Tucker md Nancy O. Clark. Bondsman James Bryan. Wit: John M. Clark. Signer Nancy O. Clark, self.

MB 3-7, 25 Nov 1856, Richard T. Tucker age 22 md Mary E. Epperson age 23. <u>Parents of groom, Saml Tucker & Mary Clark</u>. Parents of bride Wm. Epperson & Eliza Forrest.

MB 3-59, 5 Jan 1869, Robert E. Tucker age 30 md Nancy C. Blanks age 19. <u>Parents of groom Samuel & Nancy</u>. Parents of bride Richard & Catherine.

NOTE: Pittsylvania Co. 6 Dec 1834. Richard Blanks md Catharine Owen, dau of Drewry Owen & Hedrick Mahue.

The 1850 census included the following households in the Northern District: [3]

Name	Age	Calculated Birth Year	
Household 826	--	-----	
Samuel Tucker	30	1820	Farmer
			(age questioned)
Nancy	30	1820	(age questioned)
Richard T.	14	1836	
Martha C.	12	1838	
Robert E.	10	1840	
Izabella	8	1842	
Sarah	5	1844	
Devavous T.	4	1846	
John T.	2/12	1850	
Household 637	--	-----	
Richard Blanks	40	1810	
Catharine	35	1815	
Joseph	14	1836	
John	11	1839	
Elizabeth	7	1843	
William	5	1845	Hedrick Owen
Thomas	3	1847	
Nancy	1/12	1850	

(birth years were calculated from ages shown in the census)

NOTE: If Samuel & Nancy Tucker were age 30 in 1850, they would have been born ca 1820. If the ages in the 1850 census are correct, parents Samuel & Nancy would have been only ca age 16 when 1st son Richard T. was born ca 1836. However, if Samuel & Nancy were born ca 1812 as the marriage record indicates, they would have been ca age 21 when married in 1833, and ca age 24 when 1st child was born ca 1836, and ca age 38 in the 1850 census.

DB 58-378 24 Sep 1859, rec 26 Sep 1859, Logan P. Anderson, a Comr in the case of <u>Polly Craddock & c vs Elijah Tucker Exs & c</u>, to Christopher H. Jennings for $200.90, <u>98 ac. being a part of lands of est. of Elijah Tucker decd</u>, adj. F. F. Thornton & c. (See DB 59-99)

DB 59-99, 25 Feb 1860, rec 31 Aug 1860, Christopher H. Jennings & wf Elizabeth to <u>Robert E. Tucker</u>, for $200.98, <u>98 ac. it being a part of land belonging to est. of Elijah Tucker decd.</u>, adj. F. F. Thornton & c. (See DB -58-378)

NOTE: From the above deeds, the 1850 census and marriage records, it is evident that Robert E. Tucker, son of Samuel and grandson of Elijah, bought 98 ac. which formerly belonged to the estate of his grandfather.

SUMMARY: Samuel Tucker b ca 1812 in Halifax Co. Va., son of Elijah Tucker & 1st wf Betsy (Elizabeth) Barley, md 1833 Halifax Co., Va., Nancy E. Clark b ca 1812, and had issue:

Richard T. Tucker b ca 1834-36, md 1856 Halifax Go., Va., Mary E. Epperson b ca 1833 dau of William Epperson & wf Eliza Forrest.

Martha C. Tucker b ca 1838.

Robert E Tucker b ca 1839-40, md 1869 Nancy C. Blanks b ca 1850, dau of Richard Blanks & wf Catharine Owen.

Izabella Tucker b ca 1842

Sarah Tucker b ca 1844

Devavous T. Tucker b ca 1846

John T. Tucker b ca 1850

* * *

3. Chiarito, Marian Dodson, "1850 Census of Halifax County, Virginia", 1982

TR120000 - ROBERT TUCKER JR

MD FRANCES COLEMAN
SON OF CAPT ROBERT TUCKER SR
MD MARTHA

BRISTOL PARISH REGISTER [1]

Martha, dau. of <u>Robert & Frances Tucker</u> born 10 Jul 1727.

Frances, dau. of <u>Robert & Frances Tucker</u> born 11 Mar 1730.

William, son of <u>Robert & Frances Tucker</u> born 15 Apr 1733, bapt 3 Jun 1735.

NOTE: Robert Tucker Jr must have been at least age 21 when his first child was born in 1727, and must have been born by 1706.

PRINCE GEORGE CO. VA.

Patent 14-341, 17 Sep 1731, <u>Robert Tucker Jr.</u>, Pr. Geo. Co., <u>400 ac.</u> NL l.s. of Wintocomaick Cr., <u>adj. land whereon he lives</u>.

NOTE: Robert Tucker Jr must have been already living with his family on land set aside for him by his father and patented additional land adjacent to it. (See Amelia DB 1-344)

Patent 376, 28 Sep 1730, Ben Ragsdale, Pr. Geo. Co., 200 ac. NL head Sampsons Br, Winticomiack Cr. <u>adj. Robert Tucker</u>. 20 Sh.

AMELIA CO. VA.

1735 Amelia Co. was formed from that part of Prince George Co. west of Numisseen Cr.

DB 1-344, 10 Oct 1741, rec 16 Oct 1741, <u>Robert Tucker Sr to Robert Tucker Jr</u> for L100. - <u>165 1/2 ac.</u> l.s. Wintocomake Cr., bo. in pt. by the Gr. Br. against the Great Beaver Pond, the road & John Tucker's spring Br. <u>Wit</u>: John Powell, Robert Coleman & <u>John Tucker</u>. (See Patent 13-270 for Capt. Robert Tucker Sr).

WB 1-10, 20 Feb 1740, John Tally, I&A. <u>Appr</u>: <u>George Tucker</u>, Robert Cusons, <u>Robert Tucker</u>. Admr. William Tally.

WB 1-37, will of <u>William Coleman Sr.</u>, wd 2 Jun 1743, wp 21 Mar 1745. Wit: Robert Bevill, Martha x Bevill, John Powell. Exr; son Robert. Leg: Son Daniel Coleman. Son Robert Coleman - 200 ac. u.s. Wintocomake Cr. all land below great Branch. Son Joseph Coleman - 200 ac. on u.s. Wintocomake Cr. all land above great branch joining son Robert's land. Son William Coleman - 200 ac. l.s. Wintocomake Cr. on n.s. Gr. Br. Son Godphrey Coleman 200 ac. l.s. Wintocomake Cr. on n.s. Gr. Br., joining son William. <u>Dau. Frances Tucker</u>. <u>Wife Faith</u> - land & plant. where I live during Life, then to son Peter - also pers. est. during her natural life, then to be equally div. bet. two youngest sons, Godfrey & Peter.

WB 1-45, 2 May 1746. William Coleman Est. I&A. Appr: John Powell, Walter Chiles, John x Old. Exr: Robert Coleman.

WB 1-33, Oct 1745, James Coles, Est. I&A ret. by Dorothy x Cole. Apprs: Robert Tucker Jr (x), George Tucker (x), Robert Cousens.

WB 1-63, d 26 Sep 1744, p 18 May 1750, will of Robert Tucker. - names: - Exr. son Robert. - Wife Martha - son Daniel - Son Joseph - Dau. Sarah Clay - Son Robert.

WB 1-73, 15 Mar 1750. Capt. Robert Tucker Est. Inv. ret by Exr. Robert (R) Tucker. Mentions certain furniture at John Clay's.

Bonds. L200. 18 May 1750. Robert Tucker, Exr. for Robert Tucker, decd, with Abram Cock, Security.

DB 4-285, 26 Mar 1752, William Crawley to Robert Tucker, for L80.8.9, 443 ac. on l.s. of Great Branch of Wintocomaick Cr., being part of a Patent for 3,000 ac. granted to sd William Crawley, bo. Hasten's on the Gr. Br., Wolf Trap Br., Ragdall's line, Tucker Knott of Lightwood cor., Tucker's old line. Wit: Benjamin Bowles, John Applin, John Smith.

DB 4-440, 14 Jul 1752, rec. 27 Aug 1752, Benjamin Ragsdale of Dinwiddie Co. to James Tucker of county aforesaid, for L30., 200 ac. on head of Sampson's Br. of Wintocomake Cr. in Amelia Co., bo. Robert Tucker Jun cor. Wit: Pat Mullin, George Burrus, Rich x George.

WB 1-33, Will of Godfrey Coleman, wd 6 Jun 1753, wp 27 Sep 1753. Wit: Wm. x Bevill, Edward Tanner, John Archer. Exr: Bro. Peter Coleman. Leg: 2 bros. Wm. & Peter Coleman - 200 ac. left me by my father William Coleman; Bro. Peter Coleman rest of est.

WB 1-104, 24 Dec 1753, Godfrey Coleman Est. I&A. Appr: Robert x Tucker, John x Hastens, William x Hastens. Exr: Peter x Coleman.

WB 1-106, 1 May 1754, Robert Muns, Est. I&A. Appr: George x Tucker, Robert x Tucker Holman Freeman.

WB 1-186, Jan Court 1761. Walter Chiles Est. I&A. Appr: Lawrence Wills, Holman Freeman, Robert Tucker. Admr: Fendall Southerland.

DB 8-250, 20 Dec 1763, rec. 22 Dec 1763, James Tucker to Robert Tucker, for L7.10, 15 ac. on n.s. of the Main Sampson's Br., bo Robert Tuckers line, Sampson's Br. Wit: Daniel Tucker, Edward Tanner, Hezekiah Coleman. S/ James Tucker.

DB 8-254, 20 Dec 1763, rec. 22 Dec 1763, <u>Robert Tucker to James Tucker</u>, for L5, <u>12 ac.</u> on s.s. of the main Sampsjn-rs Br. at the mouth of a br. that comes through sd James Tucker's corn field, up Sampson's Br. to Robert Tucker's line, crosses Sampson's Br. <u>Wit:</u> Edward Tanner, Hezekiah Coleman, <u>Daniel Tucker</u>. S / Robert (R) Tucker.

NOTE: The effect of the above two deeds is that James Tucker (Jr) and his uncle Robert Tucker (Jr) exchanged the small acreage each owned on opposite sides of Sampson's Br. In Patent 18-389, 22 Sep 1739, Amelia Co., James Tucker (Sr) patented 400 ac. l.s. Wintocomaick Cr. <u>between his brothers Robert & John Tucker's line</u>, which he deeded to his son James Tucker (Jr) by DB 3-58 & DB 3-243. Then James Tucker Jr sold the 400 ac. (DB 3-533), and bought another 200 ac. (DB 4-440) on Sampson's Br. of Wintocomaick Cr., of which the 15 ac. is a part.

WB 2X-60, 27 Jun 1763, ret 26 Apr 1764, John Hastings Est I&A. <u>Appr:</u> Robert Tucker Sr, Daniel Coleman, Joseph Coleman. (Note: Following the death of his father in 1750, Robert Tucker Jr. was then sometimes referred to as Robert Tucker Sr.)

WB 2X-239, 21 May 176, ret. 23 Jun 1768. William Coleman Est. I&A. <u>Appr: Robert x Tucker</u>, Thos. Berry, James Bevill.

WB 2X-283. <u>Robert Tucker (Jr?)</u> wd 8 Dec 1768, wp 25 May 1769. Wit: James Old, Jesse Coleman, Richard Weeks.
<u>Exrs: Son William Tucker and son-in-law John Smith.</u>
Sec: John Clay and Edward Tanner.
Leg: <u>Wife Frances</u> - plantation I now live on with 275 1/2 ac. adj., for life or widowhood, then to <u>son, Godfrey Tucker</u>.
<u>Son William</u> - plantation he now lives on with adj. 200 ac. bet. old and new lines made by Wm. Coleman & John Smith, - all land l.s. Sampson's Br.
<u>Son Robert Tucker</u> - 278 ac. adj. his plant. beg. old line bet. him & Godfrey's land etc., bet. Robert & Daniel's land etc., to Wolf Trap Br. where John Hastens' line crosses br.
<u>Son Daniel</u> - 258 ac. adj. plantation, being all land not already mentioned n.s. Sampson's Branch.
<u>Daus. Martha Smith Frances Crowder Rachel Old</u>.

LIST OF TITHES

1736	2	----	Robert Tucker, Jun	___
1737	2	----	Robert Tucker, Jun	Cate
1738		----	Robert Tucker, Jun	Cak
1739	2	----	Robert Tucker, Jun	Cale
1740	2	----	Robert Tucker, Jun	Cabl
1743	2	----	Robert Tucker, Jun	Cale

LIST OF TITHES

1744	2	----	Robert Tucker, Jun	Cale
1747	3	----	Robert Tucker Jun	Dick, Caler
1749	4	----	Robert Tucker, William Tucker	Dick, Cato
1750	3	----	Robert Tucker, William Tucker	Dick
1751	3	----	Robert Tucker, William Tucker	Dick
1753	4	----	Robert Tucker, William Tucker	Dick, Harry
1755	6	----	Robert Tucker, William Tucker, Robert Tucker, Jun	Dick, Harry, Jenny
1756	6	----	Robert Tucker, William Tucker	Dick, Harry, Jenny, ___
1762	6	----	Robert Tucker, Sen, Dan Tucker	Dick, Harry, Jenny, Yammin
1763	7	1008½	Robert Tucker Sr List, Dan Tucker, Godfrey Tucker	Dick, Harry, Jamie, Anike
1765	7	811	Robert Tucker Sr, Daniel Tucker, Godfrey Tucker	
1767	6	533	Robert Tucker, Godfrey Tucker	Dick, Harry, Jane, Anica
1769	6	275	Robert Tucker, Godfrey Tucker	Dick, Harry, Jane, Anica

(See WB 2X-283, 1769, Robert Tucker).

NOTE: Beginning in 1763, the records showed not only the number of tithables in the household, but also the number acres of land. Also, Robert Tucker Jr was sometimes designated as Robert Tucker Sr.

SUMMARY OF LAND TRANSACTIONS FOR ROBERT TUCKER JR:

Date	Reference		Plus	Minus	Bal.
1731	Patent 14-341		400		400
1741	DB 1-344	fr father Robert	165.5		565.5
1752	DB 4-285	fr Crawley	443		1008.5
1763	DB 8-250	fr nephew James	15		1023.5
1763	DB 8-254	to nephew James		12	1011.5
1769	WB 2X-283	to son William		200	811.5
		to son Robert		278	533.5
		to son Daniel		258	275.5
		to son Godfrey		275.5	0
	Totals		1023.5	1023.5	

It is readily apparent that the above acreage balances agree with the acreage, where shown, in the tithe records.

102

NOTE: Capt. Robert Tucker Sr may have married twice, and his sons James, Robert Jr, George and John may have been sons by a 1st wife prior to 1720. It is doubtful if they were sons of Martha, who most probably was a 2nd wife of Robert Sr.

NOTE: Both Robert Jr & his brother George had a wife named Francis. It is most probable that Robert Tucker Jr md Francis Coleman, dau of William Coleman Sr because (1) Coleman named in his will dau Francis Tucker, (2) Robert Tucker Jr named in his will wife Frances & dau Francis, and (3) Robert Tucker Jr was an appraiser of est of Godfrey Coleman who was his wife's brother.

SUMMARY: Robert Tucker Jr, son of Capt Robert Tucker Sr, b before 1706 in Pr Geo Co, d 1769 in Amelia Co, md ca 1726 probably in Pr Geo Co. Frances Coleman, dau of William Coleman Sr & wf Faith, & had issue:

Martha Tucker b 1727, md John Smith.

Frances Tucker b 1730, md _____ Crowder.

Rachael Tucker b ?, md _____ Old.

William Tucker b 1733, md 1756 Mary Keatts, dau of Curtis Keatts.

Robert Tucker b ea 1739, md Sarah _____.

Daniel Tucker b by 1746, (possibly 1740), md Frances _____.

Godfrey Tucker b ca 1747, md Mary _____.

See separate chapter for each son.

* * *

1. Boddie, John B., "Births 1720-1792 From The Bristol Parish Register of. Henrico, Prince George and Dinwiddie".

TR121000 - WILLIAM TUCKER

MD MARY KEATTS
SON OF ROBERT TUCKER JR
MD FRANCES COLEMAN

BRISTOL PARISH REGISTER [2]

William Son of Robert & Frances Tucker Born 15th apr 1733 Bapt 3d June 1735.

AMELIA CO. VA.

MARRIAGE BOND, 26 Oct 1756, William Tucker md Mary Keats, Security Robert Tucker Jr, Parent Anton(?) Keats.

WB 2X-283. Robert Tucker (Jr?) wd 8 Dec 1768, wp 25 May 1769. -names: - Exrs: Son William Tucker and son-in-law John Smith. - Leg: Wife Frances - son, Godfrey Tucker - Son William - plantation he now lives on with adj. 200 ac. bet. old and new lines made by Wm. Coleman & John Smith, all land l.s. Samason's Br. - Son Robert Tucker - San Daniel - Daus. Martha Smith, Frances Crowder, Rachel Old

DB 6-201, 23 Feb 1758, Kertis Keats (sic) (Curtis Keatts) to Mary Tucker the dau. of sd Curtis Keatts, & William Tucker the husband of sd Mary & son of Robert Tucker, for natural love, good will & affection, & for 5 Sh., 200 ac. btwn Middle & Lower Sellar Forks of Deep Cr., bo. Bland's line, William's cor., Bold Br. Wit: Donal. Coleman, John Clay, Christi-. Hinton. S/ Curtis Keats. (See DB 11-170).

NOTE: On the same date, by Amelia Co. DB 6-147, 23 Feb 1758, Curtis Keatts gave to his dau. Martha Tucker & her husband Robert Tucker son of George Tucker, 200 ac. btwn Middle & Lower Fork of Deep Cr. Now whereas this Mary & Martha Keatts were sisters, their respective husbands William & Robert Tucker were first cousins. Nineteen years later in Lunenburg Co. by DB 13-23, 12 Jun 1777, Curtis Keatts gave to his dau. Tabitha Tucker & her husband William Tucker son of George Tucker, 200 ac. n.s. Couches Cr. On the same date by DB 13-pages 24-25, Curtis Keatts made similar gifts to sons John Keatts, Wm. Keatts and Charles Keatts. It appears then that Mary, Martha, Tabitha, John, Wm. & Charles Keatts are sisters and brothers.

DB 11-24, 1769, William & Mary Tucker to Robert Tucker, 200 ac. on Br. of Wintercomake Cr., plantation where he now lives, - also land l.s. of Sampson's Br. - land left to sd William Tucker by Robert Tucker his father. (See WB 2X-283 and DB 11-158).

DB 11-158, 8 Feb 1770, rec. 26 Jul 1770, <u>Robert Tucker & wf Sarah to William Tucker</u> for L400., <u>200 ac.</u> on branches of Wintocomake, which sd land was acknowledged by sd William Tucker to the Rob't last June court (?). S/ Robert Tucker, Sarah Tucker. (See DB 11-24).

NOTE: The Robert Tucker and William Tucker in the above two deeds are brothers. It appears that William sold to his brother Robert, and then bought back from him, the 200 ac. inherited from his father Robert Tucker Jr., and later sold it to Richard Newman in 1773. See DB 12-142 below.

DB 11-170, 25 Oct 1770, rec. 25 Oct 1770, <u>Mary Tucker & William Tucker</u> to Henry Dennis, for L50., <u>200 ac.</u> btwn the Middle & Lower Cellar Forks of Deep Cr., bo. Haskins cor., Thos. Bland's line, Dennis cor., a Great Branch, being part of land granted to William Chisholm by patent 20 Sep 1748, & conveyed by Chisholm to Curtis Keatts by deed 14 Sep 1751, & <u>by Keatts conveyed to Mary Tucker & William Tucker</u> 23 Feb 1758. Wit: C. W. Haskins, <u>John Appling</u>, Rich'd Hayes. S/ Mary x Tucker, William Tucker. (See DB 6-201)

DB 12-142, 14 Oct 1773, rec 20 Oct 1773, <u>William Tucker</u> to Richard Newman of Dinwiddie Co., for L250., <u>200 ac.</u> bo. William Watson, William Roach, Robert Tucker & Godfrey Tucker, <u>being the land whereon the sd William Tucker now lives</u>. Wit: James Old, Joshua Spain, John Watkins. S/ William Tucker, Mary. <u>Wife Mary relinq. dower.</u>

DB 15-76, 25 Nov 1778, <u>William Tucker & wf Mary</u> to James Southall for L50., <u>85 ac,</u> on e.s. Wintocomake Cr. <u>adj. Godfrey Tucker</u> & John Coles. Wit: David Adams, David Williams, Frederick Ford. S/ Wm. x Tucker, Mary x Tucker.

NOTE: The above 85 ac. seems to be a part of the 200 ac. which William Tucker inherited from his father, Robert Tucker Jr, and which he sold to and bought back from his brother Robert, and which he later sold to Richard Newman. However, in WR 2X-283 and in DB 11-24 above, the phrase "also land l.s. of Sampson's Br." implies his inheritance may have included land in addition to 200 ac. plantation where he now lives, (possibly this 85 ac.). But this theory is not substantiated by the tithe records below. No other deed could be found in Amelia Co. for this 85 ac.

LIST OF TITHES

1749-1756	-	---	This William Tucker appeared as a 16-yr-up tithable in the household of his father Robert Tucker Jr.
1762	1	---	William Tucker son of R.T.
1763	1	200	William Tucker

LIST OF TITHES

1767   1 400 William Tucker, son of Robt.
1769   1 200 William Tucker

William Tucker, son of Robert Tucker Jr, moved to Lunenburg Co, and did not appear on the Lists of Tithes of Amelia Co. after 1769.

LUNENBURG CO. VA.

DB 11-263, 6 May 1769, rec 11 May 1769, Gideon Moon of Lunenburg Co., to William Tucker, son of Robert Tucker of Amelia Co., for L130., 400 ac. in Lunenburg Co., bo David Siles, Gilliam. Wit: Curtis x Keatts, William Tucker, James Keatts. S/ Gideon x Moon. (See DB 17-157 & DB 18-8).

DB 17-157, 30 Oct 1795, rec 10 Dec 1795, William Tucker of Lunenburg Co. to Peter Reaves, for $520., 208 ac. on Couches Cr., bo. Cooker, Edmunds. Wit: J. Billups, Robert Tucker, N. Tucker, Thomas Ingram. S/ William Tucker. (See DB 17-202, & DB 18-161A).

DB 17-202, 11 Feb 1796, Elizabeth Tucker, wf of William Tucker relinq right of dower to land conveyed to Reaves. (See DB17-157 & DB 18-161A) (Note: This designation of Elizabeth as wife of William Tucker is most confusing, since the wife of the subject William was named Mary Keatts. This entry was recorded in the deed book over three months after the deed to which it applied).

DB 18-8, 13 Nov 1797, rec 11 Jan 1798, William Tucker to Charles Byam(?), for L100., 200 ac. bo. James Smith, Edmunds, Mary Crymes. Wit: William Tucker Senr, Peter Avery, James Old. S/ William Tucker. (See DB 18-69).

DB 18-69, 31 Mar 1798. Whereas William Tucker sold to Charles Byam(?) 200 ac. , & wf Mary was unable to come to court, court sent representative to her home & obtained her relinquishment of dower right. (See DB 18-8).

DB 18-161A, 22 Oct 1799, rec 13 Feb 1800, William Tucker, Peter Reaves & wf Nancy, to Nathan Gee, for L224., 208 ac. on Couches Cr., bo. James ___?, Edmunds, William Tucker's Mill. Wit: Sur? Tucker, Charles Byaner(?), B. Andrews. S/ William Tucker, Peter Reaves, Nancy Reaves. Memo: We have gone to the house of William Tucker & there examined Nancy Reaves, wf of Peter Reaves, & she relinq dower right on 24 Oct 1799. (See DB 17-157 & DB 17-202 above).

NOTE: The above six entries are most confusing but seem to apply to the same 400 ac. which William Tucker purchased from Gideon Moon in 1769. Why his wife was designated erroneously as Elizabeth instead of Mary in DB 17-202 is unclear. Why he sold the 208 ac. to Peter Reaves

106

& then, jointly with Peter Reaves, sold it again to Nathan Gee is unclear, unless Peter Reaves defaulted on payment. Nancy Reaves was in the home of her parents William Tucker & wf Tabitha. Why there was still 200 ac. remaining (rather than 192 ac.), after selling 208 ac. is unclear. But it does seem clear that the 208 ac. sold & the 200 ac. sold are part of the 400 ac. purchased from Gideon Moon in 1769.

There were two William Tuckers living in Lunenburg Co., who appeared on the Personal Tax Records and Land Tax Records beginning in 1782, and were recorded variously as William, William Sr, William Jr, and William (Whiskey). The designations Sr. & Jr. were most probably used to distinguish the older William son of Robert Jr, b 1733, md Mary Keatts, from his younger first cousin William son of George, b ca 1740, md Tabitha Keatts, sister of Mary Keatts. In the following personal and land tax records, William Tucker (Sr-son of Robert) who md Mary Keatts, appears to hold the 408 ac., and William Tucker (Jr-son of George) who md Tabitha Keatts, appears to hold the 400 ac, although sometimes they are shown in reverse.

YEAR	PERSONAL TAX RECORDS	LAND TAX RECORDS
1782	Wm. Tucker	Wm. Tucker 408 ac
	Wm. Tucker (Whiskey),	Wm. Tucker 200 ac.
	Hannah,Daniel, Sam	
1783	Wm. Tucker	
	Wm. Tucker	
1784	Wm. Tucker, Nelson Tucker.	
1785	Wm. Tucker Sr., Nelson Tucker.	
	Wm. Tucker (Whiskey)	
1786	William Tucker, Nelson Tucker,	
	Brister, Jude, Lewis, Hampton,	
	Jack, 2 whites age 21-up,	
	5 negroes, 2 horses, 16 cattle,	
	4 tithes.	
	Wm. Tucker, Wm. Walker,	
	Hannah, Abel, Coleman	
1787	William Tucker Sr, Neal Tucker	Wm. Tucker Sr 408 ac
	age 16-20 (perhaps Nelson?).	
	Wm. Tucker.	Wm. Tucker (Whiskey) 400 ac.
1788	William Tucker Sr.	Wm. Tucker Sr
	William Tucker (Whiskey)	Wm. Tucker (Whiskey)
1789	Wm. Tucker.	Wm. Tucker Jr(?) 408 ac.
	Wm. Tucker Jr	Wm. Tucker (Whiskey) 400 ac.
1790	Wm. Tucker.	Wm. Tucker Jr(?) 408 ac.
	Wm. Tucker (Whiskey)	Wm. Tucker (Whiskey) 400 ac.
1791	Wm. Tucker Sr.	Wm. Tucker Jr(?) 408 ac.

107

YEAR	PERSONAL TAX RECORDS	LAND TAX RECORDS
	Wm. Tucker Jr.	Wm. Tucker Jr 400 ac.
1792	Wm. Tucker Sen.	Wm. Tucker Sr 408 ac.
	Wm. Tucker Jr.	Wm. Tucker Jr 400 ac.
1793	Wm. Tucker Sr., Nelson Tucker	Wm. Tucker Sr 408 ac.
	Wm. Tucker Jr	Wm. Tucker Jr 400 ac.
1794	Wm. Tucker Sr., Nelson Tucker	Wm. Tucker Sr 400 (?) ac.
	Wm. Tucker Jr	Wm. Tucker Jr 400 ac.
1795	Wm. Tucker Sr., Nelson Tucker	Wm. Tucker Sr 400 (?) ac.
	Wm. Tucker Jr	
1796	Wm. Tucker.	Wm. Tucker 200 ac.
	Wm. Tucker	
1797	Wm. Tucker Sr.	Wm. Tucker Sr 200 ac.
	Wm. Tucker Jr.	Wm. Tucker Jr 400 ac.
1798	Wm. Tucker.	Wm. Tucker 400 ac.
1799	Wm. Tucker.	Wm. Tucker 400 ac.
1800	---	Wm. Tucker 400 ac.
1801	---	---

After selling the 208 ac. in 1795 and 200 ac. 1798, in Lunenhurg Co., we find William Tucker (Sr-son of Robert) & wife Mary & son Nelson in Halifax Co. Va.

2 Feb 1796 Louisa Tucker m James Old, Surety Nelson Tucker.

HALIFAX CO. VA.

DB 17-340, 6 Oct 1797. rec 23 Oct 1797, Ambrose Madison of Halifax Co. to William Tucker of Lunenburg Co. , for L175., 250 ac. on Cow & Childrey Cr., bo. pointers on Millstone Rd., Ezekiel Pillow, Cow Cr., Ephriam Jackson, Walter Owen, Reuben Wells, James Harris, Childrey Cr, Herbert Nunnelee. S/ Ambrose Anderson. Wit: Ezekiel Pillow, Jas Harris, John Clay.

DB 18-525, 22 Sep 1800, rec 22 Dec 1800, Reuben Wills to William Tucker, for L40, 100 ac. on Cow Cr., bo. John Carr, sd Wills, William Tucker's old line. S/ Reubin x Wills. Wit: Thomas x Walker, Freeman x Wills, James Old, Ezekiel Pillow.

DB 18-549, 9 Oct 1800, rec 22 Dec 1800, Ephriam Jackson to William Tucker for L15., 25 ac. on Cow Cr., bo. sd Tucker, Walter Owen, Joy br. S/ Ephriam Jackson. Wit: Ezk. Pillow, William Davis, James Old.

PITTSYLVANIA CO., VA

DB 14-40, Apr 1804, William Tucker Sr of Halifax Co., appoint Nelson Tucker of Pittsylvania Co. lawful attorney.

DB 14-90, 18 Jun 1804, John Balinger of Pittsylvania Co. to William

Tucker of Halifax Co., Va., for L86.8., 140 ac. in Pittsylvania Co., bo Camp Br, Scruggs, A. Meharian; also 4 ac. adj A. Meharian, total 144 ac. Wit: Nelson Tucker, Charles Bailey, Stephen Clement, William Johns, D. Hunt, John Hunt. (See Halifax Co. WB 7-228)

HALIFAX CO., VA

WB 7-228, wd 27 Mar 1806, wp 28 Jul 1806, will of William Tucker.
to wife Mary Tucker - land & plantation on n.s. Cow Creek on which I now live, for life, except 100 ac. at upper end of sd land, joining lands of Thomas Walker & Wm. Craddock; also 4 negroes Brister, Hampton, Silvey & Ursley, together with my stock of all kinds as horses, cattle & c., plantation utensils, household & kitchen furniture, &c., & after her decease, the ____ (balance) negroes & other estate as I hereafter direct.
to dau. Louise Old - all my land lying s.s. Cow Cr; also negro boy Mason already in her possession; & at wife's death, one other negro girl Silvey & increase.
to dau Sally Couch - 100 ac. on n.s. Cow Cr., joining lands of Thos. Walker & Wm. Craddock; & negro boy Griffin already in her possession.
to granddaughter Polly. D. Couch, dau. of my Sally Couch, after death of my-wife Mary - one feather bed & $30.00 in cash.
to Dau Mary Johns, after death of my wife - $5.00 in cash; also 144 ac. in Pittsylvania Co., being land purchased of John Balinger & joining land of Drury Scrugs, Thos Collins, & Wm. Clarke, & at her death, then to her three sons John Johns, Daniel Johns & Joseph Johns.
to granddaughters Sally Johns & Polly N. Johns, daus. of my sd dau. Mary Johns, after death of my wife Mary, $30.00 each in cash.
to dau. Martha Keatts - negro boy Phill already in her possession; & at death of my wife Mary, two other negroes Hampto & Ursley & her increase.
to son Nelson Tucker - negro man Lewiz; and at my wife's decease, all my land lying on n.s. of Cow Cr. except the 100 ac., disposed to dau. Sally Couch; also one large blue chest.
Remaining est. to be sold to highest bidder after decease of my wife Mary, after paying cash legacies, to be equally divided btwn my four children Louise Old, Sally Couch, Martha Keatts & Nelson Tucker.
Est not to be appraised.
Exrs: wife Mary Tucker & son Nelson Tucker. S/ William Tucker.
Wit: Claiborne x Bond, Walter x Owen, Josiah x Owen, Ezekiel Pillow, Joel Tucker, Peter Rives.

SUMMARY: William Tucker son of Robert Tucker & wife Frances Coleman, b 1733 in Prince George Co. Va., lived in Prince George, Amelia, Lunenburg & Halifax counties, d 1806 in Halifax Co. Va., md 1756 in Amelia Co. Va., Mary Keatts, dau of Curtis Keatts, and had issue:

Nelson Tucker b ca 1767, d 1843 in Pittsylvania Co. Va., md 1788 in Pittsylvania Co. Va., Martha Clark.

Louise Tucker md 2 Feb 1796 James Old.

Sally Tucker md _____ Couch, & had issue: Polly D. Couch.

Mary Tucker md _____ Johns, & had issue: John, Daniel, Joseph, Sally & Polly N. Johns.

Martha Tucker md _____ Keatts.

* * *

2. Boddie, John B., "Births 1720-1792 From The Bristol Parish Register of Henrico, Prince George and Dinwiddie".

110

TR121100 - NELSON TUCKER
MD MARTHA CLARK
SON OF WILLIAM TUCKER
MD MARY KEATTS

LUNENBURG CO. VA.

NOTE: Nelson Tucker was first listed as a 16-yr-up tithable in the household of his father William Tucker in 1784 in Lunenburg Co. However, William Tucker had lived in Amelia Co. until 1769, so Nelson was b ca 1768 in Amelia Co. He should not be confused with another Nelson Tucker b ca 1775 son of Thomas Tucker, who md 1799 Rhoda Hood.

HALIFAX CO. VA.

WB 7-228, wd 27 Mar 1806, wp 28 Jul 1806, will of William Tucker. - names - wife Mary Tucker - dau. Louise Old - dau Sally Couch - granddaughter-Polly D. Couch, dau. of my dau. Sally Couch - Dau Mary Johns - her three sons John Johns, Daniel Johns & Joseph Johns - granddaughters Sally Johns & Polly N. Johns, daus. of my sd dau. Mary Johns - dau. Martha Keatts - son Nelson Tucker - negro man Lewiz; and at my wife's decease, all my land lying on n. s. of Cow Cr. except the 100 ac. disposed to dau. Sally Couch; also one large blue chest. Remaining est. to be sold to highest bidder after decease of my wife Mary, after paying cash legacies, to be equally divided btwn my four children Louise Old, Sally Couch, Martha Keatts & Nelson Tucker. - Exrs: wife Mary Tucker & son Nelson Tucker.

DB 22-206, 2 Sep 1809, rec 23 Oct 1809, Nelson Tucker & wf Mary of Pittsylvania Co., Va. to Laben Palmer of Halifax Co., for $300., 150 ac. on n.s. Cow Cr., bo. Elijah Couch. S/ Nelson Tucker, Mary Tucker. Wit: Robert G. Tucker, Peter Reves, Gabriel Tucker. Wf Mary relinq dower right.

NOTE: It appears that Nelson Tucker sold the land in Halifax Co. which he inherited from his father William Tucker, and established his residence in Pittsylvania Co. Note also that his wife's name was recorded as "Mary", probably in error, for he married Martha Clark in 1788.

PITTSYLVANIA CO. VA.

Index to Marriage Bonds 1767-1862, p 11, 15 Dec 1788, Nelson Tucker md Martha Clark, Bondsman, Wm. Clark.

NOTE: The land tax records of Pittsylvania Co. indicate that Nelson Tucker owned tracts of 200, 10, 28 & 192 ac. on Straitstone Cr. and 200 ac. on Flyblow Cr. from 1813-1826, and another 33 ac. on Straitstone Cr beginning in 1825.

DB 8-448, John Waller gift to Nelson Tucker, negro boy James, one mare colt, in consequence of provision made for his wife Martha Tucker by will of her father Thomas Clark. Wit: James Keatts, Martha x Keatts, John Keatts.

DB 8-449, rec 19 Oct 1789, John Waller, Charles Keatts & Nelson Tucker of Pittsylvania Co. and Wm. Barber Price of Henry Co. , relinquish int. in est. of Thomas Clark decd, now in possession of Martha Clark, widow of sd decd, which by his will, at decease of widow, provision is made for a proportionate division of residuals to our wives, respectively daughters of sd decd. Wit: John Keatts, James Keatts, Martha x Keatts.

NOTE: The above deed indicates that John Waller, Charles Keatts, Nelson Tucker and William Barber Price all married daughters of Thomas Clark & wf Martha.

DB 10-263, 17 Dec 1795, rec 21 Dec 1795, Edward Flowers & wf Rebekah of Pittsylvania Co., to Nelson Tucker of Lunenburg Co., for L100, 200 ac., on l.s. south fork of Strait Stone Cr., bo. Thomas Lester decd, Henry Brown, Richard T ____.

NOTE: The designation of "Nelson Tucker of Lunenburg Co." most probably means "formerly of Lunenburg Co."

DB 10-503 20 Apr 1796, rec 19 Sep 1796, Henry Brown to Nelson Tucker , for L10., 10 ac. bo. sd Tucker, Capt. Gilbert Hunt, Thomas Lester decd. Wit: Stephen Clement, Wm. x McKinea, John Lester, D. Hunt, G. Hunt.

DB 12-409, 11 Sep 1801, rec. 21 Dec 1801. John Lester to Nelson Tucker for L14., 28 ac., bo. sd Tucker, crosses Strait Stone Cr., Capt. Isaac Clement, Wit: Philip T. Grasty, Wm. x Parham, Benjamin Stone.

DB 14-40, 16 Apr 1804, Martha Tucker of Pittsylvania Co. appoint Robert G. Tucker of Halifax Co., lawful attorney.

DB 14-40, Apr 1804, William Tucker Sr of Halifax Co., appoint Nelson Tucker of Pittsylvania Co. lawful attorney.

DB 14-210, 11 Feb 1805, rec 18 Feb 1805, Hugh Clement of Granville Co., NC, to Nelson Tucker of Pittsylvania Co., VA, for L55., 200 ac. on s.s. Strait Stone Cr., bo. Hunt, including all the land that is left out of the deed made to the sd Tucker by Edward Flowers; also one ac. adjoining sd tract bo. Hunt. S/ Stephen Clement P/A for Hugh Clement. Wit: Thomas Vaughan, Jno Welsford, John Mustain.

DB 15-468, 4 Jan 1808, rec 18 Jan 1808, Nathaniel Crenshaw, Philip S. Grasty, Samuel Stone, Nelson Tucker, & William Stone of Pittsylvania Co. to William Smith , by order of court, sold 370 ac. & out of purchase money pay & satisfy debt due James Murdock, surviving partner of himself, George Youille, Thomas Youille, late merchants & partners known by the firm of James Murcock & Co., from William Todd for L125.11.4, & William Smith purchased for L130.9.7.

DB 16-178, 13 Oct 1818, rec 17 Oct 1808, George Davis & wf Mary to Nelson Tucker, for L195., 192 ac. on Maggetty Cr. emptying into Stinking Ri. bo. Nathan Glen, Charles Baley, Joel Shelton, Thomas Davis, Gar. Lewis. (See DB 30-428)

DB 17-108, 10 May 1810, rec 18 Jun 1810 Nelson Tucker etal commrs., sold 400 ac, being part of tract whereon Edmund Tunstall now lives & being conveyed by sd John Cleaver to Thomas Tunstall, & William Tunstall became purchaser for L400.

DB 17-195, 20 Aug 1810, Nelson Tucker etal commrs. sold land, etc. not pertinent to Nelson.

DB 17-282, 16 Apr 1810, rec 15 Oct 1810, Rawley White to secure debt to Meady Anderson & to Thomas Anderson sold to Nelson Tucker & Wyatt Haley, 108 ac. on Elkhorn Cr., also negro woman Ginny, also 3 stills, all in trust.

DB 18-52, rec 15 Jan 1812, rec 15 Jun 1812, William B. Price of Pheat Co. Kentucky, Nelson Tucker & Robert Waller of Pittsylvania Co. Va., to John Waller, for $300., 200 ac. on b.s. Georges Cr., bo. Isaac Coles, Vincent Shelton, Charles Womack, excepting to Ann Bailey her interest in & to the part of sd tract lying on s.s. of Georges Cr. joining Charles Womack, which interest was devised to her by will of her former husband William Clarke, decd. Wit: Stephen Clement, John Tucker, John Shelton, Abra. Shelton. Martha Tucker wf of Nelson Tucker & Judith Waller, wf of Robert Waller, acknowledged above deed.

DB 27-123, 14 Dec 1824, rec 17 Jan 1825, George Boyd & wf Martha to Nelson Tucker, for $214.50., 33 ac. on b.s. Straitstone Cr., beginning where sd Tucker & Boyd line crosses Lynchburg Rd.

DB 30-428, 18 Oct 1828, rec 15 Dec 1828. Nelson Tucker & wf Martha to James C. Keatts for $550., 192 ac on Magotty Cr emptying into Stinking Ri, bo Coles, Jos Whitehead, Nathan Glenn, sd James G. Keatts, Richd Whitehead. (See DB 16-178)

WB 1-466, wd 1 Jan 1840, wp 18 Sep 1843, will of Nelson Tucker.
son John Tucker - all my land on w.s. Lynchburg Rd.
wf Martha - all land lying e.s. Lynchburg Rd.
grandson William C. Tucker son of my son William C. Tucker decd,
daus: Elizabeth Tucker, Polly A. Mitchell, Martha H. Priddy, Nancy P. Tucker, Susannah Waddill.
Ex: son Miles N. Tucker. Wit: Stephen Clement, George W. Coleman.

DB 51-265, 14 Jun 1848, rec 19 Jun 1848, Whereas by a decree of Circuit Superior Court btwn John Haley Plntf vs W. L. Pannill admr of N. Tucker Deft, upon a bill of Review filed by sd Pannill, the sd Rison was appointed commissioner with direction that he should by deed with special warranty, convey to sd Pannill all the real estate purchased by him under an interlocutory decree. Witnesseth that William Rison, commissioner sold to William L. Pannill the real estate purchased by him under an interlocutory decree, 528 ac, 151 ac of which Martha Tucker widow of Nelson Tucker decd has an est of dower in, on both sides of road leading from Riceville towards Bridge on both sides of Straightstone Cr, being the land formerly. owned by Nelson Tucker decd. Nelson Tucker est & Martha Tucker, by comr to William L. Pannill.

MARRIAGES

19 Aug 1816, Polly A. Tucker md James H. Mitchell.

14 Sep 1817, Martha H. Tucker md John Priddy.

Susan (Susannah) Tucker md Albert Waddill.

MARRIAGES [3]

18 Feb 1826. William C. Tucker md Mildred H. Gilbert, dau of George Gilbert who authorized the license be issued. Sur. Cornelius Gilbert. Md 21 Feb by Rev. Shadrack Mustain. p 87.

MARRIAGES [4]

26 Apr 1838, John Tucker md Sally Faris, who signs her own consent Salley Faris. Sur. Thomas R. Jenkins, Married by John W. Rosser. p 118.

21 Jun 1855, Miles N. Tucker md Mary Scruggs, Signers: Nelson Tucker, father; Patsy Tucker, mother; Drury Scruggs, father; Mildred Scruggs, mother. p 162.

SUMMARY: Nelson Tucker, son of William Tucker & wf Mary Keatts, b ca 1768 Amelia Co, lived in Lunenburg Co. until 1795, d 1843 Pittsylvania Co., md 1788 Pittsylvania Co., Martha Clark dau of Thomas Clark & wf Martha, & had issue:

Elizabeth Tucker.

Nancy P. Tucker.

Polly A. Tucker, md 1816 James H. Mitchell.

Martha H. Tucker, md 1817 John Priddy.

Susan (Susannah) Tucker, md Albert Waddill.

William C. Tucker, d before 1840, md 1826 Mildred H. Gilbert, & had issue: William C. Tucker (Jr) b before 1840.

John Tucker, md 1838 Sally Faris.

Miles N. Tucker, md 1855 Mary Scruggs, dau of Drury Scruggs & wf Mildred.

* * *

3. Williams, Kathleen Booth, "Marriages of Pittsylvania County, Virginia 1806-1830", 1965.

4. Chiarito, Marian Dodson, "Marriages Pittsylvania County, Virginia, 1831-1861", 1982.

TR121110 - JOHN TUCKER
MD SALLY FARIS
SON OF NELSON TUCKER
MD MARTHA CLARK

PITTSYLVANIA CO., VA.

WB 1-466, wd 1 Jan 1840, wp 18 Sep 1843, <u>will of Nelson Tucker</u>. -names - <u>son John Tucker - all my, land on w.s. Lynchburg Rd</u>. - wf Martha - all land lying e.s. Lynchburg Rd. - son William C. Tucker decd. - grandson William C. Tucker - daus: Elizabeth Tucker, Polly A. Mitchell, Martha H. Priddy, Nancy P. Tucker, Susannah Waddill.

26 Apr 1838, <u>John Tucker md Sally Faris</u>, who signs her own consent Salley Faris. Sur. Thomas R. Jenkins, Married by John W. Rosser. p 118.

Feb 1830. Pittsylvania Co Court Orders record that Daniel Johns, in Feb 1830, settled his guardian acounts for orphans of John Faris Sr, namely John Faris, Jane Faris, Mary Faris, Elizabeth Faris, Susan Faris, <u>Sarah Faris</u> and Samuel Faris.

SUMMARY: John Tucker, son of Nelson Tucker & wf Martha Clark, b ca 1792, m 1838 Sarah (Sally) Faris, b ca 1815, most probably orphan dau of John Faris Sr & wf Mary, and had issue:

> (information on the John Tucker family was provided to this compiler in Dec 1985 by Thomas Tucker of Danville, Va, who is great-great grandson of John Tucker)

1. William Henry Tucker, b 11 May 1839, d 1 Jun 1920, m 19 Feb 1867 Sarah Elizabeth Laine, (sister of Matilda A. Laine who m his bro Thomas John Tucker), & had issue:

> 1.1 Thomas Clark Tucker, b 19 Dec 1866, d 17 Feb 1934, m 1st 23 Dec 1891 his cousin Julia Waller b 1871, dau of Charles Edward Waller & wf Martha S. Tucker, m 2nd Lula Jenny Hodnett, b 10 May 1884. Thomas Clark Tucker had issue by his 1st wf: Elvin Clark Tucker, and had issue by his 2nd wf: Margaret Louise Tucker, Herman Johnson Tucker, Thomas Clark Tucker Jr and James Edwin Tucker.

>> 1.1.1 Elvin Clark Tucker, b 1900, d 1956 at age 56, m 1923 Elizabeth Carmel Wilbourne, (who was still living in 1985), & had issue:

>>> 1.1.1.1 Thomas Wilbourne Tucker b 15 Feb 1924, m Eva Harvey, and had no issue. (This is the Thomas Tucker who provided most of the information on the descendants of John Tucker & wf Sally Faris.)

1.1.1.2 Julian Glenwood Tucker, b 5 Feb 1925, m 4 Feb 1961 Belva Rozela Lynch, dau of Martin Luther Lynch & wf Lenora Jackson, and has issue: (information on this family provided by Mrs. Julian Tucker)

>1.1.1.2.1 Gary Allan Tucker, b 17 Jul 1963, a student at Duke University in 1985.

>1.1.1.2.2 Pamela Dawn Tucker, b 2 Oct 1969.

1.1.1.3 Leroyal Elmer Tucker, b 25 May 1927, m 18 Aug 1948 Dorothy Leona Reed & had issue: (information on this family provided by Leroyal Tucker)

>1.1.1.3.1 Patsy Lee Tucker b 1.5 Jun 1949, m James Moore from Eden, NC.

>1.1.1.3.2 Judy Diane Tucker, b 6 Jun 1951, m Buddy Patterson, bro of Debra Patterson.

>1.1.1.3.3 Dennis Reed Tucker, b 2 Feb 1954, m 1st Diane Williams, and 2nd Debra Patterson, sister of Buddy Patterson.

1.1.2 Margaret Louise Tucker, b 24 Feb 1918, m Hadley.

1.1.3 Herman Johnson Tucker, b 8 Jun 1919, d 26 Dec 1985 at Rockingham Co, NC, & had no issue.

1.1.4 Thomas Clark Tucker Jr.

1.1.5 James Edwin Tucker.

1.2. Augusta Tucker, b 1869, m 7 Jul 1890 at age 21, William B. Farthing, bro of George W. Farthing.

1.3. J. A. Tucker, b ca 1874, m 20 Nov 1901 at age 27, Pensy Glass.

1.4. Christine W. Tucker, b ca 1874, m 11 Jul 1899 at age 25, George W. Farthing, brother of William B. Farthing.

1.5. John William (Jack) Tucker, b 1877, m 20 Dec 1898 at age 21, Nellie J. Davenport & had issue:

>1.5.1. Royal Stevens (Roy) Tucker

>>1.5.1.1 Royal Stevens (Roy) Tucker, Jr.

1.6. Martha Clark Tucker, not married.

2. Thomas John Tucker, b ca 1846, m 22 Dec 1873 at age 27, Matilda A. Laine, sister of Sarah Elizabeth Laine who m his brother William Henry Tucker.

3. Joel B. Tucker, b ca 1846, m 24 Dec 1867 at age 21, Francis (East) Yeatts, widow.

4. John W. Tucker, b 1847, m 24 Apr 1869 at age 22, Sarah J. Barrett.

5. Martha S. Tucker, b ca 1847, m 10 Dec 1872 at age 25, Charles Edward Waller, & had issue:

    5.1. Julia Waller, m 23 Dec 1891 her cousin Thomas Clark Tucker.

6. Sally J. Tucker, b ca 1852, m 4 Jan 1874 at age 22, Charles H. Shelton.

7. Rebecca Tucker b ca 1857, m 14 Feb 1878 at age 21, Amos Saunders.

NOTE: All the above information on the descendants of John Tucker & wf Sally Faris was provided by others and not verified by this compiler.

TR121120 - MILES N. TUCKER

MD MARY SCRUGGS

SON OF NELSON TUCKER

MD MARTHA CLARK

PITTSYLVANIA CO., VA.

WB 1-466, wd 1 Jan 1840, wp 18 Sep 1843, will of Nelson Tucker. - names: - son John Tucker - wf Martha - William C. Tucker son of my son William C. Tucker decd. - daus Elizabeth Tucker, Polly A. Mitchell, Martha H. Priddy, Nancy P. Tucker, Susannah Waddill. Ex: son Miles N. Tucker.

MARRIAGES [1]

21 Jun 1855, Miles N. Tucker md Mary Scruggs, Signers: Nelson Tucker, father; Patsy Tucker, mother; Drury Scruggs, father; Mildred Scruggs, mother. p 162.

D3 40-163, 18 Jun 1837, rec 19 Jun 1837, Albert Waddill, indebted to Samuel Ayres, to Miles N. Tucker & George Pannill, half the debts due the observers office, 2 negro boys Dick (or Richard) & Isaac, & 230 ac. on Sandy Cr., bo. P. Waddill, Branch Waddill & Henry Richardson.

DB 49-451, 19 Mar 1842, James H. Mitchell to Miles N. Tucker & William C. Mitchell. Whereas Polly A. Mitchell, wf of sd James H. Mitchell hath relinquished her right of dower in lands now or heretofore owned by her husband sd James H. Mitchell, except that hereinafter described, & her husband desiring to support his sd wife Polly A. Mitchell for life, 181 ac., being the eastern part of tract whereon sd James H. Mitchell now resides, bo. John F. Patrick & Samuel Pannill - furthermore, James H. Mitchell convey to Miles N. Tucker & William C. Mitchell, interest in 181 ac. upon trust that they & their successors use & manage same for sole exclusive use of his wife Polly A Mitchell for life, & after her death revert to James H. Mitchell & his heirs, etc, etc.

DB 50-497, 16 Jun 1847, rec 19 Jul 1847, James H. Mitchell & wf Mary, & Miles N. Tucker of Pittsylvania Co. to Cutberth Waller of Halifax Co., for $9. & 87 1/2 cents, (looks like "Thse & 3/4 acres") (3 3/4 ac.?), bo. Waller, Pannil.

This family was not researched past 1850.

SUMMARY: Miles N. Tucker, son of Nelson Tucker & wf Martha Clark, md 1855 Pittsylvania Co, Mary Scruggs, dau of Drury Scruggs & wf Mildred.

* * *

1. Chiarito, Marian Dodson, "Marriages Pittsylvania County, Virginia, 1831-1861", 1982

TR122000 - ROBERT TUCKER

MD SARAH
SON OF ROBERT TUCKER JR
MD FRANCES COLEMAN

AMELIA CO. VA.

Robert Tucker was listed as a 16 yr old tithable in the household of his father, Robert Tucker in 1755 only, so he would have been born ca 1739. He married Sarah ____ probably ca 1762 when he was listed as a separate household.

LIST OF TITHES

1762	1	---	Robert Tucker Jun	
1765	2	---	Robert Tucker, blacksmith Isse Clay	
1767	4	278	Robert Tucker Jun, Jesse Clay, Joseph Tucker	Dener
1769	4	478	Robert Tucker, Joseph Tucker	Dinah
1770	5	278	Robert Tucker, Peter Hudson	Robin, Daniel, Dinah

(See WB 2-273, 1773, Robert Tucker).

NOTE: The identity of the Jesse Clay & Peter Hudson in the household of Robert Tucker btwn 1765-70 is not clear. Joseph Tucker is probably the younger brother of Robert.

WB 2X-283. Robert Tucker (Jr?) wd 8 Dec 1768, wp 25 May 1769. - names – Exrs: - Son William Tucker and son-in-law John Smith. - Wife Frances - son Godfrey Tucker - Son William - Son Robert Tucker - 278 ac. adj. his plant. beg. old line bet. him & Godfrey's land etc. bet. Robert & Daniel's land etc., to Wolf Trap Br. where John Hastens' line crosses br. - Son Daniel - Daus. Martha Smith, Frances Crowder, Rachel Old.

DB 11-24, 1769, William & Mary Tucker to Robert Tucker, 200 ac. on Br. of Wintercomake Cr., plantation where he now lives, - also land l.s. of Sampson's Br. - land left to sd William Tucker by Robert Tucker his father. (See WB 2X-283 and DB 11-158).

DB 11-158, 8 Feb 1770, rec. 26 Jul 1770, Robert Tucker & wf Sarah to William Tucker, for L400., 200 ac. on branches of Wintocomake, which sd land was acknowledged by sd William Tucker to the Rob't last June court (?). S/ Robert Tucker, Sarah Tucker. (See DB 11-24).

NOTE: The Robert Tucker and William Tucker in the above two deeds are brothers. It appears that William sold to his brother Robert, and then bought back from him, the 200 ac. inherited from his father Robert Tucker Jr., and later sold it to Richard Newman in 1773.

WB 2-273, 26 Oct 1773, rec. 28 May 1778. I&A Est. of Robert Tucker. Included slaves: Daniel, Bob, L___, Dinah, Mingo, Patience, Lucy, Dol, Kilcy. Made by William Hastens, Daniel Coleman & John Hastens.

NOTE: From above I&A, Robert Tucker died intestate in 1778. The 278 ac. inherited from his father apparently passed to his son & heir at law Joel Tucker. (See below).

Order Book 14-99, 22 Jan 1778, Joel Tucker son & heir at law of Robt Tucker decd, Patsy Tucker, Fanny Tucker, Anderson Tucker, Betsey Tucker & Sally Tucker, infants, by James ___, their next friend, (Complt) -vs- Martin Chandler & wf Sally, late widow of Robt Tucker, decd & adm of his estate (Deft).

NOTE: The above record identifies the children of Robert & Sarah Tucker as Joel, Anderson, Patsy, Fanny, Betsy & Sally, and indicates that Sarah Tucker, widow of Robert, married 2nd Martin Chandler.

Order Book 13-___, 22 Jan 1778, Martin Chandler is appointed guardian of Patty, Joel, Fanny, Anderson, Betsy & Sally Tucker, orphans of Robert Tucker decd whereupon he gave bond and Security according to law.

Order Book 18-86, 26 Mar 1787, Betsey Tucker, orphan of Robert Tucker, decd has the approbation of-the Court to choose her guardian, who made choice of Godfrey Tucker for her guardian. Rice Newman, Security. (Note: Godfrey Tucker was her uncle.)

Joel Tucker was probably born ca 1764. He was shown on the Personal Tax Records of Amelia Co. as one white tithable, beginning in 1785 & running through 1788. The Amelia Co. Land Tax Records show Joel Tucker orphan, holding 200 ac. in 1782. The Land Tax Alterations for 1787 record "Anderson Tucker of Joel Tucker 200, of Martin Chandler 100; Joel Tucker est. by Anderson Tucker". Although the alterations are not always clear, It appears Joel Tucker may have died intestate & without issue in 1787, and his estate passed to his brother and heir at law Anderson Tucker. Robert Tucker owned 278 ac. at his death in 1778. Joel Tucker held only 200 ac. in 1782. Anderson Tucker received in 1787, 200 ac. from Joel Tucker and 100 ac. from Martin Chandler (which apparently was approximately 1/3 dower interest of Sarah Tucker in est. of her first husband Robert Tucker decd.)

"And." (perhaps Anderson) Tucker is shown as a tithable in the household of his uncle Godfrey Tucker in 1788.

1 Jun 1804, John Holloway md Sarah Tucker. Sur. David Meredith. Md 2 Jun by Rev. William Dier. p H-3.

SUMMARY: Robert Tucker b ca 1739 son of Robert Tucker Jr & wf Frances Coleman, d 1778, md before 1764 Sarah _____ & had issue:

Joel Tucker b ca 1764, d ca 1787, without issue.

Patsy Tucker.

Fanny Tucker md _____ Southall.

Anderson Tucker b ca 1772, d 1842, without issue.

Betsy Tucker md _____ Hawks.

Sally Tucker md John Holloway.

(See chapters for Joel Tucker and Anderson Tucker.)

TR122100 - JOEL TUCKER
SON OF ROBERT TUCKER
MD SARAH

AMELIA CO. VA.

WB 2-273, 26 Oct 1773, rec. 28 May 1778. I&A <u>Est. of Robert Tucker</u>. Included slaves: Daniel, Bob, L____, Dinah, Mingo, Patience, Lucy, Dol, Kilcy. Made by William Hastens, Daniel Coleman & John Hastens.

NOTE: From above I&A, Robert Tucker died intestate in 1778. The 278 ac. inherited from his father apparently passed to his son & heir at law Joel Tucker. (See below).

Order Book 14-99, 22 Jan 1778, <u>Joel Tucker son & heir at law of Robt Tucker, decd</u>, Patsy Tucker, Fanny Tucker, Anderson Tucker, Betsey Tucker & Sally Tucker, infants, by James ____, their next friend, (Complt) -vs- Martin Chandler & wf <u>Sally, late widow of Robt Tucker decd & adm of his estate</u> (Deft).

Order Book 13-___ , 22 Jan 1778, Martin Chandler is appointed guardian of Patty, <u>Joel</u>, Fanny, Anderson, Betsy & Sally Tucker, <u>orphans of Robert Tucker decd</u> whereupon he gave bond and Security according to law.

Joel Tucker was probably born ca 1764. He was shown on the Personal Tax Records of Amelia Co. as one white tithable, beginning in 1785 & running through 1788. The Amelia Co. Land Tax Records show Joel Tucker orphan, holding 200 ac. in 1782. The Land Tax Alterations for 1787 record "Anderson Tucker of Joel Tucker 200, of Martin Chandler 100; Joel Tucker est. by Anderson Tucker". Although the alterations are not always clear, it appears Joel Tucker may have died intestate & without issue in 1787, and his estate passed to his brother and heir at law Anderson Tucker.

SUMMARY: Joel Tucker b ca 1764, son of Robert Tucker & wf Sarah ____, d 1787 intestate and without issue.

TR122200 - ANDERSON TUCKER
SON OF ROBERT TUCKER
MD SARAH

AMELIA CO. VA.

"And." (perhaps Anderson) Tucker was shown as a 16-yr-up tithable in the household of his uncle Godfrey Tucker in 1788, so he was probably b ca 1772 and became age 21 probably ca 1793.

Order Book 14-99, 22 Jan 1778, Joel Tucker, son & heir at law of Robt Tucker decd, Patsy Tucker, Fanny Tucker, Anderson Tucker, Betsey Tucker & Sally Tucker, infants, by James ____, their next friend, (Complt) -vs- Martin Chandler & wf Sally, late widow of Robt Tucker, decd & adm of his estate (Deft).

Order Book 13-___, 22 Jan 1778, Martin Chandler is appointed guardian of Patty, Joel, Fanny, Anderson, Betsy & Sally Tucker, orphans of Robert Tucker decd whereupon he gave bond and Security according to law.

Joel Tucker was probably born ca 1764. He was shown on the Personal Tax Records of Amelia Co. as one white tithable, beginning in 1785 & running through 1788. The Amelia Co. Land Tax Records show Joel Tucker orphan, holding 200 ac. in 1782. The Land Tax Alterations for 1787 record "Anderson Tucker of Joel Tucker 200, of Martin Chandler 100; Joel Tucker est. by Anderson Tucker". Although the alterations are not always clear, it appears Joel Tucker may have died intestate & without issue in 1787, and his estate passed to his brother and heir at law Anderson Tucker.

DB 20-245, 2 Mar 1796, rec. 28 Apr 1796, Anderson Tucker to John Harmon, for L200., 200 ac. in Raleigh Parish adj. Rice Newman, Burwell Coleman, David Adams, Thomas Hood, & Joel Bevill. Wit: John Newman, Martin Chandler, Thomas Harmon. S/ Anderson Tucker. (Note: Apparently this is the 200 ac. which Anderson Tucker -inherited from his deceased brother Joel Tucker).

DB 21-74, 7 Aug 1800. rec 20 Dec 1800, Robert Chappell & wf Peggy to Anderson Tucker, for L550., 375 ac., bo. Alexander Jones, Abner Osborne, Matt Farley & Nancy Finney. S/ Robert Chappell. Wit: John Holloway, Wm. Morgan, Charles Broadfoot. (See DB 21-107 for 138 ac. and DB 26-72 for 236 ac. 138 ac + 236 ac. = 374 ac.) (See also DB 32-317 for 375 ac.)

DB 21-107, 1 Nov 1799, rec 22 Jan 1301, <u>Anderson Tucker</u> to George Kidd, for L198, <u>138 ac.</u> bo. Allen Adams Jones Neal Purkinson and Bevill. S/ Anderson Tucker. Wit: Wm. Mann, Simeon Morgan, Wm. Morgan. (Note: This 138 ac. may be a part of DB 21-74 for 375 ac., leaving 237 ac. See DB 32-239 for 237 1/2 ac.)

DB 22-339, 28 May 1807, <u>Anderson Tucker</u> to Constable Qualification

DB 22-456, 1808, <u>Anderson Tucker</u> etal (tr) to John Chieves (Release D) -very complex - release of land bought in deed of trust.

DB 23-120, 1809, <u>Anderson Tucker</u> to Constable Qualification Bond

DB 26-72, 29 Jun 1822, rec 25 Jul 1822, Wm. Mann & wf Nancy of town of Petersburg, to <u>Anderson Tucker</u> of Amelia Co., for $1180., <u>236 ac.</u>, bo. Edward H. Jones, Bevel road, Samuel Morgan, George T, Samuel Morgan_?_, est. Pleasant Puckett, Mary C. Cl_?_. (difficult to read) (See DB 21-74 for 375 ac. less DB 21-107 for 138 ac. = 237 ac.) (See also DB 32-239 for 237 1/2 ac.)

DB 27-268, 1825, <u>Anderson Tucker etal (Comr)</u> to sell est. of Phillip Farley, sold to Edward Randolph, etc

DB 32-239, 30 Oct 1835, rec 26 Nov 1835, <u>Anderson Tucker</u> to Spencer A. Mann, for $800., <u>237 1/2 ac.</u> bo. Spencer A. Mann, Beaverpond Cr., Wm. Wilson. (See DB 21-74 for 375 ac. less DB 21-107 for 138 ac. = 237 ac.) (See also DB 26-72 for 236 ac.)

DB 32-317, 30 Oct 1835, rec 28 Apr 1836, <u>Anderson Tucker</u> to William Worsham, for $1,000., <u>375 ac. where Anderson Tucker now lives,</u> bo. est. of Henry Robertson, Bevills Rd, John Chieves decd, John Bland, Edward W. Watkins. (See DB 21-74)

WB 15-27, Will of <u>Anderson Tucker</u>, wd 9 Jan 1842, wp 21 Mar 1842. Leg:

(1) Benjamin Watkins Bailey - $100. for benefit of my <u>sister Sally Holloway</u> for life - then to be equally divided among the children of Benjamin W. Bailey by his present wife Mary.

(2) when my <u>nephew Robert Holloway</u> becomes 21 & establishes a blacksmith shop for himself, I give him $500. as a capital to start him in business.

(3) to <u>nephews John Holloway & William Holloway</u> who are somewhere in the western country, $500. each.

(4) to <u>children of my sister Fanny Southall,</u> $250. to be equally divided. (5) to <u>children of my, sister Betsey Hawks</u> $250. equally divided.

(6) to <u>children of Patsy Worsham, my half-sister</u> $250. equally divided. (7) to <u>children of my half-sister Nancy Reese (?)</u>, $250. equally divided.

(8) all rest of estate divided btwn my <u>3 whole sisters and 2 half sisters</u>, my half-sisters taking 1/2 share & that share to sister Sally Holloway be held in trust by B. W. Bailey.

(9) my land & personal property to be sold & divided according the foregoing provision.

Exs: friends Doct. Robert Edward Jones & David Mabin.

Wit: J. E. Leigh, John W. Knight, _____ Crowder.

NOTE: Apparently Anderson Tucker died unmarried and without issue. Apparently his half-sisters Patsy Worsham and Nancy Reese were daughters of his mother Sarah by her 2nd marriage to Martin Chandler.

WB 15-38, I&A Est. <u>Anderson Tucker</u>, 28 Mar 1812 (42?), rec 28 Apr 1812 (42?), included negro man ruptured (not named) & numerous Bonds. Appr: Robt E. Jones.

WB 15-145, Acct of Sales Est. <u>Anderson Tucker</u>, 28 Apr 1812 (42?), Rec. 20 Jun 1813 (43?) Robt E. Jones.

WB 15-334, Ex. Acct. of Est. <u>Anderson Tucker</u>, Robert E. Jones, Ex.

WB 15-549, Ex. Acct. of Est. <u>Anderson Tucker</u>, Robert E. Jones, Ex.

SUMMARY: Anderson Tucker, son of Robert Tucker & wf Sarah, b ca 1772 in Amelia Co. VA, d 1842 unmarried & without Issue in Amelia Co. VA.

TR123000 - DANIEL TUCKER

MD FRANCES (? EPPES ?)
SON OF ROBERT TUCKER JR
MD FRANCES COLEMAN

AMELIA CO. VA.

Daniel Tucker was listed as a 16-yr-up tithable in the household of his father Robert Tucker 1762-65, and perhaps earlier, so he must have been born by 1746 or earlier. He probably married in 1767 when he was listed as a separate household.

LIST OF TITHES

1762-65	-	---	Daniel Tucker included in household of father Robert Tucker
1767	1	---	Daniel Tucker son of Robt
1769	2	258	Daniel Tucker, Peter Hudson
1770	1	258	Daniel Tucker

WB 2X-283. Robert Tucker (Jr?) wd 8 Dec 1768, wp 25 May 1769. - names --Exrs: Son William Tucker and son-in-law John Smith - Wife Frances - son Godfrey Tucker - Son William - Son Robert Tucker - Son Daniel - 258 ac. adj plantation, being all land not already mentioned n.s. Sampson's Branch. - Daus. Martha Smith, Frances Crowder, Rachel Old.

WB 2X-197. William Adams, Est. I&A July Court 1767 ret. & rec. 27 Aug 1767. Appr: Robert Cousins, Sampson Meredith, Daniel Tucker.

DB 13-219, 10 Dec 1774, rec 24 Aug 1775, Daniel Tucker to Thomas Bevill, for L200., 258 ac. bo. widow Coleman's line, dividing line btwn Robert Tucker & Daniel Tucker. Wit: David Williams, William Roach, Godfrey Tucker. S/ Daniel Tucker.

NOTE: Daniel Tucker son of Robert Jr, is not to be confused with his first cousin, Daniel Tucker son of William, nor with his uncle, Daniel Tucker son of Capt Robert Sr. This Daniel Tucker seems to have sold the 258 ac. inherited from his father Robert Tucker Jr and moved to another county or state.

The subject Daniel Tucker was not further researched by this compiler. Boddie provides the following list of descendants:

BODDIE: [2]

"Daniel Tucker had a son named Ethel (Etheldred) b 1767. In 1789 when John Eppes deeded land to Richard Smith, Daniel & Ethel Tucker were witnesses (Dinwiddie O.B.4). Also John Eppes sold land to Daniel Tucker in 1789 & this deed was witnessed by Richard Smith & Ethel Tucker. He was included in the 1790 Census in Wake Co. N. C. In 1798 he purchased land on the Savannah River in Elbert Co. Ga. He was a planter & minister. Tombstones in Elberton, Ga. show that the Rev. Daniel Tucker b 14 Feb 1740, d 7 Apr 1818. Frances Tucker, wf of the Rev. Daniel Tucker, b 4 Apr 1750, d 6 Aug 1825. At right of graves - Frances, wf of Eppes Tucker, b 25 Apr 1790, d 19 May 1818 -."

Children of Daniel & Frances Tucker:

1. Ethel Tucker, b 1767, Dinwiddie Co. Va., md Rebecca Davis (dau. of Humphrey Davis), d 1851 in Chambers Co. Ala.

   a. Ethel Tucker Jr., m 17 May 1825, Nancy Davis

   b. Humphrey Davis Tucker, b 29 Sep 1791, m 1819 Edith or Eda Grant, dau of Daniel Grant.

      (1). William Tucker, b ca 1820, d 1853, m Amanda Davis.

      (2). Ethel Gaines Tucker, b 8 Sep 1820 in S.C., d 25 May 1898, md Thirza Ann Hall.

      (3). Elizabeth Rebecca Tucker, b 8 May 1822, d 2 Feb 1891.

      (4). Mary Frances Tucker, b 5 Jul 1824, d 23 Oct 1888, m Pleasant Bolton Hall.

      (5). John J. Tucker, b 31 Oct 1826, d 12 Jan 1896, m (1) Ollie Crawford, m (2) Louisa Kilpatrick.

      (6). Daniel Joseph Tucker, b ca 1830, d 6 Jan 1896 Troup Co. Ga. m 8 Feb 1853, Green Co. Ga., Elizabeth W. Hines.

         (a). Mary, d infant.

         (b). Joseph Davis Tucker, b 1 Mar 1864, d 13 Mar 1886.

         (c). William Humphrey Tucker, b 1 Jul 1872 md 19 Nov 1901 Anne Champagne, d 11 Sep 1912.

         (i). Alice Humphrey Tucker b 25 Aug 1903, m 7 Feb 1923 Robert Sheffield Towers.

   c. William Tucker, m Mary Elizabeth Grant, sister of above Edith Grant.

     d. Frances Tucker, m John Carlile, 15 Feb 1821.

"There may have been other children.

    2. Robert Tucker, b Va., d 1835 Randolph Co. Ga.

    3. Gabriel Tucker, d 1838 Franklin Co. Tenn.

    4. Daniel Tucker, b Va., d 1850 Lee Co. Ala.

    5. Eppes Tucker, b Va., d Lee Co. Ala, m (1) Frances ____, (2) Martha ____.

    6. Reuben Tucker, b 1787, Dinwiddie Co., Va., d 1831 Camden, S.C., md Jane Cannon.

    7. Sham Tucker, d 1828 Newton Co. Ga.

    8. Frances Tucker, no issue.

    9. Susannah, no issue."

NOTE: The above information was extracted from Boddie, but he did not include the sources of his information. This compiler did not further research or verify any of that data.

* * *

2. Boddie, John B., "Historical Southern Families", Vol II, pp 260-61

TR124000 - GODFREY TUCKER

MD MARY
SON OF ROBERT TUCKER JR
MD FRANCES COLEMAN

AMELIA CO. VA.

NOTE: The Amelia Co. Lists of Tithes include Godfrey Tucker as a 16-yr-up tithable in the household of his father Robert Tucker Sr. (formerly Robert Tucker Jr) from 1763 until 1769 when his father died. Tax Records are illegible 1771-1777. Godfrey Tucker is listed as a separate tax payer in his own household 1778-1788. If he was age 16 in 1763, then he was born ca 1747, and was age 21 ca 1768, and probably married ca 1768.

LIST OF TITHES & PERSONAL TAX RECORDS

1778	-	Godfrey Tucker	James
1779	-	Godfrey Tucker	Jim
1782	3	Godfrey Tucker	James, Jude
1783	3	Godfrey Tucker	
1786	1	Godfrey Tucker	
1787	1	Godfrey Tucker	
1788	3	Godfrey Tucker, And. Tucker, Robert Tucker.	

In 1788, shown with Godfrey Tucker are "And." Tucker and Robert Tucker. Robert Tucker may have been his son, but "And." is believed to be Anderson Tucker, orphan son of his brother Robert Tucker who died 1778. (See Robert Tucker and Sarah).

WB 2X-283. Robert Tucker (Jr?) wd 8 Dec 1768, wp 25 May 1769. -names: - Exrs: Son William Tucker and son-in-law John Smith. - Wife Frances - plantation I now live on with 275 1/2 ac, adj., for life or widowhood, then to son, Godfrey Tucker. - Son William - Son Robert Tucker Son Daniel - Daus. Martha Smith, Frances Crowder, Rachel Old.

DB 15-76, 25 Nov 1778, William Tucker & wf Mary to James Southall for L50., 85 ac. on e.s. Wintocomake Cr. Adj. Godfrey Tucker & John Coles. Wit: David Adams, David Williams, Frederick Ford. S/ Wm. x Tucker, Mary x Tucker.

DB 16-227, 17 Dec 1782. Godfrey Tucker to Abner Osborne for L864., 275 ac. in Raleigh Parish, on Wintocomake Cr. adj. William Foster, Martin Chandler, Newman's lines, Wintocomake Swamp, Great Br., William Foster's line, Martin Chandler's land, Newman line, spring slash. Wit: David Adams, Francis Woodward, Henry x Westbrook. S/ Godfrey Tucker.

NOTE; It is interesting that in 1770, Amelia Co. Tax Records listed a Godfrey Tucker (Patroller) as one of 6 tithables in the household of a Francis Tucker with 275 ac. of land. This seems to be the 275 1/2 ac. which Godfrey inherited from his father, and which he sold in 1782 to Abner Osborne.

DB 16-326, 10 Jan 1783, James Chappell to Godfrey Tucker for L675., 450 ac. bo. John Pryor, John Dudley, William Wilson, Emanuel Weeks, Robert Tucker. Wit: John Tucker, David Williams, Anderson Moore. S/ James Chappell.

NOTE: The 450 ac. which Godfrey Tucker purchased in 1783 apparently fell in that part of Amelia Co. which was cut off into Nottoway Co. in 1789. The Nottoway Co. Land Tax Records show Godfrey Tucker holding 424 ac. in 1789 & 1790.

NOTTOWAY CO. VA.

DB 1-200, 3 Nov 1791, Godfrey Tucker & wf Mary of Granville Co., N.C. to Abner Osborne of Nottoway Co., Va., 386.5 ac. bo, n.s. Nammozine Cr., Robert Tucker, David Tucker, Abner Osborne, Wilson, Joseph Jones, Daniel Stone, Wm. Weaks, Emanuel Weaks.

The discrepancies between 450 ac. bought in 1783, 424 ac. taxed in 1789-90 and 368.5 ac. sold in 1791 is confusing.

Could Godfrey Tucker's wife Mary have been a daughter of Abner Osborne, to whom he sold land in Amelia Co. in 1782 and in Nottoway Co. in 1791?

Apparently Godfrey Tucker & wife moved to Granville Co., N.C. This compiler has not further researched this family.

SUMMARY: Godfrey Tucker b ca 1747 in Amelia Co. Va., md Mary ____ (possibly Osborne), owned and sold land in Amelia and Nottoway Counties, moved in 1791 to Granville Co., N.C.

NOTE: The following information was graciously provided by Mary McCampbell Bell, C.G.R.S. Her proof notes are indicated in parenthesis ( ).

Godfrey Tucker b ca 1735?, probably Amelia Co, Va, d - will written 7 Feb 1827, will proved Mar 1827 (1) Elbert Co, GA, son of Robert Tucker (2,5) d 1769 (2) Amelia Co, Va. Godfrey Tucker had issue:

1. Jesse Tucker (1,3) b ca 1770-1780 (3) Amelia Co (6), d 1830-1840 (3) Ala?

2. Robert Tucker (1,3).

3. Bartlett Tucker (1,3) b ca 1773 (7) Va, or ca 1784 (3) Amelia Co, Va, d 1863 (8) Abbeville Co, SC, m 1st Martha Burch Heard (3), m 2nd Nancy (7).

4. Lucy Tucker (1) m Wiley Wall (1), ch. Jesse C. Wall (1).

* * *

PROOF NOTES of Mary McCampbell Bell

(1) Godfrey Tucker will-Elbert Co, GA, WB 1825-1829, p165

(2) <u>Historical Southern Families</u> by John B. Boddie, Vol 2, p 260

(3) Godfrey Tucker Data file DAR

(4) <u>History of Elbert Co, GA</u>

(5) Amelia Co, VA will of Robert Tucker WB 2X-173

(6) Godfrey lived in Amelia Co, VA 1782 2/8 whites

(7) 1860 census Abbeville Co, SC p 224

(8) Bartley Tucker estate papers, Abbeville Co, SC

TG130000 - GEORGE TUCKER SR

MD 1st FRANCES
MD 2nd CATHARINE
SON OF CAPT ROBERT TUCKER SR
MD MARTHA

George Tucker is believed to be one of five older sons of Capt. Robert Tucker Sr. By Amelia Co. DB 1-341-44, 10 Oct 1741, Robert Tucker Sr simultaneously deeded land to John Tucker, George Tucker and Robert Tucker Jr. This would indicate that John, George and Robert Jr were brothers and sons of Capt. Robert Tucker Sr. James Tucker was documented in Patent 18-389 as a brother of Robert and John. William Tucker was documented in Amelia Co. DB 10-51 as a brother of John. Subsequently, Robert Tucker Sr. did not include these five sons among those named in his will, except to name son Robert as executor. Robert Tucker Sr. named his wife Martha in his will, written 26 Sep 1744 (Amelia Co. WB 1-63), and she was his wife as early as 1720, when the birth of their daughter Anne was recorded in the Bristol Parish Register. Capt. Robert Tucker Sr may have married twice, and James, Robert, George & John may have been sons by his first wife prior to 1720.

George Tucker was b by 1710, m first ca 1730 Frances, and m second ca 1760 Catharine, & d ca 1784. The births of children to George and Frances Tucker are recorded in the Bristol Parish Register as early as 1731. In Amelia Co. DB 14-206 (1777) and in Lunenburg Co. WB 3-152 (1784), George's wife is named as Catharine.

BRISTOL PARISH REGISTER [1]

Hanna D (dau) of George & Frances Tucker Born 30th March 1731 Bapt 29th august.

Robert Son of George & Frances Tucker Born 3d dcer 1733.

AMELIA CO. VA.

DB 1-343, 10 Oct 1741. Robert Tucker Sr to George Tucker for L70., 200 ac. s.s. Appomattox Ri. & on u.s. Middle Cr., Wit: John Powell, Robert Coleman & Robert Tucker Jr. (See DB 14-206).

WB 1-10, 20 Feb 1740. John Tally, I&A. Appr: George Tucker, Robert Cusons, Robert Tucker, Admr: William Talley.

WB 1-33, Oct 1745, James Coles, Est. I&A ret. by Dorothy x Cole. Apprs: Robert Tucker Jr (x), George Tucker (x), Robert Cousens.

Patent 28-207, 20 Aug 1747, George Tucker, Amelia Co., 275 ac. u.s. Woody Cr. (See DB 7-662-663).

WB 1-89, Richard Chambers, wd 7 Oct 1751, wp 23 Jul 1752. <u>Wit</u>: George x Tucker, Stephen x Dodson, William Herringham. Ex: sister Ruth Chambers. Leg: sister Ruth Chambers - land & plant. where I live. If she dies without heir, to John Dodson, son of Stephen Dodson, but if he sell, next heir at law shall enter & possess same.

WB 1-106, 1 May 1754. Robert Muns, Est. I&A. <u>Appr</u>: George x Tucker, Robert x Tucker, Holman Freeman.

WB 1-118, 25 Nov 1755. Stephen Dodson, Est. I&A ret 27 Nov 1755. <u>Appr</u>: Pat Mullen, George Tucker, Robert Cousens. Admr: Charles x Cousens.

WB 1-120, 28 Oct 1756, James Clay Est. I&A. <u>Appr</u>: Daney Stanly, Holmon Freeman, George Tucker. Admr: Charles Clay Sr.

DB 7-662-663, 10 Jul 1762, rec. 22 Jul 1762, <u>George Tucker to sons William Tucker 137 1/2 ac. & Robert Tucker - 137 1/2 ac.</u>, remainder of tract Pat. 14 Feb 1756, u.s. of Indian Branch of Deep Cr. - in dividing sd Robert's land where he now lives below road & Edw. Threatts dwelling house, Dandy's (alias Davenport's) line, Jos. Gray's & sd Threatts. Wit:: to both deeds: Wm. Crawley, Wm. Walthall, Abraham Burton. (See Patent 28-207 for 275 ac.)

DB 14-206, 25 Aug 1777, <u>George Tucker & wf Catharine</u> of Raleigh Parish to John Ford, for L375., <u>200 ac.</u> on u.s. Middle Cr. on s.s. Appomattox Ri. Wit: Rice Newman, Robert Cousins, Joel Tucker, John Cousins, John Dodson. S/ George x Tucker, Catharine x Tucker. (See DB 1-343).

LIST OF TITHES - AMELIA CO.

1736	2	---	George Tucker	Josh
1737	2	---	George Tucker	Jack
1738	2	---	George Tucker	Jack
1739	1	---	George Tucker	
1740	1	---	George Tucker	
1741	1	---	George Tucker	
1743	1	---	George Tucker	
1744	1	---	George Tucker	
1743	2	---	George Tucker	Tom
1744	3	---	George Tucker	Tom, Mingo
1747	2	---	George Tucker	Mongo
1749	2	---	George Tucker	Mingo
1750	4	---	George Tucker, Robert Tucker	Mingo, Dilce
1751	4	---	George Tucker, Robert Tucker	Mingo, Bell
1752	4	---	George Tucker, Robert Tucker	Mingo, Dilcy
1753	3	---	George Tucker, Robert Tucker	Mingo

LIST OF TITHES - AMELIA CO.

1755	3	---	George Tucker, Robert Tucker	Mingo
1756	2	---	George Tucker	Mingo
1762	5	---	George Tucker, Wm Tucker, Henry Tucker	Bollice, Lande
1763	4	200	George Tucker, Henry Tucker	Ballis, Dinah
1764	2	333	George Tucker	Archa
1765	5	___	George Tucker's List, Henry Tucker, George Tucker	Battis, Lenden
1767	4	200	George Tucker Jun, Joseph Tucker	Bettis, Linder
1769	4	900	George Tucker, Jos Tucker	Bartis, Lynden
1770	5	200	George Tucker, George Tucker Jr, Jos Tucker	Battles, Linder

NOTE: George Tucker and his family had moved from Amelia Co. to Lunenburg Co. by 1782.

LUNENBURG CO., VA

LIST OF TITHES - LUNENBURG CO.

1782	George Tucker, Joel Tucker	Lender, Mol, Lucy, Isaac, Ned
1783	George Tucker, J. Tucker (Sunlight on the Southside on p 396 names George Tucker, Joel Tucker, Lewelling Tucker, with 6 slaves & 6 white tithes.)	
1784	Catharine Tucker, Lewelling, Joel & Robert Tucker	
1785	Catherine Tucker, Robert Tucker	
1785	Joel Tucker is listed as separate household	
1785	Lewelling Tucker is listed as separate household	
1786	Robert Tucker	Listed with: Linder, Moll, Lucy, Isaac, Ned, Jack, bett.
1787	Catharine Tucker, Robert Tucker	
1788	Catharine Tucker is listed as separate household through 1791	
1788	Robert Tucker is listed as separate household	

LAND TAX RECORDS:

1782	George Tucker	200 ac.
1787	George Tucker decd	200 ac
1788	George Tuckers Estate	200 ac.

136

LAND TAX RECORDS:

1789	George Tuckers Estate	200 ac.
1790	George Tuckers Estate	200 ac.
1791	George Tuckers Estate	200 ac.
1792	Joel Tucker	100 ac. from George Tuckers Estate.

DB 9-249, 8 Sep 1763, Shipeallen Puckett & wf Mary of Lunenburg Co. sold 196 ac. for L30., to George Tucker of Dinwiddie Co., bo. on s.s. of Round Meadow Br., beg. at mo. of Round Meadow Br., thence up br., part of tract whereon sd Pucket new liveth. S/ Shippeallen Pucket, Mary x Pucket. Wit: William Davis, Baxter Davis, John Davis.

NOTE: No deed for disposition of the above 196 ac. could be found, and it was not included in the estate of George Tucker Sr. at time of his death in 1784. Possibly this was another George Tucker who lived in Dinwiddie Co.

DB 13-68, 26 Sep 1777, rec 18 Jan 1778, William Davis of Amelia Co., to George Tucker of sd Co., for L230., 199 ac. in Lunenburg Co., bo. Ward Hudson, Richard Ingram, Duprey, Brizendine, Davis, Edmund. Wit: John Cureton Jr, William Tucker, Joel Tucker, John Keatts. S/ William Davis. (See DB 13-69) (See WB 3-152 in which George Tucker willed this land to wf Catharine for life & then jointly to sons Joel & Robert).

DB 13-69, Bond, William Davis of Amelia Co. bound to George Tucker Senr of sd Co. for L500. Condition of obligation is to make title to 200 ac. sold to George Tucker & to maintain same free from incumberance of his wife's right of dower. Wit: John Anderson, John Keatts, Wm. Tucker, Joel Tucker, John Cureton Jr. (See DB 13-68).

WB 3-152, wd 25 Sep 1780, wp 11 Mar 1784, "I, George Tucker the elder of Lunenbur& Co. - - ".
Leg: Wife Catharine - the use of my land & plantation - about 200 ac., all my slaves & pers. prop. during her natural life or widowhood.
Sons Joel, Lew & Robert Tucker - negro Ned to be divided equally bet. them.
Sons Joel Tucker & Robert Tucker - my land to be divided bet. them, Robert's 100 ac. to include the plantation house.
Son Lew - negro woman to be sold by exr. & money divided after paying cash legacies, the balance to him (Lew).
Dau. Milly Clay - negro girl Moll & her increase.
Dau. Biddy Tucker - negro girl Sue & her increase.
Son Lew Tucker - negro boy Isaac.
Son William Tucker & Dau. Fanny. Coleman - 1 Sh. each, having already provided for them.

<u>Sons Henry, George & Joseph Tucker</u> - 5 pounds each, after wife's decease.

<u>Five youngest children: Joel, Lew, Robert, Milly Clay & Biddy</u> - rest & residue of real & pers. est

Exrs: wife Catharine Tucker and sons William and Joel Tucker. Estate not to be appraised. S/ George x Tucker. Wit: Ward x Hudson, Richard Ingram, John Hudson, David Stokes Jr.

> CODICIL - 30 Dec 1783 - the 5 pounds devised my <u>son George, he being dead,</u> I devise to my 4 last children, namely, Obedience, Joel, Lew & Robert & their heirs.
> Wit: Nelson Tucker & William Tucker.

WB 3-172, <u>George Tucker Est.</u> I&A 8 Jul 1784. S/ Catharine Tucker, Joel Tucker.

In 1792, son Robert, and his mother Catharine, sold his 100 ac. share of his fathers estate, and the remaining 100 ac. reverted to Joel Tucker. Catharine Tucker died probably in 1792.

DB 16-196, 9 Feb 1792, rec. 9 Feb 1792, Katharine Tucker, Robert Tucker & wf Sally of Lunenburg Co., sold 100 ac. for L65. Bo. on br. of Meherrin Ri., beg. Brizendine's cor, Edmond's line, Ingram's & Stokes' line. S/ Katharine x Tucker, Robert Tucker, Sally x Tucker. (See DB 13-68 where George bought 199 ac. and WB 3-152 where George willed 200 ac. to wife Catharine for life, then 100 ac. to go to son Robert and remainder to son Joel.).

DB 18-14-A, 8 Feb 1797, rec 8 Feb 1787, Joel Tucker & wf Elizabeth sold 100 ac. in Lunenburg Co., for L100., to Josiah Thompson, bo. on north by Thomas Edmunds, on west by Rowland Hudson, south by Mary Ingram & east by Dicy Hudson. (See DB 13-68 & WB 3-152).

NOTE: George Tucker and his first wife Frances had a son named Robert Tucker who was born 3 Dec 1733, married Martha Keatts, and died intestate in 1765 (See WB 2X-90), leaving his widow Martha and at least two sons, Branch Tucker and Robert Gabriel Tucker. (See separate chapters for Robert Tucker who md Martha Keatts, for Branch Tucker and for Robert Gabriel Tucker.) Now 15 years later, George Tucker, in his will dated in 1780 and probated 1784, willed to another son Robert, 100 ac., including the plantation, but George's second wife Catharine was to have use of the land and plantation for life. Then in 1792, (DB 16-196), Katharine Tucker, Robert Tucker & wf Sally, sold the 100 ac. This must be George's other son named Robert who md Sarah (Sally) Smith in 1787 (WB 3-309).

SUMMARY CONCLUSION: George Tucker Sr, son of Capt Robert Tucker Sr of Prince George and Amelia Counties, b ca 1710 in Prince George Co., d 1784 in Lunenburg Co., md ca 1730 his first wife Frances ____ & had children named:

Hannah Tucker b 1731.

Robert Tucker the 1st, b 1733, d 1765, md ca 1756 Martha Keatts.

William Tucker b ca 1741, md ca 1763 Tahitha Keatts.

Fanny Tucker md ____ Coleman.

Henry Tucker b ca 1746.

George Tucker Jr. b ca 1749, d 1781.

Joseph Tucker b ca 1751.

George Tucker Sr md 2nd ca 1760 Catharine ____ & had children named:

Hilly Tucker md ____ Clay.

Obedience (Biddy) Tucker.

Joel Tucker b ca 1764-65, d ca 1820, md 1788 Elizabeth Clemons.

Lewellyn (Lew) Tucker, b ca 1764-65 md 1788 Ursula Pettipool.

Robert Tucker the 2nd, b ca 1766, md 1737 Sarah (Sally) Smith.

George Tucker Sr died in 1784 and his 2nd wife Catharine died probably ca 1792-93.

* * *

1. Boddie, John B., "Births 1720-1792 From The Bristol Parish Register of Henrico, Prince George and Dinwiddie"

TG131000 - ROBERT TUCKER (1)

MD MARTHA KEATTS

SON OF GEORGE TUCKER SR

MD 1ST FRANCES
MD 2ND CATHARINE

NOTE: George Tucker md 1st Frances, and their son Robert (1) was born in 1733, md Martha Keatts, and d 1765. George Tucker md 2nd Catharine, and their son Robert (2) was born after 1765, md Sarah (Sally) Smith.

BRISTOL PARISH REGISTER [2]

Robert Son of George & Frances Tucker Born 3d dcer 1733.

AMELIA CO. VA.

Robert Tucker was listed as a tithable in the household of George Tucker, beginning in 1750 and continuing through 1755, in Amelia Co. Records. He married Martha Keatts, most probably in 1756.

DB 6-147, 23 Feb 1758, Curtis Keatts to Martha Tucker dau of sd Curtis Keatts & Rob't (Robert) Tucker the husband of sd Martha & son of George Tucker, for natural love, good will & affection & for 5 Sh., 200 ac. , btwn Middle & Lower Fork of Deep Cr., bo. Dennis' cor. in Leath's line, Bolling's line, Kedoah Thones(?) her line, south fork of the Bold Br. running to the Great Seller Cr., Williams' line. Wit: Edwd Thweat, John Anderson, Thos. Jeffres. (See DB 8-196)

DB 7-662-663, 10 Jul 1762, rec. 22 Jul 1762, George Tucker to sons William Tucker - 137 1/2 ac. & Robert Tucker - 137 1/2 ac., remainder of tract Pat. 14 Feb 1756, u.s. of Indian Branch of Deep Cr. - in dividing sd Robert's land where he now lives below road & Edw. Threatts dwelling house, Dandy's (alias Davenport's) line, Jos. Gray's & sd Threatts. Wit:: to both deeds: Wm. Crawley, Wm. Walthall, Abraham Burton. (See Patent 28-207 for George Tucker and DB 17-89 below).

DB 8-196, 1763, Robert Tucker & wf Martha, dau. of Curtiss Keatts, to Christr., Haskins, for L50., _____ ac. (200 ac.) btwn Middle & Lower Seller Fk. of Deep Cr., Bland's cor, Leith's cor, Haskins' cor, Dennis' etc., part of gr. to Wm. Chishom & by deed to Keatts & by deed to Robert & Martha Tucker 23 Feb 1758. (See DB 6-147).

WB 2X-90. Robert Tucker Sr(?) Est. I&A ret & rec 28 Mar 1765. Appr: Nathan Fletcher, George Davenport, David Cordle.

DB 17-89, 23 Feb 1784, <u>Branch Tucker</u> of Lunenburg Co., to Nathan Fletcher of Nottoway Parish, Amelia Co., for L300., <u>137 ac.</u> in Nottoway Parish on b.s. Cabbin Br., bo. by est. of Benjamin Beasley, the orphans of George Davenport, William Osborne Jr., Daniel Parham & Nathan Fletcher, <u>it being the land the sd Branch Tucker intestate (?) from his father Robert Tucker decd</u>, as his at law to the sd Robert, & the sd Branch Tucker <u>warrants against the dower of his mother Martha Tucker</u>. Wit: Richard Jones Jr, Edward Jones, Thomas Jones, Peter Robertson. (See DB 7-662-663).

NOTE: From the above Est. I&A and deed, it appears that Robert Tucker died in 1765 and that Branch Tucker is a son of Robert Tucker and wife Martha. Branch Tucker was listed as a separate household tither in Amelia Co. Tax Records for 1788. (See below). There is evidence also that Branch Tucker and Robert G. (Gabriel) Tucker were brothers. See separate records for them.

LIST OF TITHES

1762	2	----	Robert Tucker, John Kent	
1763	2	137 ½	Robert Tucker	Gloucester
1768	3	3772 (probably 3-137 ½)	Martha Tucker List, Charles Cates (probably Keatts)	Gloucester, Moll
1788	1	----	Branch Tucker	

LUNENBURG CO. VA.

DB 11-235, 9 Feb 1769, rec 9 Feb 1769, Joshua Ingram of Bute Co. N.C. to <u>Martha Tucker, dau. of Curtis Keatt</u> of Amelia Co., for 5 Shillings, <u>300 ac.</u> in Lunenburg Co. on s.s Couches Cr., bo. Malone. Wit: John Ward, Richard Ingram, John Ingram. S/ Joshua Ingram. Wf Amy Ingram relinq dower. (See DB 15-39).

DB 15-39, 8 Jun 1787, rec 14 Jun 1787, <u>Martha Tucker</u> to Edward Jordan, for L180., <u>300 ac.</u> on branches of Couches Cr. S/ Martha Tucker. (See DB 11-235).

LIST OF TITHES & PERSONAL TAX RECORDS:

1769	Martha Tucker's List	0 tithes, 300 ac.
1772	Martha Tucker's List, Joseph Tucker	2 tithes.
1773	Martha Tucker, Joseph Tucker	2 tithes.
1782	Martha Tucker	Gloster, Dame.
1782	Joseph Tucker	Hannah.
1783	Martha Tucker, Branch Tucker, Robert Tucker	1 white tithe above 21, 3 negroes.
1783	Martha Tucker, B. Tucker	Gloster, Will.

LIST OF TITHES & PERSONAL TAX RECORDS:

1783	Joseph Tucker	1 white 21 yrs old,
	(This Joseph may be brother of Martha's	7 whites, 1 slave.
	deceased husband Robert, who lived in her	
	household until her son Branch reached age	
	21 in 1783, then both Joseph and Branch	
	maintained separate households).	
1784	Branch Tucker, Robert Tucker	Gloucester, Will,
		Daniel, one covering
		horse.
1786	Branch Tucker	Lucy, one stud horse,
		20/the season.
1786	Martha Tucker, Robert Tucker	Gloster, Will, Daniel.
	(Martha is no longer listed as a household	
	after 1786)	
1788	Robert G. Tucker	
	(Listed as separate household beginning in	
	1788.)	

NOTE: The above tithable & personal tax records indicate that, following the death of Robert Tucker (1), his widow Martha maintained her household until her sons Branch Tucker & Robert G. Tucker attained age 21.

NOTE: George Tucker, in his will written in 1780 (WB 3-152), did not mention his older son Robert (1), who md Martha Keatts, by his 1st wife Frances, since Robert (1) had died in 1765. However, George did name another son Robert (2), who md Sarah(Sally) Smith, by his 2nd wife Catharine. See separate chapter for Robert Tucker (2) md Sarah Smith.

SUMMARY: Robert Tucker (1), son of George Tucker Sr & 1st wf Frances _____ b 1733, d 1765, md ca 1756 Martha Keatts, dau of Curtis Keatts, & had issue:

Branch Tucker b ca 1763.

Robert Gabriel Tucker b ca 1765.

* * *

2. Boddie, John B., "Births 1720-1792 from the Bristol Parish Register of Henrico, Prince George and Dinwiddie."

142

TG131100 - BRANCH TUCKER

MD 1ST MILLICENT (MILLY) CHEATHAM
MD 2ND ELIZABETH FERRELL
SON OF ROBERT TUCKER (1)
MD MARTHA KEATTS

AMELIA CO. VA.

DB 6-147, 23 Feb 1758, Curtis Keatts to Martha Tucker dau of sd Curtis Keatts & Rob't (Robert) Tucker the husband of sd Martha & son of George Tucker, for natural love, good will & affection & for 5 Sh., 200 ac., btwn Middle & Lower Fork of Deep Cr., bo. Dennis' cor. in Leath's line, Bolling's line, Kedoah Thones(?) her line, south fork of the Bold Br. running to the Great Seller Cr., Williams' line. Wit: Edwd Thweat, John Anderson, Thos. Jeffres. (See DB 8-196).

DB 7-662-663, 10 Jul 1762, rec. 22 Jul 1762, George Tucker to sons William Tucker - 137 1/2 ac. & Robert Tucker - 137 1/2 ac., remainder of tract Pat. 14 Feb 1756, u.s. of Indian Branch of Deep Cr. - in dividing sd Robert's land where he now lives below road & Edw. Threatts dwelling house, Dandy's (alias Davenport's) line, Jos. Gray's & sd Threatts. Wit: to both deeds: Wm. Crawley, Wm. Walthall, Abraham Burton. (See Patent 28-207 for George Tucker). (See DB 17-89 below).

DB 8-196, 1763, Robert Tucker & wf Martha, dau. of Curtiss Keatts, to Christr., Haskins, for L50., ___ ac. (200 ac.) btwn Middle & Lower Seller Fk. of Deep Cr., Bland's cor, Leith's cor, Haskins' cor, Dennis' etc., part of gr. to Wm. Chishom & by deed to Keatts & by deed to Robert & Martha Tucker 23 Feb 1758. (See DB 6-147).

WB 2X-90. Robert Tucker Sr(?) Est. I&A ret & rec 28 Mar 1765. Appr: Nathan Fletcher, George Davenport, David Cordle.

DB 17-89, 23 Feb 1784, Branch Tucker of Lunenburg Co. to Nathan Fletcher of Nottoway Parish, Amelia Co., for L300., 137 ac. in Nottoway Parish on b.s. Cabbin Br., bo. by est. of Benjamin Beasley, the orphans of George Davenport, William Osborne Jr., Daniel Parham & Nathan Fletcher, it being the land the sd Branch Tucker intestate (?) from his father Robert Tucker decd, as his at law to the sd Robert & the sd Branch Tucker warrants against the dower of his mother Martha Tucker. Wit: Richard Jones Jr, Edward Jones, Thomas Jones, Peter Robertson. (See DB 7-662-663).

NOTE: From the above deed, it appears that Robert Tucker died in 1765, his wife Martha died in 1784, and that Branch Tucker was their son and heir at law, who inherited the 137 ac. Branch must have been age 21 in 1784 when he sold his inheritance, and would have been born ca 1763.

There is evidence also that Robert G. (Gabriel) Tucker was a younger brother of Branch. Both Branch and Robert G. were shown as 16-up tithables in the household of their widowed mother Martha Tucker in 1783 in Lunenburg Co. Branch was shown as a separate household in 1786, and Robert G. as a separate household in 1789. Branch Tucker was listed as a separate household tither in Amelia Co. Personal Tax Records for 1788.

PERSONAL TAX RECORD

1788   1 Branch Tucker

LUNENBURG CO. VA.

LIST OF TITHES & PERSONAL TAX RECORDS:

1782	Martha Tucker	Gloster, Dame.
1783	Martha Tucker, Branch Tucker, Robert Tucker	1 white above 21, 3 negroes, 3 white tithes
1783	Martha Tucker, B. Tucker	Gloster, Will.
1784	Branch Tucker, Robert Tucker	Gloucester, Will, Daniel, one covering horse.
1786	Branch Tucker	Lucy, one stud horse, 20/the season.
1790	Branch Tucker	
1791	Branch Tucker	
1792	Branch Tucker	
1793	Branch Tucker	
1796	Branch Tucker	

DB 13-286, 9 Dec 1779, deed dated 30 Nov., Charles Keatts of Lunenburg Co. to George Tucker of same Co., 400 ac. for L1500., in Lunenburg Co., part of a tract belonging to Curtis Keatts, adj. Evan's line, Stokes & Fontaines old lines, branch of Fucking Creek (name changed to Modesty Cr.), Robert Dixon's land, etc. to beg. S/ Charles Keatts. Wit: Richard Ingram, John Cureton, William Tucker. (See DB 15-149)

NOTE: The above deed of 400 ac. applied to George Tucker Jr, who died intestate in 1781. Robert Tucker (1) was heir at law of his brother George Tucker Jr.. Branch Tucker was heir at law of his father Robert Tucker (1), who died intestate in 1765. Branch Tucker sold that same 400 ac. to his brother Robert Gabriel Tucker by DB 15-149 below.

DB 15-149, 13 Dec 1787, rec 14 Feb 1788, Branch Tucker & wf Milley of Amelia Co. to Robert Gabriel Tucker of Lunenburg Co. for L100., 400 ac., being part of tract belonging to Curtis Keatt heretofore, bo. Evans, Stokes, Fountain, br. of Fucking Cr., Robert Dixon. Wit: Edwd Jordan, Francis Jordon, Susanna Jordon. S/ Branch Tucker. Wf Milly relinq dower right. (See DB 13-286)

DB 16-25, 18 Jan 1790, rec 10 Jun 1790, Warren Buford of York Co. S. C. to Branch Tucker of Lunenburg Co., Va., for L210., 430 ac., joining Henry Stokes, Lodowick Farmer, Arthur Herring, Ambrose Ellis, Robert Tucker. Wit: Thomas Buford, James Buford, Henry Buford, Sicily Buford. S/ Warren Buford. (See DB 16-174 & DB 16-236).

DB 16-26, 17 Jan 1790, rec 10 Jun 1790. Deed of Trust. Branch Tucker of Lunenburg Co.,Va. to Warren Buford of York Co., S. C. ref. to above deed. L210. to be paid on or before 25 Dec next ensuing. Should Branch Tucker fail to make full payment when due, then Warren Buford may dispose of land to discharge amount due. Wit: Thomas Buford, James Buford, Henry Buford, Sicily Buford. S/ Branch Tucker.

DB 16-174, 13 Oct 1790, Mary Buford wf of Warren Buford relinq right of dower to land conveyed by her husband to Branch Tucker. (See DB 16-25).

DB 16-236, 23 Dec 1791, rec 12 Jul 1792, Branch Tucker of Lunenburg to Alexander Listen, for L215., 430 ac. where Branch Tucker now lives, bo. Lodowick Farmer, Anthony Herring, Ambrose Ellis, Gabriel Tucker, Henry Stokes. Wit: John Cole, Hezekiah ____, ____ Tabb. S/ Branch Tucker. Wf Millison relinq dower right. (See DB 16-25).

DB 17-68, 10 Mar 1795, Rec 11 Jun 1795, (1) Lewis Countelou of Lunenburg Co, (2) Robert G. Tucker & Branch Tucker, (3) David Stokes, James Smith trustee for sd Robert G. Tucker, William Stokes, Branch Tucker, - - whereas, Countelou is bound to Lunenburg Court for L100., to make good the state of the orphan Lany Cokeram -- guardian for same & sd Robert G. Tucker - - joined in the bond with sd Countelou , -- also Robert G. Tucker joined on bond to James Vaughn of Pr. Edward Co. for L7.16.8, for the hire of a negro woman Hanah, the same joint on bond to Thomas Hudson of Pr. Edward for the hire of a negro fellow Sam for L10.10 the same security to Ann Stokes etc. etc.,-- a detailed deed of trust to secure debts.

DB 17-475, 7 Dec 1796, rec 7 Jun 1797. (1) Branch Tucker of Lunenburg (2) Robert G. Tucker of Lunenburg (3) James Smith of Lunenburg, Trustee. Whereas Branch Tucker indebted to Robert G. Tucker for L20. payable Dec 25, 1797, pledged negro girl.

CHESTERFIELD CO. VA. [3]

1784 <u>Branch Tucker md Millicent Cheatham</u>, dau. of Josiah Cheatham & wf Millicent Lipcomb.

PRINCE EDWARD CO. VA.

DB 9-262, 19 Mar 1787, rec 16 Apr 1787, Stanley Chaffen to <u>Branch Tucker</u>, <u>both of Pr. Edward Co.</u>, <u>400 ac.</u> on b.s. Spring Cr., bo. Ananias Hancock, Robert Dun, Daniel Hays, Robert Martin, Cotteral, Joel Elam, William Elam. S/ Stanley Chaffen, Lucy Chaffen. Wit: Nicholas David, Saml Davis, Benj Moore. (See DB 9-275 for 370 ac. & DB 9-340 for 25 ac.)

DB 9-275, 25 Apr 1793, rec 17 Jun 1793, <u>Branch Tucker & wf Millicent of Lunenbura Co.</u> to John Billups of same Co., for L110, <u>370 ac.</u> on Spring Cr. in Pr. Edward Co., bo. John Hurt, Henry Young est., Philip Johnson & Joel Elam. S/ Branch Tucker, Milicent x Tucker. Wit: P. Stokes, John Boisseau, William Cain. (See DB 9-262 & DB 9-340)

DB 9-340, 29 Apr 1791, rec 19 Jun 1792, <u>Branch Tucker of Lunenburg Co.</u> to John Hurt of Pr. Edward Co., for L50., <u>25 ac.</u> on Spring Cr., bo. sd Hurt, Henry Young. 8/ Branch Tucker. Wit: Thomas Watkins, Robert Watkins. Lee Bird. Geo Medly. (See DB 9-262 and DB 9-275)

NOTTOWAY CO. VA. [4]

DB 1-17, 25 Jul 1789, <u>Branch Tucker of Amelia Co.</u> to Thomas Rudd of Chesterfield Co. <u>307 ac.</u> on Little Sailor Cr. in Nottoway Prince Edward, it being granted to sd Tucker by a deed from James Cheatham. <u>Milly Tucker</u> relinquished her dower.

NOTE: This compiler could not find a deed from James Cheatham to Branch Tucker for 307 ac. in Nottoway, Pr. Edward or Amelia Counties. it probably fell during the period for which records were destroyed.

CHARLOTTE CO. VA. [5]

DB 5-159, 6 Mar 1781, Richard Hayes of Charlotte Co. to <u>Branch Tucker of Lunenburg. Co.</u> <u>100 ac.</u> on Wardsford Cr. in Charlotte Co.

2 Aug 1816 <u>Branch Tucker md 2nd</u> Elizabeth Ferrell, dau of William Ferrell decd.

WB 5-53, 3 Jul 1820, Inv. & Appr. of Estate of <u>Branch Tucker</u> decd, total value $156.72.

NOTE: The above indicates Branch Tucker died in 1820.

WB 12-406, 5 Jun 1851, <u>will of Elizabeth Tucker</u>. To George W. Elliott in trust, all estate real & personal of which I may die possessed or entitled to & also all lands I may acquire, particularly the land which I have this day contracted for, it being a part of the land called Brook's, which I expect to get title to. The sd trustee shall hold the sd property for benefit of my daughter <u>Mary Branch Tombs, wife of James Tombs</u>, & use sd property in the most judicious manner so as to make the best income for support of my sd daughter during her life. Neither property nor income to be liable to control of sd James Toombs. At death of sd daughter, sd property & income above support of sd daughter & her children, to be equally divided between her children. Ex: Drury A. Ferrell. S/ Elizabeth Tucker.

Mary Branch Tucker, b 1819, dau of Branch Tucker, md James Toombs 11 Apr 1843.

SUMMARY: Branch Tucker, 1st son of Robert (1) Tucker & wf Martha Keatts, b ca 1763 in Amelia Co., Va., d 1820 Charlotte Co. Va., md 1st 1784 in Chesterfield Co. Va., Millicent Cheatham, dau of Josiah Cheatham & wf. Millicent Lipcomb, md 2nd in Charlotte Co. Va. Elizabeth Ferrell, dau of William Ferrell, & had issue:

Mary Branch Tucker b 1819, md 1843 James Toombs.

* * *

3. Notes from Mrs. Faye R. Tuck

4. Notes from Mrs. Faye R. Tuck

5. Notes from Mrs. Faye R. Tuck

TG131200 - ROBERT GABRIEL TUCKER
MD 1ST DORITY (DOLLY) CLEMONS
MD 2ND MARY (POLLY) HUBBARD
SON OF ROBERT TUCKER (1)
MD MARTHA KEATTS

LUNENBURG CO. VA.

DB 15-149, 13 Dec 1787, rec 14 Feb 1788, Branch Tucker & wf Milly of Amelia Co. to <u>Robert Gabriel Tucker of Lunenburg. Co.</u> for L100., <u>400 ac.</u>, being part of tract belonging to Curtis Keatt heretofore, bo. Evans, Stokes, Fountain, br. of Fucking Cr., Robert Dixon. Wit: Edwd Jordan, Francis Jordon, Susanna Jordon. S/ Branch Tucker. Wf Milly relinq dower right. (See DB 16-308, DB 17-387).

NOTE: The 400 ac. above was land given by Curtis Keatts to his son Charles Keatts (DB 13-26) in 1777, sold to George Tucker Jr (DB 13-286) in 1779, whose estate passed through heir-at-law Robert Tucker decd, to heir-at-law Branch Tucker, then sold to his brother Robert Gabriel Tucker (DB 15-149) in 1787, then 200 ac. sold to William Hamlett (DB 16-308) in 1793 & 200 ac. sold to Josiah Thompson (DB 17-387) in 1797.

DB 16-308, 2 Mar 1793, rec 11 Apr 1793, <u>Robert Gabriel Tucker & wf Dolly</u>, to William Hamlett, for L50., <u>200 ac.</u>, bo. Ambrose, Henry Stokes, Lewis Cantelou, David Stokes, Robert G. Tucker. Wit: Branch Tucker, Spencer Minos, George Barnes. S/ Robert G. Tucker, Dolly x Tucker. Wf Dolly relinq dower right. (See DB 15-149).

DB 17-68, 10 Mar 1795, Rec 11 Jun 1795, (1) Lewis Countelou of Lunenburg Co, (2) <u>Robert G. Tucker</u> & Branch Tucker, (3) David Stokes, James Smith trustee for sd Robert G. Tucker, William Stokes, Branch Tucker, - - whereas, Countelou is bound to Lunenburg Court for L100., to make good the state of the orphan Lany Cokeram -- guardian for same & sd Robert G. Tucker - - joined in the bond with sd Countelou, -- also Robert G. Tucker joined on bond to James Vaughn of Pr. Edward Co. for L7.16.8, for the hire of a negro woman Hanah, the same joint on bond to Thomas Hudson of Pr, Edward for the hire of a negro fellow Sam for L10.10 the same security to Ann Stokes etc. etc.,-- a detailed deed of trust to secure debts.

DB 17-204, 11 Aug 1795, rec 11 Feb 1796, (1) Ambrose Ellis of Lunenburg (2) <u>Robert G. Tucker</u> (3) James Smith, trustee for sd Robert G. Tucker. Wit. that Robert G. Tucker security for Ambrose Ellis - pledged slaves, horse, cattle, hogs, etc.

DB 17-387, 9 Feb 1797, Robert G. Tucker & wf Dolly, to Josiah Thompson for L200., 200 ac. on head of Fucking Cr. bo. David Stokes decd, Samuel Shervins decd, Ambrose Ellis, William Hamlet, being the land purchased by Robert G. Tucker of Branch Tucker. (See DB 15-149).

DB 17-389, 9 Feb 1797, rec 9 Feb 1797, (1) Josiah Thompson of Nottoway Co. (2) Robert G. Tucker of Lunenburg, (3) Henry Stokes of Lunenburg - Josiah Thompson indebted to Robert G. Tucker - pledged 200 cc. on Fucking Cr., being same sold by Robert G. Tucker & wf Dolly to Josiah Thompson - Nevertheless, if Thompson fail to pay debt, then land will be sold. S/ Josiah Thompson, Robert G. Tucker, Henry Stokes. (See DB 17-387).

DB 17-475, 7 Dec 1796, rec 7 Jun 1797, (1) Branch Tucker of Lunenburg, (2) Robert G. Tucker of Lunenburg, (3) James Smith of Lunenburg, trustee, - whereas Branch Tucker inebted to Robert G. Tucker, for L20., payable Dec 1797, - pledged negro girl.

LIST OF TITHES [6]

| 1783 | Martha Tucker, Branch Tucker, Robert Tucker | 1 white tithe above 21 yrs, 3 negroes, 3 white tithes. |

PERSONAL TAX RECORDS

1783	Martha Tucker, B (Branch) Tucker	Gloster, Will.
1784	Branch Tucker, Robert Tucker	Gloucester, Will, Daniel, one covering horse.
1786	Martha Tucker, Robert Tucker	Gloster , Will, Daniel, 1 white 21 yrs, 3 negroes, 2 horses, 9 cattle, 4 tithes.
1787	Martha Tucker, Robert Gabriel Tucker above age 21	3 blacks, 2 horses 11 cattle.
1789	Robert G. Tucker	
1790	Robert G. Tucker	
1791	Robert Gabriel Tucker	
1792	Robert Gabriel Tucker	
1793	Robert Gabriel Tucker	
1794	Robert G. Tucker	
1795	Robert G. Tucker	
1796	Robert G. Tucker	
1797	Robert G. Tucker	
1798	Robert G. Tucker	

NOTE: From 1786 Tax Record above, Robert Gabriel Tucker was age 21 in 1786, therefore born ca 1765.

LAND RECORDS

1788	400 ac.	Robert G. Tucker	From B (Branch) Tucker.
1789	400 ac.	Robert C. Tucker	
1790	400 ac.	Robert G. Tucker	
1791	400 ac.	Robert Gabriel Tucker	
1792	400 ac.	Robert Gabriel Tucker	
1793	200 ac.	Robert G. Tucker	
1794	200 ac.	Robert G. Tucker	
1795	200 ac.	Robert G. Tucker	
1796	200 ac.	Robert G. Tucker	
1797	200 ac.	Robert G. Tucker	

AMELIA CO. VA.

NOTE: Although no marriage record could be found, information cited below indicates that Robert G. Tucker md Dority (Dolly) Clemons, dau. of William Clemons & wf Ama Clay. Dolly Clemons' sisters were Elizabeth Clemons who md Joel Tucker son of George, and Amey Clemons who was unmarried. Her brother was John Clemons who md Nancy Walthall.

WB 2-42, 14 Dec 1774, will of William Clemons, names: wife Amey Clemons - 200 ac. (not defined); sister Elizabeth Smith-- L20.; sister Peggy Bradshaw - L20.; sister Martha Johnson - L20.; son John Clemons - all my land. Exrs: friend Thomas Bolling Munford and my brother Thomas Apling. Acknowledged by: John Clay, William Thompson, Samuel Young, Martin Wilkinson, Sara Clay.

WB 5-405, wd 17 Dec 1795, wp 28 Sep 1797, will of Ama Clemons, names: son John Clemmon - 20 Shillings; dau. Dority Tucker -negro boy Ben; daus. Elizabeth Tucker & Dority Tucker - negroes Pallace, Frank, Phil, & Brister, to be equally divided between them, and each of the above mentioned paying my dau. Ama Clemons - L5. Rest of est. equally div. btwn two daughters Elizabeth & Dority. Exrs: David Clay & John Clay. S/ Ama Clemons. Wit: John Clay, David Clay, Martha Clay.

DB 26-42, 22 Dec 1821, Robert G. Tucker for himself & wf Dolly Tucker, Amy Clemons, & Elizabeth Tucker widow of Joel Tucker who was formerly Elizabeth Clemons, parties interested in the tract of land received in District Court of Amelia Co., of John Webb, as legatees of John Clemons, all of Halifax Co. of the one part, for $1,600. sold to Francis Dyson of Nottoway Co. of the other part, 340 ac. bo. by John Webb, Robert & William Shore, Doctr Daniel Hardoway & Francis Dyson.

NOTE: John Webb was widower of Nancy Clemons, who was dau. of John Clemons. When Nancy died without issue, the inheritance from her father John Clemons reverted to his sisters, Dolly Clemons wf of Robert G. Tucker, Elizabeth Clemons widow of Joel Tucker, and Amy Clemons who was unmarried.

HALIFAX CO. VA.

Robert G. Tucker moved his family to Halifax Co. where he bought land and resided until his death in 1833.

DB 18-262, Weakley Estate to Wm. Tucker of Lunenhurg, 666 ac. on Runaway Cr. bo. Clay's line, Robert Tucker's cor. Wit: Robert G. Tucker, Joel Tucker, Robert Tucker, Peter Rives, Wm. Vaughan.

DB 19-470, 26 Feb 1800, rec 28 Feb 1803, Benjamin Swinney to Robert G. Tucker for L50. 50 ac. adj. land where I now live. S/ Benjamin Swinney. (See DB 20-77).

DB 20-77, 27 Feb 1804. Kezia Swinney relinq right of dower to 50 ac. which her husband Benjamin Swinney sold to Robert G. Tucker by DB 19-470.

DB 19-475, 20 Nov 1802, rec 28 Feb 1803, Samuel Weakley, executor of est. of Robert Weakley, decd, of Davidson Co. Tenn, to Robert G. Tucker of Halifax Co. Va., for L257., 227 ac. on west fork of Runaway Cr., bo Robert Tucker, James Ridgeway, William Swinney, Joel Tucker. S/ Sam'l Weakley. Wit: Joel Tucker, David Logan, Robert Tucker, Simpson Chisshon.

DB 20-432, 4 Mar 1805, rec 22 Apr 1805, Robert Tucker to Robert G. Tucker, for L70., 56 ac., on w..s. of west fork of Runaway Cr., bo. Robert G. Tucker, James Ridgeway, William Tucker. S/ Robert Tucker. Wit: Charles Reaves, Joshua Stone, James Ridgeway. (See DB 21-132)

DB 21-132 4 Mar 1805, Sarah Tucker, wife of Robert Tucker, relinq dowr right to sale of 56 ac. to Robert G. Tucker by DB 20-432. (Note: The Robert Tucker & wf Sarah is most probably Robert Tucker (the 2nd), son of George Tucker and uncle of Robert G. Tucker)

DB 21-661, 23 Jul 1808, 25 Jul 1808, William Chisshen to Robert G. Tucker for L118.10., 79 ac., on Brush Cr., bo. James Buckley, sd Robert G. Tucker. S/ William Chisshen. Wit: Peter Reaves, John L. Jennings, George Glass. (See DB 21-686)

DB 21-686, 24 Sep 1808, Ann, wf of William Chisshen, relinq dower right to 79 (or 71) ac. sold to Robert G. Tucker by DB 21-661.

DB 28-169, Amey Clemons of Halifax Co., Va. appoint Robert G. Tucker of Halifax Co., my true & lawful attorney.

NOTE: This compiler did not further research the land transactions of Robert G. Tucker.

MARRIAGES [7]

26 Oct 1817, John L. Jennings md Mary Tucker. Sur. Robert G. Tucker, p 94

MB 1-123 20 Nov 1826, Robert G. Tucker md Mary Hubbard. Bondsman, Cornelius Hubbard.

WB 16-268, wd 21 Jan 1831, wp 28 Jan 1833, will of Robert G. Tucker.
Legatees: to wife Polly Tucker - all my property on plantation on Staunton Ri. including negroes Alick, Charity, Mary, Reubin.
to son Gabriel Tucker - negro Abram together with property already given him.
to son Claiborne Tucker - negro John together with property already given him.
to granddaughter Harriett Jennings - mulatto girl Milly.
to daughter now Mrs., Mary Jennings, wife of John L. Jennings Esqr - 4 negroes Fanny, Jenny, Betty, Dicey.
to sons Gabriel & Claihorne - the balance of real & personal est.,equally divided.
Exrs: sons Gabriel & Claihorne.

1850 CENSUS [8]

Name	Age	Calculated DateOf Birth	
Household 759	-	-	-
Gabriel Tucker	59	ca 1791	Farmer
Household 777	-	-	-
John L. Jennings	75	ca 1775	Farmer
Mary C.	49	ca 1801	
Thomas M. Purkins	27	ca 1823	Overseer

NOTE: Gabriel Tucker was listed in a separate household by himself in the 1850 census. Claiborne Tucker was not included in the census.

SUMMARY: Robert Gabriel Tucker, son of Robert (1) Tucker & wf Martha Keatts, b ca 1765 in Lunenburg Co, d 1833 in Halifax Co, Va, md 1st probably ca 1787 in Amelia Co., Dority (Dolly) Clemons, dau of William Clemons & wf Amy Clay of Amelia Co., md 2nd 1826 in Halifax Co., Va., Mary (Polly) Hubbard, & had issue by his 1st wf:

Gabriel Tucker b ca 1791.

Claiborne Tucker.

Mary Tucker b ca 1801, md 1817 John L. Jennings.

* * *

6. "Sunlight on the Southside", p 396.

7. Chiarito, Marian Dodson & Prendergast, James Hadley, "Marriages of Halifax County, Virginia 1801-1831",

8. Chiarito, Marian Dodson, "1850 Census of Halifax County, Virginia", 1982

TG132000 - WILLIAM TUCKER

MD TABITHA KEATTS
SON OF GEORGE TUCKER SR
MD 1st FRANCES
MD 2ND CATHARINE

AMELIA CO. VA.

LIST OF TITHES

1761	5	---	George Tucker, Wm. Tucker, Henry Tucker	Bollice, Lande
1763	1	137	Wm Tucker, son of George	
1764	5	137	Wm. Tucker	Tom, Dick, Tom, Dilce
1765	5	137	Wm. Tucker	Tom, Yull, Tom, Dilce
1767	1	202	William Tucker son of George	

NOTE: William Tucker was listed only one year, in 1761, in the household of his father George Tucker in Amelia Co. Beginning in 1763, he was listed as a separate household. Since his father deeded land to him in 1762, he must have been age 21 at that time, and he would have been born ca 1741, of Frances the 1st wife of George.

DB 7-662-663, 10 Jul 1762, rec. 22 Jul 1762, George Tucker to sons William Tucker - 137 1/2 ac. & Robert Tucker - 137 1/2 ac., remainder of tract Pat. 14 Feb 1756, u.s. of Indian Branch of Deep Cr. - in dividing sd Robert's land where he now lives below road & Edw. Threatts dwelling house, Dandy's (alias Davenport's) line, Jos. Gray's & sd Threatts. Wit: to both deeds: Wm. Crawley, Wm. Walthall, Abraham Burton. (See Patent 28-207).

DB 9-311, 1768, William Tucker & wf Tabitha of Lunenburg Co. to John Keatts-for L120., 137 /2 ac. in Amelia Co. beg. Nathan Fletcher's cor. etc.

NOTE: Amelia Co. Tithe Records show that Wm. Tucker son of George, owned 137 ac. in 1763, 1764 and 1765, and that he owned 202 ac. in 1767. He sold the 137 ac. in 1768. The 202 ac. is most probably the same as 200 ac. given to him by his father-in-law Curtis Keatts in Lunenburg Co.

LUNENBURG CO. VA.

DB 11-298, 14 Sep 1769, rec 14 Sep 1769, <u>Curtis Keatts of Lunenburg Co. to William Tucker, son of George Tucker, for natural love & affection I have for my dau. Tabitha Tucker, wf of sd William Tucker</u>, & for 5 Shillings, <u>200 ac.</u>, being 104 ac. on lower end of Bacon's tract & 96 ac. at lower end of Brag's tract joining the other. Memorandum: Sd Wm. Tucker shall not sell the above land during the life of <u>Curtis Keatts & Tabitha his wife</u>. Wit: John Ward, William Herring, Wm. Jeter. S/ Curtis x Keatts. Tahitha, wf of sd Curtis, relinq dower right. (See DB 18-208A).

Da 13-23, 12 Jun 1777, rec 12 Jun 1777, <u>Curtis Keatt, to Tabitha Tucker dau. of sd Curtis Keatt & William Tucker husband of sd Tabitha & son of George Tucker</u>, for natural love, good will & affection to Tabitha & William, & 5 shillings, <u>200 ac.</u> on n.s. Couches Cr., bo. Fontaine, Brown, Tucker, Briggs. Wit: John Keatt, William Keatt, Charles Keatt. S/ Curtis Keatt. (See DB 18-208A).

NOTE: In DB 13-pages 24-26, 12 Jun 1777, same date as above, Curtis Keatts made similar gifts to sons John Keatts, Wm. Keatts and Charles Keatts.

DB 13-24, 12 Jun 1777, rec 12 Jun 1777, <u>Curtis Keatt to son John Keatt</u>, for natural love, good will & affection & 5 shillings. 200 ac. bo. Mark Thornton, br. of Bawdy Cr., Evans, Bolton. Wit: William Tucker, Wm. Keatt, Charles Keatt. S/ Curtis Keatt.

DB 13-25, rec 12 Jun 1777, <u>Curtis Keatt to son William Keatt</u>, for natural love, good will & affection & 5 shillings, 400 ac. being part of larger tract, bo. Fontaine, Toal, Tusekiah Cr., Baker, br. of Bawdy Cr. Wit: William Tucker, John Keatt, Charles Keatt. S/ Curtis Keatt.

DB 13-26, rec 12 Jun 1777, <u>Curtis Keatt to son</u> Charles Keatt, for natural love, good will & affection & 5 shillings, part of a larger tract, containing 400 ac. bo. Evans, Stokes, Fontaine, br. of Fucking Cr. Wit: John Keatt, William Tucker, Wm. Keatt. S/ Curtis Keatt. (See DB 13-286).

NOTE: Nineteen years earlier, in Amelia Co., by DB 6-147, 23 Feb 1758, Curtis Keatts gave to his dau. Martha Tucker & her husband, Robert Tucker son of George Tucker, 200 ac. btwn Middle & Lower Fork of Deep Cr. On the same date, by DB 6-201, 23 Feb 1758, Curtiss Keatts also gave to his dau. Mary Tucker, husband of William Tucker son of Robert Tucker, 200 ac. btwn Middle & Lower Sellar Forks of Deep Cr.

WB 3-152, wd 25 Sep 1780, wp 11 Mar 1784, "I, <u>George Tucker the elder of 1.unenburg Co.</u> - names - Wife Catharine - Sons Joel, Lew & Robert Tucker - Dau. Milly Clay - Dau. Biddy Tucker - <u>Son William Tucker</u> & Dau. Fanny Coleman - 1 Sh. each, having already provided for them. - Sons Henry, George & Joseph Tucker - <u>Exrs</u>: wife Catharine Tucker and <u>sons William and Joel Tucker.</u>

NOTE: George Tucker, in the above will, stated he had already made provision for son William Tucker. See Amelia Co. DB 7-662-663 for gift of 137 1/2 ac. and DB 9-311 for sale of the 137 1/2 ac.. William Tucker & wf Tabitha then received two gifts from her father Curtis Keatts of 200 ac. each, by Lunenburg Co. DB 11-298 & DB 13-2, which they sold by DB 18-208A.

DB I8-208A, 14 Dec 1799, rec 13 Feb 1300, <u>William Tucker & wf Tabitha</u> to Joshua Gee, for L400., <u>400 ac.</u> on Couches Cr. bo. Tucker, Lowery, Stokes, Davis, McKay, Smith, including all land not condemed in erection of the mill that now belongs to Nathan Gee. Wit: Edwd P. Boman, Davd Street, Lew Jones. S/ William Tucker, Tabitha Tucker. (See DB 11-298 for 200 ac. & DB 13-23 for 200 ac.)

There were two William Tuckers living in Lunenburg Co., who appeared on the Personal Tax Records and Land Tax Records beginning in 1782, and were recorded variously as William, William Sr, William Jr, and William (Whiskey). The designations Sr. & Jr. were most probably used to distinguish the older William son of Robert Jr, b 1733, md Mary Keatts, from his younger first cousin William son of George, b ca 1741, md Tabitha Keatts, sister of Mary Keatts. In the following personal and land tax records, William Tucker (Sr-son of Robert) who md Mary Keatts, appears to hold the 408 ac., and William Tucker (Jr-son of George) who md Tabitha Keatts, appears to hold the 400 ac.

YEAR	PERSONAL TAX RECORDS	LAND TAX RECORDS
1782	Wm. Tucker	Wm. Tucker 408 ac
	Wm. Tucker (Whiskey),	Wm. Tucker 200 ac.
	Hannah,Daniel, Sam	
1783	Wm. Tucker	
	Wm. Tucker	
1784	Wm. Tucker, Nelson Tucker	
1785	Wm. Tucker Sr., Nelson Tucker.	
	Wm. Tucker (Whiskey)	
1786	William Tucker, Nelson Tucker,	
	Brister, Jude, Lewis, Hampton, Jack,	
	2 whites age 21-up, 5 negroes,	
	2 horses, 16 cattle, 4 tithes.	

YEAR	PERSONAL TAX RECORDS	LAND TAX RECORDS
	Wm. Tucker, Wm. Walker, Hannah Abel, Coleman	
1787	William Tucker Sr, Neal Tucker age 16-20 (perhaps Nelson?).	Wm. Tucker Sr 408 ac.
	Wm. Tucker.	Wm. Tucker (Whiskey) 400 ac
1788	William Tucker Sr.	Wm. Tucker Sr
	William Tucker (Whiskey)	Wm. Tucker (Whiskey)
1789	Wm. Tucker.	Wm. Tucker Jr(?) 408 ac
	Wm. Tucker Jr	Wm. Tucker (Whiskey) 400 ac.
1790	Wm. Tucker.	Wm. Tucker Jr(?) 408 ac
	Wm. Tucker (Whiskey)	Wm. Tucker (Whiskey) 400 ac.
1791	Wm. Tucker Sr.	Wm. Tucker Jr(?) 408 ac.
	Wm. Tucker Jr	Wm. Tucker Jr 400 ac.
1792	Wm. Tucker Sen.	Wm. Tucker Sr 408 ac.
	Wm. Tucker Jr	Wm. Tucker Jr 400 ac.
1793	Wm. Tucker Sr.	Wm. Tucker Sr 408 ac.
	Nelson Tucker	
	Wm. Tucker Jr	Wm. Tucker Jr 400 ac.
1794	Wm. Tucker Sr.	Wm. Tucker Sr 400 (?) ac.
	Nelson Tucker	
	Wm. Tucker Jr	Wm. Tucker Jr 400 ac.
1795	Wm. Tucker Sr.	Wm. Tucker Sr 400 (?) ac.
	Nelson Tucker	
	Wm. Tucker Jr	
1796	Wm. Tucker.	Wm. Tucker 200 ac.
	Wm. Tucker	
1797	Wm. Tucker Sr.	Wm. Tucker Sr 200 ac.
	Wm. Tucker Jr.	Wm. Tucker Jr 400 ac.
1798	Wm. Tucker.	Wm. Tucker 400 ac.
1799	Wm. Tucker.	Wm. Tucker 400 ac.
1800	--	Wm. Tucker 400 ac.
1801	--	--

After selling the 208 ac. in 1795 and 200 ac. 1798, in Lunenhurg Co., William Tucker (Sr-son of Robert) & wife Mary & son Nelson moved to Halifax Co. Va.

After selling the 400 ac. in 1799, the subject William Tucker (Jr-son of George) & wife Tabitha moved to Halifax Co. Va.

HALIFAX CO. VA.

DB 18-262, 30 Sep 1799, rec 25 Dec 1799, Elinor Weakley, Samuel Weakley & wf Sally, to <u>William Tucker</u> <u>for L475.</u>, <u>666 ac.</u> on Runaway Cr. bo. Clay, Robert Weakley, Frederick Farmer, Robert Tucker, James Ridgeway, Daniel Mays(?). S/ Elinor x Weakley, Samuel Weakley, Sarah Weakley. Wit: Robert G. Tucker, Joel Tucker, Robert Tucker, Peter Reyes, William Vaughan. Sally Weakley, wife of Samuel Weakley reling dower right.

DB 18-490, 3 Dec 1800, rec 26 Jan 1801, <u>William Tucker</u> to Peter Reaves, for L150., <u>320 ac.</u> on e.s. Runaway Cr., bo. Daniel Clay, Fleming Hodges. S/ William Tucker, Wit: Joel Tucker, Robert Tucker, Henry Tucker.

DB 20-235, 21 Jul 1804, Isham Britton to <u>William Tucker</u>, for L129, negro man slave named Peter.

DB 20-612, 7 Jul 1805, rec 23 Sep 1805, Samuel Weakley, Executor for est of Robert Weakley decd, to <u>William Tucker</u>, for $100., <u>74 ac.</u> on Brush Cr., bo. William Chissher, James Ridgeway, S/ Samuel Weakley Est.. Wit: Peter Reves, Wm. Royster, Richard Maynard. (See DB 21-398)

DB 21-397, 5 Jan 1807, rec 29 Apr 1807, William Pringle & wf Barbary to <u>William Tucker</u>, for L100., <u>100 ac.</u> bo. Farnbrough, Joel Tucker, Davis, Glass, Wilson. S/ William Pringle. Wit: Sam'l Powell, Booker Shelton, Peter Reves, Robt G. Tucker. Wife Barbery relinq dower right. (See WB 10-305)

DB 21-398, 6 Jan 1807, rec 27 Apr 1807, <u>William Tucker</u> to William Pringle, for L74., <u>74 ac.</u> S/ William Tucker. Wit: Peter Reves, Rob't G. Tucker, Elijah Couch. (See DB 20-612)

WB 10-305, wd 5 Jun 1814, wp 22 Jan 1816, will of <u>William Tucker</u>.
wife Tahitha Tucker - 100 ac, on Runaway Cr.
grandson William T. Rives
<u>dau. Nancy Rives</u>
granddau. Nancy Rives
granddau. Elizabeth Rives
grandson Peter Rives
Ex: William T Rives;
Wit: N. Tucker, Robert G. Tucker, Gabriel Tucker, Claiborne Tucker.

SUMMARY: William Tucker, son of George Tucker & 1st wf Frances, b 1741 in Amelia Co., d 1816 in Halifax Co., md ca 1763 Tahitha Keatts, dau of Curtis Keatts & wf Tahitha, & had issue of one daughter and no sons:

Nancy Tucker md Peter Rives, and had issue:

William T. Rives,

Nancy Rives,

Elizabeth Rives

Peter Rives.

TG133000 - HENRY TUCKER SR

MD NANCY (ANN)
SON OF GEORGE TUCKER SR
MD 1ST FRANCES
MD 2ND CATHARINE

LUNENBURG CO. VA.

WB 3.-152, wd 25 Sep 1780, wp 11 Mar 1784, "I, George Tucker the elder of Lunenburg Co." - names - Wife Catharine - Sons Joel, Lew & Robert Tucker - Dau. Milly Clay - Dau. Biddy Tucker - Son William Tucker & Dau. Fanny Coleman - Sons Henry George & Joseph Tucker - 5 pounds each, after wife's decease.

NOTE: The subject Henry Tucker is not to be confused with another Henry Tucker of Amelia Co., who was listed in 1762, only, as a 16-yr-up tithable in the household of his father Matthew Tucker Sr, son of Francis Tucker the Elder, another Tucker Family line. That Henry Tucker was listed as a separate household beginning in 1763, was born ca 1742, attained age 16 ca 1758, attained age 21 ea 1763, and bought land adjacent to his father Matthew Tucker in 1766 (DB 9-26), and was on Amelia Co. Land Tax Records 1782-1796.

NOTE: George Tucker did not deed or will any land to his son, the subject Henry Tucker, in either Amelia or Lunenburg Co. Henry Tucker was most probably one of the older sons of George and his 1st wife Frances. He was listed as a 16-yr-up tithable in the household of his father George Tucker from 1762 through 1765 in Amelia Co., & was probably born ca 1746, became age 16 ca 1762, became age 21 ca 1767, and was ca age 34 in 1780 when his father's will was written. List of Tithables was incomplete 1757-61. He was no longer listed after 1765, either in the household of his father or separately, and no deeds were found for him in either Amelia or Lunenburg Co.

However, a Henry Tucker appeared in Halifax Co. VA in 1800, as a witness, along with Joel & Robert Tucker, to a deed for William Tucker, all of whom were brothers of the subject Henry Tucker. He also bought land in 1800 in the same area of Halifax Co. The subject Henry Tucker would have been ca age 54 at that time.

HALIFAX CO., VA.

DB 18-490, 3 Dec 1800, rec 26 Jan 1801, William Tucker to Peter Reaves, for L150., 320 ac. on e.s. Runaway Cr., bo. Daniel Clay, Fleming Hodges. S/ William Tucker, Wit: Joel Tucker, Robert Tucker, Henry Tucker.

DB 18-352, 27 Mar 1800, rec 28 Apr 1800, Lodwick Tally to <u>Henry Tucker Senr,</u> both of Halifax Co., for L130., <u>250 ac.</u>, bo. Wm. Robertson, Wm. Green, Thomas Farnbrough, crossing Millstone Rd., William Gates. Wit: Beverly Sydnor, Isaac Early, Crawford Tucker. S/ Lodwick x Talley. Polly, wf of Lodwick, relinq dower. (See DB 19-299 for 50 ac., DB 21-22 for 24 1/4 ac., DB 23-185 for 9 ac.)

DB 19-299, 15 Feb 1802, rec 28 Jun 1802, <u>Henry Tucker Senr</u> to Robert Sales, for L40., <u>50 ac.</u> bo. Wm. Robertson, William Green, Thos Williams, Millstone Rd. Wit: Henry Robertson, Randolph x Tucker, Henry x Tucker. S/ Henry x Tucker. <u>Wife Ann relinq dower.</u> (See DB 18-352)

DB 21-22, rec 23 Dec 1805, <u>Henry Tucker</u> to Jesse Talley for L24.5., <u>24 1/4 ac.</u>, bo. a branch, Sydnor, Buckner. S/ Henry Tucker.

DB 23-135, 23 Aug 1811, rec 26 Aug 1811, <u>Henry Tucker Senr</u> to Robert Sails, for $18., <u>9 ac.</u> on s.s. Millstone Rd., <u>being part of land whereon Henry Tucker now lives</u>, bo. Henry Tucker, Robert Sailes. Wit: Peter Reaves, Dudley Glass, John Glass, Crawford Tucker. S/ Henry x Tucker. (See DB 18-352)

WB 10-383, wd 1 Feb 1816, wp 22 Apr 1816, <u>will of Henry Tucker,</u> being old & infirm & weak of body, but sound of mind & memory,
to beloved <u>wife Nancy Tucker,</u> for life, tract of land I now live on, bo. Sydnor & Barley's line, up Old Spring Br to head, Sail's line, both sides of Glass's Road. Also, all my personal estate with exception of one of the dwelling houses on the premises reserved for my
son <u>Randolph Tucker</u> who is to support my sd wife her lifetime - further that personal estate be disposed of agreeable to wishes of wf Nancy Tucker after selling a sufficient quantity to raise $20.00, which I give
to <u>dau. Elizabeth Martin</u>.
to <u>son Henry Tucker</u> - balance of my lands lying north of above described lines on condition he pay $100.00 to my executor.
to<u> son Randolph Tucker</u> - all that part of my land laying between the above described line and Glass's Road, after his mother's death.
Balance of my lands laying south of Glass's Road, after wife's death, to be sold for best price & money divided equally btwn <u>three sons Claiborne Ellington Tucker, Crufford (sic) (?Crawford) Tucker, & Anderson Tucker.</u>
Ex: Son Randolph Tucker. S/ Henry x Tucker, L.S.
Wit: Wm. Sydnor, William Barley, Joseph Epperson.

MARRIAGES [1]

22 Dec 1800. Ganaway Martin md Betsy Tucker. Sur Henry Tucker. p 43.

MARRIAGES [2]

MB 1-47, 22 Apr 1801. Randolph Tucker md Nancy Ridgeway. Sur. James Ridgeway. p 47.

MB 1-50, 13 Feb 1802. Crawford Tucker md Peggy Hubbard, dau of John Hubbard who consents. Sur. Moses Bond. Wit. Moses Bond & Randolph Tucker. p 50.

MB 1-61, 17 Apr 1805, Henry Tucker md Elizabeth Green, Sur. Randolph Tucker, Wit Randolph Tucker & Crawford Tucker. William Green consents. No relationship given. p 61.

26 Oct 1818. John Green md Dolly Talley, dau of Lodwick Talley who consents. Sur. John Sibley, Wit. Anderson Talley & John Sibley. p 96.

SUMMARY: Henry Tucker Sr son of George Tucker Sr & 1st wf Frances, b ca 1746 probably in Amelia Co., d 1816 Halifax Co., Va., md probably in Lunenburg Co. Nancy (Ann) _____ & had issue:

Elizabeth (Betsy) Tucker md 1800 Ganaway Martin

Randolph Tucker md 1801 Nancy Ridgeway.

Crawford Tucker md 1802 Peggy Hubbard.

Henry Tucker (Jr) md 1805 Elizabeth Green.

Claiborne Ellington Tucker.

Anderson Tucker.

* * *

1. Knorr, Catherine Lindsay "Marriages of Halifax County, Virginia, 1753-1800" 1957

2. Chiarito, Marian Dodson & Prendergast, James Hadley, "Marriages of Halifax County, Virginia 1801-1831" 1985

TG133100 - RANDOLPH TUCKER

MD NANCY RIDGEWAY
SON OF HENRY TUCKER SR
MD NANCY (ANN)

HALIFAX CO., VA.

MARRIAGES [3]

MB 1-47, 22 Apr 1801. <u>Randolph Tucker md Nancy Ridgeway</u>. Sur. James Ridgeway. p 47.

DB 19-299, 15 Feb 1802, rec 28 Jun 1802, Henry Tucker Senr to Robert Sales, for L40., 50 ac. bo. Wm. Robertson, William Green, Thos Williams, Millstone Rd. Wit: Henry Robertson, <u>Randolph x Tucker</u>, Henry x Tucker. S/ Henry x Tucker. <u>Wife Ann relinq dower</u>.

WB 10-383, wd 1 Feb 1816, wp 22 Apr 1816, <u>will of Henry Tucker</u>, - names - <u>wife Nancy Tucker</u> - <u>one of the dwelling houses on the premises reserved for my son Randolph Tucker who is to support my sd wife her lifetime</u> - dau. Elizabeth Martin - son Henry Tucker - <u>son Randolph Tucker - all that part of my land laying between the above described line and Glass's Road after his mother's death</u>. - Ex: Son Randolph Tucker.

The subject Randolph Tucker did not appear in the 1850 census of Halifax Co., Va. and was not researched further.

SUMMARY: Randolph Tucker son of Henry Tucker & wf Nancy (Ann) _____ , b probably ca 1780 in Lunenhurg Co., md 1801 Halifax Co., Va., Nancy Ridgeway.

* * *

3. Chiarito, Marian Dodson & Prendergast, James Hadley, "Marriages of Halifax County, Virginia 1801-1831" 1985

TG133200 - CRAWFORD TUCKER

MD PEGGY HUBBARD
SON OF HENRY TUCKER SR
MD NANCY (ANN)

HALIFAX CO., VA.

DB 18-352, 27 Mar 1800, rec 28 Apr 1800, Lodwick Tally to Henry Tucker Senr, both of Halifax Co., for L130., 250 ac., bo. Wm. Robertson, Wm. Green, Thomas Farnbrough, crossing Millstone Rd., William Gates. Wit: Beverly Sydnor, Isaac Early, Crawford Tucker. S/ Lodwick x Talley. Polly, wf of Lodwick, relinq dower.

MARRIAGES [4]

MB 1-50, 13 Feb 1802. Crawford Tucker md Peggy Hubbard, dau of John Hubbard who consents. Sur. Moses Bond. Wit. Moses Bond & Randolph Tucker. p 50.

DB 21-47, 1 Jan 1806, rec 27 Jan 1806, Crafford (sic) (?Crawford) Tucker to Robert Sails, for L40, 43 3/4 ac. on Millstone Rd., bo. Robertson, Williams.

DB 23-135, 23 Aug 1811, rec 26 Aug 1811, Henry Tucker Senr to Robert Sails, for $18., 9 ac. on s.s. Millstone Rd., being part of land whereon Henry Tucker now lives, bo. Henry Tucker, Robert Sailes. Wit: Peter Reaves, Dudley Glass, John Glass, Crawford Tucker. S/ Henry x Tucker.

WB 10-383, wd 1 Feb 1316, wp 22 Apr 1816, will of Henry Tucker, - wife Nancy Tucker - son Randolph Tucker - dau. Elizabeth Martin - son Henry Tucker - Balance of my lands laying south of Glass's Road, after wife's death, to be sold for best price & money divided equally btwn three sons Claiborne Ellington Tucker, Crufford (sic) (?Crawford) Tucker, & Anderson Tucker.

The subject Crawford Tucker did not appear in the 1850 census of Halifax Co., Va. and was not researched further.

SUMMARY: Crawford Tucker son of Henry Tucker Sr & wf Nancy (Ann) _____, b probably ca 1781 in Lunenburg Co., md 1802 Halifax Co., Va. Peggy Hubbard.

* * *

4. Chiarito, Marian Dodson & Prendergast, James Hadley, "Marriages of Halifax County, Virginia 1801-1831" 1985

TG133300 - HENRY TUCKER JR

MD ELIZABETH GREEN
SON OF HENRY TUCKER SR
MD NANCY (ANN)

HALIFAX CO., VA.

MARRIAGES [5]

MB 1-61, 17 Apr 1805, <u>Henry Tucker md Elizabeth Green</u>, Sur. Randolph Tucker, Wit. Randolph Tucker & Crawford Tucker. William Green consents. No relationship given. p 61.

Following is the will of Henry Tucker Sr.

WB 10-383, wd 1 Feb 1816, wp 22 Apr 1816, <u>will of Henry Tucker</u>, - <u>wife Nancy Tucker</u> - son Raldolph Tucker -dau. Elizabeth Martin - <u>son Henry Tucker - balance of my. lands lying north of above described lines on condition he pay $100.00 to my executor</u>. - sons Claiborne Ellington Tucker, Crufford (?Crawford) Tucker, & Anderson Tucker.

Following is the will of Henry Tucker Jr.

WB 18-518, wd 16 May 1838, wp 27 Aug 1838, <u>will of Henry Tucker</u>. after payment of debts, bal. of est. to beloved <u>wife Elizabeth Tucker</u> for life, & at her death, my land equally divided btwn <u>three sons Thomas, James & John</u>. Bal. of est. to be sold & proceeds divided btwn all my children, ie. three sons named & <u>dau. Nancy Hall</u>. Ex: son James Tucker Wit: Wm. Sydnor, Allen Robertson, John Green s/ Henry x Tucker.

Henry Tucker Jr's sons Thomas and John did not appear in the 1850 census of Halifax Co., Va. and were not researched further. See separate chapter on James Tucker.

SUMMARY: Henry Tucker Jr son of Henry Tucker Sr & wf Nancy (Ann) _____, b probably ca 1784 in Lunenburg Co, d 1838 Halifax Co, Va, md 1805 Halifax Co, Va, Elizabeth Green & had issue:

Thomas Tucker.

James Tucker b ca 1807, md Sarah Fuqua, dau of Joseph Fuqua.

John Tucker.

Nancy Tucker md _____ Hall.

* * *

5. Chiarito, Marian Dodson & Prendergast, James Hadley, "Marriages of Halifax County, Virginia 1801-1831" 1985

TG133310 - JAMES TUCKER

MD SARAH FUQUA
SON OF HENRY TUCKER JR
MD ELIZABETH GREEN

HALIFAX CO., VA.

WB 22-352, 21 Jul 1829, wp 27 Aug 1829, Oct Court 1829, <u>will of Joseph H. Fuqua</u>, names son James - my tract of land, wife (not named) $200. dau Armon(?) - negro girl Maria, $200., bay horse named Jim. dau Betsy - negro woman Lucy, gray horse named Jack. <u>dau Sally Tucker, wife of James Tucker</u> - negro girl already given to her. These words or the like effect the sd Joseph H. Fuqua declared in the presence of the witnesses whose names are hereto subscribed. with the intention that the same should stand for and be his last will & testament. 25 Jul 1829. A. L. Peters, John M. Arendall.

On 27 Aug 1829, Court, Ordered that <u>Mary P. Fuqua</u>, John T. Fuqua, Jos H. Fuqua Jr, David W. Fuqua, William G. Fuqua, <u>James Tucker & Sarah his wife</u>, Elizabeth B. Fuqua, Armon E. Fuqua, & James B. Fuqua, the widow & next of kin of sd decd, be summoned to appear at the next court, to contest the same if they please.

At another court held 23 Oct, the sd will was again presented, & thereupon the next of kin in their proper persons and by their attorney, waive all opposition to the sd will, whereupon the same was proved by the oath of Alexander Peters and Jno M. Arendall, & on motion of John A. McGraw, certificate is granted him for obtaining letters of Administrtation with the nuncupative will annexed in due form.

WB 18-518, wd 16 May 1838, wp 27 Aug 1838, <u>will of Henry Tucker</u>. after payment of debts, bal. of est. to beloved <u>wife Elizabeth Tucker</u> for life, & at her death, my land equally divided btwn three <u>sons</u> Thomas, <u>James</u> & John. Bal. of est. to be sold & proceeds divided btwn all my children, ie. three sons named & dau. Nancy Hall. Ex: .son James Tucker Wit: Wm. Sydnor, Allen Robertson, John Green s/ Henry x Tucker.

DB 48-227, 16 Nov 1842, rec 29 Nov 1842, whereas James Tucker is indebted to Joseph H. Fuqua for $500., James Tucker sold to Giles McGraw, his interest in the estate of the late Henry Tucker decd which was assigned as dower to Elizabeth Tucker, widow of Henry Tucker, & also his interest in real estate now in possession of Joseph H. Fuqua & devised by him the sd Fuqua in right of his late wife Catharine Fuqua who was Catharine Younger -also cattle, stock, household furniture, grain, tobacco, etc. Wit: Armistead Lacy, Patrick F. Henry, Jno. S. Priddy. S/ James x Tucker.

The Birthdates Of The James Tucker Family Are Calculated From Ages Shown In The 1850 Census: [6]

Name	Age	Calculated Birthdate	
Northern District			
Household 5	--	--	--
James Tucker	43	ca 1807	Farmer
Sarah W.	34	ca 1816	
Elizabeth A.	12	ca 1838	
Susan F.	8	ca 1842	
Sarah W.	6	ca 1844	
Mary P.	4	ca 1846	
Alice A.	9/12	ca 1850	
Elizabeth	70	ca 1780	

NOTE: Elizabeth Tucker, age 70, is most probably mother of James Tucker, and widow of Henry Tucker Jr.

SUMMARY: James Tucker son of Henry Tucker (Jr) & wf Elizabeth Green, b ca 1807 probably in Halifax Co Va., md probably ca 1837 Sarah Fuqua, b ca 1816, dau of Joseph H. Fuqua Sr & wf Catherine Younger, and had issue:

Elizabeth A. Tucker b ca 1838.

Susan F. Tucker b ca 1842.

Sarah W. Tucker b ca 1844.

Mary P. Tucker b ca 1846.

Alice A. Tucker b ca 1850.

* * *

6. Chiarito, Marian Dodson, "1850 Census of Halifax County, Virginia", 1982

TG133400 - CLAIBORNE ELLINGTON TUCKER

SON OF HENRY TUCKER SR

MD NANCY (ANN)

HALIFAX CO., VA.

DB 26-62, 1 Apr 1816, rec 22 Apr 1816, Philamon Hawkins to <u>Claiborne Tucker</u>, for $80.00, <u>40 ac.</u>, bo. Peter Reves, James Monroe, Harbert Nunnelle, it being the land Hawkins purchased of Matthew Farmer. Wit: Elisha Abbott, Lydia Abbott, Alex W. Crews. S/ Philemon Hawkins, wife Mary Hawkins. (See DB 29-96 for 41.5 ac.)

DB 29-96, 25 Dec 1820, rec 25 Dec 1820, <u>Claiborne Tucker</u> to Merit Talbot, for $100.00, <u>41.5 ac.</u> on headwaters of Bradley Cr. bo Herbert Nunnallee, James Monroe & sd Merit Talbot. (See DB 26-62 for 40 ac.)

WB 10-383, wd 1 Feb 1816, wp 22 Apr 1816, <u>will of Henry Tucker</u> - names: -<u>wife Nancy Tucker</u> - son Randolph Tucker dau. Elizabeth Martin - son Henry Tucker - Balance of my lands laying south of Glass's Road, after wife's death, to be sold for best price & money divided equally btwn three <u>sons</u> Claiborne Ellington Tucker, Crufford (sic) (?Crawford) Tucker, & Anderson Tucker].

The subject Claiborne Tucker was not included in the 1850 census of Halifax Co, Va., and was not further researched.

SUMMARY: Claiborne Ellington Tucker son of Henry Tucker Sr & wf Nancy (Ann) _____.

TG134000 - GEORGE TUCKER JR

SON OF GEORGE TUCKER SR
MD 1st FRANCES
MD 2nd CATHARINE

AMELIA CO. VA.

George Tucker (Jr) was listed as a 16-yr-up tithable in the household of his father George Tucker (Sr) in Amelia Co. in 1765 and in 1770, so he was probably born ca 1749, and attained age 21 ca 1770. He died in 1781 in Lunenburg Co., prior to the death of his father.

LUNENBURG CO. VA.

DB 13-286, 30 Nov 1779, rec 9 Dec 1779, Charles Keatt to George Tucker, both of Lunenburg Co. for L1,500., 400 ac., being part of tract belonging to Curtis Keatt heretofore, bo. Evans, Stokes, Fontaine, br. of Fucking Cr. Robert Dixon. Wit: Richd Ingram, John Curetan, William Tucker. S/ Charles Keatt.

WB 3-76, 10 May 1781, Inv. & Appr. Est. of George Tucker Jr., by Lyd. Bacon & John Cureton & _____ Murrell.

NOTE: The above inventory indicates that George Tucker Jr died in 1781.

LAND TAX RECORDS

1782	George Tucker Jr, decd. Est.	400 ac.
1787	George Tucker Jr. decd. Est.	400 ac.
1788	George Tucker Jr. decd. Est.	400 ac.

What disposition was made of his 400 ac. estate after 1788 is not clearly determined. However, see DB 1.5-149, 1787, where Branch Tucker, nephew of George Tucker Jr, sold this same 400 ac. Apparently George Tucker Jr's estate passed to his heir-at-law brother Robert Tucker decd, and then to Robert's son, Branch Tucker. See chapter for Branch Tucker.

WB 3-152, wd 25 Sep 1780, wp 11 Mar 1784, "I, George Tucker the elder of Lunenburg Co." - names: - Wife Catharine - Sons Joel, Lew & Robert Tucker - Dau. Milly Clay - Dau. Biddy Tucker - Son William Tucker & Dau. Fanny Coleman - Sons Henry, George & Joseph Tucker - 5 pounds each, after wife's decease.

> CODICIL - 30 Dec 1783 - the 5 pounds devised my son George he being dead, I devise to my 4 last children, namely, Obedience, Joel, Lew & Robert & their heirs.

SUMMARY: George Tucker. Jr, son of George Tucker Sr & 1st wf Frances _____ , b ca 1749, d 1781, without issue.

TG135000 - JOSEPH TUCKER

MD LUCY
SON OF GEORGE TUCKER SR
MD 1ST FRANCES
MD 2ND CATHARINE

LUNENBURG CO. VA.

DB 12-161, 22 Jul 1772, rec 13 Aug 1772, Thomas Harding to Joseph Tucker, for L41.10., 200 ac. & plantation whereon William Purdue now lives, on s.s. Willingham's Rd. Wit: John Ward, William Tucker, Drewery Morrell(?). S/ Thomas' Harding. (See DB 13-11).

DB 13-10, 23 May 1776, Rec 13 May 1777, James Beuford Senr of Cumberland Parish of Lunenburg Co. to Joseph Tucker of same parish, for L50., 200 ac. on Whites Br., bo. Thomas Beuford, Thomas Tabb, Richard Evans, John Eppes. Wit: Thomas Hardy, Peter x Beuford, Elizabeth Hardy. S/ James Beuford Senr. (See DB 14-139)

DB 13-11, 12 May 1776, rec 13 Mar 1777, Joseph Tucker to Ambrose Beuford, for L50., 200 ac. bo. Vineham's Rd, William Herring, Mark Andrews, Daniel Melone, Thomas Hardy. Wit: John Barry, Robert x Beasley, Daniel x Melone. S/ Joseph Tucker. Wf. Lucy relinq dower right. (See DB 12-161).

DB 14-139, 9 Dec 1784, Joseph & Lucy Tucker for L70. sold to John Eppes, 200 ac. in Lunenburg Co. beg. Wm. Ellis' & adj Thos. Buford, Rev. James Craig, Robt. Chappell & sd John Eppes, whereon sd Tucker now lives. S/ Joseph Tucker, Lucy x Tucker. (See DB 13-10).

WB 3-152, wd 25 Sept 1780, wp 11 Mar 1784, " I, George Tucker the elder of Lunenburg Co." - names – wife Catharine - Sons Joel, Lew & Robert Tucker - Dau. Milly Clay - Dau. Biddy Tucker - Son William Tucker & Dau. Fanny Coleman - Sons Henry, George & Joseph Tucker - 5 pounds each, after wife's decease.

LIST OF TITHES [7]

1772	Martha Tucker's List, Joseph Tucker	2 tithes
1773	Martha Tucker's List, Joseph Tucker	2 tithes
1783(?)	Joseph Tucker, (21 years old)	7 whites, 0 blacks, 1 21 yr. old, 1 slave.

PERSONAL TAX RECORDS

1782	Joseph Tucker	Hannah
1783	Joseph Tucker	
1784	Joseph Tucker	

1782   200 ac. Joseph Tucker
1785   200 ac. Joseph Tucker

NOTE: George Tucker did not deed or will any land to his son Joseph Tucker, in either Amelia or Lunenburg Co. He was probably one of the older sons by his 1st wf Frances. He was listed in Amelia Co. as a 16-yr-up tithable in the household of his father George Tucker from 1767 through 1770, after which George Tucker moved to Lunenburg Co. If he was age 16 in 1767, he would have been born in 1751, and would have been age 21 in 1772, which is the year he first bought land in Lunenburg Co. (DB 12-161).

In a list of tithes in Lunenburg Co. for 1772-1773, a Joseph Tucker is shown in the household of Martha Tucker's List. This is most probably the subject Joseph Tucker, who was brother of Martha's deceased husband Robert Tucker. In another list of tithes labeled as year 1783(?) (probably should be 1773), Joseph Tucker is shown as 21 years old in a separate household.

Our subject Joseph Tucker b 1751, is not to be confused with his first cousin Joseph Tucker b 1733 son of John Tucker, or with his uncle Joseph Tucker b 1722 son of Capt Robert Tucker Sr.

SUMMARY: Joseph Tucker, son of George Tucker Sr & 1st wife Frances,b ca 1751 in Amelia Co., md probably in 1772, Lucy ___ and was still living in 1784 when he was named in his father's will, and when he sold his land in Lunenburg Co.

* * *

7. Bell, Landon C., "Sunlight on the Southside"

TG136000 - JOEL TUCKER (SR)

MD ELIZABETH CLEMONS
SON OF GEORGE TUCKER SR
MD 1ST FRANCES
MD 2ND CATHARINE

LUNENBURG CO. VA.

DB 13-68, 26 Sep 1777, rec 18 Jan 1778, William Davis of Amelia Co., to George Tucker of sd Co., for L230., 199 ac. in Lunenhurg Co., bo. Ward Hudson, Richard Ingram, Duprey, Brizendine, Davis, Edmund. Wit: John Cureton Jr, William Tucker, Joel Tucker, John Keatts. S/ William Davis. (See WB 3-152 in which George Tucker willed this land to wf Catharine for life & then jointly to sons Joel & Robert).

WB 3-152, wd 25 Sep 1780, wp 11 Mar 1784, "I, George Tucker the elder of Lunenburg Co." -names: - Wife Catharine - the use of my land & plantation ... about 200 ac., all my slaves & pers. prop. during her natural life or widowhood. - Sons Joel Tucker & Robert Tucker - my land divided bet. them, Robert's 100 ac. to include the plantation house. - Sons Joel, Lew & Robert Tucker - negro Ned to he divided equally bet. them. - Dau. Milly Clay - Dau. Biddy Tucker - Son William Tucker - Dau. Fanny Coleman - Sons Henry, George & Joseph Tucker -
Exrs: wife Catharine Tucker and sons William and Joel Tucker.

> CODICIL - 30 Dec 1783 - the 5 pounds devised my son George, he being dead, I devise to my 4 last children, namely, Obedience, Joel, Lew & Robert & their heirs.

WB 3-172, George Tucker Est. I&A 8 Jul 1784. S/ Catharine Tucker, Joel Tucker.

PERSONAL TAX RECORDS

1782	Joel Tucker	Listed in household of George Tucker, with slaves Lender, Moll, Lucy, Isaac, Ned.
1783	Joel Tucker	Listed in household of George Tucker.
1784	Joel, Lewelling & Robert Tucker	Listed in household of Catherine Tucker.
1785	Joel Tucker	Listed as a separate household.
1786	Joel Tucker	Joice & Clary, 3 tithes, 1 white, 2 negroes, 1 horse.
1787	Joel Tucker	1 white, 2 blacks, 1 horse.
1788	Joel Tucker	
1789	Joel Tucker	
1790	Joel Tucker	

PERSONAL TAX RECORDS

1791 Joel Tucker
1792 Joel Tucker
1793 Joel Tucker
1794 Joel Tucker
1795 Joel Tucker
1796 Joel Tucker
1797 Joel Tucker
1798 Joel Tucker

DB 18-I4-A, 8 Feb 1798, rec 8 Feb 1798, Joel Tucker & wf Elizabeth sold 100 ac. in Lunenburg Co., for L100., to Josiah Thompson, bo. on north by Thomas Edmunds, on west by Rowland Hudson, south by Mary Ingram & east by Dicy Hudson. (See DB 13-68 & WB 3-152 for George Tucker).

AMELIA CO. VA.

Marriages, p T-2, 25 Nov 1788, Joel Tucker md Elizabeth Clements, who signs her consent Elizabeth Clemons. Witness to consent John Clemons & Ama Clemons. Sur: John Clemons.

NOTE: Elizabeth Clemons, Amey Clemons, Dority (or Dorothy or Dolly) Clemons, and John Clemons were children of William Clemons and wife Ama Clay, who was daughter of John Clay and wife Sarah Tucker, who was daughter of Capt Robert Tucker Sr and wife Martha. Elizabeth Clemons married Joel Tucker son of George & 2nd wf Catharine of Lunenburg Co. Dolly Clemons married Robert Gabriel Tucker, son of Robert, nephew of subject Joel, and grandson of George. See following.

WB 5-405, wd 17 Dec 1795, wp 28 Sep 1797, will of Ama Clemons, names: son John Clemmon - 20 Shillings; dau. Dority Tucker -negro boy Ben; daus. Elizabeth Tucker & Dority Tucker - negroes Pallace, Frank, Phil, & Brister, to be equally divided between them, and each of the above mentioned paying my dau. Ama Clemons - L5. Rest of est. equally div. btwn two daughters Elizabeth & Dority. Exrs: David Clay & John Clay. S/ Ama Clemons. Wit: John Clay, David Clay, Martha Clay.

WB 5-437, 22 Feb 1798, I&A Est. Amey Clemons decd rec.

WB 2-42, 14 Dec 1774, will of William Clemons, names: wife Amey Clemons - 200 ac. (not defined); sister Elizabeth Smith - L20.; sister Peggy Bradshaw - L20.; sister Martha Johnson - L20.; son John Clemons - all my land. Exrs: friend Thomas Bolling Munford and my brother Thomas Apling. Acknowledged by: John Clay, William Thompson, Samuel Young, Martin Wilkinson, Sara Clay.

WB 3-201, 12 Oct 1782, will of John Clay Sr - names - son John Clay Jr - dau Amy Clements - wf Sarah Clay - daus Sarah, Martha, Dorothy & Phebe.

DB 26-42, 22 Dec 1821, Robert G. Tucker for himself & wf Dolly Tucker, Amy Clemons, & Elizabeth Tucker widow of Joel Tucker who was formerly Elizabeth Clemons, parties interested in the tract of land received in District Court of Amelia Co., of John Webb, as legatees of John Clemons, all of Halifax Co. of the one part, for $1,600. sold to Francis Dyson of Nottoway Co. of the other part, 340 ac. bo. by John Webb, Robert & William Shore, Doctr Daniel Hardoway & Francis Dyson.

NOTE: John Webb was widower of Nancy Clemons, who was dau. of John Clemons. When Nancy died without issue, the inheritance from her father John Clemons reverted to his sisters, Dolly Clemons wf of Robert G. Tucker, Elizabeth Clemons widow of Joel Tucker, and Amy Clemons who was unmarried.

NOTE: The subject Joel Tucker is not to be confused with his first cousin Joel Tucker son of William Tucker & wf Ann, a brother of George Tucker. This compiler, B. DeRoy Beale made that error on pages 23, 27 and 172 of his book "The Beale Family of Halifax County, Virginia", 1979, where he erroneously identified his ancestor Joel Tucker Sr who married Elizabeth Clemons, as the son of William Tucker of Amelia Co. who married Ann ____. However, that Joel Tucker Sr , son of William, married 1st Usley Chappell, and 2nd Nancy Moore, and lived in Amelia, Nottoway and Halifax Counties. See separate chapter.

NOTE: The subject Joel Tucker, was son of George Tucker Sr & 2nd wf Catharine, who lived in Amelia Co. through 1770, and moved to Lunenburg Co. Joel Tucker married in 1788 in Amelia Co., Elizabeth Clemons, dau. of William Clemons & wf Ama Clay. Joel Tucker & wf Elizabeth sold in 1798 the 100 ac. in Lunenburg Co. which he inherited from his father George Tucker Sr. They moved to Halifax Co., Va. where he bought and sold land, raised his family and died 1820.

HALIFAX CO. VA.

DB 18-370, 20 Feb 1800, rec 23 Jun 1800, Joshua Compton & wf Amy to Joel Tucker for L50., 100 ac. on Runaway Cr., bo. sd Tucker's line. S/ Joshua x Compton. Wit: Robert G. Tucker, Benjamin (B) Swinne, Dole (or Doc) Tucker. (Note: The notation "bo. sd Tucker's line" implies Joel Tucker owned land prior to this date. This most probably refers to DB 18-396, which was dated 1 Jan 1800 prior to this deed, but recorded 28 Jul 1800 after this deed.)

DB 18-396, 1 Jan 1800, rec 28 Jul 1800, heirs & representatives of John Simpson estate to <u>Joel Tucker</u> for $50., <u>40 ac.</u> on Runaway Cr., bo. John Stone, Joshua Compton, Robert Weakley. (See DB 24-229).

DB 19-476, 20 Nov 1802, rec 28 Feb 1803, Samuel Weakley, executor of est of Robert Weakley decd of Davidson Co. Tenn., to <u>Joel Tucker</u> of Halifax Co., for L216., <u>270 ac.</u> on Runaway Cr., bo. Benjamin Swinney, Robert G. Tucker, crosses west fork of Runaway Cr., Robert Farnbrough, Barnett Farmer. S/ Sam'l Weakley. Wit: David Logan, Robert Tucker, Robt G. Tucker, Simpson x Chisshen.

DB 20-5, 24 Oct 1803, rec 24 Oct 1803, John Stow to <u>Joel Tucker</u> for L30., <u>60 ac.</u> on west fork of Runaway Cr., bo. sd Tucker, Joshua Compton, John P. Swinney. S/ John. Stone. Wit: Robert G. Tucker, William Chisshen, James Swinney.

DB 21-307, 24 Dec 1806, rec 26 Jan 1807. Robert Farnbrough to <u>Joel Tucker</u> for L90., <u>100 ac.</u> in the waters of east fork of Runaway Cr., bo. Barnett Farmer, Thomas Hodges, Charles Wilson. S/ Robert Farnbrough. Wit: Rob't G. Tucker, William C. Tucker, Wm. Barnes.. Hannah, wf of Robert Farnbrough, relinq dower right. (See DB 24-229 & DB 27-36).

DB 24-229, 23 Apr 1813, <u>Joel Tucker</u> for $200., to his <u>son</u> William C. Tucker, 145 ac. on waters of Runaway Cr., it being the same conveyed from Robert Farnbrough to Joel Tucker with an addition of all the land btwn sd tract & the first br. of Runaway Cr. to the west. (See DB 21-307 above for 100 ac. & possibly DB 18-396 above for 40 ac.).

DB 27-26, 16 Oct 1817, James McCaffery to <u>Joel Tucker</u> for L50., <u>50 ac.</u> upon Brush Cr.

DB 27-36, 19 Jan 1818, <u>William C. Tucker to his father Joel Tucker</u> for $700., <u>145 ac.</u> on waters of Runaway Cr., it being same tract conveyed by Robert Farnbrough to sd Joel Tucker, with an addition of all the land btwn sd tract & the first hr. of Runaway Cr. to the west. (See DB 18-396, DB 21-307 & DB 24-229).

DB 27-274, 30 Nov 1818, Joshua Clay & wf Dolly & John Clay & wf. Melison, to <u>Joel Tucker</u> for $820., a tract of land lying on b.s. Childrey Cr. (number acres not shown). (probably 300 ac. as shown on land tax records of 1819).

WB 12-50, wd 6 Dec 1820, wp 25 Dec 1820, <u>will of Joel Tucker Sr of Halifax Co, Va.</u> Wit: Frederick Clay, James x Clay.

Exrs: <u>Son William C. Tucker</u> and Ezekiel Pillow.

Leg: <u>Wife Elizabeth Tucker</u> - all my estate except such as is otherwise disposed of in this will, both real & personal, for life or widowhood.

To each of my children at age 21 or marriage - such negroes as may he spared and which children may require, to be deducted from each child's share of estate.

To my several daus. - reserve the two smallest rooms of my dwelling house for their use until they are securely married.

To <u>three daus. Dolly Clay, Elizabeth Tucker & Amy Tucker</u> - three 50-ac. tracts of land, that is, one tract of 50 ac. bought of James McCaffrey, one tract est. of 50 ac. bought of James Eastham, and one tract est. of 50 ac. bought of Joshua Clay - the three daughters <u>to draw lots</u> for the three tracts.

At death or marriage of wf Elizabeth Tucker, my personal property to be divided amongst my children as follows:

Three daus. - one likely negro apiece.

<u>Son John Tucker</u> - negro boy Sonie.

<u>Son George</u> - negro boy Ase.

<u>Son Thomas</u> - two negro children John & Edmund.

Rest of personal property equally divided btwn my children.

<u>Son William C. Tucker</u> - as I have heretofore given him that part of land I allotted for him, I now give him no land.

<u>Son Worstnam Tucker</u> - 200 ac. beg. at br. running into Runaway Cr.

<u>Son Thomas Tucker</u> - remainder of tract whereon I now live

<u>Sons John & George Tucker</u> - all the land I bought of Joshua Clay, (except what I have given to my daus.).

LAND TAX RECORDS

1819	Joel Tucker	50 ac.	Brush Cr.
1819	Joel Tucker	145 ac.	Runaway Cr., fr Wm. C. Tucker
1819	Joel Tucker	300 ac.	Childrey Cr., fr J. Clay decd.

1822	Dolly Clay	50 ac.	Runaway Cr.
1822	Eliza Tucker	50 ac.	Runaway Cr.
1822	Amy Tucker	50 ac.	
1822	Worstnam Tucker	200 ac.	
1822	John & George Tucker	405 ac.	
1822	Thomas Tucker	300 ac.	

The two daughters Dolly Clay & Elizabeth Tucker are shown on 1822 land tax records as holding 50 ac. each on Runaway Cr, and Amy Tucker holding 50 ac., location not shown. Joel Tucker's will specified one of these lots was bought of James McCaffrey, another was to be taken from the acreage bought of Joshua Clay (no. ac. not specified in that deed). The other 50 ac. lot was specified as that bought of James Eastman. This compiler could find no deed for land bought of James Eastman. DB 18-396 included 40 ac. on Runaway Cr. bought of Simpson Estate & DB 20-5 included 60 ac. on Runaway Cr. bought of John Stow. It is not clear which 50 ac. lot went to Dolly, Elizabeth and Amy.

The daughter Elizabeth Tucker, who married Charles Beal, died 1830, leaving infant son Joel Thomas Beal(e), and infant daughter Mary Beal who died infant 1833. Charles Beal died 1836. Joel Thomas Beal(e) md Elizabeth Ann Tucker, dau of John C. Tucker & wf Mary (Polly) R. Godby.

The acreage willed to sons John & George was specified as "all the land I bought of Joshua Clay except what I have given to my daus." Land tax records of 1819 show Joel Tucker holding a 300 ac. tract on Childrey Cr. from J. Clay decd. But land tax records of 1822 show John & George holding 405 ac. It would appear that the land bought of Joshua Clay would have consisted of 455 ac. (50 ac. to one of the daughters + 405 ac. to John & George).

The acreage willed to Thomas Tucker was specified as "remainder of tract whereon I now live". The land tax records of 1822 showed Thomas Tucker holding 300 ac. According to Chancery Court Suit, Box 12, 1846, Thomas Tucker died an infant intestate & his land & personal property reverted to his heirs at law.

The son Worstnam Tucker, named in the will of Joel Tucker Sr, is the same as Joel W. Tucker who married Judith Barber.

The marriages of some of the children of Joel and Elizabeth Tucker are recorded in Halifax County Marriage Books:

MB 1-82, 22 Mar 1813, Dolly (Dorothy) Tucker md Charles Clay.

MB 1-105, 17 Dec 1821, Elizabeth A. Tucker md Charles Beal. (See "The Beale Family of Halifax County, Virginia" 1978, by B. DeRoy Beale).

MB 1-117, 22 Oct 1824, John C. Tucker md Polly R. Godby, signed by Christian Godby, parent; Bondsman, Archibald Comer Jr.

MB 1-132, 11 Aug 1829, Joel W. Tucker md Judith Barber. Bondsman & Witness David Barber. Signer Shadrack Barber father. (Note: The index & register were recorded as John W. Tucker, but original mariage document clearly showed Joel W. Tucker. bdb)

MB 1-170, 28 Oct 1842, Amy Tucker md Nathanial Dews.

The heirs of Joel Tucker Sr sold among themselves the remaining estate, as per the two deeds following:

DB 55-287, 26 Nov 1853, John C. Tucker & wf Mary, Charles Clay & wf Dolly, Joel T. Beal & wf. Ann, for $367.50, to William C. Tucker, Joel W. Tucker, & George W. Tucker, 147 ac., taken from the tract of land of the late Joel Tucker decd.

DB 55-297, 18 Oct 1853, William C. Tucker & wf Martha, John C. Tucker & wf. Mary, Joel W. Tucker & wf Judith, George W. Tucker & wf Lisa, Joel T. Beal & wf Ann, for $730., to Charles Clay, 292 ac. on Runaway Cr.

SUMMARY OF LAND TRANSACTIONS:

Year	References		Plus	Minus	Bal
1800	DB 18-370	fr Compton	100		100
1800	DB 18-396	fr Simpson Est.	40		140
1803	DB 19-476	fr Weakley Est.	270		410
1803	DB 20-5	fr Stowe	60		470
1806	DB 21-307	fr Farnbrough	100		570
1813	DB 24-229	to son Wm. C.		145	425
1817	DB 27-26	fr McCaffery	50		475
1818	DB 27-36	fr son Wm. C.	145		620
1818	DB 27-274	fr Clay (land tax)	300		920
1820	WB 12-50	to dau Dolly Clay		50	870
		to dau Eliz. Tucker		50	820
		to dau Amy Tucker		50	770
		to son Worstnam		200	570
		to son Thomas(land tax)		300	270
		to sons John/George(l.t.)	___	405	(135)
			1065	1200	
		discrepancy	135	___	
			1200	1200	
		fr son Thomas decd est	300		300
1853	DB 55-287	distribution		147	153
1853	DB 55-297	distribution	___	292	(139)
			1500	1639	
		discrepancy	139	___	
			1639	1639	

This compiler is unable to account for the discrepancies.

Chancery Court Suit — Beale vs Tucker, Box 12, 1846 --- <u>Joel Tucker died some years ago</u>, leaving widow Elizabeth Tucker & children Dolly Clay, John Tucker, George Tucker, Amy Tucker Joel Tucker, & Elizabeth Beal wife of Charles Beal, & Thomas Tucker & William C. Tucker. --- Soon after death of testator, his dau. Elizabeth Beal died leaving husband Charles Beal & two children Joel & Mary Beal. -- Some time after her death, the testator's son Thomas Tucker died an infant intestate leaving no wife, child or other descendant. ---- Testator's son W. C. Tucker alone qualified as executor. --- On 10 Dec 1830, Elizabeth Tucker widow of testator, in consideration that her children & grandchildren have covenanted to pay all her debts, & in consideration that her children or their husbands, & grandchildren Joel & Mary Beal by their guardian Wm. C. Tucker, have covenanted to pay her annually during her lifetime, $7.14 each, has agreed to surrender to them all the property of every kind which belonged to her husband, reserving to herself for life one bed & furniture, relinquishing the right she has thereto as well under the will of her husband as under the statutes of distributions as one of the next of kin of her deceased son Thomas Tucker. --- Persons interested in the property desire that same be sold & debts of testator & Elizabeth Tucker may be paid out of the proceeds due of the sale, & residue divided among those entitled thereto.

The birthdates of the Joel Tucker Sr family
are calculated from ages shown in the 1850 Census: [1]

Name	Age	Calculated Birthdate
William C. Tucker	61	ca 1789
Dolly Clay	52	ca 1798
Joel W. Tucker	52	ca 1798
John C. Tucker	49	ca 1801
Amy Dews	48	ca 1802
George W. Tucker	44	ca 1806

SUMMARY: Joel Tucker Sr, son of George Tucker Sr & 2nd wf Catharine, b ca 1764-65 in Amelia Co, d ca 1820 in Halifax Co, Va, md 1788 in Amelia Co, Elizabeth Clemons, dau of William Clemons & wf Ama Clay, & had issue:

William C. Tucker b ca 1789, md Martha ____.

Dolly Tucker h ca 1798, md 1813 Charles Clay.

Joel W. (Worstnam) Tucker b ca 1798, md 1829 Judith Barber.

John C. Tucker b ca 1801, md 1824 Mary (Polly) R. Godby

Amy Tucker b ca 1802, md 1842 Nathaniel Dews.

Elizabeth A. Tucker b ca 1805, d prior to 1830, md 1821 Charles Beal.

George W. Tucker b ca 1806, md 1st Harriett P ____, 2nd Lisa ____.

Thomas Tucker, b after 1809, d prior to 1830, unmarried.

See separate chapter for each of the sons of Joel Tucker Sr & wife Elizabeth Clemons.

* * *

1. Chiarito, Marian Dodson, "1850 Census of Halifax County, Virginia"

TG136100 - WILLIAM C. TUCKER

MD MARTHA
SON OF JOEL TUCKER SR
MD ELIZABETH CLEMONS

HALIFAX CO., VA.

WB 12-50, wd 6 Dec 1820, wp 25 Dec 1820, will of Joel Tucker Sr - names: - Exrs: Son William C. Tucker and Ezekiel Pillow. - Wife Elizabeth Tucker - three daus. Dolly Clay, Elizabeth Tucker & Amy Tucker - Son John Tucker - Son George - Son Thomas - Son William C. Tucker - as I have heretofore given him that part of land allotted for him I now give him no land. - Son Worstnam Tucker.

The son Thomas Tucker, named in the will of Joel Tucker Sr, died without issue, and the land which he inherited (300 ac. from land tax records) reverted back to the estate of Joel Tucker and his heirs at law. Apparently the 145 ac. which Joel bought back from son William C. also remained in the estate. The surviving heirs apparently sold among themselves 147 ac. and 292 ac. as per the deeds following:

DB 24-229, 23 Apr 1813, Joel Tucker for $200., to his son William C. Tucker, 145 ac. on waters of Runaway Cr., it being the same conveyed from Robert Farnbrough to Joel Tucker with an addition of all the land btwn sd tract & the first br. of Runaway Cr. to the west. (See DB 21-307 for 100 ac. & possibly DB 18-396 for 40 ac. for Joel Tucker Sr. See also DB 27-36 below).

DB 27-36, 19 Jan 1818, William C. Tucker to his father Joel Tucker for $700., 145 ac. on waters of Runaway Cr., it being same tract conveyed by Robert Farnbrough to sd Joel Tucker, with an addition of all the land btwn sd tract & the first br. of Runaway Cr. to the west. (See DB 24-229 & DB 55-287)

NOTE: The meaning of the DB 24-229 and DB 27-36 is not clear, since Joel Tucker Sr stated in his will that he had already allotted land to his son William C. Tucker. Since Joel Tucker Sr bought back the 145 ac. from son William C. Tucker, for 3.5 times the amount he sold it for, perhaps the net result is that he gave him cash in lieu of land.

DB 55-287, 26 Nov 1853, John C. Tucker & wf Mary, Charles Clay & wf Dolly, Joel T. Beal & wf Ann, for $367.50, to William C. Tucker, Joel W. Tucker, & George W. Tucker, 147 ac., taken from the tract of land of the late Joel Tucker decd. (See DB 61-61)

DB 55-297, 18 Oct 1853, <u>William C. Tucker & wf Martha</u>, John C. Tucker & wf Mary, Joel W. Tucker & wf Judith, George W. Tucker & wf Lisa, Joel T. Beal & wf Ann, for $730., to Charles Clay, 292 ac. on Runaway Cr. (Note: Apparently this was the same as 300 ac. which Joel Tucker Sr willed to his son Thomas Tucker who died infant, and which reverted back to the estate & heirs of Joel Tucker Sr)

DB 61-61, 9 Nov 1867, pursuant to order July term 1867, commissioners divided land & assigned Lot No. 1 of 56 ac. to Judith Tucker, widow of Joel Tucker, and her children Shederick B. Tucker, Geo. W. Tucker, Dodson Tucker and Ann Foster formerly Tucker, & Elizabeth Tucker formerly Tucker; <u>lot No 2 of 62 ac. to Wm. C. Tucker</u>; and Lot No. 3 of 58 ac. to Geo. W. Tucker. (56 + 62 + 58 = 166 ac. See D13 55-287 for 147 ac.)

While the above deeds to which William C. Tucker was a party, involved the estate of his father Joel Tucker Sr, the following deeds pertain to William C. Tucker in his own right.

DB 24-492, 24 Jan 1814, rec 24 Jan 1814, Description of negro girl Betty, age 14 or 15, brought into the commonwealth by <u>William C. Tucker</u>.

DB 25-11, 15 Jun 1814, rec 25 Jul 1814, Description of slave girl Caty, age 9, brought into state by <u>William C. Tucker</u>.

DB 25-588, 31 Aug 1815, rec 15 Mar 1816. James Eastham, deputy sheriff of William Royall sheriff of Halifax Co., to <u>William C. Tucker</u> for $52.06, <u>50 ac.</u> (part of 230 ac. with delinquent taxes by Robert Davis).

DB 25-595, 31 Aug 1815, rec 16 Mar 1816, James Eastham, deputy sheriff of William Royall sheriff of Halifax Co., to <u>William C. Tucker</u> for $3.07, <u>19 ac.</u> (part of 400 ac. with delinquent taxes by Redman Cody). (See DB 28-77)

DB 28-77, 24 Aug 1819, rec 24 Aug 1819, <u>William C. Tucker</u> of Halifax Co. to Henry Wade Sr of Pittsylvania Co., for $4., <u>19 ac.</u>, being the 19 ac. sold off 400 ac. in name of Redman Cody & sold by James Eastham Deputy Sheriff for William Royall Sheriff, at Halifax Courthouse 31 Aug 1815, conveyed to sd Henry Wade Sr, such title invested in me by sd Eastham deed. (See DB 25-595)

DB 37-497, 25 Jan 1830, rec 25 Jan 1830, Royal Daniel Jr to secure debt to <u>William C Tucker</u>, sold to Davis G. Tuck, <u>298 1/2 ac on Banister Ri, formerly belonging to William C. Tucker</u>, bo road leading to Terry's bridge, Mrs. Daniel, Mrs. Petty, Mill Cr, Henry Thomas, William Trunklin.

DB 37-657, ___ Jan 1830, rec 28 Jun 1830, Frances Daniel to secure debt to <u>William C. Tucker</u>, sold to Davis G. Tuck, <u>150 3/4 ac, on Banister Ri, formerly belonging to William C. Tucker</u>, bo road to Terry's bridge, John Stevens, Mrs. Petty,

NOTE: The above two deeds, DB 37-497 & DB 37-657 refer to 298 1/2 ac + 150 3/4 ac. = 449 1/4 ac. on Banister Ri, as formerly belonging to William C. Tucker. No deeds were found for the purchase or sale by William C. Tucker for this land.

DB 42-224, 27 Feb 1835, rec 25 Mar 1835, William Holt, Clerk of Halifax Co. Court, to <u>William C. Tucker</u>, <u>126 ac.</u> on Aarons Cr, charged on the books of Commissioner of Revenue as James Burchen to raise tax charged hererto for year 1832.

DB 43-406, 5 Jul 1836, rec 25 Oct 1836, Irby Atkinson & wf Jane to <u>William C. Tucker</u> for $200., <u>100 ac</u> on waters of Hyco, bo Mrs Johnson.

DB 54-542, 29 Sep 1852, rec 1 Oct 1852, James L. Blackwell & wf Lucy, for $3,000., to <u>William P. Tucker & William C. Tucker</u>, <u>3 ac.</u> on b.s. Hyco Ri, with mill dam & mill house & other appurtenances, including one ac on south of Hyco adj dam & 2 ac on north side.

NOTE: This compiler did not further research deeds for William C. Tucker after 1852.

NOTE: Joel Tucker Sr, father of William C. Tucker, died in 1820. William C. Tucker was executor of his father's estate. Elizabeth Tucker, sister of William C. Tucker, md Charles Beal, and she died in 1830. William C. Tucker was appointed guardian of their infant children Joel Thomas Beal and Mary Beal. Mary Beal died in 1833. Charles Beal died in 1836, and William C. Tucker was administrator of his estate. William C. Tucker settled the estate of his father Joel Tucker Sr., the estate of his brother-in-law Charles Beal, and the guardianships of his neice Mary Beal and his nephew Joel Thomas Beal, as evidenced by the following deeds, minutes and administrations.

DB 31-639, rec. 27 Oct 1823: "On 16 Jun 1823, Charles Beal & Elizabeth A. Beal, formerly Elizabeth Tucker, sold for $500., the whole of their interest in the estate of Joel Tucker, deceased, except the lands of the father of the said Elizabeth Beal, formerly Elizabeth Tucker, to <u>William C. Tucker</u>." Wit: Richard Thornton, Joel W. Tucker, George W. Tucker.

M 4-273, Nov 1830, <u>William C. Tucker</u> is appointed guardian of Joel and Mary Beal, infant children of Charles Beal. George W. Tucker & Elisha Hodge surety & bond acknowledged in the penalty of $2,000.

M 3-296. 1830. The court doth order Wm. C. Tucker to render an account of his administration of the est. of Joel Tucker decd - - the court doth further order the commissioners - - assign to the plaintiff Amy Tucker, one negro as equal in value as may be to the negro hereto delivered to her sisters Dolly Clay and Elizabeth Beal respectively - - and also that they do ascertain the value of the slaves received by Elizabeth Beal - - and the court not deciding at this time, anything in relation to the alleged sale by Charles Beal to the defendant William C. Tucker, doth give liberty to either of the said parties to file a bill against the other for establishing his rights.

M 6-25, 1833. Mary Beal, one of the plaintiffs, having departed this life - order William C., Tucker - to pay - to Charles Beale in right of his wife Elizabeth Beale decd as the sole representative of his dau. Mary Beal decd, the sum of $303.55., with interest, & to Joel Beal the sum of $75.00, with interest; but out of the sum to be paid to Charles Beal, the sd William C. Tucker will retain the sum of $26.75 paid by him as the Guardian of the sd Mary Beal decd, and that he make report for a final decree.

M 6-162, 1834, An acct of Wm. C. Tucker, grdn of Joel Beal, ret. & rec.

M 6A-276, 1836, On motion of William C. Tucker certificate is granted him for obtaining - administration of the estate of Charles Beal decd.

M 12-89, 1844. It is ordered - to examine, state & settle the acct. current of William C. Tucker admr. of Charles Beal decd & report.

M 12-121, 1844, It is ordered that commissioner Terry do examine, state & settle the acct. current of William C. Tucker, admr of Charles Beal decd.

M 12-121, 1844, It is ordered that commissioner Terry do examine, state & settle the acct. current of Wm. C. Tucker Grdn of Joel Beal.

M 13-2, 1845, Acct current of Wm. C. Tucker Adm. of Charles Beal decd, ret. & ord. to lie one term. Acct current of same, guardian of Joel T. Beal, retd & OR.

M 13-20, 1845, An acct. current of Wm. C. Tucker, admr. of Charles Beal deed, no exception taken & OR.

WB 18-245. The inv. of est. of Charles Beal decd 25th day of Nov 1836: William C. Tucker adm.

WB 21-31. Agreeably to decree of July Court 1842, commissioner has stated & settled the guardian acct. of William C. Tucker, Guardian of Joel Beal. At court 25 Aug 1845, acct. curr. of William C. Tucker Guardian of Joel Beal was ret. & OR.

WB 21-41. At a court 25 Aug 1845, acct of <u>William C. Tucker, Adm. of Charles Beall</u> decd was ret. & OR. At another court on 22 Sep, no exceptions being taken, the sd acc. curr. was OR.

WB 30-606 16 Jun 1873, <u>will of William C. Tucker</u> names:
Granddaughter Isabella Tucker.
Grandson John W. Tucker.
Grandson Wilber F. Tucker.
Grandson William B. Tucker.
Grandson Walter Tucker.
<u>Son Walter S. Tucker</u>, appointed trustee for his children.
Granddaughter Fannie M. Jennings.
colored Wash Tucker.
<u>Brother George W. Tucker</u>.

MB 3-22, 14 Sep 1864, William P. Tucker, age 49, widowed, md Mildred H. Harris, age 45. Parents of groom <u>William C. & Martha</u>. Parents of bride Thomas H. & Ann L.

NOTE: This compiler could find no marriage record for the subject William C. Tucker, but his wife is identified as Martha in many deeds cited. Since she was not mentioned in his will, she most probably died prior to 1873. Although only one son, Walter S. Tucker, is named in his will, the above marriage record indicates that William C. & Martha Tucker had another son named William P. Tucker, age 49 in 1864. He was included in the 1850 census as age 33, so he was b ca 1815-17. There are many deeds in Halifax Co, VA in the name of William P. Tucker & Tucker & Rogers, which this compiler did not research.

<u>The birthdates of the William C. Tucker family are calculated from ages shown in the 1850 Census:</u> [2]

Name	Age	Calculated Birthdate	
<u>Southern District</u>	--	---	---
<u>Household 518</u>	--	---	---
William C. Tucker	61	ca 1789	
Martha	55	ca 1795	
Walter S.	17	ca 1833	
Household 1003			
William P. Tucker	33	ca 1817	Merchant
Ann M.	27	ca 1823	
Martha F.	10	ca 1840	
Lorenzo L.	8	ca 1842	

SUMMARY: William C. Tucker, son of Joel Tucker Sr & wf Elizabeth Clemons, b ca 1789 in Lunenburg Co., d 1873 in Halifax Co. Va., md Martha ____, b ca 1795, d before 1873, & had issue:

William P. Tucker, b ca 1815-17, md 1st Ann M. ____, md 2nd 1864 Mildred H. Harris, & had issue:

1. Martha F. Tucker b ca 1840.

2. Lorenzo L. Tucker b ca 1842.

Walter S. Tucker b ca 1833, & had issue:

1. Isabella Tucker

2. John W. Tucker

3. Wilber F. Tucker

4. William B. Tucker

5. Walter Tucker

6. Fannie M. Tucker md Jennings.

* * *

2. Chiarito, Marian Dodson, "1850 Census of Halifax County, Va."

TG136200 - JOEL W. TUCKER

MD JUDITH BARBER
SON OF JOEL TUCKER SR.
MD ELIZABETH CLEMONS

HALIFAX CO. VA.

WB 12-50, wd 6 Dec 1820, wp 25 Dec 1820, <u>will of Joel Tucker Sr</u> - names: - Exrs: Son William C. Tucker and Ezekiel Pillow. - <u>Wife Elizabeth Tucker</u> - three daus. Dolly Clay, Elizabeth Tucker & Amy Tucker - Son John Tucker - Son George - Son Thomas - Son William C. Tucker - <u>Son Worstnam Tucker - 200 ac. beg. at br. running into Runaway Cr.</u> - Son Thomas Tucker.

The son Worstnam Tucker, named in the will of Joel Tucker Sr, is the same as Joel W. Tucker who married Judith Barber.

MB 1-132, 11 Aug 1829, Joel W. Tucker md Judith Barber. Bondsman & Witness, David Barber. Signer, Shadrack Barber, father.

NOTE: The above marriage is recorded in the Halifax Co. VA male index and female index to marriages, and in Marriage Register Book 1, in the name of "John W. Tucker". However, the original marriage record is plainly written in two places as "Joel W. Tucker", but was folded and labeled on the outside as John W. Tucker. This compiler called this error to the attention of the Court Clerk in September 1985, who noted the error on the indexes and register.

MB 1-44, 25 Dec 1800, Shadrack Barber md Sally Winfree.

MB 2-73, 14 Sep 1871, Thomas Barber, widower, md Patsy A. Martin. His parents Shadrick & Sallie. Her parents Zachariah & Edy.

WB 33-313, will of Thomas Barber, names wife Patsy Barber, brother David Barber, niece dau of Silas Barber, <u>children of Judith Tucker</u> & children of Newton Barber decd.

DB 41-298, 21 Dec 1833(?), rec 23 Dec 1823(?), (1) Joshua P. Farmer, (2) <u>Joel W. Tucker</u>, (3) Samuel B. Pillow, whereas Joshua P. Farmer is indebted to Sa. B. Pillow for $35., pledge household furniture, etc.

DB 44-59, 26 May 1837, rec 30 May 1837, (1) <u>Joel W. Tucker & wf</u> (2) Zebedee Petty (3) Peter Barksdale & c. (4) James Adkisson & c., for $667.99 by bond, & to James Adkisson & c. for $454.40 by bond, also for $164.96 by bond as security for Shadrick Barber --- <u>Joel W. Tucker</u> to secure debts, sold to Zebedee Petty, <u>200 ac. on Runaway. Cr.</u> adj John F. Farmer & others, Negro man Godfrey age 33, negro girl Sally age 12, horses, cattle, household furniture, farm equipment, tobacco, corn, etc. --- <u>in trust</u>. Wit: Dabney Glass, P. B. Sydnor, Jesse Adams. (SJJ—DB 44-

520 & DB 46-425).

DB 44-520, 23 Dec 1837, rec 22 Jan 1838, (1) <u>Joel W. Tucker</u> (2) Essos(?) H. Clarke (3) Wm. Jennings, whereas sd Tucker is indebted to sd Jennings, for $97.00, sd Tucker sold to sd Clarke, negro man Godfrey, sd Tucker to remain in possession of sd property until default is made. Wit: Christopher Nunnally, R. Jennings, Peter Barksdale.

DB 46-425, 23 Dec 1840, rec 28 Dec 1840, Zebedee Petty to Richard Thornton, <u>204.5 ac. on Runaway Cr., it being the land conveyed to Zebedee Petty by. Joel W. Tucker & wf 25 May 1837, and disposed of at public auction to pay debt</u>. (Note: recorded as 200 ac. in WB 12-50 & DB 44-59).

DB 52-549, 26 Jun 1848, rec 26 Jun 1848, <u>Joel W. Tucker,</u> to secure debts to William C. Tucker, George W. Tucker, John C. Tucker, sold to Richard Thornton, <u>my interest in undivided land of est of Joel Tucker decd.</u>, bo by Richard Thornton, Claibon Tucker, Micajah Wyatt & others, plus 2 cows & calves, two beds & furniture, one cupboard, two chests, one folding table, dressing table, nine chairs, together with all household furniture, plantation tools, growing crops.

The son Thomas Tucker, named in the will of Joel Tucker Sr, died without issue, and the land which he inherited (300 ac. from land tax records) reverted back to the estate of Joel Tucker and his heirs at law. Apparently the 145 ac. which Joel Sr bought back from son William C. also remained in the estate. The surviving heirs apparently sold among themselves 147 ac. and 292 ac.

DB 55-287, 26 Nov 1853, John C. Tucker & wf Mary, Charles Clay & wf Dolly, Joel T. Beal & wf Ann, for $367.50, to William C. Tucker, <u>Joel W. Tucker,</u> & George W. Tucker, 147 ac., taken from the tract of-land of the late Joel Tucker decd. (See DB 61-61 for 56 + 62 + 58 = 166 ac.)

DB 55-297, 18 Oct 1853, William C. Tucker & wf Martha, John C. Tucker & wf Mary, <u>Joel W. Tucker & wf Judith</u>, George W. Tucker & wf Lisa, Joel T. Beal & wf Ann, for $730., to Charles Clay, 292 ac. on Runaway Cr.

This compiler did not research what happened to Joel W. Tucker & wf Judith after he pledged the 200 ac. inherited from his father to pay debts. However, from the following deed, it appears that Joel W. Tucker d ca 1867.

The land tax records show Judith Tucker holding 147 ac. on Childrey Cr. for life from 1858-1865. Could this possibly be the same 147 ac. which was bought jointly by her husband Joel W. Tucker and his brothers William C. Tucker & George W. Tucker in 1853 (DB 55-287)? And could it possibly be the same land which was divided between them as

166 ac. in 1867 (DB 61-61 below)?

DB 61-61, 9 Nov 1867, pursuant to order July term 1867, commissioners divided land & assigned Lot No. 1 of 56 ac. to Judith Tucker, widow of Joel Tucker, and her children Shederick B. Tucker, Geo. W Tucker, Dodson Tucker and Ann Foster formerly Tucker, & Elizabeth Tucker formerly Tucker; lot No 2 of 62 ac. to Wm. C. Tucker; and Lot No. 3 of 58 ac. to Geo. W. Tucker. (56 62 f 58 = 166 ac. See DB 55-287 for 147 ac.)

The birthdates of the Joel W. Tucker family are calculated from ages shown in the 1850 Census: [3]

Name	Age	Calculated Birthdate
Household # 846	--	---
Joel W. Tucker	52	ca 1798
Judith	40	ca 1810
Shadrick	16	ca 1834
George	14	ca 1836
Ann	12	ca 1838
Elizabeth	10	ca 1840
Elias	8	ca 1842

MB 3-18, 22 Nov 1861, George W. Tucker age 25, md Frances Adams widow age 37. Parents of groom Joel W. & Judith Tucker. Parents of bride Dudley & Polly Glass.

MB 3-7, 28 Aug 1865, Shaderick B. Tucker age 31, md Catherine S. Craddock age 25 with parents consent.

SUMMARY: Joel W. Tucker, son of Joel Tucker Sr & wf Elizabeth Clemons, b ca 1798 in Lunenhurg Co, Va., d ca 1867 in Halifax Co. Va., md Judith Barber, dau of Shadrack Barber & wf Sally Winfree, and had issue:

Shaderick B. Tucker b 1834, md 1865 Catherine S. Craddock.

George W. Tucker b 1836, md 1861 Frances Adams, widow, dau of Dudley Glass & wf Polly.

Ann Tucker b 1838, md _____ Foster.

Elizabeth Tucker b 1840, md _____ Tucker.

Elias Tucker b 1842.

Dodson Tucker.

* * *

3. Chiarito, Marian Dodson, "1850 Census of Halifax County, Virginia", 1982

TG136300 - JOHN C. TUCKER

MD MARY (POLLY) R. GODBY
SON OF JOEL TUCKER SR
MD ELIZABETH CLEMONS

HALIFAX CO. VA.

WB 12-50, wd 6 Dec 1820, wp 25 Dec 1820, will of Joel Tucker Sr - names: - Son William C. Tucker and Ezekiel Pillow. - Wife Elizabeth Tucker - three daus. Dolly Clay, Elizabeth Tucker & Amy Tucker - Son John Tucker - negro boy Sonie. Son George - Son Thomas - Son William C. Tucker - Son Worstnam Tucker - Son Thomas Tucker - Sons John & George Tucker - all the land I bought of Joshua Clay, (except what have given to my daus.).

MB 1-117, 22 Oct 1824. John C. Tucker md Polly R. Godby, signed by Christian Godby, parent, Bondsman: Archibald Comer Jr.

Polly R. Godby, also known as Mary, was the daughter of Rufus Russell Godby who married Christian (Kitty) Lacy. Christian (Kitty) Lacy was the daughter of Thomas Lacy Sr who married Catherine Evans. Catherine Evans was the daughter of John Evans of Goochland Co.

WB 13-23,rec 25 Aug 1823, will of Russell Godby of Halifax Co, Va. - names: - wf Christian Godby - dau Martha Cole - dau Caty Comer - dau Nancy Godby - dau Polly Godby - grandson Edmund Godby.

WB 6-422, rec 12 Dec 1802, will of Thomas Lacy Sr - names: - children of my deceased son Elisha Lacy: Tatum, Elisha, Thomas & Betsy Epps Lacy. - son Matthew Lacy - gr-dau Betsy Roberts, dau of sd Matthew Lacy - son Reubin Lacy - dau Drucilla Pound - dau Magdaline Abbott - dau Christian Godby - dau Sally King.

Lacy [1] identified the subject Thomas Lacy as "Thomas Lacy IV of Halifax County Virginia, son of Thomas Lacy III (ca 1705/8-), the elder son of Thomas Lacy II (ca 1683/4-) & Ann (Burnley) Lacy, son of Thomas Lacy I of New Kent & Hanover Counties, Va, immigrant from Wales. - Thomas Lacy IV b ca 1728 possibly Hanover Co, Va, d 12-12-1802 Halifax Co, Va. - md Catherine Evans ca 1749 in Goochland Co, the residence of their parents - who was dau of John Evans a Welshman - whose will rec 20 May 1755, Goochland Co WB 7-3, named my son-in-law Thomas Lacy and my dau Catheren his wife."

DB 44-558, 1 Mar 1838, John C. Tucker & wf Mary R. for $218.75, sold to Thomas Lacy, one-fourth part of 250 ac., which formerly belonged to estate of Russell Godby decd, & bo. by Archer Comer, Joseph C. Terry, Allen Willingham, Lacy Epps & others.

The number acres of land which Joel Tucker Sr willed jointly to his sons John & George Tucker is uncertain. Although the will stated it was "all the land I bought of Joshua Clay except that given to daughters", the DB 27-274 from Joshua Clay did not identify number of acres. The land tax book of 1819 showed Joel Tucker holding 300 ac. on Childrey Cr., from J. Clay decd. But the land tax book of 1822 showed John & George Tucker holding 405 ac. However, in DB 46-265 below, George sold to John 211 ac., which may have been George's portion of the land inherited jointly from their father.

DB 46-265, 30 Apr 1840, George W. Tucker & wf Harriett P. for $600., sold to <u>John C. Tucker, 211 ac.</u> on headwaters of Childrey Cr.

DB 51-506, 26 Oct 1846, Archibald Rowlett & wf Rebecca, for $75., to <u>John C. Tucker 37 1/2 ac.</u> bo. James Tucker, Frederick Clay, John C. Tucker & others.

The son Thomas Tucker, named in the will of Joel Tucker Sr, died without issue, and the land which he inherited (300 ac. from land tax records) reverted back to the estate of Joel Tucker and his heirs at law. Apparently the 145 ac. which Joel bought back from son William C. also remained in the estate. The surviving heirs apparently sold among themselves 147 ac. and 292 ac. as per the two deeds following:

DB 55-287, 26 Nov 1853, <u>John C. Tucker & wf Mary</u>, Charles Clay & wf Dolly, Joel T. Beal & wf Ann, for $367.50, to William C. Tucker, Joel W. Tucker, & George W. Tucker, 147 ac., taken from the tract of land of the late Joel Tucker decd.

DB 55-297, 18 Oct 1853, William C. Tucker & wf Martha, <u>John C. Tucker & wf Mary</u>, Joel W. Tucker & wf Judith, George W. Tucker & wf Lisa, Joel T. Beal & wf Ann, for $730., to Charles Clay, 292 ac. on Runaway Cr.

DB 57-400, 19 Dec 1857, Henry C. Clarke & wf Elizabeth, for $360., to <u>John C. Tucker, 126 ac.</u>, adj. Robert Jennings & D. Richard Thornton on waters of Childrey Cr. (See DB 59-398).

DB 59-398, 21 May 1861, <u>John C. Tucker & wf Polly</u>, for $175., to James H. Davis, all the land on which he now resides, containing <u>126 ac.</u> bo. by Carr & Poindexter, Robert Jennings, Richard Thornton est & Alexander Peters' children. (See DB 57-400).

DB 62-417, 12 Dec 1871, <u>John C. Tucker & wf sold to</u> Harriett Tucker, <u>200 ac.</u>

DB 62-418, 8 Dec 1871, <u>John C. Tucker</u> for $875., to Joel T. Beal & James H. Davis, <u>all my lands except the part sold to Harriett R. Tucker, containing, 293 ac.</u>.

DB 62-663, 3 May 1872. Survey & division of lands belonging to <u>John C. Tucker</u>, conveyed by deed to his children & lying on the waters of Childrey Cr., Halifax Co. Va., containing <u>566 ac.</u>:

    Lot # 1 assigned to Harriett Tucker, containing 204 ac.

    Lot # 2 assigned to James Davis, containing 173 ac.

    Lot # 3 assigned to Joel T. Beal, containing 189 ac.

<u>The birthdates of the John C. Tucker family</u>
<u>are calculated from ages shown in the 1850 Census:</u> [2]

Name	Age	Calculated Birthdate
Household # 772	---	---
John C. Tucker	49	ca 1801
Polly	46	ca 1804
Harriett R.	19	ca 1831
Gabriel H.	12	ca 1838
James Davis	29	ca 1821
Catharine L.	18	ca 1832
Household # 773	---	---
Joel T. Beal	27	ca 1823
Elizabeth A.	23	ca 1827
Charles L.	4	ca 1846
Joshua R.	2	ca 1848
Joel P. Tucker	18	ca 1832

MB 1-176 7 Dec 1844, Joel T. Beal md Elizabeth Ann Tucker. (See "The Beale Family of Halifax County, Virginia", 1978, by B. DeRoy Beale)

MB 1-191 7 Mar 1850, James Davis md Catharine L. Tucker.

The family cemetery of Joel T. Beale is located on his homeplace on Route 603, just east of the community of Republican Grove, and includes the following tombstone inscriptions:

    Joel T. Beale, born Oct 20, 1817, died Jun 15, 1901.

    Annie E. Beale, born Mar 15, 1820, died May 18, 1878.

NOTE: The birthdates on the tombstones of both are in error. Joel T. Beale was most probably b ca 1823 as per the 1850 census. His parents Charles Beal & wf Elizabeth A. Tucker were md Dec 17, 1821 (MB 1-105). Annie E. (Tucker) Beale was most probably b ca 1827 as per 1850 census. Her parents, the subject John C. Tucker & wf Mary (Polly) R. Godby were md Oct 22, 1824 (MB 1-117). Elizabeth Ann Tucker and Annie E. Beale are one and the same person. Also located in this cemetery are the unmarked graves of Joel & Elizabeth Ann Beale's oldest son, Charles Lacy Beale and his wf Adeline M. Tucker, dau of James Tucker & wf Sarah Bass.

SUMMARY: John C. Tucker, son of Joel Tucker Sr & wf Elizabeth

Clemons, b ca 1801, d 1872, md 1824 Mary (Polly) R. Godby, b ca 1804, dau of Rufus Russell Godby & wf Christian (Kitty) Lacy, and had issue:

Elizabeth Ann (or Annie E) Tucker b ca 1827, md 1844 Joel Thomas Beale b ca 1823, son of Charles Beal & wf Elizabeth Tucker.

Harriett R. Tucker b ca 1831, never married.

Catharine L. Tucker b ca 1832, md 1850 James H. Davis b ca 1821.

Gabriel H. Tucker b ca 1838, probably died infant after 1850.

NOTE FROM THIS COMPILER:

Shadrack Beal (c1764-1815) & wf Mary (Molly) Farris (dau of Joseph Farris Sr) were my gr-gr-gr-grandparents.

Charles Beal (ca1790-1836) & wf Elizabeth Tucker (dau of Joel Tucker & wf Elizabeth Clemons) were my gr-gr-grandparents.

Joel Thomas Beale (1823-1901) & wf Elizabeth Ann Tucker (dau of John C. Tucker & wf Mary (Polly) R. Godby) were my gr-grandparents.

Charles Lacy Beale (1846-1885) & wf Adeline Tucker (dau of James Tucker & wf Sarah (Sally) Bass) were my grandparents.

Charlie Joel Beale (1876-1958) & wf Anna Lee Owen (dau of Henry Edmund Owen & wf Alice Ann Clements) were my parents.

I, being Barkley DeRoy Beale (1924-). (See "The Beale Family of Halifax County, Virginia", 1978)

* * *

1. Lacey, Wesley Hubert & Lacy, Howell Edison, "The Thomas Lacy III Family of Hanover and Buckingham Counties, Virginia", 1983

2. Chiarito, Marian Dodson, "1850 Census of Halifax County, Virginia"

TG136400 - GEORGE W. TUCKER
MD 1ST HARRIETT P
MD 2ND LISA
SON OF JOEL TUCKER SR
MD ELIZABETH CLEMONS

HALIFAX CO. VA.

WB 12-50, wd 6 Dec 1820, wp 25 Dec 1820, <u>will of Joel Tucker Sr</u> - names: - Exrs: Son William C. Tucker and Ezekiel Pillow. - <u>Wife Elizabeth Tucker</u> - three daus. Dolly Clay, Elizabeth Tucker & Amy Tucker - <u>Son George - negro boy Ase</u> - Son Thomas - Son William C. Tucker - Son Worstnam Tucker - Son Thomas Tucker - <u>Sons John & George Tucker - all the land I bought of Joshua Clay. (except what I have given to my daus.).</u>

The number acres of land which Joel Tucker Sr willed jointly to his sons John & George Tucker is uncertain. Although the will stated it was "all the land I bought of Joshua Clay except that given to daughters", the DB 27-274 from Joshua Clay did not identify number of acres. The land tax book of 1819 showed Joel Tucker holding 300 ac. on Childrey Cr., from J. Clay decd. But, the land tax hook of 1822 showed John & George Tucker holding 405 ac. However, in DB 46-265 below, George sold to John 211 ac., which may have been George's portion of the land inherited jointly from their father. Subsequently, he bought land and moved to the Southern District of Halifax Co., Va.

DB 46-265, 30 Apr 1840, <u>George W. Tucker & wf Harriett P.</u> for $600., to John C. Tucker, <u>211 ac.</u> on headwaters of Childrey Cr.

DB 51-577, 29 Dec 1846, rec 14 Jan 1847, Robert M. Scott & wf Susan W. Scott, to <u>George W. Tucker</u>, for $215., <u>21.5 ac.</u> south of Dan Ri, north of Milton road & west of M__?__ Rd.

DB 54-566, 4 Aug 1852, rec 12 Nov 1852, Jno T Garland & wf Christiana J. Garland, George Williamson & wf Eliza A. Williamson of Caswell Co., N.C., for $180., to <u>George W. Tucker, 60 ac.</u> on s.s. of Dan Ri. in Halifax Co., Va., on the Main Stage Road leading fr Halifax Courthouse to Milton, N.C., adj sd George W. Tucker, __?__, Byrd, Rogers & c.

DB 55-228, 28 Sep 1853, rec 10 Oct 1853, Samuel Pate & wf Susan, for "Three hundred & fifty one 12 1/2 dollars" (sic) to <u>George W. Tucker, 17 89/160 ac</u> on s.s. Dan Ri., east of & adj road leading from the Milton Stage Road to Roxboro, bo. Susan Thaxton, Bo__?__.

194

DB 55-253, 6 Apr 1853, rec 24 Nov 1853, Bedford Brown & wf Mary L. Brown of Fauquier Co, Va., for $30., to George W. Tucker, all their interest, being 7.5 ac. in a certain undivided tract of land known as the Edwards tract of 60 ac., the interest conveyed being 1/4 part of the 1/2 which was devised by Mrs. Isabella Glenn decd to sd Mary L. Brown, on main road fr Rogers Ferry in Halifax Co., Va. to Milton, N.C., adj Byrd Rogers, George W. Tucker.

The son Thomas Tucker, named in the will of Joel Tucker Sr, died without issue, and the land which he inherited (300 ac. from land tax records) reverted back to the estate of Joel Tucker and his heirs at law. Apparently the 145 ac. which Joel Sr bought back from son William C. also remained in the estate. The surviving heirs apparently sold among themselves 147 ac. and 292 ac. as per the two deeds following:

DB 55-287, 26 Nov 1853, John C. Tucker & wf Mary, Charles Clay & wf Dolly, Joel T. Beal & wf Ann, for $367.50, to William C. Tucker, Joel W. Tucker, & George W. Tucker, 147 ac., taken from the tract of land of the late Joel Tucker decd.

DB 55-297, 18 Oct 1853, William C. Tucker & wf Martha, John C. Tucker & wf Mary, Joel W. Tucker & wf Judith, George W. Tucker & wf Lisa, Joel T. Beal & wf Ann, for $730., to Charles Clay, 292 ac. on Runaway Cr.

DB 61-61, 9 Nov 1867, pursuant to order July term 1867, commissioners divided land & assigned Lot No. 1 of 56 ac. to Judith Tucker, widow of .Joel Tucker, and her children Shederick B. Tucker, Geo. W. Tucker, Dodson Tucker and Ann Foster formerly Tucker, & Elizabeth Tucker formerly Tucker; lot No 2 of 62 ac. to Wm. C. Tucker; and Lot No. 3 of 58 ac. to Geo. W. Tucker. (56 + 62 + 58 = 166 ac. See DB 55-287 for 147 ac.)

Apparently George W. Tucker was married twice. DB 46-265 in 1840 records his wife's name as Harriet P. Apparently she died prior to 1850, for she was not listed with him in the 1850 census. DB 55-297, in 1853 records his wife's name as Lisa. Neither marriage for this George W. Tucker is recorded in Halifax Co. However, the marriage of his son William A. Tucker is recorded.

The birthdates of the George W. Tucker family
are calculated from ages shown in the 1850 Census: [3]

Name	Age	Calculated Birthdate
George W. Tucker	44	ca 1806
Martha A.	20	ca 1830
William A.	19	ca 1831
Elizabeth M.	13	ca 1837

The birthdates of the George W. Tucker family
are calculated from ages shown in the 1850 Census: [3]

Name	Age	Calculated Birthdate
Mary J.	8	ca 1842

MB 3-12, 25 Jan 1859, <u>Wm, A. Tucker</u>, age 25, md Emma S. Bruce, age 25. <u>Parents of groom Geo. W. & H. P. Tucker</u>. Parents of bride Edward & H Bruce.

SUMMARY: George W. Tucker, son of Joel Tucker Sr & wf Elizabeth Clemons, b ca 1806, md 1st ca 1829, Harriett P ____ d before 1850, md 2nd before 1853 Lisa ____ and had issue by his 1st wf:

Martha A. Tucker b ca 1830.

William A. Tucker, b ca 1831, md 1859 Emma S. Bruce, dau of Edward Bruce.

Elizabeth M. Tucker b ca 1837.

Mary J. Tucker b ca 1842.

* * *

3. Chiarito, Marian Dodson, "1850 Census of Halifax County, Virginia", 1982.

TG136500 - THOMAS TUCKER
(UNMARRIED)
SON OF JOEL TUCKER SR
MD ELIZABETH CLEMONS

HALIFAX CO. VA.

WB 12-50, wd 6 Dec 1820, wp 25 Dec 1820, will of Joel Tucker Sr - names: - Exrs: Son William C. Tucker and Ezekiel Pillow. - Wife Elizabeth Tucker - three daus. Dolly Clay, Elizabeth Tucker & Amy Tucker Son John Tucker - Son George - Son Thomas - two negro children John & Edmund. - Son William C. Tucker - Son Worstnam Tucker - Son Thomas Tucker - remainder of tract whereon I now live.

Land Tax Book of Halifax Co. for 1822, 1823 & 1824 showed Thomas Tucker holding 300 ac. on Childrey Cr.

Chancery Court Suit - Beale vs Tucker, Box 12, 1846 -- Joel Tucker died some years ago, leaving widow Elizabeth Tucker & children Dolly Clay, John Tucker, George Tucker, Amy Tucker & Joel Tucker, & Elizabeth Beal wife of Charles Beal, & Thomas Tucker & William C. Tucker. --- Soon after death of testator, his dau. Elizabeth Beal died leaving husband Charles Beal & two children Joel & Mary Beal. --- Some time after her death, the testator's son Thomas Tucker died an infant intestate leaving no wife, child or other descendant. --- Testator's son W. C. Tucker alone qualified as executor. --- On 10 Dec 1830, Elizabeth Tucker widow of testator, in consideration that her children & grandchildren have covenanted to pay all her debts, & in consideration that her children or their husbands, & grandchildren Joel & Mary Beal by their guardian Wm. C. Tucker, have covenanted to pay her annually during her lifetime, $7.14 each, has agreed to surrencer to them all the property of every kind which belonged to her husband, reserving to herself for life one bed & furniture, relinquishing. the right she has thereto as well under the will of her husband as under the statutes of distributions as one of the next of kin of her deceased son Thomas Tucker. -- Persons interested in the property desire that same be sold & debts of testator & Elizabeth Tucker may be paid out of the proceeds due of the sale, & residue divided among those entitled thereto.

Since Thomas Tucker died without issue, and his mother relinquished any right to his distribution, the land which he owned (300 ac. from land tax records) reverted back to the estate of Joel Tucker Sr and his heirs at law. Since this action was taken by Elizabeth Tucker in Dec 1830, Thomas Tucker died prior to that date as a legal infant, never having attained age 21; therefore he was born probably several years after 1809.

SUMMARY: Thomas Tucker, son of Joel Tucker Sr & wf Elizabeth Clemons, b after 1809, d before 1830 unmarried.

TG137000 - LEWELLING TUCKER

MD URSULLA PETTIPOOL
SON OF GEORGE TUCKER SR
MD 1ST FRANCES
MD 2ND CATHARINE

LUNENBURG CO. VA.

WB 3-152, wd 25 Sep 1780, wp 11 Mar 1784, "I, <u>George Tucker the elder of Lunenburg Co.</u>" - names - <u>Wife Catharine</u> - <u>Sons Joel, Lew & Robert Tucker - negro Ned to be divided equally bet. them</u>. - <u>Son Lew - negro woman to be sold by exr. & money divided after paying cash legacies, the balance to him (Lew)</u>. - Dau. Milly Clay - Dau. Biddy Tucker - <u>Son Lew Tucker - negro boy Isaac</u>. - Son William Tucker - Dau. Fanny Coleman - Sons Henry, George & Joseph Tucker - <u>Five youngest children</u>: Joel, <u>Lew</u>, Robert, Milly Clay & Biddy - rest & residue of real & pers. est.

> CODICIL - 30 Dec 1783 - the 5 pounds devised my son George, he being dead, I devise to my <u>4 last children</u>, namely, Obedience, Joel, <u>Lew</u> & Robert & their heirs.

PERSONAL TAX RECORDS

1783	George Tucker, Joel Tucker, Lewelling Tucker 6 white tithes, 6 negroes.
1784	Catharine Tucker, Lewelling, Joel & Robert Tucker.
1785 - 1814	Lewelling Tucker was listed as a separate household from 1785 through 1814.

LAND TAX RECORDS

1793	Lewellin Tucker	182
1794	Lewellin Tucker	182
1798	Lewelling Tucker	200
1799	Lewelling Tucker	200
1800	Lew Tucker	200

George Tucker did not deed or will any land to his son Lewelling Tucker in either Amelia or Lunenburg Co. Lewelling was among the four last children of George & his 2nd wf Catharine, was b in Amelia Co, and was first listed as a 16-yr-up tithahle in the household of his father in 1783 in Lunenburg Co. His father died in 1784 and he was listed with his mother Catharine Tucker in 1784. He was listed as a separate household beginning in 1785, though he may not have been age 21 at that time. If he was age 21 in 1785, then he was born ca 1764. However, if he was age 16 in 1783, then he was born ca 1767, and was most likely age 21 when he married in 1788.

MB 3-309, 24 Jan 1788, Lew Tucker md Assula Pettipool, by Thomas Crymes.

DB 16-295, 14 Feb 1793. Isaac & Ann Brizendine of Charlotte Co., Va., to Lewelling Tucker of Lunenburg Co., 182 ac. for L60., on br. of Couches Cr., adj Joseph Smith, Thos. Dupree, Joseph Smith, John Edmunds, James Cooper & Thos. Stevenson. Wit: Richard Brizendine, Thos. Tisdale, Wm. Tisdale. (See DB 16-470).

DB 16-470, 12 Jun 1794, rec 12 Jun 1794, Lewelling Tucker & wf Ursuley, to Joseph Smith Senr, for L65., 182 ac. on branches of Couches Cr. joining Joseph Smith & Susanna Dupree on the south, Thomas Edmunds on the west, James Cooper on the north & Thomas Stevenson on the east. Wit: John Smith, Branch Jones, Tomy Bigger. S/ Lewelling Tucker, Ursuley x Tucker. (See DB 16-295)

DB 17-510, 17 Jun 1797, rec 13 Jul 1797, James Cooper & wf Frances to Lieu Tucker (perhaps Lewelling Tucker), for L135., 200 ac., bo. Peter Reaves, William Tucker, John Smith, Thomas Lowry & Thomas Edmunds. Wit: Geo. Craighead, James Cooper, Elared Williams, Richard Stone. S/ James Cooper, Frances Cooper, who relinq dower right.

DB 18-224-A, 15 Aug 1800, Lewelling Tucker & wf Ursley to John Smith, 100 ac., bo. sd Smith, Thomas _____, Joshua _____, Nathan _____, Thomas Edwards. (Note: How Lewelling Tucker obtained this 100 ac. is not clear. It may be part of the 200 ac. bought of James Cooper by DB 17-510).

DB 18-256-A. 26 Nov 1800, rec. 9 Apr 1801, Pleasant & Nancy Craddock to Lewelling Tucker of Lunenburg Co., 151 ac., bo. John Gordon, the legatee of John Neal decd, Peter Saunders, William Craighead. (See DB 19-70, DB 19-233A for 100 ac. & DB 21-115 for 51 ac.)

DB 19-70, 9 Jul 1801, rec 11 Feb 1802, Lewelling Tucker to secure debt to Pleasant Craddock, sold to Joseph Yarbrough, 151 ac., bo John Gordon, the legatees of John Neal, Peter Landrum, ____ Craighead Sen, & ____ deGraffenreid. (See DB 18-256-A)

NOTE: Apparently the above debt was paid and deed became void. See DB 19-233A & DB 21-115.

DB 19-233A, 12 Apr 1804, rec 19 Apr 1804, Lewellin Tucker & wf Ursely, for $733., to Jaimy Vaughan, 100 ac. on Reedy Cr. (See DB 18-256A)

DB 21-45A, 24 Apr 1804, Ursely Tucker, wf of Lewellin Tucker relinquish dower right to land conveyed to Jaimy Vaughan on 12 Apr 1804.

DB 21-115, 4 Mar 1807, rec 10 Sep 1807, <u>Lewelling Tucker & wf Urcillia</u>, for $300., to Josiah Alderson, <u>51 ac.</u> whereon Lewelling Tucker now lives, bo. Peter Lamkin, Jno. Gordon, Tocharnir Graffenreidt. (See DB 18-256A)

DB 22-24A, 1 Jul 1808, rec. 9 Feb 1809. <u>Lew Tucker,</u> to secure debt to Horatio Winn, sold to Richard Ellis, trustee, one negro slave named Pat and her future increase.

DB 22-57, 12 Oct 1809, <u>Ursula Tucker wf of Lewelling Tucker</u> relinq dower right to 51 ac. sold to Josiah Alderson on 14 Mar 1807. (See DB 21-115)

HALIFAX CO. VA.

MB 1-69, 29 Apr 1808, <u>Lewallen Tucker md Nancy Kirk.</u> Bondsman William Kirk.

DB 22-164, __ Aug 1809, rec 28 Aug 1809. Thomas Dodson Jr & wf Mary to <u>Lewalin</u> Tucker, both of Halifax Co., Va., for L140., <u>217 ac.</u> on Hunting Cr., bo. Palmer, Gordon. S/ Thomas Dodson Jr.

DB 23-261, 28 Oct 1811, rec 25 Nov 1811. <u>Lewallen Tucker</u> of Halifax Co., to Charles Gilcrist of Campbell Co., for L154., <u>270 ac.</u> on Hunting Cr., bo. Legon, Seamore, Wallis, Hudson. S/ Lewallen x Tucker. Wit: James Eastham, Thomas Dobson Sr.

NOTE: Since "Lewallen" Tucker married in Halifax in 1808, and "Lewelling" Tucker of Lunenburg still had wife Ursula in 1809 (DB 22-57), they do not appear to be one and the same person. They may be father and son, but this was not further researched by this compiler.

SUMMARY: Lewelling (Lew) Tucker, son of George Tucker Sr & 2nd wf Catherine ____, b ca 1767 in Amelia Co, md ca 1788 in Lunenburg Co., Ursulla Pettipool.

TG138000 - ROBERT TUCKER (2)

MD SARAH SMITH
SON OF GEORGE TUCKER SR
MD 1ST FRANCES
MD 2ND CATHARINE

NOTE: George Tucker md 1st Frances, and their son Robert (1) was born in 1733, md Martha Keatts, and d 1765. George Tucker md 2nd Catharine, and their son Robert (2) was born after 1765, md Sarah (Sally) Smith.

LUNENBURG CO. VA.

DB 13-68, 26 Sep 1777, rec 18 Jan 1778, William Davis of Amelia Co., to George Tucker of sd Co., for L230., 199 ac. in Lunenburg Co., bo. Ward Hudson, Richard Ingram, Duprey, Brizendine, Davis, Edmund. Wit: John Cureton Jr, William Tucker, Joel Tucker, John Keatts. S/ William Davis. (See WB 3-152 in which George Tucker willed this land to wf Catharine for life & then jointly to sons Joel & Robert).

WB 3-152, wd 25 Sep 1780, wp 11 Mar 1784, "I, George Tucker the elder of Lunenburg Co." -names: - Wife Catharine - the use of my land & plantation ... about 200 ac., all my slaves & pers. prop. during her natural life or widowhood. - Sons Joel, Lew & Robert Tucker - negro Ned to be divided equally bet. them. - Sons Joel Tucker & Robert Tucker - my, land to be divided bet. them, Robert's 100 ac. to include the plantation house. Dau. Milly Clay - Dau. Biddy Tucker - Son William Tucker - Dau. Fanny Coleman - Sons Henry, George & Joseph Tucker - Five youngest children: Joel, Lew, Robert, Milly Clay & Biddy - rest & residue of real & pers. est.
> CODICIL - 30 Dec 1783 - the 5 pounds devised my son George, he being dead, I devise to my 4 last children, namely, Obedience, Joel, Lew & Robert & their heirs.

WB 3-172, George Tucker Est. I&A 8 Jul 1784. S/ Catharine Tucker, Joel Tucker.

Marriage WB 3-309, 27 Nov 1787, Robert Tucker md Sarah Smith, by Thomas Crymes.

DB 16-196, 9 Feb 1792, rec. 9 Feb 1792, Katharine Tucker, Robert Tucker & wf Sally of Lunenburg. Co., sold 100 ac. for L65. Bo. on br. of Meherrin Ri., beg. Brizendine's cor, Edmond's line, Ingram's & Stokes' line. S/ Katharine x Tucker, Robert Tucker, Sally x Tucker. (See DB 13-68 where George bought 199 ac. and WB 3-152 where George willed 200 ac. to wife Catharine for life, then 100 ac. to go to son Robert and remainder to son Joel.).

PERSONAL TAX RECORD

1782	George Tucker, Joel Tucker	Lender, Mol, Lucy, Isaac, Ned.
1783	George Tucker, J. Tucker	
1784	Catherine Tucker, Lewelling, Joel & <u>Robert Tucker</u>	
1785	Catherine Tucker, Robert Tucker	
1786	Robert Tucker	Linder, Moll, Lucy, Isaac, Ned, Jack, Bett,1 white age 21, 7 negroes, 4 horses, 12 cattle, 3 tithes.
1787	Catharine Tucker, Robert Tucker (above 21)	7 blacks, 4 horses, 10 cattle
1788	Robert Tucker	
1789	Robert Tucker	
1790	Robert Tucker	
1791	Robert Tucker	

Robert Tucker was first listed as a tithable in the household of his mother Catharine in 1784. Assuming he was age 16 in 1784, then he would have been born ca 1767-68, and age 21 in 1788. But he was listed as above 21 in 1787 and he married in Nov 1787, so he was born ca 1766.

This Robert Tucker (2), son of George Tucker & 2nd wf Catharine, does not appear on the Lunenhurg Co. Personal Tax Records after 1791, nor on the Land Tax Records. In 1792 he sold the 100 ac. in Lunenhurg Co., inherited from his father, and moved to Halifax Co., Va.

HALIFAX CO. VA.

DB 18-262, 30 Sep 1799, rec 25 Dec 1799, Elinor Weakley, Samuel Weakley & wf Sally, to William Tucker for L475., 666 ac. on Runaway Cr. <u>bo.</u> Clay, Robert Weakley, Frederick Farmer, <u>Robert Tucker</u>, James Ridgeway, Daniel Mays(?). S/ Elinor x Weakley, Samuel Weakley, Sarah Weakley. Wit: Robert G. Tucker, Joel Tucker, <u>Robert Tucker</u>, Peter Reves, William Vaughan. Sally Weakley, wife of Samuel Weakley relinq dower right.

DB 18-526, 11 Dec 1800, rec 26 Jan 1801, Samuel Weakley executor for est. of Robert Weakley decd of Davidson Co., Tenn., to <u>Robert Tucker of Halifax Co., for L140., 251 ac.</u> on west fork of Runaway Cr., bo. at a beach on e.s. of cr. at mouth of a br., the ___ marked with the letters FR & the figures 1783, William Tucker's land, Tedrick Farmer's land. S/ Samuel Weakley's Est. Wit: Rob't G. Tucker, Joel Tucker, Barret T. Farmer. (See DB 20-432 & DB 25-513).

DB 20-432, 4 Mar 1805, rec 22 Apr 1805, <u>Robert Tucker</u> to Robert G. Tucker, for L70., <u>56 ac.</u>, on w.s. of west fork of Runaway Cr., bo. Robert G. Tucker, James Ridgeway, William Tucker. S/ Robert Tucker. Wit: Charles Reaves, Joshua Stone, James Ridgeway. (See DB 13-526, DB 21-132, & DB 25-513).

DB 21-132, 13 Jun 1806. <u>Sarah Tucker, wife of Robert Tucker</u>, relinq dower right to sale of 56 ac. to Robert G. Tucker by DB 20-432.

D3 20-470, 23 Nov 1804. James Smith to <u>Robert Tucker</u>, for L110., a negro woman slave named Judah. S/ John Smith. Wit: Peter Barksdale, William Sydnor, John Jennings.

DB 25-513 1 Nov 1815, <u>Robert Tucker & wf Sarah</u> for $1,050., to Shadrack Barber, <u>210 ac.</u> on Runaway Cr, bo. Joel Tucker, William Tucker. (See DB 18-526 & DB 20-432).

NOTE: This compiler has not further researched this Robert Tucker & wf Sarah (Sally) Smith.

SUMMARY: Robert Tucker son of George Tucker Sr & 2nd wf Catharine, b ca 1766 in Amelia Co., Va., md 1787 in Lunenburg Co., Sarah Smith, moved to Halifax Co. Va. ca 1799.

TJ140000 - JOHN TUCKER SR

MD SARAH OLD

SON OF CAPT ROBERT TUCKER SR

MD MARTHA

PRINCE GEORGE CO. VA.[1]

p 577, 9 Oct 1733, Richard Tally of Pr. Geo. Co. to John Tucker, for L20., land s.s. Appomattox Ri., 144 ac., part of patent dated 1723, bo. by river & Cattale Br. & Allen Howard. Mary, wife of Richard Tally, ack. dower rt. Wit: Wm. Green, Jeffrey Hawks, Jo___ Hawks. Rec. 9 Oct 1733. (See Amelia Co. DB 2-259).

NOTE: John Tucker must have attained age 21 when he bought land in 1733, so he was born ca 1712.

AMELIA CO. VA.

Patent 16-67, John Tucker, 26 Jul 1735, Amelia Co., 200 ac. l.s. Winkomaick Cr.

DB 1-341. 10 Oct 1741, rec. 16 Oct 1741. Robert Tucker Sr to John Tucker for L100. - 165 1/2 ac. l.s. Wintocomake Cr. bo. in pt. by sd John Tucker's spring br. & the rd to John Tucker's sp. br. Wit: John Powell, Robert Coleman & Robert Tucker Jr. (See Patent 13-270 for Capt Robert Tucker. Sr) (See WB 2X-304)

NOTE: By DB 1-341, DB 1-342 and DB 1-343, Robert Tucker Sr simultaneously deeded land to John Tucker, George Tucker and Robert Tucker Jr on 10 Oct 1741, so we can conclude they are his sons. Since he had already deeded land to them, there was no need to include them in his will, although he did name son Robert as executor. There is ample evidence from patents and deeds that James, Robert Jr, George, John, William, Joseph & Daniel Tucker were brothers, and sons of Capt. Robert Tucker Sr.

DB 2-259, d 21 Feb 1745, John Tucker to John Waller for L60, 144 ac., s.s. Appomattox Ri., bo. Goose Island, Richard Talley's div. line, crossing Cattail Br., Eggleston's line crossing Bolling's meadow to Charles Cousens line & the ri. Rec. Feb 21, 1745. (See Pr. Geo. Co. Deed p 577, and Amelia Co. DB 2-442).

DB 2-440, 29 Nov 1746, Richard Talley to Patrick Mullin (Mullen), for L200., four tracts: (1) 181 ac. s.s. Appomattox Ri., bo. by ri. below Winterocth (sic), Ford & the ri.; (2) 99 ac. bo. by John Talley Sr's upper cor. on Appomattox Ri., Cattail Br., Richard Talley's former cor. & the ri.; (3) 60 ac. being part of a larger tract of 204 ac., adj. to above tract; the other part Talley conveyed to John Tucker Sr.; (4) 18 ac. beg. at John

Talleys Point on bank of ri, as it meanders to mouth of Cattail Run. Rec. 20 Feb 1746. Wife Mary rel. dower. (See Pr. Geo Co. Deed p 577 & Amelia Co. DB 2-259).

DB 2-442, 14 Jan 1746, John Waller Sr., Planter to Patrick Muller of Henrico Co., Va., for L64.10. Wit: Richard x Talley, Mary x Talley & Thomas x Talley. Two tracts: (1) 144 ac. s.s. Appomattox Ri., being part of larger Pat. of 204 ac. to Richard Talley on 5 Sep 1723, & signed by Hugh Drisdall, Governor, & sold by sd Talley to John Tucker; (2) 60 ac. being Pat, to Patrick Muller before, beg. at Richard Talley's upper cor. on the ri, Allen Howard's line & the ri. Rec. 20 Feb 1746. Wife Ann Waller rel. dower. (See Pr. Geo Co. Deed p 577 & Amelia Co. DB 2-259).

DB 5-282, 1 Mar 1755, John Ornsby to John Tucker, Planter for L55., 408 ac., being part of a tract of 4,154 ac. patented to John Ornsby 20 Jul 1748, on the branches of Cellar Cr., bo. Peter ___, Cornel Bland, Curtis Caters. Wit: William Tucker, Joseph Tucker, William Talley Jnr. S/ John Ornsby. (See DB 10-51).

WB 2X-16, Walter Chiles Est. Acct. for 1761 ret & rec 25 Feb 1762. Examined 30 Nov 1761 by Abraham Green, Wm. Crawley, Laurence Wills. Adm. Fendall Southerland. Names mentioned: Thomas Whitworth, Walter Scott, Thomas Green, John Tucker (overseer), John Smith, Wm. Crawley, Stephen Dance, Claiborne Anderson, Wm. Black, Robert Kennon, Sterling Thornton, Thornton Pryor.

LUNENBURG CO. VA.

DB 9-207, 11 Aug 1763, William White of Lunenburg Co. to John Tucker of Amelia Co., 292 ac. in Lunenburg Co., for L50., beg. James Bilbors cor. to Charles ?upussas line, Murrys line, Burwell's line, Ravencrofts line. Wit: Thos. Green, Zachariah Bevil (or Bell), Jeremiah Glen. (Note: This area became Mecklenburg Co. in 1765. See Mecklenburg Co. DB 1-32 for 296 ac.)

NOTE: John Tucker's brother James Tucker bought land adj Ravenscrofts line in 1760 (DB 6-326). His brother George Tucker lived and died in Lunenburg Co. His brother William Tucker patented and sold land in Lunenburg Co, but there is no evidence he lived there.

MECKLENBURG CO. VA.

DB 1-32, 19 Mar 1765, rec 13 May 1765, John Tucker to Edward Bevil, 296 ac., bo. Edward Bevil, Abraham Burton, James Tucker, Bilbor, William Murphy. Wit: Thos. Green, Wm. Murphey, Abraham Burton. (See Lunenburg Co. DB 9-207 for 292 ac.).

DB 1-33, 20 Mar 1765, rec. 13 May 1765, Edward Bevill to John Tucker, for L50., 150 ac. on n.s. Allens Cr., bo. Thomas Green, Bilbow. S/ Edward Bevill. Wit: Wm. Parker, Thos. Green, Wm. Johnson. (See DB 1-499).

DB 1-499, 9 May 1767, rec 14 Sep 1767, John Tucker to Hezekiah Coleman, for L50., 150 ac. bo. Thomas Green, John Farlow, William Parker, Joseph Southerlin, Whitter. Wit: W. Murphey, Spence Waddy, Richard x Talley. S/ John x Tucker. (See DB 1-33)

NOTE: Although John Tucker bought and sold land in Lunenhurg and Mecklenburg counties, there is no evidence he lived in either county.

AMELIA CO. VA.

WB 2X-80, John Powell Est., I&A d 7 Nov 1764, ret & rec 24 Jan 1765. Appr: John Booth, John x Old, John Tucker.

DB 10-51, 16 Jul 1768, rec. 22 Sep 1763, John Tucker Sen of Raleigh Parish to his brother William Tucker, for L85., 200 ac. in Nottoway Parish, joining lands of Peter Randolph Bland Christopher, _____ Haskins & John Clark, it being the upper end or part of 400 ac. which sd John Tucker purchased of the Rev., John Osborne, bo. Christopher Haskins, John Clark, including all the land btwn sd line & the line run btwn sd John Tucker & Rev. John Osborne. Wit: John Clay, Ch' Clay, Robert Stanfield. Wf Sarah relinq. dower. S/ John x Tucker, Sarah. (See DB 5-282).

NOTE: John Tucker Sen and William Tucker Sen were brothers and sons of Capt Robert Tucker Sr. See DB 5-282 for John Tucker and DB 14-407 for William Tucker. Also, John Clay was brother-in-law to John and William Tucker, having married their sister Sarah Tucker.

WB 2X-242, will of John Old (x), wd 8 Mar 1767, wp 28 Jul 1768. Wit: John Powell, William Morgan, Agness x Powell. Ex: wife Mary Old, James Old, Edward Old. Sec: Peter Jones, Pasch Greenhill. Leg: wife Mary Old - plant. I now live on & personality. Sons: James, Edward, John, William, Charles, Thomas & Joshua. Daus: Ann Clay; Sarah Tucker (negro boy Daniel); Mary Old; Phibe Old; Judith Old (gives them all negroes, etc.). Two separate inventories - one for est. in Amelia Co., and another for est. in Dinwiddie Co. Va. (515 ac. on White Oak Cr., etc.)

WB 2X-304, <u>will of John x Tucker</u>, d 15 Jul 1768, wp 23 Nov 1769. Wit: William Tucker, Robert Tucker. Exr: wife Sarah Tucker & Robert Tucker son of my brother Robert. Sec: John Willson.
Leg: <u>Wife Sarah - during her life the plantation I now live on & all land that side div. line with houses</u>; & likewise negro girl Nan for life & afterward to either of my grandchildren (not named) as she thinks proper; also my h.h. goods, etc. for life, then to be equally div. among my children.
<u>Son Joseph Tucker</u> - one cow.
<u>Son John Tucker</u> - <u>200 ac. where he now lives</u>, & negro woman Jane & negro boy Ned after my wife's death or marriage.
<u>Son William Tucker</u> - <u>plantation I now live on containing 166 ac.</u>, after my wife's death, but he may do what he thinks proper on the land his side of dividing line; also negro boy Phil, his bed, 4 head cattle & his hogs.
<u>Son Lewis Tucker</u> - negro boy Shib, if he pay 5 pounds to me or my wife Sarah before Dec 25 next, or he shall be sold to pay the debt & remainder returned to him; and for his <u>other legacies he has already received</u>.
Estate not to be appraised. S/ John Tucker.
Robert Tucker refused to act as executor.

NOTE: The will of John Tucker (with wife Sarah) includes proof that he is brother of Robert Tucker Jr (with wife Frances), in that he appointed as one of his executors, Robert Tucker son of "my brother Robert". Also DB 10-51 above includes proof that John Tucker and William Tucker were brothers.

WB 2X-310, John Tucker Sr. Inv. ret & rec 25 Jan 1770.

SUMMARY OF LAND TRANSACTIONS
IN PRINCE GEORGE-AMELIA:

Year	References	Plus	Minus	Bal
1733	Pr. Geo. Deed p 577	144		144
1735	Patent 16-67	200		344
1741	DB 1-341 fr father Robert (1)	166		510
1745	DB 2-259 to Waller		144	366
1755	DB 5-282 fr Ornsby (2)	408		774
1768	Adjustment (2)		8	766
1768	DB 10-51 to bro. Wm.		200	566
1769	WB 2X-304 to son John		200	366
1769	to son Wm.		166	200
1769	to son Lewis (3)		200	0
		918	918	

(1) recorded as 166 1/2 ac. in DB 1-341, as 166 ac. in WB 2X-304.
(2) recorded as 408 ac in DB 5-282, as 400 ac in DB 10-51.
(3) son Lewis is shown on List of Tithes as holding 200 ac in 1767,

which possibly is same 200 ac. patented to father John in 1735, (Patent 16-67) and possibly the same willed to Lewis as "his other legacies he has already received". However, no deed could be found for 200 ac. from John to son Lewis.

LIST OF TITHES

1749	2	---	John Tucker, Joseph Tucker	
1750	3	---	John Tucker, Joseph Tucker	Joan
1751	4	---	John Tucker, Joseph Tucker, John Tucker	Jane
1752	4	---	John Tucker, Joseph Tucker, John Tucker	Jane
1753	5	---	John Tucker, Joseph Tucker, John Tucker, William Tucker	Jenne
1755	5	---	John Tucker, Joseph Tucker, John Tucker, William Tucker	Jenne
1756	6	---	John Tucker, Joseph Tucker, John Tucker, William Tucker, Lewis Tucker	Gin
1764	2	75 (775?)	John Tucker, Lewis Tucker	
1765	3	566	John Tucker, John Hudson	Janey
1767	2	166	John Tucker Sen	Jame
1769	3	166	John Tucker, Wm. Waller	Jane

(See WB 2X-304, 1769, John Tucker).

NOTE: The acreage balances in the summary of land transactions correspond with the acreage, where shown, in the list of tithes.

NOTE: The birthdates of the sons of John Tucker (Sr) are estimated based upon their being included as a tithable at age 16, as follows:

Joseph age 16 in 1749, b 1733;

John (Jr) age 16 in 1751, b 1735;

William age 16 in 1753, b 1737;

Lewis age 16 in 1756, b 1740.

SUMMARY: John Tucker (Sr), son of Capt Robert Tucker Sr, b ca 1712 Prince George Co, d 1769 Amelia Co., and ca 1733 Sarah Old, dau of John Old & wf Mary, & had issue:

Joseph Tucker b by 1733.

John Tucker (Jr) b ca 1735.

William Tucker b ca 1737.

Lewis Tucker b ca 1740.

* * *

1. Weisiger, Benjamin B., III, "Prince George County, Virginia Records 1733-1792"

TJ141000 - JOSEPH TUCKER

SON OF JOHN TUCKER SR

MD SARAH OLD

AMELIA CO. VA.

WB 2X-304, <u>will of John x Tucker</u>, d 15 Jul 1768, wp 23 Nov 1769. - names: - Exr: wife Sarah Tucker & Robert Tucker son of my brother Robert. - <u>Wife Sarah - Son Joseph Tucker - one cow</u>. - Son John Tucker - Son William Tucker - Son Lewis Tucker.

Joseph Tucker was listed as a 16-yr-up tithable in the household of his father John Tucker (Sr) 1749-56, so he was born ca 1733, and attained age 21 ca 1754. He received no land by deed or will from his father John Tucker Sr in either Amelia, Lunenburg or Mecklenburg Co. Nothing more is known of this Joseph Tucker.

This Joseph Tucker should be clearly distinguished from other Joseph Tuckers:

(1) his uncle Joseph Tucker, b 17 Jun 1722, age 21 in 1743, son of Capt. Robert Tucker Sr (md Martha). But that Joseph & wf Prudence purchased & sold land in Amelia Co. in 1742 (DB 1-436) & in 1774 (DB 13-189), and moved to Prince Edward Co.

(2) his first cousin Joseph Tucker, b ca 1751, son of George Tucker of Amelia and Lunenburg Counties. That Joseph Tucker & wf Lucy bought and sold land in Lunenburg Co btwn 1772-1779.

(3) a Joseph Tucker b ca 1691, who surveyed land in Pr. Geo. Co. (now Amelia Co.) in 1712, and patented land in Pr. Geo. Co. (now Dinwiddie Co.) btwn 1718-1755. That Joseph patented land adj. Robert Wynne (Patent 14-23, 1730) and most probably md Lucretia Wynne, dau of Maj. Robert Wynne, and lived in Dinwiddie Co.

(4) a Joseph Tucker Jr, b ca 1724, who patented land in 1745 & 1756 in Pr. Ceo. Co. (now Dinwiddie Co.).

(5) the Joseph Tucker of Dinwiddie, who in 1779 in Amelia Co., as Joseph Tucker Jr md Ann Sollard dau of Charles Sollard, and who in 1789 in Nottoway Co. (DB 1-19) received a gift of slaves from his father-in-law Charles Sollard.

SUMMARY: Joseph Tucker son of John Tucker & wf Sarah Old, b ca 1733 in Prince George Co., was still living in 1768 when named in his father's will.

TJ142000 - JOHN TUCKER JR

MD MARGARET
SON OF JOHN TUCKER SR
MD SARAH OLD

AMELIA CO. VA.

WB 2X-304, <u>will of John x Tucker</u>, d 15 Jul 1768, wp 23 Nov 1769. - names: - Exr: wife Sarah Tucker & Robert Tucker son of my brother Robert. <u>Wife Sarah</u> - Son Joseph Tucker - <u>Son John Tucker - 200 ac. where he now lives</u>, & negro woman Jane & negro boy Ned after my wife's death or marriage. - Son William Tucker - Son Lewis Tucker.

DB 7-349, 27 Nov 1760, William Crowder to <u>John Tucker of Raleigh Parish</u>, for L65., <u>200 ac.</u> on l.s. Sweathouse Cr., of Deep Cr., bo. John Old's cor. in Thomas Booth's line, Dyson's cor. Wit: Rob't Marshall, John x Farley, Abraham Burton. S/ William Crowder. (See Nottoway Co. DB 1-561)

DB 11-380, 11 Feb 1772, rec 27 Feb 1772, <u>John Tucker of Nottoway Parish</u>, to John Tabb of Raleigh Parish, for L12. & 1/2 Penny, <u>100 ac.</u> - to secure debt - , bo William Tucker, Thomas Mitchell & Theodorick Bland, and land where sd Tucker now lives. Wit: Rowlett Price, John Beadell, Thos. Bedel. S/ John Tucker. (Note: Apparently the debt was paid, for this seems to be same land sold in DB 12-111 below).

DB 12-111, 25 Sep 1772, rec 3 Oct 1772, <u>John Tucker</u> to Frederick Leonard for L60., <u>100 ac.</u> on branches of Lower Seller Cr., adj William Tucker, Peter Randolph Bland, Theodorick Bland, sd John Tucker. Wit: C. W. Haskins, Balaam Jones, George Still, John Bythisa. <u>Wf Margaret</u> reling dower. S/ John Tucker, Margaret Tucker.

NOTE: DB 12-111 above and DB 18-55 below establish John Tucker's wife as Margaret and his daughter as Nancy.

DB 18-55, 24 Jan 1787, <u>John Tucker to dau. Nancy Tucker</u>, for natural love & affection and also for better maintenance, <u>?</u> <u>ac.</u> bo. adj. land of Theodorick Bland, Frederick Leonard, William Cabiness, & William Grigg Featherstone - with all household & kitchen furniture & all stocks of horses, cattle, sheep & hogs. Wit: Peter Bland, Randall x Simmons, Richard Bland Jr, Edward Bland. S/ John x Tucker. (See also Nottoway Co. DB 2-56)

Note: Although the number of acres is not shown in the above deed, apparently it is the remaining 100 ac. of 200 ac. inherited from his father John Tucker Sr, after selling 100 ac. to Frederick Leonard. This land lay in the area of Amelia Co. which was cut off into Nottoway Co. in 1789.

(See Nottoway Co. DB 2-56)

LIST OF TITHES - AMELIA CO.

1751-1756	-	---	John Tucker (Jr) is listed as 16-yr-up tithable in household of his father John Tucker (Sr)
1766	1	200	John Tucker
1767	1	200	John Tucker

LAND TAX RECORDS - AMELIA CO.

1782-1788   John Tucker Jr   200 ac.

Since John Tucker Jr was listed as a 16-yr-up tithable in the household of his father John Tucker Sr, beginning in 1751, he was born ca 1735, and attained age 21 ca 1756.

The land where the subject John Tucker Jr (son of John Tucker Sr) lived, lay in the Nottoway Parish area of Amelia Co. which in 1789 became Nottoway Co.

NOTTOWAY CO., VA.

DB 1-196, 6 Oct 1791, rec 6 Oct 1791, Benjamin Bennett of Nottoway Co. to John Tucker of sd county, 33 ac., bo. branch along Sterling William's line, Manual Weeks, William Bennett. S/ Benjamin Bennett. Wit: Edmd Wills, Samuel Morgan, Daniel Mayes, Jr. Margaret wf of Benjamin Bennett reling dower right.

DB 1-340, 3 Oct 1793, rec 3 Oct 1793, Britton Moore to John Tucker, 100 ac. bo. William Battes, Capt. Philip Jones decd, sd John Tucker, Col. Bland decd. S/ Briton x Moore, Wit: Wm. Cahaniss. (See DB 2-56)

DB 1-401, 5 Dec 1793, rec 4 Sep 1794, John Tucker Senr of Nottoway Co. for L20., to Nancy Tucker, 2 Bay Mares & all my corn & fodder. S/ John x Tucker, Wit: John Hall.

DB 1-561, 13 Aug 1796, rec 1 Sep 1796, John Tucker of Nottoway Co. to Grief. Ellington, 155 ac., bo. sd Tucker, Robert Tucker, Hawks, Peter Jones, Philip Jones est., Bates, Blodget. S/ John Tucker. Wit: Devoreus(?) Hightower, William S. Feoard(?). Wife was prively examined & assented, but her name was blank in the memo attached.) (See Amelia Co. DB 7-349 for 200 ac.)(200-155=45)

DB 2-56. 3 Jan 1798, rec 1 Feb 1798, John Tucker & daughter Nancy Tucker of Nottoway Co., to Tapley Mahanes, 100 ac. bo. Lew Clark, William Cabiness, Martha Blodgett. S/ John x Tucker, Nancy x Tucker, Wit: James David, Pierce Baseheech, Charles Griggs. (See DB 1-340)

NOTE: At this date, John Tucker's land holding included 45+33=78 ac. See Land Tax Records.

LAND TAX RECORDS - NOTTOWAY CO.

1789 - 91	John Tucker	200 ac.
1792 - 93	John Tucker	200 ac. + 33 ac.
1794 - 96	John Tucker	200 ac. + 33 ac. + 100 ac.
1797 - 98	John Tucker	45 ac. + 33 ac. + 100 ac. (200-155=45)
1799 -1814	John Tucker	45 ac. + 33 ac.
		(Lower Celler Cr. adj. Grief Ellington)
1815	John Tucker Sr	- explanation of changes - 78 ac. formerly charged to John Tucker Sr is taken off the book as the sd Tucker has been decd seven years and the land transferred to other persons.

NOTE: The above explanation of change to land tax records indicates the subject John Tucker died ca 1808. Although the Nottoway Co. land tax records showed land holdings for a John Tucker Sr and a John Tucker Jr, there is no evidence the subject John Tucker had a son. It appears the subject John Tucker (ca 1735-1808 son of John Sr & wf Sarah) had designated himself as Sr at this time, and his first cousin John Tucker (ca 1747-1815 son of William Sr & Ann) was designated as Jr.

NOTE: Sorting out the various John Tuckers was most difficult. By careful analysis of the passage of number of acres of land and names of slaves, I was able to distinguish one from the other and establish relationships.

See John Tucker Sr (1712-1769) who was son of Capt Robert Tucker Sr, and who md Sarah Old, and who was father of the subject John Tucker Jr (1735-1808).

See also John Tucker Sr (1747-1815) who was son of William & Ann Tucker, and grandson of Capt Robert Tucker Sr, and who md Mary _____.

See also John Tucker Jr (1786-1807) who was most probably orphaned son of William Tucker Jr, but whose guardian was his uncle John Tucker Sr (William Jr's brother) and who most probably md his guardian's dau Patty (Martha) Tucker.

All of them lived in the area of Amelia Co. which became Nottoway Co. in 1789. All of this was even more confusing because a separate Francis Tucker family line, who also lived in Amelia and Nottoway Counties, also included several generations of John Tuckers.

SUMMARY: The subject John Tucker Jr, son of John Tucker Sr & wf Sarah Old, b ca 1735 Amelia Co, d ca 1808 Nottoway Co., attained age 21 ca 1756, md Margaret ____ and had issue:

Nancy Tucker.

TJ143000 - WILLIAM TUCKER

MD SUSANNA
SON OF JOHN TUCKER SR
MD SARAH OLD

AMELIA CO. VA.

William Tucker was listed as a 16-yr-up tithable in the household of his father John Tucker (Sr) 1753-1756, so he was b ca 1737, and attained age 21 ca 1758.

LIST OF TITHABLES

1762	1	---	William Tucker son of John
1763	1	---	William Tucker son of John
1765	1	---	William Tucker son of John
1767	1	---	William Tucker son of John
1769	1	---	William Tucker son of John
1770	1	166	William Tucker son of John

WB 2X-304, will of John x Tucker, d 15 Jul 1768, wp 23 Nov 1769. - names: - Exr: wife Sarah Tucker & Robert Tucker son of my brother Robert. - Wife Sarah - Son Joseph Tucker - Son John Tucker - Son William Tucker - plantation I now live on containing 166 ac., after my wife's death, but he may do what he thinks proper on the land his side of dividing line; also negro boy Phil, his bed, 4 head cattle & his hogs. - Son Lewis Tucker.

NOTE: What happened to this William Tucker son of John and the 166 ac. is unclear. The 166 ac. was half of original Patent 13-270 in 1727 for 331 ac. to Capt. Robert Tucker Sr., who deeded 166 ac. to his son John Tucker Sr in 1741 (DB 1-341), who willed 166 ac. to his son, the subject William Tucker in 1768-69. This land lay on l.s. Wintocomaick Cr. in Amelia Co., but no disposing deed could be found and no tract of 166 ac. appears in the land tax records of Amelia Co. beginning in 1782. However, while he was still a tithable in Amelia Co in 1770, William Tucker and his brother Lewis Tucker bought land in Prince Edward Co beginning in 1764, and in Pittsylvania Co. beginning in 1779.

PRINCE EDWARD CO., VA.

DB 2-243, rec 15 Oct 1764, John Avary to William Tucker, both of Raleigh Parish of Amelia Co, for L20, 174 ac. on l.s. Sandy Ri in Prince Edward Co., bo Samuel Pincham, being part of a patent to Charles Burks for 574 ac. 20 Jul 1741. (See DB 3-376)

DB 3-376, rec 16 Jul 1768, rec 21 Nov 1768, <u>Wm. Tucker to Lewis Tucker</u>, both fr Raleigh Parish of Amelia Co., for L50, <u>174 ac.</u> in Prince Edward Co., being the land that William Tucker purchased of John Avary. Wit: John Clay, Charles Clay, Robert Stanfield. (See DB 2-243)

PITTSYLVANIA CO., VA.

DB 5-236, 21 Sep 1779, John Cox of Henry Co, Patrick Parish, to <u>William Tucker</u> of Amelia Co. Nottoway Parish, for L1,350., <u>810 ac</u> on b.s. Mill Cr & Pigg River rd in Pittsylvania Co., being land where sd John Cox formerly lived, adj William Payne, Thomas Jones.

NOTE: William Tucker appeared on the first Personal Tax Records of Pittsylvania Co. in 1782, as 1 white tithable. His son Robert first appeared in 1783, but as a 0 tithable, and was first listed as 1 white tithable in 1785, but he married in 1782, so he was born probably ca 1761. His son Daniel had not attained tithable status through 1790, but was on the 1815 tax list as 1 tithable, and sold land in 1806, so he was born probably between 1769-1785. His brother Lewis Tucker appeared on the tax lists of 1786-1788.

MARRIAGES [2] 1 Jan 1732, Robert Tucker md Martha Shelton. Sur. Joseph Akin. Signs her own consent, p 4.

DB 7-28, 3 Apr 1783, rec 15 Apr 1783, <u>William Tucker to Robert Tucker</u>, for love & affection & L5., <u>200 ac.</u> on draughts & branches of Mill Cr., bo. Phebe Tucker, Arch'd Gordon, Thomas Payne, sd Robert Tucker.

NOTE: The identity of Phebe Tucker is not determined.

DB 8-90, __ May 1787, rec 16 Sep 1787, <u>William Tucker</u> of Cambden Parish, Pittsylvania Co., to Walter Hurcherson of sd co., <u>100 ac.</u>, bo., sd Tucker, William Payne, Edmund Payne, Pigg Ri. Rd.

DB 8-330, 15 Jan 1789, rec 19 Jan 1789, <u>William Tucker to Robert Tucker (his son)</u>, for love & affection he bears to his son & for 5 shillings, negro woman Jenny & her future increase. S/ William Tucker. Wit: Nelson Tucker, William Shelton, Thos. Payne.

DB 8-383, 13 Sep 1787, rec 20 Apr 1789, <u>William Tucker</u> to Charles Keatt, for L150., <u>300 ac.</u> on b.s. Mill Cr, Pig River Road & Courthouse Rd, being the upper part of land John Cox formerly lived on & conveyed by Cox to sd Tucker by deed 21 Sep 1779, bo. Legrand, Thomas Payne, Courthouse Rd, Robert Tucker, sd William Tucker, Pig Ri. Rd, Edmund Payne, Thomas Jones, Ben Shelton.

DB 11-244, 16 Dec 1797, rec 15 Jan 1798, <u>William Tucker to Robert Tucker</u>, for L6.18., <u>100 ac.</u> on b.s. Mill Cr., bo. Jones, Wm. Payne, Key, , <u>being the land William Tucker now lives on</u>. S/ William Tucker. Wit: Armistead Shelton, William Shepherd, Benja Shelton.

26 Feb 1800, 4 Aug 1802, rec 21 Oct 1805, <u>will of William Tucker</u>. Names <u>wife Susanna</u>, her dau Jellica Haymes, my <u>son Robert</u>, my <u>dau Mary Elden</u>, my <u>dau Milly Williams</u>, John Williams son of Milly Williams, my <u>son Daniel</u>, <u>dau Susanna Tucker</u>, granddau Elizabeth Tucker (dau of Susanna). To my son Daniel Tucker - all the land that I possess at his mother's death. Ex: Colo. William Clark, Armistead Shelton, Thomas Payne.

NOTE: The above implies that William Tucker married Susanna Haymes, possibly a widow, who had a daughter Jellica Haymes, by her first husband.

SUMMARY: William Tucker, son of John Tucker Sr & wf Sarah Old, b ca 1737 in Amelia Co, Va., d ca 1805 in Pittsylvania Co., Va., md ca 1760 probably in Amelia Co., Susanna ____, and had issue:

>   Robert Tucker, b ca 1761, md 1782 Martha Shelton.
>
>   Daniel Tucker.
>
>   Mary Elden Tucker.
>
>   Milly Tucker md ____ Williams, & had issue John Williams.
>
>   Susanna Tucker, who had issue Elizabeth Tucker.

* * *

2. Knorr, Catherine Lindsay, "Marriages of Pittsylvania County, 1767-1805", 1956

TJ143100 - ROBERT TUCKER

MD MARTHA SHELTON
SON OF WILLIAM TUCKER
MD SUSANNA

PITTSYLVANIA CO., VA

MARRIAGES [3] 1 Jan 1782, <u>Robert Tucker md Martha Shelton</u>. Sur. Joseph Akin. Signs her own consent, p 4.

DB 7-28, 3 Apr 1783, rec 15 Apr 1783, William Tucker to <u>Robert Tucker</u>, for love & affection & L5., <u>200 ac.</u> on draughts & branches of Mill Cr., bo. Phebe Tucker, Arch'd Gordon, Thomas Payne, sd Robert Tucker.

DB 8-330, 15 Jan 1789, rec 19 Jan 1789, William Tucker to <u>Robert Tucker (his son)</u>, for love & affection he bears to his son & for 5 shillings, negro woman Jenny & her future increase. S/ William Tucker. Wit: Nelson Tucker, William Shelton, Thos. Payne.

DB 11-244, 16 Dec 1797, rec 15 Jan 1798, William Tucker to <u>Robert Tucker</u>, for L6.18., <u>100 ac.</u> on b.s. Mill Cr., bo. Jones, Wm. Payne, Key, , being the land William Tucker now lives on. S/ William Tucker. Wit: Armistead Shelton, William Shepherd, Benja Shelton.

26 Feb 1800, 4 Aug 1802, rec 21 Oct 1805, <u>will of William Tucker</u>. Names <u>wife Susanna</u>, her dau Jellica Haynes, <u>my son Robert</u>, my dau Mary Elden, my dau Milly Williams, John Williams son of Milly Williams, my son Daniel, dau Susanna Tucker, granddau Elizabeth Tucker (dau of Susanna). To my son Daniel Tucker - all the land that I possess at his mother's death. Ex: Colo. William Clark, Armistead Shelton, Thomas Payne.

SUMMARY: Robert Tucker, son of William Tucker & wf Susanna, b ca 1761 probably in Amelia Co., md 1782 Pittsylvania Co., Martha Shelton.

* * *

3. Knorr, Catherine Lindsay, "Marriages of Pittsylvania County, 1767-1805", 1956

TJ143200 - DANIEL TUCKER

SON OF WILLIAM TUCKER

MD SUSANNA

PITTSYLVANIA CO., VA.

26 Feb 1800, 4 Aug 1802, rec 21 Oct 1805, <u>will of William Tucker</u>. Names <u>wife Susanna,</u> her dau Jellica Haymes, my son Robert, my dau Mary Elden, my dau Milly Williams, John Williams son of Milly Williams, my son Daniel, dau Susanna Tucker, granddau Elizabeth Tucker (dau of Susanna). To my <u>son Daniel Tucker - all the land that I possess at his mother's death</u>. Ex: Colo. William Clark, Armistead Shelton, Thomas Payne.

NOTE: William Tucker purchased 810 ac. in 1799, deeded away 700 ac., leaving 110 ac. at his death which he willed to son Daniel. (See DB 20-354 for 114 ac.)

DB 15-89, 16 Jun 1806, <u>Daniel Tucker</u>, Joshua Hardy & wf (Jursmisna ?) to Jacob Saunders, for L145. <u>68 1/2 ac.</u> on b.s. Mill Cr., bo. sd Tucker, Thomas Jones, Henry Kay. Wit: Samuel Fuqua, Thomas C. Stone.

NOTE: Daniel Tucker had not attained tithable status through 1790, but was on the 1815 tax list as 1 tithable, and was at least age 21 when he sold the above land in 1806, so he was horn probably between 1769-1785 in Amelia Co. No deed was found for the purchase of this land, so it was probably inherited jointly by Daniel Tucker & Joshua Hardy. None of the deeds for Daniel Tucker named a wife, and no marriage record was found. But does the above deed suggest that Daniel Tucker was married to Joshua Hardy's sister, or that they married sisters, and jointly inherited land? This was not further researched.

DB 20-349, 16 Dec 1816, rec 20 Jan 1817, John Williams to <u>Daniel Tucker</u>, for $390., <u>94 ac.</u> on Flat Br. of Cherrystone Cr., bo. Hardy, Moore, Pig Ri. Old Rd., Yates, Obadiah Taylor. Keesee. (See DB 23-53)

DB 20-354, 26 Dec 1816, rec 20 Jan 1817, <u>Daniel Tucker</u> to Thos. B. Jones for $421., <u>114 ac.</u>, bo. sd Jones, n.s. Mill Cr. Pig Ri. Rd. S/ Daniel Tucker, Wit: John Williams, William Fitzgerald, Allen Jones. (Note: This probably was the land willed to Daniel by his father William Tucker.) (See Will)

DB 23-53, __ Jun 1819, rec 20 Dec 1819, <u>Daniel Tucker</u> to Anthony D. Haden, for $400., <u>94 ac.</u> on Flat Br. of Cherrystone Cr., on which sd Tucker now lives. bo Hardy, Moore, Pig Ri old Rd, John Yeatts, Obadiah Taylor, Keesee. S/ Daniel Tucker. Wit: Obadiah Taylor, Munford Taylor, Jno Taylor, Isham Bays. (See DB 20-349)

DB 23-454, 16 Jun 1820, rec 17 Jul 1820, Fanny Goodman to <u>Daniel Tucker</u>, for $220., <u>80 ac</u>, on b.s. long br. of Whitethorne Cr., bo. Beverley S. Shelton, Richard G. Keatts, John Butcher & Benjamin Dodd, being land deeded from Benjamin Dodd to sd Fanny Goodman. (See DB 28-253)

DB 28-253, 10 Sep 1826, rec 18 Sep 1826, <u>Daniel Tucker</u> to Tunstall Shelton Jr., for $155., <u>80 ac.</u> on b.s. of long br. of Whitethorne Cr. , bo. John Butcher, Richard G. Keatts, Elizabeth Walton & Benjamin Dodd, being land Benjamin Dodd sold to Fanny Goodman. S/ Daniel Tucker. Wit: Wm. Lewis Jr, Daniel Shelton, James F. Shelton. (See DB 23-454)

DB 28-254, 16 May 1826, rec 18 Sep 1826. Tunstall Shelton Jr, to secure debt to <u>Daniel Tucker</u>, in trust, to Thompson Robertson, <u>80 ac.</u> on b.s. long br. of Whitethorne Cr., bo. Benjamin Dodd, John Butcher,, Richard G. Keatts, Elizabeth Walton.

SUMMARY: Daniel Tucker son of William Tucker & wf Susanna, b probably btwn 1769-1785 in Amelia Co, known to have lived in Pittsylvania Co. 1802-1826.

TJ144000 - LEWIS TUCKER

MD ELIZABETH
SON OF JOHN TUCKER SR
MD SARAH OLD

AMELIA CO. VA.

Lewis Tucker was listed as a 16-yr-up tithable in the household of his father John Tucker Sr in 1756-64, so he must have been born ca 1740, and attained age 21 ca 1761.

LIST OF TITHABLES

1766	1	---	Lewis Tucker
1767	1	200	Lewis Tucker
1769	1	___	Lewis Tucker

WB 2X-304, will of <u>John x Tucker</u>, d 15 Jul 1768, wp 23 Nov 1769. - names: - Exr: wife Sarah Tucker & Robert Tucker son of my brother Robert. - <u>Wife Sarah</u> - Son Joseph Tucker - Son John Tucker - Son William Tucker - <u>Son Lewis Tucker - negro boy. Shib, if he pay 5 pounds to me or my wife Sarah before Dec 25 next, or he shall be sold to pay the debt & remainder returned to him. and for his other legacies he has already received</u>.

NOTE: Although John Tucker did not will any land in 1768-69 to his son Lewis, Amelia Co. List of Tithables shows Lewis Tucker holding <u>200 ac. in 1767</u>. This is possibly the same 200 ac. on l.s. Wintocomaick Cr. which John Tucker received by Patent 16-67 in 1735 in Amelia Co., and possibly the same referred to in his will for Lewis as "other legacies he has already received".

This compiler could find no further reference to this Lewis Tucker, b ca 1740, son of John and Sarah, nor the 200 ac which he held in Amelia Co. in 1767. However Lewis Tucker appears, along with his brother William, in Prince Edward Co in 1768 and Pittsylvania Co. in 1786-1788.

PRINCE EDWARD CO., VA.

DB 3-376, rec 16 Jul 1768, rec 21 Nov 1768, <u>Wm. Tucker to Lewis Tucker</u>, both fr Raleigh Parish of Amelia Co., for L50, <u>174 ac.</u> in Prince Edward Co., being the land that William Tucker purchased of John Avary. Wit: John Clay, Charles Clay, Robert Stanfield. (DB 4-250)

DB 4-250, 18 Aug 1772, rec 19 Oct 1772. <u>Lewis Tucker & wf Elizabeth</u> to Hezekiah Coleman, both of Amelia Co., for L55., <u>174 ac</u> on Sandy Ri in Prince Edward Co., bo Richard Burks, Daniel Lewelling & George Forrest. Wit: John Gorsham, Godfrey Tucker, Jesse Coleman. (See DB 3-376)

PITTSYLVANIA CO., VA

Elizabeth Tucker appeared on the Personal tax records of Pittsylvania Co. in 1782, Lewis Tucker in 1783-1788, and Lewallen Tucker in 1789-1790, but neither appeared on the Land Tax Records. Also Merrymonwright Tucker appeared on the Personal Tax Records in 1789-90, Colston Tucker in 1815-1820, and Edmond Tucker in 1820. On the Land Tax Records, Colson Tucker held 100 ac. on Sandy Cr 1822-1826. (Lewis Tucker's older brother William Tucker owned land in Pittsylvania Co. beginning in 1779, and died there ca 1804.)

NOTE: Lewis Tucker and Lewallen Tucker were most probably the same person, per information in the following deeds.

DB 14-467, 26 Nov 1805, rec 16 Dec 1805, William Irby, collector, Pittsylvania Co, to William Price Sr, for L20., 91 ac. which was assessed in the name of Lewis Tucker of Pittsylvania which was sold for the low payment of tax due there, bo. William Price, Geo. Robertson, James Foulkes, Clay.

NOTE: No deed was found for purchase of 91 ac. by Lewis Tucker.

DB 24-32, 7 Jan 1820, rec 15 Apr 1821. We, Ludicy Tucker, Patsy Gravely late Patsy Tucker, Merriman Tucker & William Gravely, give to Colson Tucker the interest we have in 100 ac. on waters of Sandy Cr. btwn lines of Price, Fulks, Clay & others, being land formerly decreed to Lewalland Tucker.

DB 26-15, 19 Nov 1823, Coulston Tucker, indebted to Thos S. Shelton, sold to Atkinson Lovelace, land (no. acres not shown), bo. Wm. Guin, Matthew Clay, Charles Clay, it being land which Lewis Tucker died seized possessed of & sd Coulston Tucker being by law one of the legatees of sd Lewis Tucker decd, & by purchase of the other legatees the rightful owner of same for which a suit is now depending in Superior of Pittsylvania Co. in behalf of sd C. Tucker against William Thomas.

NOTE: The two deeds above indicate that Lewis (Lewallen) Tucker had died before 1820, leaving heirs Ludicy Tucker, Patsy Gravely, Merriman Tucker & Coulson Tucker.

MARRIAGES: [4]

16 Sep 1817. Coulson Tucker m Judith Warren, who gives her own consent as Judah Warren. Sur. Saunders Warren. Md by Rev. James Beck (Minister says 15 Sep) p 64.

Nothing more is known of the subject Lewis Tucker.

SUMMARY: Lewis Tucker, son of John Tucker Sr & wf Sarah Old, b ca 1740 in Amelia Co, d before 1820 in Pittsylvania Co., md prior to 1772 Elizabeth ___, and had issue:

Ludicy Tucker.

Patsy Tucker md Gravely.

Merriman Tucker.

Coulson Tucker b probably before 1796 in Pittsylvania Co., md 1817 Pittsylvania Co. Judith Warren.

* * *

4. Williams, Kathleen Booth, "Marriages of Pittsylvania County, Virginia 1806-1330", 1965

TW150000 - WILLIAM TUCKER SR

MD ANN
SON OF CAPT ROBERT TUCKER SR
MD MARTHA

AMELIA CO. VA.

LIST OF TITHABLES

1736 -1738	--	---	William Tucker listed in household of Robert Tucker	
1740	--	---	William Tucker	
1743	--	---	Wm Tucker	
1744	--	---	Wm Tucker	
1747	--	---	Wm Tucker	
1749	--	---	Wm Tucker	
1750	--	---	William Tucker	
1752	--	---	William Tucker	
1753	--	---	William Tucker	
1755	2	---	William Tucker	Lydia
1756	3	---	William Tucker, Daniel Tucker	Teddy
1762	4	---	William Tucker, Wm Tucker	Dick, Lydia
1763	5	---	William Tucker, William Tucker, John Tucker	Dick, Sedy
1764	5	644	William Tucker Sr, William Tucker, John Tucker	Dick, Lidda
1765	6	644	William Tucker, John Tucker	Dick, Lydia
1767	7	644	William Tucker Sen, John Tucker, Robert Tucker, Jesse Tucker	Dick, Jack, Liddy
1769	6	844	William Tucker Sen, John Tucker, Robert Tucker	Dick, Jack, Lydia
1770	6	844	William Tucker Sen, Jno Tucker, Robt Tucker	Dick, Jack, Lydia
1782	13	---	William Tucker Sen	Dick, Dinah, Hanah, Buck, Charles, Stephen, Mick, Peter, Moll, Eve, Major, Agnes, Lydia
1783	3	---	William Tucker	
1784	6	---	William Tucker Sr	

(See WB 3-300, 1785, William Tucker)

NOTE: William Tucker was listed as a 16-yr-up tithable in the household of his father Capt. Robert Tucker Sr from 1736-38 in Amelia Co., and was listed as a separate household and a 21-yr-old tither in 1740. Therefore he was born before 1720 in Pr. Geo. Co., married Ann ____ before 1740, and began buying and patenting land in 1742 in Amelia Co. The lists of tithables identify the sons of William Tucker Sen to be Daniel, William Jr, John, Robert, & Jesse Tucker. Other sons named in his will include David and Joel Tucker. Jesse Tucker must have died a minor, for no other reference to him was found.

DB 1-438, 19 Nov 1742, Chas. Williamson of Pr. Geo. Co. to William Tucker for L14.5, 189 ac. l.s. Seller fk. of Deep Cr. & a valley s.s. Reedy Br. & sd. br. DB 1-438, 19 Nov 1742, Chas. Williamson of Pr. Geo. Co. to William Tucker for L14.5, 189 ac, l.s. Seller fk. of Deep Cr. & a valley s.s. Reedy Br. & sd. br.

Patent 22-443, 1 Aug 1745, William Tucker, Amelia Co. 300 ac. l.s. Deep Cr. (See DB 2-265). Patent 22-443, 1 Aug 1745, William Tucker, Amelia Co. 300 ac. l.s. Deep Cr. (See DB 2-265).

DB 2-263, 20 Dec 1745, Uriah x Cliswells (Cliswell) to William Tucker, for L27, 280 ac. l.s. Seller Fork of Deep Cr., bo. Short, Hawks, Williams, Celler Cr. Wit: Joseph Tucker, Elias x Morgan & John Clay. Wife Elizabeth rel. dower.

DB 2-265, 21 Mar 1745, William Tucker to John Mayton for L20, 300 ac. l.s. Deep Cr., bo. William Coleman, Peter Jones, Abraham Jones, Munford, being land Pat, to sd Tucker on Aug 1, 1745. Wit: John Clay, John x Ellington & Uriah Cliswell. Wife Ann rel. dower. (See Patent 22-443).

Patent 25-273, 12 Jan 1746, William Tucker Amelia Co. 400 ac. b.s. Kitts Horsepen Br., lower fork Seller Cr. (See DB 2-547).

DB 2-547, 16 Oct 1747, William Tucker to Thomas Moran for L25, 400 ac. b.s. Kitts Horsepen Br. of Lower Fork of Seller Cr., bo. Christopher Hinton, Munford, Baldwin, Bland, being Pat. to sd Tucker on 12 Jan 1746. Wit: Thomas Pain Jr., Charles Hunley & John x Stigall. Wf Ann rel. dower. (See Patent 25-273).

Patent 28-276, 1 Oct 1747, William Tucker, Amelia Co. 400 ac. btwn the Swethouse & Seller Creeks. (See DB 3-219). (See DB 10-76 for Daniel Tucker son of Capt Robert Tucker Sr).

DB 3-219, rec. 4 Mar 1748, <u>William Tucker for love & affection I have & care unto William Gallemore</u> and for his better advancement in the world, <u>400 ac.</u>, btwn Swethouse & Seller Creeks, bo. Charles Clay, Abraham Jones, Abraham Hanks, Jo Hanks, Rich'd Jones. Wit: <u>John Clay</u>, Henry Jones, William Jones. (See Patent 28-276). (See DB 10-76 for Daniel Tucker son of Capt Robert Tucker Sr)

NOTE: The relationship of William Gallemore to William Tucker is not clear. He may he a son-in-law, or a brother-in-law. William Gallemore & wf Mary sold the same 400 ac. to John Cordle by DB 8-232, 1763; which John Cordle & wf Ann sold to John Clay by DB 9-267, 1767, which John Clay & wf Sarah (sister of William Tucker Sr & Daniel Tucker) sold to Daniel Tucker by DB 10-76, 1768.

WB 1-31, 24 Feb 1753, Ann Cape, Est. sale acct. ret. <u>Apprs</u>: Richard Dennis, <u>William Tucker</u>, Peter Jones. Adm: Pat Mullen.

LUNENBURG CO. VA.

Patent 31-57, 20 Sep 1751, <u>William Tucker, Lunenburg Co.</u>, <u>350 ac.</u> b.s. Meadow Cr. adj. Walker's land. (See DB 4-500)

Patent 33-57, 16 Aug 1756, <u>William Tucker, Lunenburg Co.</u>, <u>400 ac.</u> upper br. of Dry Cr. adj. Nicholas Hudson. (See DB 7-65 below).

DB 4-500, 2 Oct 1756, rec .5 Jul 1757. <u>William Tucker of Amelia Co.</u> to Abram Smith of Dinwiddie Co., for L25., <u>350 ac. in Lunenburg Co.</u> on b.s. of Meador Cr., <u>it being patented to William Tucker,</u> bo. Waker's cor., River's cor. Wit: Abra. Cocke Junr, Peter Smith, William Cross, John Hightower Jr. S/ William Tucker. (See Patent 31-57)

DB 7-65, 8 May 1761, <u>William & Ann Tucker of Amelia Co.</u> to Thos. Wilmut of Pr. Edward Co., for L54, <u>400 ac. in Lunenburg Co.</u>, on upper br. of Dry Cr., beg. Nicho. Hudson's in Wynn's line, John Mitchell's cor. Ann relinq. dower int. (See Patent 33-57 above).

NOTE: Although William Tucker patented and then sold land in Lunenburg Co., there is no evidence he ever lived in that county.

AMELIA CO. VA.

DB 8-183, 21 Aug 1763, rec. 25 Aug 1763. <u>Allen Hinton to William Tucker</u> for L30, <u>105 ac.</u> btwn the Sweathouse Fork & the Lower Seller Fork of Deep Cr., it being part of 400 ac. formerly pat. to Christopher Hinton, bo. Francis Bolling. Wit: William Hall, Thomas Powell, William Covington. S/ Allin Hinton, Rosamond Hinton. (See WB 3-300)

DB 8-238, rec., 24 Nov 1763, <u>Robert Hinton & wf Elizabeth to William Tucker</u> for L13., <u>70 ac.</u> on head of Sweathouse Cr., adj. Col. Bland, being part of a tract patented to Christopher Hinton Senr. 2 Jan 1737. S/ Robert x Hinton, Eliz'a x Hinton. (See WB 3-300).

DB 10-51, 16 Jul 1768, rec. 22 Sep 1768, John Tucker Sen of Raleigh Parish to his brother William Tucker, for L85, 200 ac. in Nottoway Parish, joining Peter Randolph Bland, Christopher ____ Haskins, & John Clark, it being the upper part of 400 ac., which sd John Tucker purchased of the Rev. John Orsborne, bo. Christopher Haskins, John Clark, including all the land btwn sd line & line run btwn sd John Tucker & Rev. John Osborne. Wit: John Clay, Ch. Clay, Robert Stanfield. Wife Sarah Relinq. dower. S/ John x Tucker, Sarah. (See DB 14-407)

NOTE: The above deed indicates that John Tucker Sr & William Tucker Sr were brothers and therefore sons of Capt. Robert Tucker Sr, although they are not named in his will (WB 1-63). See DB 5-282 for John Tucker Sr, DB 14-407 for William Tucker Sr. Also see Patent 18-389 for James Tucker, in which James, Robert and John Tucker are shown to be brothers. Also see DB 1-341-344, in which John, Robert and George Tucker are shown to be brothers and sons of Capt Robert Tucker Sr.

DB 11-199, 25 Jul 1770, John Hamlin & wf Philadelphia to William Tucker Sen for L109, 545 ac. being the greater part in Amelia Co. & lesser in Dinwiddie Co., on head of Namaseen Cr., bo. Pryor's cor. & Tucker's cor. Wit: Sam'l Wills, Daniel Tucker, R. Bradfute.

DB 14-407, 25 Aug 1788, William Tucker Sen of Raleigh Parish to John Caudle Purkinson & Betty Perkinson of Nottoway Parish, for L200., 200 ac. bo. on north & west by Peter Randolph Bland, on east by John Tucker & Kedrick Leonard, & on south by Lew Clark. Wit: Hezekiah Bevill, Thomas Hood, John Hood. S/ William x Tucker, Ann x Tucker. (See DB 12-211 for John Tucker, son of John Tucker). (See DB 10-51)

WB 3-300, will of William Tucker, 8 Feb 1785, (date recorded not shown). Ex: sons Daniel Tucker, John Tucker & Robert Tucker.
Leg: son Daniel Tucker, land ___ ac. on n.s. of Licking Br. to David Granbitt's cor, Cellar Cr., being all the land I have on that side the new line - plus negro Arthur.
Son William Tucker - all my lands below the aforesaid Liking Br, & the br. called Mirey Br., fr. one br. to the other north & south course, that is, on the e.s. of that line - plus negro Nancy.
Son John Tucker - land which I purchased of Allen Hinton & Robert Hinton - also 25 ac. most convenient to him of the land I purchased of William Watson.
Son Robert Tucker & son David Tucker - land which I purchased of William Watson, except those 25 ac. already bequeathed to son John Tucker, to be divided between them by running a line they think proper - also to son Robert Tucker - negro Jack, and to son David Tucker - negro Beck & her increase.
Dau. Mary Chappell - negro Jency & her increase.

Dau. Sarah Olds' three children - (negro) Fanny & her increase and (negro) Majors(?).

Dau. Anne Tucker - negroes Hannah & Rachel & their increase.

Wife Ann -land I now live on for life & remainder of my estate not before mentioned, but at her death:

Son David Tucker to have negro Moll & incr.

Son William Tucker to have negro Charles.

Son John Tucker to have negro Peter.

Son Robert to have negro Missse & incr.

Son David to have negro Stephen.

Dau. Mary Chappell to have negro Abner.

Son Joel Tucker - the land whereon I now live & four negroes Dick, Dinah, Cale & Peg & incr. & all remainder of my estate not already mentioned, except bed & furniture, one cow & calf & side saddle, which I give to dau. Ann Tucker.

Estate not to be appraised. Wit: David Williams, Richard Hawkes, John Hawkes. S/ William x Tucker.

NOTE: For land purchased by William Tucker: from Allen Hinton see DB 8-183; from Robert Hinton see DB 8-233; from William Watson (unable to find deed, but see DB 11-199 fr John Hamlin).

SUMMARY OF LAND TRANSACTIONS IN AMELIA CO.:

Year	Source		Plus		Minus	Bal
1742	DB 1-438 fr Williamson	(5)	189			189
1745	Patent 22-443	(1)	300			489
1745	DB 2-263 fr Cliswell	(5)	280			769
1745	DB 2-265 to Mayton			(1)	300	469
1746	Patent 25-273	(2)	400			869
1747	DB 2-547 to Moran			(2)	400	469
1747	Patent 28-276	(3)	400			869
1748	DB 3-219 to Gallemore			(3)	400	469
1763	DB 8-183 fr Allen Hinton	(7)	105			574
1763	DB 8-238 fr Robert Hinton	(7)	70			644
1768	DB 10-51 fr bro. John	(4)	200			844
1770	DB 11-199 fr Hamlin (a)	(6)	545			1389
1788	DB 14-407 to Perkinson		___	(4)	200	1189
	BALANCE		2489		1300	
1788	(?) WB 3-300:			(5)	125	1064
	to son Daniel (b)					
	to son William (c)			(5)	244	820
	to son John			(7)	105	715
	to son John			(7)	70	645
	to son John (a)			(6)	25	620

229

SUMMARY OF LAND TRANSACTIONS IN AMELIA CO.:

Year	Source	Plus	Minus	Bal
	to son Robert (a)	(6)	320	300
	to son David (a)	(6)	300	100
	to son Joel (d)			

(a) Although William Tucker's will stated he left to sons John, Robert & David the land he bought of William Watson, no such deed could be found. However, the Land Tax records show Robert holding 545 ac. in 1782, from which 200 ac. went to David in 1787, 25 ac. was deducted in 1788 (to John ?), leaving 320 ac. on Namozine Cr. which Robert held 1789-1813 in Nottoway Co. This 545 ac. was purchased by William Tucker Sr from John Hamlin by DB 11-199 in 1770, and is possibly that referred to as being bought of William Watson.

(b) Land Tax records show Daniel holding 125 ac. in Amelia Co. 1782-88, & 125 ac. in Nottoway Co. 1789-1807.

(c) Land Tax records show William holding 244 ac. in Amelia Co. 1782-87, and it going to Joel Tucker in 1788.

(d) Land Tax records show Joel holding 244 ac. in Amelia Co. in 1788, & 244 ac. in Nottoway Co. in 1789-95; then holding 207 ac. 1796-1798; then estate 147 ac. 1799-1819. The reduction totaling 97 ac. was probably William's share which was sold by his heir Kennon Tucker, leaving 147 ac. as Joel's share. The remaining 100 ac. is not accounted for.

MARRIAGES - AMELIA CO., VA. [1]

7 Dec 1778	Robert Tucker to Mary Hawks	Sec. Daniel Tucker
19 Feb 1780	William Old to Sarah Tucker	Sur. Robert Frend, p 0-1
14 Feb 1782	David Tucker to Fanny Old.	Sec. Robert Tucker

MARRIAGES . HALIFAX CO., VA.

17 Oct 1799, Joel Tucker md Usley Chappell.

MB 1-66, 24 Apr 1807, Joel Tucker md Nancy Moore, Bondsman Anderson Moore.

SUMMARY: William Tucker Sr, son of Capt Robert Tucker Sr & wf Martha. of Pr. Geo. & Amelia Co., b before 1720 in Pr. Geo. Co., d after 1785 in Amelia Co., md Ann _____ before 1740 and had issue:

Daniel Tucker b ca 1740 Amelia Co.

William Tucker Jr b before 1746 Amelia Co.

John Tucker b ca 1747 Amelia Co.

Jesse Tucker b ca 1750 Amelia Co., named as 16-yr-up tithable in 1767 only, must have died minor.

Robert Tucker b 1751 Amelia Co., md 1778 Amelia Co., Mary Hawks, dau. of Joshua & Angelica Hawks.

David Tucker b ca 1761 Amelia Co., md 1st 1782 Amelia Co., Fanny Old.

Joel Tucker b ca 1762 Amelia Co., m 1st 1799 Halifax Co., Usley Chappell (probably dau. of Robert Chappell), md 2nd 1807 Halifax Co., Nancy Moore, dau of Anderson Moore.

Mary Tucker md _____ Chappell. Sarah Tucker md 1780 William Olds.

Ann Tucker.

* * *

1. Williams, Kathleen B., "Marriages of Amelia County, Virginia, 1735-1815", 1961

TW151000 - DANIEL TUCKER

MD ELSEY
SON OF WILLIAM TUCKER SR
MD ANN

AMELIA CO. VA.

LIST OF TITHABLES

1756	-	---	Daniel Tucker listed with William Tucker	
1767	1	__	Daniel Tucker, son of Wm	
1769	1	__	Daniel Tucker, son of Wm	
1770	3	__	Daniel Tucker, son of Wm	Dick, Annaca

PERSONAL TAX RECORDS

1782	4	Daniel Tucker	Dick, Anarcha
1783	4	Daniel Tucker	
1784	5	Daniel Tucker	
1785	5	Daniel Tucker	
1787	1	Daniel Tucker	
1788	2	Daniel Tucker, Daniel Tucker	
1789	1	Daniel Tucker	

NOTE: Daniel Tucker was listed as a 16-yr-up tithable in the household of his father William Tucker first in 1756, tithable records were missing 1757-61, and he was not listed with his father in 1762. Thus Daniel Tucker was born ca 1740, became age 21 ca 1761, and was listed as a separate household beginning in 1767. In 1788, two Daniel Tuckers were listed in the same household, indicating there may have been a Daniel Tucker Jr., b ca 1772, However, no further record is found of a Daniel Tucker Jr in either Amelia or Nottoway Co.

WB 3-300, will of William Tucker, 8 Feb 1785, (date recorded not shown). -names: - Ex: sons Daniel Tucker, John Tucker & Robert Tucker. - son Daniel Tucker, land ____ ac. on n.s. of Licking. Br. to David Granbitt's cor, Cellar Cr., being all the land I have on that side the new line - plus negro Arthur. - Son William Tucker - Son John Tucker - Son Robert Tucker - son David Tucker - Dau. Mary Chappell - Dau. Sarah Olds' three children - Dau. Anne Tucker - Wife Ann - Son Joel Tucker - dau. Ann Tucker.

NOTE: The land which Daniel Tucker inherited from his father William Tucker Sr fell in Nottoway Co. which was cut off from Amelia Co. in 1789. Land Tax Records indicate this consisted of 125 ac.

LAND TAX RECORD - AMELIA CO.

1782   Daniel Tucker   125 ac.
1787   Daniel Tucker   125 ac.
1788   Daniel Tucker   125 ac.

NOTTOWAY CO. VA.

LAND TAX RECORDS

1789 -1795   Daniel Tucker   125 ac.
1796 -1798   Daniel Tucker   125 + 37 ac.
1799 -1807   Daniel Tucker   125 + 37 + 60 ac.

DB 1-456, 3 Jun 1795, rec 4 Jun 1795, Kennon Tucker & wf Lucy of Nottoway Co. to Daniel Tucker, 37 ac., bo. Peter Jones, Uriah's branch. S/ Kennon x Tucker, Lucy x Tucker. Wit: Peter Jones Senr, Pleasant Bevill, Joshua Hawks Senr. (See DB 3-493)

DB 2-25, 4 Oct 1797. rec 7 Jun 1798. Cannon Tucker & wf Lucy of Nottoway Co. to Daniel Tucker, 60 ac. bo. on east by Peter Jones & Richard Hawks, on west & south by William Greenhill, & on north by Daniel Tucker. S/ Cannon Tucker, Lucy x Tucker. Wit: Charles Morton, Joshua Hawks Sen, John Hawks, John Spain. (See DB 3-179)

For identification of Kennon (or Cannon) Tucker & wf Lucy, see chapter on William Tucker Jr.

DB 3-179, 1805, rec 4 Sep 1806, Daniel Tucker of Nottoway Co. to Martha Hawks, for L100., 60 ac. bo Richard Hawks, Archer Jones. S/ Daniel Tucker. (See DB 2-25)

DB 3-493, 7 Dec 1808, rec 5 Jan 1809, Daniel Tucker & wf Elsey to Archer Jones for L330., 165 ac. bo. Archer Jones, Rialis Branch, Martha Hawks. S/ Daniel Tucker, Elsey Tucker. Wit: Joshua Hundley, Francis Cardwell, Richd Walthall. On 5 Jan 1809, Elsey Tucker reling dower right. (See WB 3-300 and land tax record for 125 ac. & DB 1-456 for 37 ac., totalling 162 ac.)

SUMMARY OF LAND TRANSACTIONS:

Year	Transaction	Plus	Minus	Bal
1785	WB 3-300 fr father's will	123		125
1795	DB 1-456 fr Kennon Tucker	37		162
1797	DB 2-25 fr Kennon Tucker	60		222
1805	DB 3-179 to Martha Hawks		60	162
1808	DB 3-493 to Archer Jones		165	0

NOTE: Daniel Tucker had sold all his land in Nottoway Co. by 1808, at which time he was ca age 68. Nothing more is known by this compiler of this Daniel Tucker.

NOTE: The subject Daniel Tucker b ca 1740 son of William Tucker & wf Ann, should not be confused with his cousin Daniel Tucker (1740-1818) son of Robert Tucker Jr & wf Frances, nor with his uncle Daniel Tucker b 1725 son of Capt Robert Tucker Sr & wf Martha.

NOTE: A Daniel Tucker bought 325 ac. in Mecklenburg Co. in 1778, md 1787 in Mecklenburg Co. Jincy Cardin, dau of John Cardin, & died 1824 in Mecklenburg Co., leaving widow Jane. But that Daniel Tucker was not the same as the subject Daniel Tucker whose wife was named Elsey in 1809 when he sold his land in Nottoway Co. (See DB 3-493)

SUMMARY: Daniel Tucker, son of William Tucker Sr & wf Ann of Amelia Co., b ca 1740 in Amelia Co., lived in the area of Amelia Co. which became Nottoway Co. in 1789, was married to wife Elsey in 1809, when he sold his land in Nottoway Co.

He may have had a son Daniel Tucker Jr b ca 1772 (?).

TW152000 - WILLIAM TUCKER JR

MD LUCY SPAIN
SON OF WILLIAM TUCKER SR
MD ANN

AMELIA CO. VA.

LIST OF TITHABLES

1762-	-	---	William Tucker listed with his father William Tucker
1764			
1765	1	400	Wm Tucker Jun
1767	1	__	Wm Tucker Jun
1769	1	__	William Tucker son of Wm
1770	1	100	William Tucker son of Wm

PERSONAL TAX RECORDS

1782	4	William Tucker Jun	Nancy, Aggy, Milly
1783	2	William Tucker	
1784	2	William Tucker Jr	
1785	3	William Tucker	
1786	0	William Tucker decd	
1787	0	William Tucker est	

This compiler is unable to reconcile the 400 ac. in 1765 and the 100 ac. in 1770, shown on the tithe records.

NOTE: In the Lists of Tithables and Personal Tax Records of Amelia Co., William Tucker Jr was listed as a tithable in the household of his father William Tucker Sen in 1762-1764. Between 1765 and 1785 he was listed as a separate household as either William Tucker Jun or William Tucker son of Wm. In 1786, he was listed as William Tucker deceased, and in 1787 as William Tucker estate. From the above we may conclude he was born ca 1744, became age 21 ca 1765, and died 1786.

DB 15-409, 27 Aug 1780, <u>Wm. Tucker</u> to Rice Newman for L4000., <u>40 ac. with a plantation whereon I (Wm. Tucker) now live</u>. Wit: Robert French. S/ William Tucker. The condition of above obligation is such that if Wm. Tucker pay to Rice Newman on or before 25 Dec 1781 the L4000., then the above obligation to be void & sd Tucker shall have full power & authority to sell the above land any time btwn this & 25 Dec 1781 to pay above debt. Wit: Robert French, Jesse Ellington, Hopkins Muse. S/ William Tucker.

Following is the will of William Tucker Sr:

WB 3-300, <u>will of William Tucker</u>, 8 Feb 1785, (date recorded not shown). - names: - Ex: sons Daniel Tucker, John Tucker & Robert Tucker. - son Daniel Tucker - <u>Son William Tucker - all my lands below the aforesaid Liking Br. & the br. called Mirey Br. fr. one br. to the other north & south course, that is, on the e.s. of that line - plus negro Nancy.</u> - John on Son Robert Tucker - son David Tucker - Dau. Mary Chappell - Sarah Olds' three children - Dan. Anne Tucker - <u>Wife Ann</u> - Son Joel Tucker.

Following is the appraisal of estate of William Tucker Jr, who died 1786.

WB 4-6. Rec. 28 Sep 1786. Appraisal of <u>est. of William Tucker Jun, decd,</u> Included negro woman Nancy, girl Aggy, girl Milly, girl Patt. Total value L178.4.5 1/2. Appr: Joshua Hawks, Richard Hawks, Daniel Pitchford.

LAND TAX RECORDS-AMELIA CO.

1785	William Tucker Jr	244 ac.	
1788	Joel Tucker	244 ac.	(1788 alterations say "Wm Tucker 244 by Joel Tucker, Joel Tucker D of William Tucker 244".)

NOTTOWAY CO. VA.

LAND TAX RECORDS-NOTTOWAY CO.

1791-1795	Joel Tucker	244 ac.
1796-1798	Joel Tucker	207 ac.
1799-1819	Joel Tucker est	147 ac.

NOTE: The land which William Tucker Sr willed to his son William Tucker Jr lay in the area of Amelia Co. which was cut off into Nottoway Co. in 1789. The Land Tax records of Amelia Co. show William Tucker Jr "holding" 244 ac. in 1782 & 1787. The 1788 alterations show 244 ac. going from William Tucker to Joel Tucker. The Nottoway Co. Land Tax show Joel Tucker "holding" the 244 ac. 1789-1795. The probable meaning of this is that the 244 ac. which William Tucker Jr "held", included not only his inheritance, but also the inheritance of his younger brother Joel, who was to receive his inheritance at the death of his mother. No deed was found for the transfer of this land.

NOTE: There is no marriage record for William Tucker Jr in Amelia or Nottoway Co. and since he died without a will, it is most difficult to identify his family. However, other records identify his wife as Lucy Spain and children as Kennon Tucker, William N. Tucker, Mary Tucker and John Tucker (known as John Tucker Jr while under the guardianship of his uncle known as John Tucker Sr).

CO 2-261, <u>Kennon Tucker, William Tucker, John Tucker</u> by Kennon Tucker his next friend, & <u>Mary Tucker</u> - vs - <u>Lucy Tucker admx of William Tucker decd</u>. Appointed commissioners Peter Jones (R), Archer Jones, Lew Jones & Abner Osborne to <u>divide estate of sd decd among complainants</u> equally, after assigning one equal third part thereof to defendant widow for life as her dower in sd est. & return report.

CO 2-395, 11 Nov 1799, <u>Kennon Tucker, William Newman Tucker, John Tucker</u> by <u>Kennon</u> Tucker his next Friend, and <u>Mary Tucker</u>, plaintants - vs - <u>Lucy Tucker admx of William Tucker</u>, defendant. This day came complaintants by their attorney, & commissioners appointed by this court to <u>divide est of William Tucker decd</u> equally amongst the complaintants after assigning one equal third part thereof to the defendant widow of sd William as her dower - having returned their part - ordered that same be made final - & that complaintants enjoy their several shares allotted them, & that defendant enjoy for life her third of her husbands est allotted to her by sd commissioners.

Nottoway Co. records appear to indicate that William Tucker Jr, decd in 1786, had a brother named John and an orphan son named John, and that William Jr's brother John, became guardian of William Jr's son John.

WB 1-452, rec 3 Sep 1801, Debit John Tucker son of <u>William Tucker decd</u>, in acct with John Tucker Guardian Credit.

WB 1-501, 2 Sep 1802, John Tucker acct with John Tucker Guardian.

WB 2-26 1 Sep 1803, John Tucker <u>Orphan of Wm. Tucker</u> to John Tucker Gdn.

NOTE: The above documents would indicate that orphan John Tucker had not attained his majority in 1803. Because they lived in the same household, the uncle was referred to as John Tucker Sr and the nephew as John Tucker Jr. See separate chapters for John Tucker Jr and Martha (Patty) and John Tucker Sr and Mary (Polly).

HALIFAX CO., VA.

DB 7-162, 26 Oct 1825, rec 3 Nov 1825. <u>Lucy Tucker</u> of Halifax Co., Va. for love & affection to John Tucker of aforesaid Co., & for $1., gave to John Tucker all <u>her interest as legatee in land which Joshua Spain of Nottoway Co., died possessed of</u>. Wit Thomas E. Old, Catharine Walker, Wiley Chappell. Recorded in Halifax Co., Va. 22 Sep 1823.

SUMMARY: William Tucker Jr, son of William Tucker Sr & wf Ann, b ca 1744 Amelia Co, d 1786 Amelia Co, md probably in Amelia Co. after 1765, Lucy Spain dau of Joshua Spain, and had issue:

Kennon (Cannon) Tucker b ca 1774 in Amelia Co., md probably ca 1795 in Nottoway Co., Lucy _?_.

William Newman Tucker

Mary Tucker

John Tucker (Jr) b ca 1783 in Amelia Co.

TW152100 - KENNON TUCKER

MD LUCY
SON OF WILLIAM TUCKER JR
MD LUCY SPAIN

AMELIA CO., VA.

WB 4-6. Rec. 28 Sep 1786. <u>Appraisal of est. of William Tucker Jun, decd.</u> Included negro woman Nancy, girl Aggy, girl Milly, girl Patt. Total value L178.4.5 1/2. Appr: Joshua Hawks, Richard Hawks, Daniel Pitchford.

LAND TAX RECORDS

1785	William Tucker Jr	244 ac.	
1788	Joel Tucker	244 ac.	(1788 alterations say "Wm Tucker 244 by Joel Tucker, Joel Tucker D of William Tucker 244".)

NOTTOWAY CO. VA.

1789 Nottoway Co. was formed from Amelia Co.

LAND TAX RECORDS-NOTTOWAY CO.

1791-1795	Joel Tucker	244 ac.
1796-1798	Joel Tucker	207 ac.
1799-1819	Joel Tucker est.	147 ac.

NOTE: The land which William Tucker Sr willed to his son William Tucker Jr lay in the area of Amelia Co. which was cut off into Nottoway Co. in 1789. The Land Tax records of Amelia Co. show William Tucker Jr "holding" 244 ac. in 1782 & 1787. The 1788 alterations show 244 ac. going from William Tucker to Joel Tucker. The Nottoway Co. Land Tax show Joel Tucker "holding" the 244 ac. 1789-1795. The probable meaning of this is that the 244 ac. which William Tucker Jr "held", included not only his inheritance, but also the inheritance of his younger brother Joel, who was to receive his inheritance at the death of his mother. No deed was found for the transfer of this land from William Tucker (Jr) to Joel Tucker. However, when Joel Tucker's land tax holding was reduced in 1796 by 37 ac. from 244 ac. to 207 ac., and further reduced in 1799 by 60 ac. from 207 ac. to 147 ac., we find the following deeds recorded:

DB 1-456, 3 Jun 1795, rec 4 Jun 1795, <u>Kennon Tucker & wf Lucy of Nottoway Co, to Daniel Tucker, 37 ac.</u>, bo. Peter Jones, Uriah's branch. S/ Kennon x Tucker, Lucy x Tucker. Wit: Peter Jones Senr, Pleasant Bevill, Joshua Hawks Senr.

DB 2-2.5, 4 Oct 1797. rec 7 Jun 1798. <u>Cannon Tucker & wf Lucy of Nottoway Co. to Daniel Tucker, 60 ac.</u> bo. on east by Peter Jones & Richard Hawks, on west & south by William Greenhill, & on north by Daniel Tucker. S/ Cannon Tucker, Lucy x Tucker. Wit: Charles Morton, Joshua Hawks Sen, John Hawks, John Spain.

Now who was Kennon (or Cannon) Tucker? And why would he sell 37 + 60 = 97 ac., being part of the land "held" by Joel Tucker? This compiler contends that Kennon (or Cannon) Tucker was a son of William Tucker Jr, decd, whose land was held by Joel Tucker. When Kennon came of age & married, he sold his inheritance of 97 ac. to his uncle Daniel Tucker.

This theory is supported by two entries in Nottoway Co. Court Order Book 2:

CO 2-261, <u>Kennon Tucker</u>, William Tucker, John Tucker by Kennon Tucker his next friend, & Mary Tucker - vs - <u>Lucy Tucker admx of William Tucker decd</u>. Appointed commissioners Peter Jones (R), Archer Jones, Lew Jones & Abner Osborne to <u>divide estate of sd decd among complainants</u> equally, after assigning one equal third part thereof to defendant for life as her dower in sd est. & return report.

CO 2-395, 11 Nov 1799, <u>Kennon Tucker</u>, William Newman Tucker, John Tucker by Kennon Tucker his next friend, and Mary Tucker, plaintants - vs - <u>Lucy Tucker admx of William Tucker</u>, defendant. This day came complaintants by their attorney, & commissioners appointed by this court to <u>divide est of William Tucker decd</u> equally amongst the complaintants after assigning one equal third part thereof to the defendant widow of sd William as her dower - having returned their part - ordered that same be made final - & that complaintants enjoy their several shares allotted them, & that defendant enjoy for life her third of her husbands est allotted to her by sd commissioners.

If Kennon Tucker was age 21 when he sold land in 1795, he was b ca 1774. This compiler has found no further record of Kennon Tucker.

SUMMARY: Kennon Tucker son of William Tucker Jr & wf Lucy Spain, b ca 1774 in Amelia Co., md ca 1795, probably in either Amelia or Nottoway Co., Lucy _____.

TW152200 - WILLIAM NEWMAN TUCKER

MD ELIZABETH
SON OF WILLIAM TUCKER JR
MD LUCY SPAIN

AMELIA CO., VA.

WB 4-6. Rec. 28 Sep 1786. Appraisal of est. of William Tucker Jun, decd. Included negro woman Nancy, girl Aggy, girl Milly, girl Patt. Total value L178.4.5 1/2. Appr: Joshua Hawks, Richard Hawks, Daniel Pitchford.

NOTTOWAY CO., VA.

CO 2-261, Kennon Tucker, William Tucker, John Tucker by Kennon Tucker his next friend, & Mary Tucker - vs - Lucy Tucker admx of William Tucker decd. Appointed commissioners Peter Jones (R), Archer Jones, Lew Jones & Abner Osborne to divide estate of sd decd among complainants equally, after assigning one equal third part thereof to defendant for life as her dower in sd est. & return report.

CO 2-395, 11 Nov 1799, Kennon Tucker, William Newman Tucker, John Tucker by Kennon Tucker his next friend, and Mary Tucker, plaintants - vs - Lucy Tucker admx of William Tucker, defendant. This day came complainants by their attorney, & commissioners appointed by this court to divide est of William Tucker decd equally amongst the complainants after assigning one equal third part thereof to the defendant widow of sd William as her dower - having returned their part - ordered that same be made final - & that complainants enjoy their several shares allotted them, & that defendant enjoy for life her third of her husbands est allotted to her by sd commissioners.

NOTE: William N. Tucker was at least age 21 in 1799 when he was party to a court action, and was born probably before 1778.

DB 2-131, 3 Apr 1800, rec 3 Apr 1800. Lucy Hawks of Nottoway Co. to William N. Tucker, 60 ac., bo on east by Daniel Mann & Bass, on west by John Clay & Bland, on north by L. Jones & on south by Edward Johnson. Wit Archer Jones, Daniel Tucker, Cannon x Tucker. (See WB 2-162 for 6 ac & DB 2-269 for 54 ac.)

DB 2-162, 22 Apr 1800, rec 4 Sep 1800. William N. Tucker to Edward Johnston, 6 ac. by Henry Randolph on the west & Archer Bass on the east & adj sd Edward Johnston. Wit John Clay Jr, John Clay, Emanuel x Wicks. (See DB 2-131)

DB 2-269, 1 Oct 1800, rec 4 Feb 1802, William N. Tucker (also shown as William Newman Tucker) of Nottoway Co., to Pleasant Bevil, 54 ac., bo Henry Randolph, John Bland, Lin(?) Jones, Daniel Mann, Archer Bass, being part of tract which sd Tucker purchased of Lucy Hawks. Wit Edwd Bland, E. H. Dennis, H. Randolph. (See DB 2-131)

No other deeds were found for William N. Tucker in Nottoway Co. after 1800. Later references to a William N. Tucker are found in Halifax Co., Va beginning in 1835.

HALIFAX CO., VA.

WB 17-399, 1835, Inv est William N. Tucker.

WB 18-507, 3 Apr 1835, rec 23 Jul 1838. acct sales est William N. Tucker. Names mentioned Elizabeth Tucker, Polly Tucker.

1850 CENSUS [1]

Name	Age	Calculated Birthyear
Northern District	---	---
Household 43	---	---
Elizabeth Tucker	40	ca 1810
Elijah B.	15	ca 1835

LAND TAX RECORDS

1856-1864 Wm. N. Tucker Est, 124 ac. Terrible Cr.

DB 58-276, 2 May 1859, Elijah B. Tucker to Armistead Lacy, my interest in 124 ac. belonging to my father William N. Tucker's estate, now in the possession of my mother Elizabeth Tucker, widow of sd Wm. N. Tucker decd, in trust, to secure James L. Kirk as his security on a delivery bond to P. W. Newlin & Son for $73.56. (See DB 58-590)

DB 58-509, 15 Jan 1860, rec 23 Jan 1860, Eligy B. Tucker to James W. Woodall, his interest in a certain piece of land joining Mathew Richardson, Mrs. N. C. Holland & c, in trust, to secure a debt to John W. Canada for $53.00.

DB 58-590, 10 Dec 1859, rec 9 May 1860, Elijah B. Tucker to James E. Tucker for $75.00, 124 ac. bo. Ann Hill, Mathew Richardson & c, being the land on which the late Wm. N. Tucker died, now occupied by Elizabeth Tucker.

DB 59-71, 8 Aug 1860, rec 8 Aug 1860, Elijah B. Tucker to James D. Clay, trustee, one Bay Horse, all my growing crops of corn, fodder, shecks & Tobacco, in trust, to secure a debt due James E. Tucker upon an open acct, supposed to be about $200.

This compiler did not further research the William N. Tucker family, nor identify James E. Tucker.

SUMMARY: William N. Tucker son of William Tucker Jr & wf Lucy Spain, b probably before 1778 in Amelia Co., d ca 1835 in Halifax Co., VA, md Elizabeth _____ b ca 1810 & had issue:

Elijah B. Tucker b ca 1835.

* * *

1. Chiarito, Marian Dodson, "1850 Census of Halifax County, Virginia", 1982

TW152300 - JOHN TUCKER JR

MD MARTHA (PATTY) TUCKER
SON OF WILLIAM TUCKER JR
MD LUCY SPAIN

AMELIA CO., VA.

WB 4-6. Rec. 28 Sep 1786. Appraisal of est. of William Tucker Jun, decd. Included negro woman Nancy, girl Aggy, girl Milly, girl Patt. Total value L178.4.5 1/2. Appr: Joshua Hawks, Richard Hawks, Daniel Pitchford.

NOTTOWAY CO., VA.

1789. The area where William Tucker Jr lived in Amelia Co., became Nottoway Co.

CO 2-261, Kennon Tucker, William Tucker, John Tucker by Kennon Tucker his next friend, & Mary Tucker - vs - Lucy Tucker admx of William Tucker decd. Appointed commissioners Peter Jones (R), Archer Jones, Lew Jones & Abner Osborne to divide estate of sd decd among complainants equally, after assigning one equal third part thereof to defendant for life as her dower in sd est. & return report.

CO 2-395, 11 Nov 1799, Kennon Tucker, William Newman Tucker, John Tucker by Kennon Tucker his next friend, and Mary Tucker, plaintants - vs - Lucy Tucker admx of William Tucker, defendant. This day came complaintants by their attorney, & commissioners appointed by this court to divide est of William Tucker decd equally amongst the complaintants after assigning one equal third part thereof to the defendant widow of sd William as her dower - having returned their part - ordered that same he made final - & that complaintants enjoy their several shares allotted them, & that defendant enjoy for life her third of her husbands est allotted to her by sd commissioners.

Nottoway Co. records appear to indicate that William Tucker Jr, decd in 1786, had a brother named John and an orphan son named John, and that William Jr's brother John, became guardian of William Jr's son John.

WB 1-452, rec 3 Sep 1801, Debit John Tucker son of William Tucker decd, in acct with John Tucker Guardian Credit.

WB 1-501, 2 Sep 1802, John Tucker acct with John Tucker Guardian.

WB 2-26 1 Sep 1803, John Tucker Orphan of Wm. Tucker to John Tucker Gdn.

The above documents would indicate that orphan John Tucker had not attained his majority in 1803. Further identification of John Tucker orphan of William Tucker is difficult. However, this may be another case in which Sr-Jr did not mean father-son. It may be that John Tucker, brother of William Jr, was then the senior John, and became known as John Sr, while William Jr's orphan son John, was then the junior John and became known as John Jr. For we find that John Sr deeded land to John Jr, but did not identify him as a son. See following deed.

DB 4-457, 2 Nov 1814,, rec 2 Mar 1815, John Tucker & wf Mary of Nottoway Co. to <u>John Tucker Jr</u> of same County, for L100., <u>80 ac. bo.</u> Samuel Perkins, <u>John Tucker Sr, Godfrey Tucker, Robert Tucker</u>, Grief Ellington. S/ John Tucker.

DB 4-470 Apr 1815, rec 5 May 1815, Commissioners Samuel Morgan, Peter Perry & <u>John Tucker Jr</u> appointed to sell 106 ac. belonging to heirs of Sterling Williams decd & divide proceeds btwn his heirs, & sold the land to Godfrey Tucker for $547.60, payable in 12 months, bo. John Tucker Sr, William Wicks, Emanuel Wicks.

NOTE: The above deeds suggests that John Tucker Jr, was at least age 21 in 1814, so he was b before 1793. If he was son of William Jr who died 1786, he certainly was born before 1786 (possibly as early as 1783-see Halifax Co. 1850 census). Also, DB 4-457 did not identify John Jr as a son of John Sr, and DB 4-544. cited later, does not include John Jr as a son-heir of John Sr. So this John Tucker Jr may have been, instead, the orphan of William Tucker Jr, for whom John Tucker was guardian in 1801-03, cited above.

See also the following deed.

DB 4-544, 17 Jan 1816, rec 1 Feb 1816, Joel Tucker Jr of Halifax Co., Va., John E. Tucker & wf Polly, <u>John Tucker & wf Patty of Nottoway Co.</u> to Godfrey Tucker of Nottoway Co., for $480., 96 3/4 ac., <u>it being all the land which the late John Tucker Senr dec'd, died possessed of</u>, except 32 1/4 ac. of the same tract which sd Godfrey Tucker inherited from his father the sd John Tucker Senr, in Nottoway Co., bo. William Wicks, Sam'l Perkins, sd John Tucker and the land which Godfrey Tucker purchased from the estate of the late Sterling Williams decd. S/ Joel Tucker, John E Tucker, Polly x Tucker, John Tucker, Patty x Tucker. Acknowledged by Polly Tucker having a dower right, & <u>Patty Tucker having a right of inheritance</u> in the land conveyed.

The above deed identifies the heirs of John Tucker Sr as: Polly (Mary?) Tucker having a dower right; Patty (Martha?) Tucker having a right of inheritance; Joel Tucker Jr of Halifax Co.; and Godfrey Tucker. (For further discussion of this deed, see chapter on John Tucker & wf. Mary, son of William Tucker Sr & wf Ann.) This compiler contends that the John Tucker (with wf Patty) was known as John Tucker Jr, that he was the orphaned son of William Tucker Jr, and that he married Patty Tucker dau of John Tucker Sr who was the guardian of John Tucker Jr.

DB 4-469, 4 May 1815, John Tucker Jr & Peter Perry, bound for $200., condition that John Tucker Jr is appointed a Constable in Nottoway Co.

DB 4-470 Apr 1815, rec 5 May 1813, Commissioners Samuel Morgan, Peter Perry & John Tucker Jr appointed to sell 106 ac. belonging to heirs of Sterling Williams decd & divide proceeds btwn his heirs, & sold the land to Godfrey Tucker for $547.60, payable in 12 months, bo. John Tucker Sr, William Wicks, Emanuel Wicks, Robert Tucker. (See DB 4-544)

The Nottoway Land Tax Records for 1820-21 also show 80 ac. going from John Tucker Jr to Godfrey Tucker as 89 ac. Unfortunately, Nottoway Deed Book 9, which covers this period, is missing.

CO 9-71, 1 Apr 1824. John Spain, Newman Spain, Thomas B. Spain, William Spain, John Tucker, & Rebecca Spain - vs - Thomas P. Spain. Order to divide land of Joshua Spain Snr decd, est 204 3/4 ac., equally to John, Newman, Thomas B., William, Rebecca & Thomas P. Spain & John Tucker.

DB 7-162, 26 Oct 1825, rec 3 Nov 1825. Lucy Tucker of Halifax Co. Va. for love & affection to John Tucker of aforesaid Co., & for $1., gave to John Tucker all her interest as legatee, in land which Joshua Spain of Nottoway Co., died possessed of. Wit Thomas E. Old, Catharine Walker, Wiley Chappell. Recorded in Halifax Co., Va. 22 Sep 1823. (See DB 8-365)

DB 8-365, 10 Nov 1828, rec 5 Nov 1829, John Tucker & wf Martha of Halifax Co., to William Spain Jr of Nottoway Co., for $40., 29 ac. in Nottoway Co, bo Reuben Hawks, Thomas B. Spain, Samuel Scott. (See DB 7-162)

NOTE: The above deeds identify Lucy Tucker as: daughter of Joshua Spain, as wife of William Tucker Jr, and as mother of John Tucker who married Martha (Patty). The above 29 ac was Lucy Tucker's 1/7 share of 204.75 ac of Joshua Spain's estate (CO 9-71) which she gave (DB 7-162) to her son John Tucker.

HALIFAX CO., VA.

1850 CENSUS:

Birthdates of the John Tucker family
are calculated from ages shown in the census): [2]

Name	Age	Calculated Birthdate	
Southern District	--	---	---
Household # 174	--	---	---
John Tucker	67	ca 1783	Planter
Martha	75	ca 1775	
Robert A.	36	ca 1814	Overseer
Elizabeth T.	27	ca 1823	
William S	7	ca 1843	
James F.	5	ca 1845	
Henry	4	ca 1846	
Sarah	2	ca 1848	

John Tucker who was age 67 in the 1850 census was b ca 1783. It is assumed that Martha, age 75 in 1850 census, was his wife and was b ca 1775, eight years senior to her husband. Patty and Patsy were nicknames for Martha. It appears that John Tucker Jr in Nottoway DB 4-457 and John Tucker & wf Patty in Nottoway DB 4-544, are the same as John Tucker & wf Martha in Halifax 1850 census. His will also appears in Halifax Co.

WB 26-510, 15 Jun 1849, rec 26 Sep 1859. will of John Tucker. wife Martha & son Robert A. Tucker - land whereon I now reside to be enjoyed by them jointly during her life, & at her death to son R. A. Tucker & his heirs. Remainder of est to wf Martha for life, then to dau Mary, wf of James Walker - 1/3 part, son Robert A. Tucker - 2/3 part. Exor: son Robert A. Tucker. S/ John Tucker, Wit: Nathaniel W. Carlton, Alillian Old.

SUMMARY: John Tucker Jr, son of William Tucker Jr & wf Lucy Spain, b ca 1783 in Amelia Co, d 1859 in Halifax Co, Va, md probably ca 1804 in Nottoway Co. Patty (Martha) Tucker, dau of John Tucker (Sr) & wf Mary (Polly), & had issue:

Mary Tucker md James Walker.

Robert A. Tucker b ca 1814 probably Nottoway Co, md Elizabeth T. ____ b ca 1823, & had issue:

1. William S. Tucker b ca 1843.

2. James F. Tucker b ca 1845.

3. Henry Tucker b ca 1846.

4. Sarah Tucker b ca 1848.

* * *

2. Chiarito, Marian Dodson, "1850 Census of Halifax County, Virginia", 1982

TW153000 - JOHN TUCKER SR

MD MARY
SON OF WILLIAM TUCKER SR
MD ANN

AMELIA CO. VA.

NOTE: In the Lists of Tithables for Amelia Co., John Tucker is listed as a 16 yr-up tithable in the household of his father William Tucker Sr from 1763-1770. Thus John Tucker was born ca 1747, and was age 21 ca 1768.

WB 3-300, will of William Tucker, 8 Feb 1785, (date recorded not shown). -names: - Ex: sons Daniel Tucker, John Tucker & Robert Tucker. - son Daniel Tucker - Son William Tucker - Son John Tucker - land which I purchased of Allen Hinton, & Robert Hinton - also 25 ac. most convenient to him of the land I purchased of William Watson. - Son Robert Tucker - son David Tucker Dau. Mary Chappell - Dau. Sarah Olds' three children - Dau. Anne Tucker - Wife Ann - Son John Tucker to have negro Peter - Son Joel Tucker.

NOTE: For land purchased by William Tucker: from Allen Hinton see DB 8-183 - 105 ac.; from Robert Hinton see DB 8-238 - 70 ac.; from William Watson (unable to find deed from Watson, but see DB 11-199 for 545 ac. purchased from John Hamlin).

DB 8-183, 21 Aug 1763, rec. 25 Aug 1763. Allen Hinton to William Tucker for L30, 105 ac. btwn the Sweathouse Fork & the Lower Seller Fork of Deep Cr., it being part of 400 ac. formerly pat. to Christopher Hinton, bo. Francis Bolling. Wit: William Hall, Thomas Powell, William Covington. S/ Allin Hinton, Rosamond Hinton. (See DB 15-220)

DB 8-238, rec., 24 Nov 1763, Robert Hinton & wf Elizabeth to William Tucker, for L13 70 ac. on head of Sweathouse Cr., adj. Col. Bland, being part of a tract patented to Christopher Hinton Senr. 2 Jan 1737. S/ Robert x Hinton, Eliz'a x Hinton.

DB 11-199, 25 Jul 1770, John Hamlin & wf Philadelphia to William Tucker Sen, for L109, 545 ac. being the greater part in Amelia Co. & lesser in Dinwiddie Co., on head of Namaseen Cr., bo. Pryor's cor. & Tucker's cor. Wit: Sam'l Wills, Daniel Tucker, R. Bradfute.

NOTE: The land which John Tucker inherited from his father William Tucker Sr included 105 ac. purchased from Allen Hinton, 70 ac. purchased from Robert Hinton, plus 25 ac. purchased from John Hamlin, totaling 200 ac. This land lay in the area of Amelia Co. which was cut off to form Nottoway Co. in 1789.

DB 15-220, 25 Nov 1779, Thomas Bonner & wf Elizabeth to John Tucker, for L800., 106 ac. on both sides of Swethouse Cr., bo. Watson's cor. & line, Bennet's line. S/ Thos. Bonner, Elizabeth Bonner. (See DB 16--24).

DB 15-356, 27 Jul 1780, William Munford to John Tucker son of William Tucker of Cellar Cr. Whereas Thomas Bomar late by his indenture of mortgage 25 Jun 1772 to secure pmt to Wm. Munford (land) on b.s. Swethouse Cr. (acres not shown) & whereas Thomas Bonner (Bomar?) satisfied all debts which sd Wm. Munford had against him - sold to John Tucker for LI5., (bounds & acres not shown). S/ Wm. Munford. (Note: in the mortgage Bomar to Munford, DB 11-455, bounds are shown as Swethouse Cr., Watson's line, Bennet's line, but number of acres was not shown there either).

DB 16-24, 2 Nov 1781, John Tucker to David Williams, 106 ac. b.s. Swethouse Cr., bo. Bennet's line, John Tucker, Robert Tucker, Emanual Weeks, Benjamin Bennet. Wit: Dan Tucker, Sterling Williams. S/ John Tucker. (See Amelia Co. DB 15-220 & Nottoway Co. DB 4-470).

LAND TAX RECORDS - AMELIA CO.

1782   John Tucker   100 ac.
1788   John Tucker   200 ac.

NOTTOWAY CO. VA.

LAND TAX RECORDS - NOTTOWAY CO.

1789 -1814 John Tucker Jr, 200 ac.
1815   John Tucker Sr, 120 ac. (80 ac. to John Tucker Jr from John Tucker Sr)
1816   (-32 1/4 ac. to Godfrey Tucker fr John Tucker's est
            (-96 3/4 ac. to Godfrey Tucker fr Joel Tucker & others which was charged to John Tucker Sr, Celler Cr. adj. Grief Ellington.
            (- 9 ac. - overrun by new survey.)
            NOTE: 32 1/4 + 96 3/4 + 9 = 120 ac. in est. of John Tucker Sr.

The following three records indicate the subject John Tucker was guardian to his nephew John Tucker son of William Tucker.

WB 1-452, rec 3 Sep 1801, Debit John Tucker son of William Tucker decd, in acct with John Tucker Guardian Credit.

WB 1-501, 2 Sep 1802, John Tucker acct with John Tucker Guardian.

WB 2-26, 1 Sep 1803, John Tucker Orphan of Wm. Tucker to John Tucker Gdn.

DB 4-457, 2 Nov 1814,, rec 2 Mar 1815, John Tucker & wf Mary of Nottoway Co. to John Tucker Jr of same County, for L100., 80 ac. bo. Samuel Perkins, John Tucker Sr, Godfrey Tucker, Robert Tucker, Grief Ellington. S/ John Tucker.

NOTE: The above deed did not identify John Tucker Jr as a son of John Tucker Sr, and DB 4-544. cited later, did not include John Tucker Jr as an heir of John Tucker Sr. So this John Tucker Jr may be, instead, the orphan of William Tucker Jr, for whom John Tucker was guardian in 1801-03, cited above. (See chapter on William Tucker Jr)

DB 4-470 Apr 1815, rec 5 May 1815, Commissioners Samuel Morgan, Peter Perry & John Tucker Jr appointed to sell 106 ac, belonging to heirs of Sterling Williams decd & divide proceeds htwn his heirs, & sold the land to Godfrey Tucker for $547.60, payable in 12 months, bo. John Tucker Sr, William Wicks, Emanuel Wicks, Robert Tucker. (See Amelia Co. DB 16-24 & Nottoway Co. DB 4-544)

NOTE: If Godfrey Tucker was age 21 in 1815, he was b ca 1794.

NOTE: The 106 ac. which John Tucker Sr bought from Thomas Bonner in 1779 (Amelia DB 15-220) and sold to David Williams in 1781 (Amelia DB 16-24), to which Sterling Williams was a witness, seem to be the same 106 ac. which the heirs of Sterling Williams sold to Godfrey Tucker in 1817 (Nottoway Co. DB 4-470). This acreage was overstated by 18 ac. and shows up as 88 ac. on the land tax records for Godfrey Tucker beginning in 1817.

CO 1-44 - Indenture of sale btwn Godfrey Tucker, David Williams, Jane Williams, Sterling Williams & Benedict Jackson, proved by witnesses Anderson Moore, Francis Lewis & Abraham Seward.

The above court order refers to DB 4-470, and seems to identify the heirs of Sterling Williams who sold the 106 ac. to Godfrey Tucker.

WB 4-5, 26 Oct 1815, rec 3 Oct 1816, Inventory of est. of John Tucker decd, by Godfrey Tucker, administrator, included household furnishings & farm equipment and slaves Becky, Archer, Ussey, Dick, William, & Washington.

NOTE: The above inventory indicates the subject John Tucker Sr died intestate in 1815.

DB 4-544, 17 Jan 1816, rec 1 Feb 1816, <u>Joel Tucker Jr of Halifax Co.,</u> <u>Va., John E. Tucker & wf Polly, John Tucker & wf Patty of Nottoway</u> <u>Co, to Godfrey Tucker of Nottoway Co.,</u> for $480. <u>96 3/4 ac., it being all</u> <u>the land which the late John Tucker Senr dec'd died possessed of,</u> except 32 1/4 ac. of the same tract which sd Godfrey Tucker inherited from his father the sd John Tucker Senr, in Nottoway Co., bo. William Wicks, Sam'l Perkins, sd John Tucker, and the land which Godfrey Tucker purchased from the estate of the late Sterling Williams decd. S/ Joel Tucker, John E Tucker, Polly x Tucker, John Tucker, Patty x Tucker. Acknowledged by <u>Polly Tucker having a dower right, & Patty Tucker</u> <u>having a right of inheritance</u> in the land conveyed. (See DB 4-470)

NOTE: The meaning of the above DB 4-544 is most confusing. It appears that:

(1) the John Tucker Sr was the same John Tucker whose est. I&A was recorded in WB 4-5, dated 26 Oct 1815, rec. 3 Oct 1816, with Godfrey Tucker Administrator.

(2) John Tucker Sr inherited 200 ac. from his father William Tucker Sr. He sold 80 ac. to a John Tucker Jr (not identified as a son), leaving 120 ac. in his estate.

(3) His son Godfrey Tucker claimed 32 1/4 ac. as his inheritance, which is approximately 1/4, leaving 87 3/4 ac. as the remaining 3/4. This was overrun by 9 ac. and adjusted to 96 3/4 ac. which the remaining heirs then sold to Godfrey.

(4) Polly Tucker who had a dower interest, must he the same as Mary Tucker widow of John Tucker Sr, who subsequently had married a John E. Tucker

(5) Patty (Martha?) Tucker who had a right of inheritance must he a dau of John Tucker Sr, who married yet another John Tucker.

(6) John Tucker Jr is not included among the heirs of John Tucker Sr, but as the husband of Patty who was an heir, and he may he the orphan of William Tucker for whom John Tucker Sr was guardian.

(7) Joel Tucker Jr of Halifax Co., Va. was most probably son of John Tucker Sr, but was known as Joel Jr because he was younger than an uncle Joel Tucker who held 147 ac. in the same area of Nottoway Co. 1789-1819. The Joel Jr is most probably the same Joel Tucker Jr who was named (but not as a son) in the will of Joel Tucker Sr in 1854 in Halifax Co. (WB 24-177).

(8) Thus the heirs of John Tucker Sr at his death seem to he:

(a) widow Mary (Polly) who later married John E. Tucker,

(b) son Godfrey,

(c) son Joel Jr,

(d) dau Patty (Martha).

From DB 4-544, Mary (Polly) Tucker, widow of John Tucker Sr, subsequently married one John E. Tucker (identity unknown). The Nottoway Land Tax Records show John E. Tucker holding land beginnig in 1816. Unfortunately Land Tax Records after 1836 and Deed Book 9 and Deed Books 11-beyond are missing, so we have only the following documents to support the land transactions of John E. Tucker:

LAND TAX RECORDS

1816-19	John E. Tucker	91 + 19 = 110 ac.
1820-27	John E. Tucker	110 ac.
1828-30	John E. Tucker	99 1/8 + 4 = 103 1/8 ac.
1831-32	John E. Tucker	103 1/8 ac.
1833-36	John E. Tucker	103 1/8 + 63 = 166 1/8 ac.

DB 7-346, 27 Feb 1827, rec 2 Mar 1827, Edward Bland to John E. Tucker for $32., 4 ac. on Leath's Cr, adj sd John E. Tucker , bo. Jones.

DB 7-347, 7 Feb 1827, rec 2 Mar 1827, John E. Tucker to Edward Bland for $54., 10 7/8 ac. adj. sd Edward Bland.

John E. Tucker is also named as a legatee of slaves in the will of Joel Tucker Sr (Halifax Co Va WB 24-77, probated 23 Jan 1854)

SUMMARY: John Tucker Sr, son of William Tucker Sr & wf Ann of Amelia Co, b ca 1747 in Amelia Co, d 1815 in Nottoway Co, md Mary (Polly) and had issue:

Godfrey Tucker b ca 1794.

Joel Tucker Jr.

Patty (Martha) Tucker md a John Tucker (most probably John Tucker Jr, orphaned son of William Tucker Jr, under guardianship of the subject John Tucker Sr.)

TW153100 - JOEL TUCKER JR
MD SALLY CLEMENTS
SON OF JOHN TUCKER SR
MD MARY

NOTTOWAY CO., VA.

DB 4-544, 17 Jan 1816, rec 1 Feb 1816, <u>Joel Tucker Jr of Halifax Co. Va.</u>, John E. Tucker & wf Polly, John Tucker & wf Patty of Nottoway Co, to Godfrey Tucker of Nottoway Co., for $480., <u>96 3/4 ac., it being all the land which the late John Tucker Senr dec'd, died possessed of, except 32 1/4 ac. of the same tract which sd Godfrey Tucker inherited from his father the sd John Tucker Senr</u>, in Nottoway Co., bo. William Wicks, Sam'l Perkins, sd John Tucker, and land which Godfrey Tucker purchased from the estate of the late Sterling Williams decd. S/ Joel Tucker, John E Tucker, Polly x Tucker, John Tucker, Patty x Tucker. Acknowledged by <u>Polly Tucker having a dower right & Patty Tucker having a right of inheritance</u> in the land conveyed. (See DB 4-470)

NOTE: The meaning of the above DB 4-544 is most confusing. It appears that:

(1) the John Tucker Sr was the same John Tucker whose est. I&A was recorded in WB 4-5, dated 26 Oct 1815, rec. 3 Oct 1816, with Godfrey Tucker Administrator.

(2) John Tucker Sr inherited 200 ac. from his father William Tucker Sr. He sold 80 ac. to a John Tucker Jr (not identified as a son), leaving 120 ac. in his estate.

(3) His son Godfrey Tucker claimed 32 1/4 ac. as his inheritance, which is approximately 1/4, leaving 87 3/4 ac. as the remaining 3/4. This was overrun by 9 ac. and adjusted to 96 3/4 ac. which the remaining heirs then sold to Godfrey.

(4) Polly Tucker who had a dower interest, must he the same as Mary Tucker widow of John Tucker Sr, who subsequently had married a John E. Tucker

(5) Patty (Martha?) Tucker who had a right of inheritance must he a dau of John Tucker Sr, who married yet another John Tucker.

(6) John Tucker Jr is not included among the heirs of John Tucker Sr, but as the husband of Patty who was an heir, and he may he the orphan of William Tucker for whom John Tucker Sr was guardian.

(7) Joel Tucker Jr of Halifax Co., Va. was most probably son of John Tucker Sr, but was known as Joel Jr because he was younger than an uncle Joel Tucker who held 147 ac. in the same area of Nottoway Co. 1789-1819. The Joel Jr is most probably the same Joel Tucker Jr who was named (but not as a son) in the will of. Joel Tucker Sr in 1854 in

Halifax Co. (WB 24-177).

(8) Thus the heirs of John Tucker Sr at his death seem to be:

(a) widow Mary (Polly) who later married John E. Tucker,

(b) son Godfrey,

(c) son Joel Jr,

(d) dau Patty (Martha).

HALIFAX CO. VA

MB 1-75, 17 Nov 1810. Joel Tucker Jr md Sally Clements, Bondsman Benjamin Clements.

DB 29-341 rec 28 May 1821 Thomas Clay Sr to Joel Tucker Jr, for $85., 20 1/2 ac. adj. Anderson's Rd. & being part of tract whereon Thomas Clay now resides, formerly Locketts, bo. Anderson's Rd, where the lines of Obed(?) Hendrick, Williams, Hughes & sd Thomas Clay intersect, William Parker, Joel Tucker, Hendricks.

DB 34-160 rec 29 Sep 1826, William Parker Sr to Joel Tucker for $715.60, 119.1 ac. on waters of Chestnut(?) Cr. bo. Clay's line.

DB 34-575, 27 Apr 1827, rec 25 Jun 1827, Obediah Hendrick to Joel Tucker Sr, for $30., 3 1/2 ac. on w.s. Little Polecat Cr.. Wit: George W. Wood, Joel Tucker Jr, Andrew Anderson.

DB 36-431, 25 Oct 1828, rec 27 Oct 1828, (1) William Tucker, (2) Joel Tucker Jr (3) David Tucker, to secure debt of William Tucker to David Tucker for $524.48, pledged horses, cows, household furniture and equipment, etc. Wit: James O. Tucker, Joel Tucker.

WB 24-177, wd 25 Nov 1839, wp 23 Jan 1854, will of Joel Tucker Sr. Wife Nancy Tucker - all tract of land lying west of the road and on which I now live with all houses, furniture, 6 negroes of her choice, a horse of her choice, my carryall, 1/3 part of stock. Residue of negroes divided in 6 parts & equally divided between James O. Tucker, Joel Tucker Jun, John E. Tucker, Robert Tucker, John Tucker & Jane B. Stimpson. (Note: both John E. Tucker & John Tucker appeared as shown) Land lying east of the road with all stock be sold & money distributed as follows: $150.00 to wife Nancy Tucker, $100.00 to Martha Dickie, $50.00 to Martha Watson, $50.00 equally divided btwn two nieces Nancy Tucker & Martha Tucker; $50.00 to Joel Tucker Jr; $50.00 equally div. btwn Sarah Ford & Mary Ford. Ex. not to give bond or security & est. not to be appraised. Ex: James O. Tucker & John Tucker. S/ Joel Tucker.

NOTE: For a further discussion of this will, see chapter on Joel Tucker Sr son of William Tucker Sr & wf Ann.

NOTE: The subject <u>Joel Tucker Jr</u> is believed by this compiler, to be <u>not the son of Joel Tucker Sr, but the son of John Tucker Sr & wf Mary (Polly)</u> of Nottoway Co. In Nottoway DB 4-544, he is included among the heirs of John Tucker Sr. In Halifax WB 24-177, he is named in the will of Joel Tucker Sr, but not identified as a son.

The following account claims that Joel Tucker Jr and Robert A. Tucker are sons of Joel Tucker Sr. This was apparantly based upon them being "named" in the will of Joel Tucker Sr, but that will did not identify either of them as a son, and this account offers no other citation of proof.

> STOKES CO. N.C. (Book Stokes Co., Heritage, N. C.)
> Joel Tucker Sr from Halifax Co. Va - 2 sons Robert A. Tucker & Joel Tucker Jr. Joel Tucker Jr b 1790 d 1853, will Dec 1844 (1854?)Halifax Co., Va. Joel was residing with his son Benj. in Stokes Co., N. C. 1850 Census. Children Gabriel W. Tucker, b 1813 died post 1880 Benjamin C. Tucker b 1815, died post 1880. Benjamin C. Tucker was a farmer & carpenter born in Halifax Co. Va., md 1st Sicily Simmons 2 Jul 1833, Stokes Co,.N.C. md 2nd Elizabeth Hill 24 May 1845, Stokes Co.,N.C.

The above account is believed by this compiler to be incorrect in part, for the following reasons:

Robert A. Tucker is identified in WB 26-510 (1859) as son of John Tucker & wf Martha, and is shown with his family in the 1850 census of Halifax Co. as age 36 overseer in the household #174 of his parents John & Martha Tucker. [3]

Joel Tucker Jr is identified in Nottoway Co. DB 4-544 as an implied heir of John Tucker Sr & wf Mary (Polly).

SUMMARY: Joel Tucker Jr, probably son of John Tucker Sr & wf Mary (Polly), b 1790 probably in Nottoway Co., d 1853 probably in Stokes Co. NC, md 1810 in Halifax Co., Va., Sally Clements, probably dau of Benjamin Clements & wf Sarah, & had issue: (per citation above but not verified by this compiler)

> Gabriel W. Tucker b 1813, probably in Halifax Co., Va., d post 1880.

> Benjamin C. Tucker b 1815, probably in Halifax Co., Va., d post 1880, probably in Stokes Co., NC., md 1st 1833 Stokes Co., NC, Sicily Simmons, md 2nd 1845 Stokes Co., NC, Elizabeth Hill.

TW153200 - GODFREY TUCKER

SON OF JOHN TUCKER SR

MD MARY

NOTTOWAY CO., VA.

LAND TAX RECORDS - NOTTOWAY CO.

1789 -1814 John Tucker Jr, 200 ac.

1815 John Tucker Sr, 120 ac. (80 ac. to John Tucker Jr from John Tucker Sr)

1816 (-32 1/4 ac. to Godfrey Tucker fr John Tucker's est.

(-96 3/4 ac. to Godfrey Tucker fr Joel Tucker & others which was charged to John Tucker Sr , Celler Cr. adj. Grief Ellington.

(- 9 ac. - overrun by new survey.)

NOTE: 32 1/4 + 96 3/4 + 9 = 120 ac. in est. of John Tucker Sr

1815 -1816 Godfrey Tucker, 106 ac fr Sterling Williams est.

1817 -1819 Godfrey Tucker, 88 ac (charged with 18 ac. too much which is taken off) (106-18=88)

1816 -1819 Godfrey Tucker, 88 ac. plus 32 1/4 ac. (fr John Tuckers est.) plus 96 3/4 ac. (fr Joel Tucker & others which was charged to John Tucker Sr, Celler Cr. adj. Grief Ellington) = 217 ac.

1820 -1830 Godfrey Tucker, 217 ac.

1821-1830 Godfrey Tucker, 217 ac. plus 89 ac. - over 9 ac. (Land Tax entry says fr "John N. Tucker"; explanation of changes at end of report says fr "John Tucker Jr".) 217 + 89 = 306 ac. (Note: Deed Books 5 & 6 btwn 1816-1825 have been destroyed, but by DB 4-457, 1814, John Tucker & wf Mary sold 80 ac. to John Tucker Jr.)

1831-1836 Godfrey Tucker, 306 ac.

1837-1839 Godfrey Tucker, 306 ac. plus 30 ac. (fr Robert Pollard, Cellar Cr. adj J. F. Ellington) = 336 ac.

1840 Godfrey Tucker, 336 ac.

1841-1850 Godfrey Tucker est. 336 ac.

DB 4-457, 2 Nov 1814,, rec 2 Mar 1815, John Tucker & wf Mary of Nottoway Co. to John Tucker Jr of same County, for L100., 80 ac. bo. Samuel Perkins, John Tucker Sr, Godfrey Tucker, Robert Tucker, Grief Ellington. S/ John Tucker.

DB 4-470 Apr 1815, rec 5 May 1815, Commissioners Samuel Morgan, Peter Perry & John Tucker Jr appointed to sell 106 ac. belonging to heirs of Sterling Williams decd & divide proceeds btwn his heirs, & sold the land to Godfrey Tucker for $547.60, payable in 12 months, bo. John Tucker Sr, William Wicks, Emanuel Wicks.

NOTE: If Godfrey Tucker was age 21 in 1815, he was b ca 1794.

NOTE: The 106 ac. which John Tucker Sr bought from Thomas Bonner in 1779 (Amelia DB 15-220) and sold to David Williams in 1781 (Amelia DB 16-24, to which Sterling Williams was a witness), seem to be the same 106 ac. which the heirs of Sterling Williams sold to Godfrey Tucker in 1817 (Nottoway Co. DB 4-470). This acreage was overstated by 18 ac. and shows up as 88 ac. on the land tax records for Godfrey Tucker beginning in 1817.

CO 1-44 - Indenture of sale btwn Godfrey Tucker, David Williams, Jane Williams, Sterling Williams & Benedict Jackson, proved by witnesses Anderson Moore, Francis Lewis & Abraham Seward.

The above court order refers to DB 4-470, and seems to identify the heirs of Sterling Williams who sold the 106 ac. to Godfrey Tucker.

WB 4-5, 26 Oct 1815, rec 3 Oct 1816, Inventory of est. of John Tucker decd, by Godfrey Tucker administrator, included household furnishings & farm equipment and slaves Becky, Archer, Ussey, Dick, William, & Washington.

NOTE: The above inventory indicates the subject John Tucker Sr died intestate in 1815.

DB 4-544, 17 Jan 1816, rec 1 Feb 1816, Joel Tucker Jr of Halifax Co., Va., John E. Tucker & wf Polly, John Tucker & wf Patty of Nottoway Co, to Godfrey Tucker of Nottoway Co., for $480., 96 3/4 ac., it being all the land which the late John Tucker Senr dec'd, died possessed of, except 32 1/4 ac. of the same tract which sd Godfrey Tucker inherited from his father the sd John Tucker Senr, in Nottoway Co., bo. William Wicks, Sam'l Perkins, sd John Tucker, the land which Godfrey Tucker purchased from the estate of the late Sterling Williams decd. S/ Joel Tucker, John E Tucker, Polly x Tucker, John Tucker, Patty x Tucker. Acknowledged by Polly Tucker having a dower righter & Patty. Tucker having a right of inheritance in the land conveyed. (See DB 4-470)

NOTE: The meaning of the above DB 4-544 is most confusing. It appears that:
(1) the John Tucker Sr was the same John Tucker whose est. I&A was recorded in WB 4-5, dated 26 Oct 1815, rec. 3 Oct 1816, with Godfrey Tucker Administrator.
(2) John Tucker Sr inherited 200 ac. from his father William Tucker Sr.

He sold 80 ac. to a John Tucker Jr (not identified as a son), leaving 120 ac. in his estate.

(3) His son Godfrey Tucker claimed 32 1/4 ac. as his inheritance, which is approximately 1/4, leaving 87 3/4 ac. as the remaining 3/4. This was overrun by 9 ac. and adjusted to 96 3/4 ac. which the remaining heirs then sold to Godfrey.

(4) Polly Tucker who had a dower interest, must be the same as Mary Tucker widow of John Tucker Sr, who subsequently had married a John E. Tucker.

(5) Patty (Martha?) Tucker who had a right of inheritance must he a dau of John Tucker Sr, who married yet another John Tucker.

(6) John Tucker Jr is not included among the heirs of John Tucker Sr, but as the husband of Patty who was an heir, and he may be the orphan of William Tucker for whom John Tucker Sr was guardian.

(7) Joel Tucker Jr of Halifax Co., Va. was most probably son of John Tucker Sr, but was known as Joel Jr because he was younger than an uncle Joel Tucker who held 147 ac. in the same area of Nottoway Co. 1789-1819. The Joel Jr is most probably the same Joel Tucker Jr who was named (but not as a son) in the will of Joel Tucker Sr in 1854 in Halifax Co. (WB 24-177).

(8) Thus the heirs of John Tucker Sr at his death seem to be:

(a) widow Mary (Polly) who later married John E. Tucker,

(b) son Godfrey,

(c) son Joel Jr,

(d) dau Patty (Martha).

NOTE: In 1837, the land tax records show an additional 30 ac. added to Godfrey Tucker fr Robert Pollard, Cellar Cr adj J. F. Ellington. Deed Book 9 (1828 -1839) has been destroyed, so this transaction could not he verified. Also destroyed are Deed Books 11 and beyond (1841 -) Will Books 9 and beyond (1846 -), Land Tax Records after 1850, and marriage records, so no further identification of Godfrey Tucker or disposition of his estate of 336 ac. is known to this compiler. But by 1850 he had inherited or bought the 200 ac. plus 106 ac. formerly owned by his father John Tucker Sr, plus an additional 30 ac.

SUMMARY: Godfrey Tucker, son of John Tucker Sr & wf Mary (Polly), b ca 1794 in Nottoway Co., Va., was last known to have had an estate of 336 ac. in Nottoway Co. 1841-1850.

TW154000 - ROBERT TUCKER

MD MARY HAWKS
SON OF WILLIAM TUCKER SR
MD ANN

AMELIA CO. VA.

LIST OF TITHABLES

1767 -1770 Robert Tucker is listed as 16-yr-up tithable in the household of William Tucker. If he was age 16 in 1767, then he was born ca 1751, and attained age 21 ca 1772, or possibly earlier. He was most probably age 21 in 1771 when he deeded land, and no longer appeared as a tithable in the household of his father. Thus he would have been born ca 1750, and age 16 ca 1766.

PERSONAL TAX RECORDS

1782	11	Robert Tucker	Will, Hannah, Sue, Tom, Sall, Sily, Silvy, Lucy, Tab Judy
1783	3	Robert Tucker	
1784	2	Robert Tucker	
1785	1	Robert Tucker	
1786	1	Robert Tucker	
1787	1	Robert Tucker	
1790	0	Robert Tucker	

DB 11-263, 15 Apr 1771, Stephen Dance & wf Phebe, of Dinwiddie Co., to Rob't Tucker of Amelia Co., for L50, 135 ac. bo. Rob't Bolling's line, James Bevill's cor. & line, a branch, Daniel Tucker's line. Wit: Matthew Dance, William Roach, David x Tucker. S/ Stephen Dance, Phebe Dance.

NOTE: This compiler has found no deed disposing of the above 135 ac. The only entry in the land tax records, beginning in 1782, for a Robert Tucker was 545 ac. in Nottoway Parish.

Marriage Bonds, 7 Dec 1778, Robert Tucker md Mary Hawks, Security: Daniel Tucker.

WB 2-151, wd 21 Jul 1770, wp 28 Sep 1775, will of Joshua Hawks of Raleigh Parish, Planter, to: son Richard Hawks - all land n.s. Reedy Br. that he lives on, plus 5 shillings sterling; son John Hawks - all land s.s. of sd Br. in the fork; son Joshua Hawks - remainder of sd tract that contains the plantation whereon I now live; son George Hawks - 150 ac. whereon he has built his house on the Meadow Br.; sons John & Joshua - remainder of tract that George has built on, equally divided btwn them; dau. Frances Simmons - negro girl Rachel, plus 5 shillings sterling; dau. Mary Hawks - 1 feather bed & furniture; dau. Rebecca Hawks - 1 feather bed & furniture; dau. Lewsee Hawks - feather bed & furniture; <u>wife Angelica Hawks</u> - all my estate that I am possessed with at my decease, real & personal of negroes, stock, horses, hogs, cattle & sheep, & household & kitchen furniture, for life, & afterward, equally divided btwn my six children named here: George, John, Joshua, Mary, Rebeckah, & Lewsee Hawks. Exors: wf Angelica Hawks & son George Hawks. <u>Wit: John Clay John Clay Jr</u>, William Adams.

WB 3-300, <u>will of William Tucker</u>, 8 Feb 1785, (date recorded not shown) - <u>Ex:</u> sons Daniel Tucker, John Tucker & <u>Robert Tucker</u>. - son Daniel Tucker - Son William Tucker – Son John Tucker - <u>Son Robert Tucker & son David Tucker - land which I purchased of William Watson, except those 25 ac. already bequeathed to son John Tucker, to be divided between them by running a line they think proper - Son Robert - negro Jack</u> - Dau. Mary Chappell - Dau. Sarah Olds' three children - Dau. Ann Tucker - <u>Wife Ann</u> - <u>Son Robert to have negro Missse & incr.</u> - Son Joel Tucker.

DB 17-300, rec 22 Dec 1785, -- Whereas sd <u>Angelica Hawkes desiring a div. of est. of her late husb. Joshua Hawkes decd, should be made agreeable to his will - for natural love & affection unto</u> John Hawks, Joshua Hawks, <u>Robert Tucker & wf Mary</u>, Rebecca Hawks, heirs of George Hawks decd, heirs of Lucy Hawks decd - - and for their better support & maintenance & further consid. of L25., to be paid annually for use of the lands, <u>I have given up, released & quitclaim (to above named children) all my right, title & interest in est. of my late husb.</u>, to be divided among them agreeable to the will of <u>sd Joshua</u> - S/ Angelica Hawks. <u>Wit</u>: David Williams, <u>Joel Tucker, Daniel Tucker</u>.

LAND TAX RECORDS - AMELIA CO.

1782	Robert Tucker	545 ac.	
1787	Robert Tucker	345 ac.	(-200 ac. to David Tucker)
1788	Robert Tucker	320 ac.	(- 25 ac. (?)to John Tucker)

NOTTOWAY CO., VA.

LAND TAX RECORDS - NOTTOWAY CO.

1789 -1801	Robert Tucker	320 ac.
1802 -1814	Robert Tucker Sr	320 ac. on Namozine Cr.
1815 -1817	Robert Tucker Sr est.	320 ac.
1818 -1836	Robert Tucker Sr est.	177.5 ac.
1816 -1839	William Tucker	57 3/4 ac. fr Reuben Weeks Trustee, on Namozene Cr. adj Reuben Weeks est
1814 -1819	Joel Tucker est	147 ac.

NOTE: Robert Tucker Sr apparently died ca 1815 when his land tax records were described as "estate" He was listed as Robert Tucker Sr beginning in 1802, which implies he had a son Robert Jr. b ca 1802.

NOTE: It is most difficult to reconcile the number acres of land Robert Tucker inherited from his father William Tucker Sr. William Tucker Sr bought 545 ac. on Namozine Cr. in Amelia Co. in 1770 from John Hamlin. This was most probably the acreage referred to in will of William Tucker Sr as "purchased of William Watson", with 25 ac. going to John & remainder divided between Robert and David.

Robert Tucker "held" 545 ac. in 1782, which was reduced by 200 ac. (to David) in 1787, and reduced by another 25 ac. (possibly to John) in 1788, leaving 320 ac. Robert then held the 320 ac. on Namozine Cr adj Richard Hawks until his death in 1815. So it appears that Robert's inheritance from his father consisted of 320 ac.

Between 1817-1818, the land holding of Robert Tucker estate was reduced 320 ac. - 142.5 ac. = 177.5 ac. Unfortunately, Deed Books 5 & 6 which cover a period between 1816-1825 have been destroyed. However, changes to the 1817 Land Tax Records explain that Robert Tucker's heirs sold 84 3/4 ac. to Grief Ellington. The 177.50 ac. - 84.75 ac. = 57.75 ac. to account for. Changes to the 1826 Land Tax Records explain that William Tucker bought from Reuben Weeks (Wicks) 57 3/4 ac. on Namozine Cr adj Reuben Weeks (Wicks) est. And DB 10-346 below explains that the heirs of Robert Tucker had sold 57 3/4 ac. to Reuben Wicks, who sold it to William Tucker, who died intestate, and the 57 3/4 ac. reverted to his brother Robert Tucker decd, and then to his heirs. The Land Tax Records show William Tucker holding 57 3/4 ac. 1826-1836. William Tucker was probably b ca 1804 & died ca 1839.

DB 10-331, 6 Dec 1839, rec 6 Feb 1840, Robert Tucker & wf Prudence Tucker, Robert T. Old & wf Nancy T. Old, William D. Old, Nancy Tucker, & Martha Tucker, all of Halifax Co., Va., to George W. Pugh of Nottoway Co., for $397.50., 147 ac. lying btwn Richmond Rd & Namozine Cr, bo. William B. Wilson Sr, John Fitzgerald, Thomas Dean, it being a part of the land that the said Robert Tucker, Robert L. Old, William D. Old, Nancy Tucker, & Martha Tucker inherited from their father and grandfather Robert Tucker Sr decd who died in Nottoway Co., the sd Robert Tucker, Martha Tucker & Nancy Tucker being children of sd Robert Tucker decd, & the sd William D. Old & Robert T. Old being grandchildren of sd Robert Tucker Sr.

NOTE: Although Deed Books 5 & 6 (1816-1825) have been destroyed, the Land Tax Records show Joel Tucker est. of 147 ac. no longer existed after 1819. Apparently that 147 ac. was sold in 1820 and came into the est of Robert Tucker Sr in 1839.

DB 10-346, 6 Dec 1839, rec 23 Apr 1840, Robert Tucker & wf Prudence Tucker, Robert T. Old & wf Nancy P. Old, William D. Old, Nancy Tucker & Martha Tucker, for $200, to Thomas H. Grinstead, 57 3/4 ac. bo. Richmond Rd, Tucker, Wicks, Blom(?), it being a part of the land the sd Robert Tucker, Nancy Tucker, Martha Tucker, Robert T. Old, & William Old inherited from their brother and uncle William Tucker decd, who died in Nottoway Co., & the sd Robert Tucker, Nancy Tucker & Martha Tucker, being brother and sister to sd William Tucker decd, & the sd William Old & Robert T. Old being nephews of sd William Tucker decd., & the sd tract of land is <u>a part of the land which formerly belonged - to Robert Tucker Sen decd</u> and was purchased by the sd William Tucker decd in his lifetime from Reuben Wicks who had purchased it of sd Robert Tucker Sr's heirs, the sd William Tucker decd died without heir and without a will which entitled the parties hereto to the sd land.

NOTE: Although Robert Tucker Sr (son of William) died ca 1815 intestate, the two deeds above identify his heirs as: William Tucker decd; Robert Tucker Jr & wf Prudence; a deceased daughter who married an Old & their children; Robert T. Old & wf Nancy P.; and William D. Old; and daughters Nancy and Martha Tucker, all of whom moved to Halifax Co. Va.

SUMMARY: Robert Tucker, son of William Tucker Sr. & wf Ann, b ca 1751 in Amelia Co. Va., md 1779 in Amelia Co., Mary Hawkes, dau. of Joshua Hawkes & wf Angelica, and lived in the area of Amelia Co. which was cut off to form Nottoway Co. in 1789, d ca 1815 intestate in Nottoway Co. and had issue:

Robert Tucker Jr. b ca 1802, md Prudence.

William Tucker b ca 1805, d ca 1839 intestate without issue.

(dau) Tucker md _____ Old & had issue:

1. Robert T. Old md Nancy P. ___

2. William D. Old.

Nancy Tucker.

Martha Tucker.

TW154100 - ROBERT TUCKER

MD PRUDENCE CHAPPELL
SON OF ROBERT TUCKER
MD MARY HAWKS

NOTTOWAY CO., VA.

DB 10-331, 6 Dec 1839, rec 6 Feb 1840, <u>Robert Tucker & wf Prudence Tucker</u>, Robert T. Old & wf Nancy T. Old, William D. Old, Nancy Tucker, & Martha Tucker, all of Halifax Co., Va., to George W. Pugh of Nottoway Co., for $397.50., <u>147 ac.</u> lying btwn Richmond Rd & Namozine Cr, bo. William B. Wilson Sr, John Fitzgerald, Thomas Dean, it being a part of the land that the said Robert Tucker, Robert L. Old, William D. Old, Nancy Tucker, & Martha Tucker <u>inherited from their father</u> and grandfather Robert Tucker Sr decd who died in Nottoway Co., <u>the sd</u> Robert Tucker, Martha Tucker & Nancy Tucker <u>being. children of sd Robert Tucker decd</u>, & the sd William D. Old & Robert T. Old being grandchildren of sd Robert Tucker Sr.

DB 10-346, 6 Dec 1339, rec 23 Apr 1840, <u>Robert Tucker & wf Prudence Tucker</u>, Robert T. Old & wf Nancy P. Old, William D. Old, Nancy Tucker & Martha Tucker, for $200, to Thomas H. Grinstead, <u>57 3/4 ac.</u> bo. Richmond Rd, Tucker, Wicks, Blom(?), it being a part of the land the sd Robert Tucker, Nancy Tucker, Martha Tucker, Robert T. Old, & William Old <u>inherited from their brother</u> and uncle William Tucker decd, who died in Nottoway Co., & the <u>sd Robert Tucker</u>, Nancy Tucker & Martha Tucker, <u>being brother</u> and sister <u>to sd William Tucker decd</u>, & the sd William Old & Robert T. Old being nephews of sd Willlam Tucker decd, & the sd tract of land is a part of the land which <u>formerly belonged to Robert Tucker Sen decd</u> and was purchased by the sd William Tucker decd in his lifetime from Reuben Wicks who had purchased it of sd Robert Tucker Sr's heirs, the sd William Tucker decd died without heir and without a will which entitled the parties hereto to the sd land.

NOTE: Although Robert Tucker (son of William) died ca 1815 intestate, the two deeds above identify his heirs as: Robert Tucker Jr & wf Prudence; a daughter who married an Old & their children Robert T. Old & wf Nancy P. and William D. Old: daughters Nancy and Martha Tucker, all of whom moved to Halifax Co. Va.; and William Tucker who died intestate without issue ca 1839.

HALIFAX CO., VA.

NOTE: The following marriages, wills and census records are included to indicate the many intermarriages between the Tucker, Chappell, & Light families, and to identify the legatees in the will of Robert Tucker who md Prudence Chappell.

17 Oct 1799, Joel Tucker md Usley Chappell

MB 1-66, 23 Apr 1807, Joel Tucker md Nancy Moore. Bondsman Anderson Moore.

MB 1-75, 4 Dec 1810, James O. Tucker md Mary Light. Bondsman Joel Light, Witnesses Joel Light & John Light Jr, Signer John Light, father.

MB 1-75, 17 Nov 1810, Joel Tucker Jr md Sally Clements. Bondsman Benjamin Clements.

MB 1-86, 28 Mar 1814, William Tucker md Agnes Powell. Bondsman Watson A. Powell. Witness Joel Tucker Jr. Signer Thomas A. Powell, father.

MB 1-108, 30 Jan 1821, <u>Robert Tucker md Prudence Chappell</u>. Bondsman Joel Tucker, Witnesses Joel Tucker & Wm. Dicker, Signer Robert Chappell father.

MB 1-155, 18 Dec 1836, John L. Tucker md Orra Chappell. Bondsman Edwin S. Hurt. Witnesses Octavia Chappell & Edwin S. Hurt. Signer Robert Chappell.

WB 15-25, 1 Feb 1826, wp Jul 1829, <u>will of Robert Chappell</u>. son Joel Chappell - slaves. son Robert Chappell - 424 ac whereon I now live & slaves. <u>daus Martha Dickey & Prudence Tucker & their heirs – my tract of land called Kings, equally divided, plus slaves</u>. grandau Martha C. Tucker - slaves - but if she die w/o child, then to sons Joel & Robert Chappell & <u>daus Martha Dickey & Prudence Tucker</u> equally divided. grandau Polly T. Chappell - slave. grandau Nancy Holland - $1,200. to heir & next of kin of my deceased son John Chappell - remainder of est., that is 3/5 to sons Joel & Robert, & 2/5 to <u>daus Martha Dickey &Prudence Tucker</u>. Exors: Joel Chapel]. & Robert Chappell. S/ Robert Chappell. Wit: John Tucker, George A. Wood, Thomas Osborn.

WB 19-578, 17 Jun 1837, wp 25 Oct 1841, <u>will of Nancey Powell</u>. land whereon I reside be sold by executor, & proceeds divided in 4 equal parts to: 1/4 to son William W. Powell, 1/4 to son John W. Powell, 1/4 to son Thomas A. Powell & 1/4 equally div btwn children of son James M. Powell. to <u>dau Agness W. Tucker</u> & heirs - $100. cash. Exor: son Thomas A. Powell. S/ Nancey Powell,

WB 22-66, 1848 1 May 1846, wp 22 May 1848, <u>will of Temperance Light</u>. to Orry Tucker, wf of John L. Tucker, my bed & bed clothes, one chest & one trunk to bro. Joel Light - land on Terrible cr which fell to me in div. of est of my deceased father John Light, it being lot No. 9 in the platt, & on which my sd bro. has been building. to bro. William Light - remainder of est, together with my interest in dower of my mother-in-law Jemima H. Light. S/ Temperance x Light. Wit: Giles McCraw, John A. McCraw, Albert W. Barksdale.

> CODICIL - 10 Nov 1847. Revoke 2nd item. Lot No. 9 to remain in possession of Nancy Light & children of Joel Light during life of sd Nancy wf of Joel, & at her death to her son Charles Light.

WB 1A-133, _ ___ 1849, wp 8 Jun 1852, <u>will of Taney Clay</u>. to friends William W. Wood & Drury Wood - all my slaves, and all my interest in <u>my father's (Thomas Clay) est</u>. to friends Mary Duttie (Dickie?) & Ursula Dutti - $40. each & my bed which is at their fathers William Duttie, & also my large pitcher & two tumblers at Robert Tuckers in my chest. to Octavia Chappell - $10. to Hellen Chappell - $10. to sister Dorothy Franklin - my best clothes. to <u>Robert Tucker & wf Prudence</u> - 3 pieces of gold now in my chest at sd Robert Tucker's house. Exors: William Wood & Drury Wood. S/ Tany x Clay. Wit: Thomas J. Wood, Robert H. Carlton.

> On 8 Jun 1852, will was produced in court & Mart R. Franklin & wf & William Clay opposed the proof, but witnesses appeared & court ordered to be recorded.

WB 23-568 4 Jul 1850, wp 26 Jul 1852, <u>will of James O. Tucker</u>. Land I bought of Wm. Ives & wf be sold to pay my debts. to wf <u>Mary Tucker</u> - 200 ac. where we all now reside & all the property thereon & all that may fall into my est, for life or widowhood, that she may be the better able to keep her family together and specialy girls. S/ James O. Tucker. And I do further will that Stephen D. Tucker or one of my sons that may suit the best, may assist my wife Mary Tucker in the management of the est to try and keep everything in good order, and at my wife's decease, I desire that what property there is should be equally divided among all <u>my children</u>, taking in consideratrion some advances that has been made to some (<u>except John L. Tucker</u>) who has had more than his share already. S/James O. Tucker. Certificate granted to Stephen D. Tucker to obtain letters of administration.

WB 26-463, 26 Oct 1854, rec 25 Jul 1859, <u>will of Robert Chappell</u>. son Thomas Chappell. dau Octavia Chappell. dau Helen R. Chappell. dau Janetta Hart, wf of Edwin S. Hart. dau Orra Tucker. Exor: Thomas Leigh.

    CODICIL - 25 Aug 1858.

    CODICIL - 7 Jan 1859 - Dau Octavia Chappell having died. five grandchildren Thales O. Tucker, Eugenia D. Tucker, Sally H. Hart,, Sally R. Tucker & Prudence A. Tucker.

1850 CENSUS: [1]

	Name	Age	Calculated Birthdate
Southern District		--	---
155	William Dickey	69	ca 1781
	Ursley	25	ca 1825
	Ellen Tucker	8	ca 1842
270	Robert Tucker	59	ca 1791
	Prudence	48	ca 1802
	Nancy	60	ca 1790
271	William Old	36	ca 1814
	Robert T. Old	31	ca 1819
	William	11	ca 1839
	James	9	ca 1841
1150	Robert Chappell	69	ca 1781
	Joanna	66	ca 1784
	Thomas	45	ca 1805
	Octavia	40	ca 1810
	Ona	38	ca 1812
	Helen	26	ca1824
	Thuler Tucker	14	ca 1836
	Jennett	10	ca 1840
	Sarah	7	ca 1843
	Prudence	3	ca 1847
	Nancy Miller	50	ca 1800

NOTE: In the above census records, Nancy Tucker (age 60) is sister of Robert Tucker. William Old (age 36) & Robert T. Old (age 31) are sons of. Robert Tucker's deceased sister, and therefore nephews of Robert Tucker. William Old (age 11) & James Old (age 9) are most probably children of Robert T. Old. Robert & Joanna Chappell are most probably parents of Robert Tucker's wife Prudence. Thomas, Octavia, Ona & Helen Chappell are most probably sisters of Prudence. Ursula Dicker (Ursley Dickey)(age 25) is dau of William Dickey & wf Martha Chappell (sister of Prudence). Some of these names appear as legatees in the will of Robert Tucker following.

WB 24-561, wd 3 Mar 1855, wp 23 Apr 1855, <u>will of Robert Tucker</u>.

to Octavio & _____? Chappell - $70. ea.

to Thomas Chappell, Orra Tucker, Ginnella Hart - $50. ea.

to John L. Tucker's dau. Prudence Ann - $100. to be deposited in hands of Thomas Chappell & held in trust for her benefit.

to niece Ursula Dicker - $100.

to Agnes J. & Mary A. Tucker - $20. ea.

to sister Nancy Tucker, for life - bal. of my est, both real & personal. At decease of my sister Nancy Tucker, to 2 nephews Wm. D. & Robert T. Old - all the property loaned to sister Nancy Tucker for life.

Ex: Thomas J. & George W. Wood, with no security required. S/ Robert Tucker. Wit: Thomas J. Wood, C. J. Craddock.

NOTE: Apparently Robert Tucker died without issue, for he left his land to his sister Nancy for life, then to his nephews William D. & Robert T. Old, sons of his deceased sister who md _____ Old. Other legatees are identified in the 1850 census as cited above. The identity of the remaining legatees is not clear.

SUMMARY: Robert Tucker Jr, son of Robert Tucker Sr & wf Mary Hawks, b ca 1791 in Nottoway Co. Va, d 1855 in Halifax Co. Va., md 1821 in Halifax Co., Va., Prudence Chappell, dau of Robert Chappell & wf Joanna, and had no issue.

* * *

1. Chiarito, Marian Dodson, "1850 Census of Halifax County, Virginia"

TW154200 - WILLIAM TUCKER
SON OF ROBERT TUCKER
MD MARY HAWKS

NOTTOWAY CO., VA.

DB 7-118, 4 Jul 1825, rec 4 Aug 1825. Edward Bland Trustee for Reuben Wicks, to <u>William Tucker</u>, for $207.90, <u>57 3/4 ac.</u>

NOTE: If William Tucker was age 21 when he bought land in 1825, he was born ca 1804.

LAND TAX RECORDS

1826-1839 William Tucker, 57 3/4 ac. fr Reuben Weeks Trustee, on Namozene Cr. adj. Reuben Weeks est.

DB 10-346, 6 Dec 1839, rec 23 Apr 1840, Robert Tucker & wf Prudence Tucker, Robert T. Old & wf Nancy P. Old, William D. Old, Nancy Tucker & Martha Tucker, for $200, to Thomas H. Grinstead, 57 3/4 ac. bo. Richmond Rd, Tucker, Wicks, Blom(?), it being a part of the land the sd Robert Tucker, Nancy Tucker, Martha Tucker, Robert T. Old, & William Old <u>inherited from their brother and uncle William Tucker decd, who died in Nottoway Co.</u>, & the sd <u>Robert Tucker, Nancy Tucker & Martha Tucker, being brother and sister to sd William Tucker decd.,-& the sd William Old & Robert T. Old being nephews of sd William Tucker decd.</u>, & the sd tract of land is a part of the land which formerly belonged to Robert Tucker Sen decd and was purchased by the sd William Tucker decd in his lifetime from Reuben Wicks who had purchased it of sd Robert Tucker Sr's heirs, the sd William Tucker decd died without heir and without a will which entitled the parties hereto to the sd land.

NOTE: Although Robert Tucker (son of William) died ca 1815 intestate, the two deeds above identify his heirs as: Robert Tucker Jr & wf Prudence; a daughter who married an Old & their children Robert T. Old & wf Nancy P. and William D. Old: daughters Nancy and Martha Tucker, all of whom moved to Halifax Co. Va.; and <u>William Tucker</u> who died intestate without issue ca 1839.

SUMMARY: William Tucker, son of Robert Tucker & wf Mary Hawks, b ca 1804 in Nottoway Co., Va., d 1839 Nottoway Co., intestate, unmarried and without issue.

TW155000 - DAVID TUCKER

MD 1ST FRANCES (FANNY) OLD
MD 2ND MARY WOOD
MD 3RD CHRISTIANA BERGER
SON OF WILLIAM TUCKER SR
MD ANN

AMELIA CO. VA.

Marriage Bond dated 14 Feb 1782 for <u>David Tucker md Fanny Old</u>. Security Robert Tucker.

PERSONAL TAX RECORDS

1783	2	David Tucker
1784	2	David Tucker
1785	1	David Tucker
1786	1	David Tucker)
1786	1	David Tucker)
1787	1	David Tucker
1788	1	David Tucker)
1788	1	David Tucker Jun.)

NOTE: David Tucker was most probably age 21 when he married in 1782, so he was born ca 1761. Tithable records were missing or incomplete 1771-81, when he would have been listed as 16-yr-up tithable in the household of his father, William Tucker Sr. He was listed as a separate household first in 1783, another indication he had attained age 21. In 1786, two David Tuckers were listed as separate households. In 1788 the list included a David Tucker and a David Tucker Jr, who had also attained age 21. The meaning of this is not clear, but they surely were not father-son. The subject David Tucker moved to Halifax Co, VA in 1793, (along with his brothers Robert and Joel) and died there in 1843, but did not name a son David Jr in his will. However, there is recorded in Halifax Co in 1805 (MB 1-61) the marriage of a David Tucker (to Mary Wood) who, if he were then age 21, would have been b ca 1784. It would appear he might be the son of our subject David Tucker, who was md 1st to Fanny Old in 1782. But it is more probable that this was the second marriage of our subject David Tucker. The marriage in Pittsylvania Co. in 1823 of David Tucker to Christiana Berger, is most likely his third marriage.

WB 3-300, <u>will of William Tucker</u>, 8 Feb 1785, (date recorded not shown). - names: - son Daniel Tucker - Son William Tucker - Son John Tucker - <u>Son Robert Tucker & son David Tucker - land which I purchased of William Watson, except those 25 ac. already bequeathed to son John Tucker, to be divided between them by running a line they think proper - also to son David Tucker - negro Beck & her increase.</u> - Dau. Mary Chappell - Dau. Sarah Olds' three children - Dau. Anne Tucker - Wife Ann - <u>Son David Tucker to have negro Moll & incr.</u> - <u>Son David to have negro Stephen</u>. Son Joel Tucker -

The subject David Tucker son of William & Ann appeared in the land tax records beginning in 1787.

LAND TAX RECORDS - AMELIA CO.

| 1787 | David Tucker | 200 ac. (from Robert Tucker) |
| 1788 | David Tucker | 200 ac. |

NOTTOWAY CO. VA.

1789 Nottoway Co. was formed from Amelia Co.

The land which David Tucker inherited from his father William Tucker Sr fell in the area which became Nottoway Co.

LAND TAX RECORDS - NOTTOWAY CO.

1789	David Tucker	26 ac. (possibly 226 ac.)
1790	David Tucker	26 ac. (possible 226 ac.)
1791	David Tucker	200 + 26 (= 226 ac.)
1792	David Tucker	94 ac. (226 - 132 = 94 ac.)
1793	David Tucker	94 ac.

DB 1-142, 18 Feb 1791, rec 2 Jun 1791, <u>David Tucker of Nottoway Co.</u> to Richard Hawks. <u>132 ac.</u> on b.s. Nammosine Cr., <u>bo. Robert Tucker,</u> Morgan, Peter Jones, <u>John Tucker</u>. S/ David Tucker. Wit: Abnew Osborne, Robert Tucker, Greif Ellington. s/ David Tucker. <u>Wf Frances</u> relinq dower.

DB 1-352, 11 Dec 1793, rec 20 Jan 1794, <u>David Tucker & wf Fanny</u> of Nottoway Co. to Richard Hawks, <u>145.5 ac.</u> on Namosene Cr., <u>bo.</u> Abner Osborne, Bevil, the county line, McFarlane, sd Richard Hawks, <u>Robert Tucker</u>. S/ David Tucker, Fanny x Tucker. Wit: Robert Tucker, John Tucker, George Foster.

NOTE: It is most difficult to reconcile the number acres of land David Tucker inherited from his father William Tucker Sr. It may be a co-incidence, but William Tucker Sr bought 545 ac. on Namozine Cr. in Amelia Co. in 1770 from John Hamlin. His son Robert Tucker "held" 545 ac. in 1782, which was reduced by 200 ac. (to David) in 1787, and reduced by another 25 ac. (possibly to John) in 1788, leaving 320 ac.

which Robert held on Namozine Cr. Possibly this is the acreage referred to in will of William Tucker Sr as "purchased of William Watson", with 25 ac. going to John & remainder divided between Robert and David.

The land tax records of Nottoway Co indicate David Tucker held two tracts of 200 ac. & 26 ac. 1789-91. Where he obtained the 26 ac. is not clear, unless it was the 25 ac. actually willed to his brother John. In 1791 he sold 132 ac. on Namozine Cr, leaving 94 ac. on Land Tax Records for 1792-93. Then in 1793 he sold 145.5 ac. on Namozine Cr. Where he obtained the additional 51.5 ac. is not clear. He does not appear on the land tax records of Nottoway Co. after 1793, but bought land in Halifax Co. Va. beginning in 1793.

HALIFAX CO., VA.

NOTE: The following Halifax Co. deed in 1793-4 refers to David Tucker of "Mealy Co." This is most probably the David Tucker from Amelia-Nottoway Co. who sold land in 1793 in Nottoway Co.

DB 16-103, 17 Dec 1793, rec 24 Feb 1794. Enock Farmer & wf Sarah to David Tucker of Mealy Co (Amelia Co.?), for L75., 150 ac. on b.s. badluck Cr. S/ Enock Farmer, Sarah x Farmer. Wit: Hawkins Landrum, Richard Walne, Nancy Chappell.

DB 20-163, 3 Jan 1801, rec 25 Jun 1804. Robert Easley & wf Nancy to David Tucker, for L20.14., 17 1/4 ac. on b.s. Badluck Cr., being part of land of John Easley decd, & joins land of David Tucker &c. S/ Robert Easley, Nancy Easley, Wit: Epa Sydnor, Joel Tucker, Thomas Davenport Jr.

NOTE: David Tucker's wife Frances (Fanny) Old, named in Amelia Co. DB 1-142 (1791) & DB 1-352 (1793), must have died prior to 1801, since she did not relinquish a dower right in Halifax Co. DB 20-163 in 1801. The following seems to he his second marriage to Mary Wood, but she must have died prior to 1809, for she did not relinquish a dower right in DB 22-110 in 1809.

MB 1-61, 29 Jul 1805, David Tucker md Mary Wood. Bondsman John Wood Jr. Signer Mary Wood self.

DB 21-598, 22 Feb 1808, rec 22 Feb 1808, John Toler & wf Rebecah to David Tucker, for L165., 200 ac. on b.s. Bad Luck Cr. bo. John Switti, crossing Bad Luck Cr. S/John Toler, Rehecah Toler. Wit: Wm. Cole, Benjamin Clements, James O. Tucker. (See DB 23-397)

DB 21 673, 25 Jul 1808. I, John Toler, appoint William Cole & David Tucker lawful attorneys.

DB 22-110, 20 Jan 1809, rec 26 Jun 1809, <u>David Tucker & Joel Tucker</u> to Jesse Talley Sr., for L112.9., <u>86.5 ac.</u> bo. Chappell's corner, Anderson Rd., a branch. S/ Joel Tucker, David Tucker. Nancy Tucker, wife of sd Joel Tucker, relinq dower right. (See DB 26-11).

DB 23-397, 27 Apr 1812, rec 27 Apr 1812. <u>David Tucker to James O. Tucker</u>, for L160. , <u>200 ac.</u> b.s. Bad Luck Cr., bo. John Smith. S/ David Tucker. Wit: Joel Tucker, James Old, Richd Jones. (See DB 21-598)

DB 26-11, 25 Mar 1816, rec 25 Mar 1816, <u>Joel Tucker & David Tucker</u> to Jacob Chany, for $500., <u>225 ac.</u> on s.s. Banister Ri., bo. Powell, Clemmons, Chappell. S/ Joel Tucker, David Tucker. Wit: Joel Tucker Jr., Daniel Clark, Andrew Anderson. (See DB 22-110).

NOTE: How Joel & David Tucker came into joint possesion of the 86.5 ac. (DB 22-110) and 225 ac. (DB 26-11), total 311.5 ac., is not clear. However, the first land bought in the name of Joel Tucker only, 117 ac. (DB 16-403 in 1795) & 200 ac. (DB 17-175 in 1797), total 317 ac. may be the same as 311.5 ac sold by Joel & David.

PITTSYLVANIA CO., VA.

Pittsylvania Co. Index to Marriages, page 79, 13 Oct 1823, <u>David Tucker md Christiana Berger</u>, bondsman Daniel Berger, signed Jacob Berger Sr.

DB 39-202, 16 Nov 1836, Wm. Risen to David Berger Sr, Samuel Berger, David Berger Jr, of Pittsylvania Co., trustees for <u>Christina Tucker wf of David Tucker of Halifax Co.</u>,for $900., <u>175 ac.</u> on <u>Pigg Ri,</u> called the Goldmine Tract, bo. Morning Robertson, William Toles, Walter Coles.

HALIFAX CO., VA

DB 34-234. 24 Nov 1826, rec 1 Dec 1826, <u>David Tucker & wf Christiana</u> to Armistead Barksdale for $835., <u>173 3/10 ac.</u> on b.s. Bad Luck Cr. (See DB 16-103 for 150- ac. & DB 20-163 for 17 1/4 ac., total 167 1/4 ac.)

DB 36-431, 25 Oct 1828, rec 27 Oct 1828, (1) William Tucker, (2) Joel Tucker Jr (3) <u>David Tucker</u>, to secure debt of William Tucker to <u>David Tucker</u> for $524.48, pledged horses, cows, household furniture and equipment, etc. Wit: James O. Tucker, Joel Tucker.

DB 37-673, 28 Jun 1830, rec 28 Jun 1830, <u>David Tucker & wf Christian</u> to Robert Tucker, for $700., <u>117.5 ac.</u> on Chestnut Cr., bo. Joel Cole, Clay.

DB 37-675, 28 Jun 1830, rec 3 Jul 1830, Robert Tucker & wf Prudence, and William Dickie & wf Martha, to <u>David Tucker</u>, for $290.80, <u>63,3 (or 43,3) ac</u> on Miny (or Miry) Cr., bo Crenshaw.

NOTE: The following marriage records seem to apply to the children of

David Tucker and his 1st wf Fanny Old.

MB 1-69, 24 Oct 1808, Solomon Simpson md Sally Tucker. Sur. David Tucker.

NOTE: Sally Tucker appears to be dau of David Tucker, but she is not named in his will.

MB 1-75, 4 Dec 1810, James O. Tucker md Mary Light. Bondsman Joel Light. Witnesses Joel Light & John Light Jr. Signer John Light, father.

MB 1-75, 17 Dec 1810, Thomas Hittson md Patsy (Martha?) Tucker, dau of David Tucker who consents. Sur. James O. Tucker. Wit. James O. Tucker & Jincy B. Tucker. Md Dec 20th th the Rev. Joel Tucker.

NOTE: The identification of Rev. Joel Tucker is not determined by this compiler.

MB 1-78, 28 Oct 1811, Drewry B. Wood md Jincy Tucker. Sur. David Tucker. Md 28 Oct by Rev. Joel Tucker who says Jincy B.

MB 1-86, 28 Mar 1814, William Tucker md Agnes Powell. Bondsman Watson A. Powell. Witness Joel Tucker Jr. Signer Thomas A. Powell, father.

MB 1-95, 13 Nov 1817, Isaac Stimson md Rachael Tucker. Sur. David Tucker. Wit. Boolerd Bohannon & Henry Stimson., Erasmus Stimson consents for son, Isaac. Md 15 Nov by the Rev. J. Tucker.

WB 20-177, wd 25 Nov 1841, wp 23 Jan 1843, <u>will of David Tucker</u>.
<u>wife Christiana</u> - $1,000.00 being proceeds from sale of negro woman & children, acquired by my marriage with her also the money assigned to me in right of my wife in division of estate of her father (blank) Berger, plus interest to my death; also interest on proceeds of sale of my real & personal property. At death of wife, whole estate equally divided among <u>my children, viz James O. Tucker, Jeney B. Stimpson, Martha Hillson & William Tucker</u>, having hereto given to my <u>dau.</u> Rachael Stimpson all that I intend to give to her, nothing is given her by this will. Ex: friend William Holt S/ David Tucker.

NOTE: In MB 1-75 (1810), Jincy B. Tucker was witness to marriage of David's dau Patsy (Martha) Tucker to Thomas Hittson. In MB 1-78 (1811) Jincy B. Tucker md Drewry B. Wood. In W3 20-177 (1841), David Tucker's will named dau Jeney B. Stimpson. In WB 24-177 (1839) Joel Tucker Sr's will named Jane B. Stimpson.

DB 49-382, 24 Feb 1844, rec 27 Feb 1844, William Holt, <u>Executor of will of David Tucker decd</u> to John Grammar, for $339.40, <u>63.8 ac</u> on Miry Cr, bo Dickie, Crenshaw, <u>being the land upon which David Tucker formerly resided</u>.

SUMMARY: David Tucker, son of William Tucker Sr & wf Ann, b ca 1761 in Amelia Co., d 1843 in Halifax Co., VA, md 1st 1782 in Amelia Co. Frances (Fanny) Old, lived in the area of Amelia Co. which became Nottoway Co in 1789, and moved to Halifax Co. VA in 1793. The marriage in 1805 in Halifax Co, VA, of David Tucker to Mary Wood may be his second marriage. If this is true, then David Tucker's marriage in 1823 in Pittsylvania Co. to Christiana Berger dau of Jacob Berger Sr, may be his third marriage. David Tucker had issue, most probably all by his first wf:

Sally Tucker, md 1808 Solomon Simpson. (may be dau of David)

James O. Tucker, md 4 Dec 1810, Mary Light, dau of John Light.

Martha (Patsy) Tucker, md 1810 Thomas Hittson (or Hillson).

William Tucker, md 1814 Agnes Powell, dau of Thomas A. Powell.

Rachael Tucker, md 1817 Isaac Stimpson.

Jeney B. (Jincy B.) (Jane B.) Tucker md 1st 1810 Drewry B. Wood, md 2nd __?__ Stimpson.

TWI55100 - JAMES O. TUCKER

MD MARY LIGHT
SON OF DAVID TUCKER
MD 1ST FANNY OLD
MD 2ND MARY WOOD
MD 3RD CHRISTIANA BERGER

HALIFAX CO., VA.

MB 1-75, 4 Dec 1810, James O. Tucker md Mary Light. Bondsman Joel Light. Witnesses Joel Light & John Light Jr. Signer John Light, father.

NOTE: If James O. Tucker was age 21 when he married in 1810, he was b ca 1789.

DB 23-397, 27 Apr 1812, rec 27 Apr 1812. David Tucker to James O. Tucker, for L160., 200 ac. b.s. Bad Luck Cr., bo. John Smith. S/ David Tucker. Wit: Joel Tucker, James Old, Richd Jones.

DB 30-28 James O. Tucker was a commissioner to sell est of John Wyatt decd.

DB 31-468, 4 Apr 1823, rec 23 Jun 1823, Richard Epperson, to secure debt to James Cole, sold to James O. Tucker, 200 ac, on Sandy Cr, bo. William W. Womack, John Ferguson, Thomas & Samuel Dixons, also negro man Hal, woman Taminy(?), & child Charles, & stock of cattle, sheep & hogs.

DB 33-536, 1 Jan 1826, John Light Jr & wf Tabitha, to James O. Tucker, for $274., 66 ac., being the lot assigned to sd John Light as one of the legatees of John Light decd, adj. Agnes Carr. (See DB 46-50)

DB 33-549, 11 Feb 1826, John Light & wf Tabitha, Joel Chappell & wf Tabitha, Robert Chappell & wf Joanna, James O. Tucker & wf Mary, Stephen Light, Temperance Light, Joel Light & Agnes Carr, to William Light, for $500., all their rights & interest in parcel of land now in possession of Jemima H. Light, widow of John Light on Terrible Cr. which was assigned to sd Jemima(?) H. Light as her dower & to which she is entitled to life estate, containing 127 ac. Rec 27 Feb 1826.

DB 36-517, 13 Dec 1828, rec 13 Dec 1828, William Tucker & wf Agness, formerly Angess Powell, to secure debt to James O. Tucker, sold to William W. Powell, their interest in land on Sandy Cr occupied by Mrs. Nancy Powell as her dower in the lands of Thomas A Powell decd, plus other items.

DB 36-698, 21 Mar 1829, rec 23 Mar 1829, John Mills Sr to secure debt to John B. Mills, sold to James O. Tucker in trust, certain stock, furniture & personal property.

DB 43-1, 24 Dec 1835, rec 22 Feb 1836, William Penick & James Bruce (by agent James Atkisson) for $350., to James O. Tucker 150 ac., bo John Mills, George Carter, Henry Wilson, John Phelps. Wit: James Atkisson, Tho. Davenport. (See WB 23-568 will of James O. Tucker) (See DB 52-326)

DB 45-255, 27 Oct 1838, rec 30 Nov 1838, William Ives & wf Frances, formerly Frances Smith, to James O. Tucker, for $230., "all our interest (it being 2/3, [our 1/3 part], & Nicholas Ives & wf Sally, 1/3 part) in 101 ac, on Sandy Cr, whereon Phebe Smith widow of John Smith Junr now resides, & whereof sd John Smith Junr died seized, which land we have had divided among us, --to wit, our 2/3 laid off on the n.s., Lot No. 3 of 38 3/4 ac, the dower in the center lot, No. 2 of 40 1/2 ac, ---the sd tract of land & all our interest in the dower--", bo by sd Tucker. (Note: Just how many acres was sold is not clear to this compiler. See WB 23-568 will of James O. Tucker, by which this land was to be sold to pay debts.)

DB 46-50, 14 Oct 1839, James O. Tucker & wf Mary to John L. Tucker, for $500., lots # 6 & 7 in div of lands of John Light Sr decd, lot # 6 of 66 ac. pur. by James O. Tucker fr John Light Jr & lot # 7 of 43 1/2 ac. allotted to sd James O. Tucker, the 2 lots containing an aggregate of 109 1/2 ac. Rec 15 Oct 1839. (See DB 33-536)

WB 20-177, wd 25 Nov 1841, wp 23 Jan 1843, will of David Tucker. wife Christiana - $1,000.00 being proceeds from sale of negro woman & children, acquired by my marriage with her; also the money assigned to me in right of my wife in division of estate of her father (blank) Berger, plus interest to my death; also interest on proceeds of sale of my real & personal property. At death of wife, whole estate equally divided among my children, viz James O. Tucker, Jeney B. Stimpson, Martha Hinson & William Tucker, having hereto given to my dau. Rachael Stimpson all that I intend to give to her, nothing is given her by this will Ex: friend William Holt S/ David Tucker.

DB 52-326, 22 Sep 1847, rec 22 Nov 1847, James O. Tucker to David B. Tucker, for $300. 150 ac. bo. Henry Wilson decd. William T. Weatherford, Absalem Jones, being formerly owned by Richard Carter decd & afterward by John & James Turpins & conveyed by them to William Penick, who sold to James Atkisson who sold to James O. Tucker. S/ James O. Tucker, Wit: C. J. Clardy, S. D. Tucker, J. W. Tucker, Thomas W. Tucker. (See DB 43-1)

NOTE: Who were David B. Tucker, J. W. Tucker & Thomas W. Tucker? Probably they were sons of James O. Tucker, not named in his will, along with Samuel D. Tucker and John L. Tucker.

WB 23-568 4 Jul 1850, wp 26 Jul 1852, will of James O. Tucker. Land I bought of Wm. Ives & wf be sold to pay my debts. to wf Mary Tucker - 200 ac. where we all now reside & all the property thereon & all that may fall into my est, for life or widowhood, that she may be the better able to keep her family together and specialy girls (not named). S/ James O. Tucker. And I do further will that Stephen D. Tucker or one of my sons that may suit the best, may assist my wife Mary Tucker in the management of the est to try and keep everything in good order, and at my wife's decease, I desire that what property there is should be equally divided among all my children (not named), taking in consideratrion some advances that has been made to some (except John L. Tucker who has had more than his share already). S/James O. Tucker. Certificate granted to Stephen D. Tucker to obtain letters of administration.

NOTE: The above will seems to identify Stephen D. Tucker and John L. Tucker as sons of James O. Tucker, and to imply there may have been other children, not named. (See DB 52-326 for names of other probable sons: David B. Tucker, J. W. Tucker & Thomas W. Tucker, although they are not included in the 1850 Census of Halifax Co.)

DB 66-266, 12 May 1878, rec 27 May 1878, S. D. Tucker, commr, for $750., grant to Agnes J. Tucker, 200 ac on Bad Luck Cr, being the land which the late James O. Tucker died seized.

MB 1-175, 9 May 1843, Stephen D. Tucker md Elizabeth R. Cole. Bondsman & Witness J. C. Cole. Signer Martha J. Cole, mother.

MB 3-13, 30 Nov 1859, James G. Tucker age 25 md Mary F. Wood age 22. Parents of groom James O. & Mary Tucker. Parents of bride D. B. & A. E. Wood.

The birthdates of members of the James O. Tucker family are calculated from ages shown in the 1850 Census: [1]

Name	Age	Calculated Birthdate
Southern District	--	---
1178 Stephen Tucker	33	ca 1817
Elizabeth	25	ca 1825
Martha	6	ca 1844
Mary	4	ca 1846
Jane	3/12	ca 1850
Eleanor Cole	20	ca 1830

SUMMARY: James O. Tucker, son of David Tucker & 1st wf Frances (Fanny) Old, b ca 1789 in either Amelia or Nottoway Co., d 1852 in Halifax Co., Va., md 1810 in Halifax Co., Va., Mary Light, dau of John Light & wf Jemima, & had issue:

John L. Tucker b ca 1815, md 1836 Orra Chappell, dau of Robert Chappell & wf Joanna Light.

Stephen D. Tucker b ca 1817, md 1843 Elizabeth R. Cole, dau of Martha J. Cole.

James G. Tucker b ca 1834, md 1859 Mary F. Wood, dau of D. B. & A. E. Wood.

Daughters (not named).

Other Possible Sons:

David B. Tucker.

J. W. Tucker.

Thomas W. Tucker.

* * *

1. Chiarito, Marian Dodson, "1850 Census of Halifax County, Virginia"

279

TW155110 - JOHN L. TUCKER
MD ORRA CHAPPELL
SON OF JAMES O. TUCKER
MD MARY LIGHT

HALIFAX CO., VA.

MB 1-155, 18 Dec 1836, John L. Tucker md Orra Chappell. Bondsman Edwin S. Hunt (or Hurt), Witnesses Octavia Chappell & Edwin S. Hunt (or Hurt). Signer Robert Chappell.

NOTE: If John L. Tucker was age 21 when he married in 1836, he was b ca 1815.

DB 43-414, 18 Oct 1836, rec 25 Oct 1836, Joel Chappell & wf Tabitha to John L. Tucker, for $174., 45 ac. on Terrible Cr, adj Wm M Bates, Joseph H Fuqua, Agnes Carr, & Fielding Bomar, it being the land sd Joel Chappell inherited from est of late John Light decd. (See DB 53-52)

DB 46-50, 14 Oct 1839, James O. Tucker & wf Mary to John L. Tucker, for $500., lots # 6 & 7 in div of lands of John Light Sr decd, lot # 6 of 66 ac. pur. by James O. Tucker fr John Light Jr & lot # 7 of 43 1/2 ac. allotted to sd James O. Tucker, the 2 lots containing an aggregate of 109 1/2 ac. Rec 15 Oct 1839. (See DB 33-536)

DB 47-377, 24 Feb 1841, rec 1 Mar 1842, Agness Carr to John L. Tucker, for $275., 77 ac on north fork of Terrible Cr & known as Lot No. 5 in division of land of John Light Sr, which sd lot was assigned to sd Agness Carr, bo on north & south by sd John L. Tucker, on west by Joseph H Fuqua & Wm Bates, & on east by Fielding Bomar. (See DB 50-449 for 73 ac)

DB 48-327, 14 Jan 1843, rec 23 Jan 1843, William Taylor sold to John L. Tucker certain personal property plus his interest in est which sd Taylor holds or may be entitled to in right of his wife Nancy Taylor late Nancy Brown, in est. of Fleming Brown decd.

DB 50-449, 14 Dec 1844, rec 27 May 1825, John L. Tucker & wf Orra to James M. Bates, for $401.50, 73 ac., bo creek on Bates line, Fuqua, Terrible Cr. (See DB 47-377 for 77 ac)

DB 53-52, 22 Jan 1849, rec 22 Jan 1849, John L. Tucker to secure debts, sold to Stephen D. Tucker & Wm. H. Wood, 162 ac. on Terrible Cr, bo Joel Light, James M. Baker, Wm Bomar & William Light, also negro woman Lucinda & her child Ephriam, negro man Manuel, 1 bay horse, 1 bay mare, 1 gray mare, 2 yoke oxen, 1 oxcart, all plantation tools & utensils, household & kitchen furniture, crops on hand --, 2 milk cows & 3 yearlings, stock of hogs -- but upon special trust, sd John L. Tucker shall he permitted to remain in possession of property until 1 Jun 1849. (See DB 43-414 for 45 ac, DB 46-50 for 109 1/2 ac, total 154.5 ac. See also DB 54-21)

DB 54-18, 28 Oct 1850, <u>Robert Chappell</u>, in consideration of natural love & affection for <u>dau Orra Tucker (wf of John L. Tucker)</u>, & in order to provide for the support & maintenance of her and her children as well, sold to James Atkisson of Carrol Co, Tennesee, negro man Manuel, negro girl Chanty, 2 horses, 3 beds, 1 wagon & sundry other articles, for the separate use of sd Orra Tucker & her children, free from control of her husband John L. Tucker, and sd Atkisson shall permit sd Orra Tucker to have possession of sd property during her natural life, & at her death, shall divide sd property equally among her children.

DB 54-21, 1 Nov 1850, rec 1 Nov 1850, <u>John Tucker & wf Orra A.</u> & Stephen D. Tucker & Wm W. Wood, sold to Alexander Yuille & James S. Easley, <u>162 ac.</u> (See DB 53-52)

DB 54-195, Apr 1851. Acct. sales of property of <u>John L. Tucker</u> sold by S. D. Tucker & Wm. W. Wood, Trustees, 13 Nov 1849.

NOTE: From above deed, and the will of James O. Tucker, it appears John L. Tucker died ca 1851.

WB 23-568 4 Jul 1850, wp 26 Jul 1852, <u>will of James O. Tucker</u>. Land I bought of Wm. Ives & wf be sold to pay my debts. to <u>wf Mary Tucker</u> - 200 ac. where we all now reside & all the property thereon & all that may fall into my est, for life or widowhood, that she may be the better able to keep her family together and specialy girls. S/ James O. Tucker. And I do further will that Stephen D. Tucker or one of my sons that may suit the best, may assist my wife Mary Tucker in the management of the est to try and keep everything in good order, and at my wife's decease, I desire that what property there is should be equally divided among <u>all my children (not named)</u>, taking in consideratrion some advances that has been made to some (except <u>John L. Tucker</u> who has had more than his share already). S/James O. Tucker. Certificate granted to Stephen D. Tucker to obtain letters of administration.

<u>1850 CENSUS</u>

<u>The birthdates of members of the John L. Tucker family are calculated from ages shown in the 1850 Census:</u> [2]

	Name	Age	Calculated Birthdate
<u>Southern District</u>		--	---
1150	Robert Chappell	69	ca 1781
	Joanna	66	ca 1784
	Thomas	45	ca 1805
	Octavia	40	ca 1810

The birthdates of members of the John L. Tucker family
are calculated from ages shown in the 1850 Census: [2]

Name	Age	Calculated Birthdate
Southern District	--	---
Ona	38	ca 1812
Helen	26	ca 1824
Thuler Tucker(male)	14	ca 1836
Jennett	10	ca 1840
Sarah	7	ca 1843
Prudence	3	ca 1847
Nancy Miller	50	ca 1800

NOTE: Thuler, Jennett, Sarah & Prudence Tucker in household of Robert Chappell are children of John L. Tucker & wf Orca (or Orra) Chappell, who was dau of Robert Chappell (Jr) & wf Joanna Light. See citations in three wills below.

WB 22-66, 1848 1 May 1846, wp 22 May 1848, will of Temperance Light. to Orry Tucker wf of John L. Tucker, my bed & bed clothes, one chest & one trunk. to bro. Joel Light - land on Terrible Cr which fell to me in div. of est of my deceased father John Light, it being lot No. 9 in the platt, & on which my sd bro. has been building. to bro. William Light - remainder of est, together with my interest in dower of my mother-in-law Jemima H. Light. S/ Temperance x Light. Wit: Giles McCraw, John A. McCraw, Albert W. Barksdale.

CODICIL - 10 Nov 1847. Revoke 2nd item. Lot No. 9 to remain in possession of Nancy Light & children of Joel Light during life of sd Nancy wf of Joel, & at her death to her son Charles Light.

WB 26-463, 26 Oct 1854, rec 25 Jul 1859, will of Robert Chappell son Thomas Chappell. dau Octavia Chappell. dau Helen R. Chappell. dau Janetta Hart, wf of Edwin S. Hart. dau Orra Tucker. Exor: Thomas Leigh.

CODICIL - 25 Aug 1858.
CODICIL - 7 Jan 1859 - Dau Octavia Chappell having died. five grandchildren Thales O. Tucker, Eugenia D. Tucker, Sally H. Hart, Sally R. Tucker & Prudence A. Tucker.

WB 24-561, wd 3 Mar 1855, wp 23 Apr 1855, <u>will of Robert Tucker</u>. to Octavio & __? Chappell - $70. ea. to Thomas Chappell, <u>Orca Tucker</u>, Ginnella Hart - $50. ea. <u>to John L. Tucker's dau. Prudence Ann</u> - $100. to be deposited in hands of Thomas Chappell & held in trust for her benefit. to niece Ursula Dicker - $100. to Agnes J. & Mary A. Tucker - $20. ea. to sister Nancy Tucker, for life - bal. of my est, both real & personal. At decease of my sister Nancy Tucker, to 2 nephews Wm. D. & Robert T. Old - all the property loaned to sister Nancy Tucker for life. Ex: Thomas J. & George W. Wood, with no security required. S/ Robert Tucker. Wit: Thomas J. Wood, C. J. Craddock.

SUMMARY: John L. Tucker b ca 1815, son of James O. Tucker & wf Mary Light, d ca 1851, md 1836 Orra Chappell, dau of Robert Chappell & wf Joann Light, & had issue:

Thales (or Thuler) Tucker (son) b ca 1836.

Eugenia D (or Jennett) Tucker b ca 1840.

Sally R (or Sarah) Tucker b ca 1843.

Prudence Ann Tucker b ca 1847.

* * *

2. Chiarito, Marian Dodson, "1850 Census of Halifax County, Virginia"

TW155120 - STEPHEN D. TUCKER

MD ELIZABETH R. COLE

SON OF JAMES O. TUCKER

MD MARY LIGHT

HALIFAX CO., VA.

MB 1-175, 9 May 1843, <u>Stephen D. Tucker md Elizabeth R. Cole</u>. Bondsman & Witness J. C. Cole. Signer Martha J. Cole, mother.

<u>The birthdates of members of the Stephen D. Tucker family
are calculated from ages shown in the 1850 Census:</u> [3]

Name	Age	Calculated Birthdate
<u>Southern District</u>	--	---
1178 Stephen Tucker	33	ca 1817
Elizabeth	25	ca 1825
Martha	6	ca 1844
Mary	4	ca 1846
Jane	3/12	ca 1850
Eleanor Cole	20	ca 1830

WB 23-568 4 Jul 1850, wp 26 Jul 1852, <u>will of James O. Tucker</u>. Land I bought of Wm. Ives & wf be sold to pay my debts. to<u> wf Mary Tucker</u> - 200 ac. where we all now reside & all the property thereon & all that may fall into my est, for life or widowhood, that she may be the better able to keep her family together and specialy girls. S/ James O. Tucker. And I do further will that <u>Stephen D. Tucker or one of my sons</u> that may suit the best, may <u>assist my wife Mary Tucker in the management of the est</u> to try and keep everything in good order, and at my wife's decease, I desire that what property there is should be equally divided among <u>all my children (not named)</u>, taking in consideratrion some advances that has been made to some (except John L. Tucker who has had more than his share already). S/James O. Tucker. <u>Certificate granted to Stephen D. Tucker obtain letters of administration</u>.

NOTE: The above will identifies Stephen D. Tucker and John L. Tucker as sons of James O. Tucker, and implies there may have been other children, not named. (See DB 52-326 for names of other probable sons: David B. Tucker, J. W. Tucker & Thomas W. Tucker.)

DB 53-52, 22 Jan 1849, rec 22 Jan 1849, John L. Tucker to secure debts, sold to <u>Stephen D. Tucker</u> & Wm. H. Wood, <u>162 ac.</u> on Terrible Cr, bo Joel Light, James M Baker, Wm Bomar & William Light, also negro woman Lucinda & her child Ephriam, negro man Manuel, 1 bay horse, 1 bay mare, 1 gray mare, 2 yoke oxen, 1 oxcart, all plantation tools & utensils, household & kitchen furniture, crops on hand --, 2 milk cows & 3 yearlings, stock of hogs -- but upon special trust, sd John L. Tucker shall be permitted to remain in possession of property until 1 Jun 1849. (See DB 43-414 for 45 ac, DB 46-50 for 109 1/2 ac, total 154.5 ac. See also DB 54-21)

DB 54-21, 1 Nov 1850, rec 1 Nov 1850, John L. Tucker & wf Orra A. & <u>Stephen D. Tucker</u> & Wm W. Wood, sold to Alexander Yuille & James S. Easley, <u>162 ac.</u> (See DB 53-52)

SUMMARY: Stephen D. Tucker, son of James O. Tucker & wf Mary Light, b ca 1817, md 1843 Elizabeth R. Cole, dau of Martha J. Cole & had issue:

Martha Tucker b ca 1844.

Mary Tucker b ca 1846.

Jane Tucker b ca 1850.

* * *

3. Chiarito, Marian Dodson, "1850 Census of Halifax County, Virginia"

TW155200 - WILLIAM TUCKER

MD AGNESS POWELL
SON OF DAVID TUCKER
MD 1ST FANNY OLD
MD 2ND MARY WOOD
MD 3RD CHRISTIANA BERGER

HALIFAX CO, VA

MB 1-86, 28 Mar 1814, <u>William Tucker md Agnes Powell</u>. Bondsman Watson A. Powell. Witness Joel Tucker Jr. Signer Thomas A. Powell, father.

DB 36-431, 25 Oct 1828, rec 27 Oct 1828, (1) <u>William Tucker</u>, (2) Joel Tucker Jr (3) David Tucker, to secure debt of William Tucker to David Tucker for $524.48, pledged horses, cows, household furniture and equipment, etc. Wit: James O. Tucker, Joel Tucker.

DB 36-517, 13 Dec 1828, rec 13 Dec 1828, <u>William Tucker & wf Agness</u>, formerly Agness Powell, to secure debt to James O. Tucker, sold to William W. Powell, their interest in land on Sandy Cr occupied by Mrs. Nancy Powell as her dower in the lands of Thomas A. Powell decd, plus other items.

Will File 1, will of Thomas A. Powell names <u>Agness Tucker</u>

WB 19-578, 17 Jun 1837, wp 25 Oct 1841, <u>will of Nancey Powell</u>. Land whereon I reside he sold by executor, & proceeds divided in 4 equal parts to: 1/4 to son William W. Powell, 1/4 to son John W. Powell, 1/4 to son Thomas A. Powell & 1/4 equally div btwn children of son James M. Powell. to <u>dau Agness W. Tucker</u> & heirs - $100. cash. Exor: son Thomas A. Powell. S/ Nancey Powell.

WB 20-177, wd 25 Nov 1841, wp 23 Jan 1843, <u>will of David Tucker</u>. wife Christiana - $1,000.00 being proceeds from sale of negro woman & children, acquired by my marriage with her; also the money assigned to me in right of my wife in division of estate of her father (blank) Berger, plus interest to my death; also interest on proceeds of sale of my real & personal property. At death of wife, whole estate equally divided among <u>my children</u>, viz James O. Tucker, Jeney B. Stimpson, Martha Hillson & <u>William Tucker</u>, having hereto given to my dau. Rachael Stimpson all that I intend to give to her, nothing is given her by this will Ex: friend William Holt S/ David Tucker.

DB 66-266, 12 May 1878, rec 27 May 1878, S. D.Tucker, comrnr, for $750., grant to <u>Agnes J. Tucker</u>, 200 ac on Bad Luck Cr, being the land which the late <u>James O. Tucker died seized</u>.

NOTE: Agnes J. Tucker in the above deed probably is not the same Agness W. Tucker, wife of the subject William Tucker. If Agness Powell was ca age 16 when married in 1814, she was born ca 1798, and would have been ca age 80 in 1878. If William Tucker was ca age 21 when married in 1814, he was born ca 1793. His father David Tucker moved from Nottoway to Halifax Co in 1793. Agness Tucker was still living in 1837 when named in her mothers's will, which implied she had children heirs. William Tucker was still living in 1841 when named in his father's will. Neither is included in the 1850 census of Halifax Co, and this compiler has not further researched this family.

SUMMARY: William Tucker, son of David Tucker & 1st wf Fanny Old, b ca 1793 in Nottoway or Halifax Co., m 1814 Agness Powell, dau of Thomas A. Powell & wf Nancey, and probably had issue (names unknown).

TW156000 - JOEL TUCKER SR

MD 1ST USLEY CHAPPELL
MD 2ND NANCY MOORE
SON OF WILLIAM TUCKER SR
MD ANN

AMELIA CO. VA.

WB 3-300, <u>will of William Tucker</u>, 8 Feb 1785, (date recorded not shown).-names: - son Daniel Tucker - Son William Tucker - Son John Tucker - Son Robert Tucker - son David Tucker - Dau. Mary Chappell - Dau. Sarah Olds' three children - Dau. Anne Tucker - <u>Wife Ann</u> - land I now live on for life - <u>Son Joel Tucker – the land whereon I now live & four negroes Dick, Dinah, Cale & Peg & incr. & all remainder of my estate not already mentioned</u>.

NOTE: Joel Tucker must have been an infant under age 16 when his father William Tucker Sr wrote his will in 1785, for he was never listed as a tithable in the household of his father. While William Sr willed specific lands to each of his other sons, he left the land whereon he lived to his wife Ann for life, and afterward to son Joel. It is difficult to determine how many acres went to Joel. There are no deeds for Joel, and the Land Tax Records are complex.

Apparently William Tucker Sr, prior to writing his will, had given custody of his lands to his sons, for in 1782, the land tax records indicate: William Tucker est. 47 ac., Daniel 125 ac. and William Jr 244 ac. all in Raleigh Parish; and John 100 ac. and Robert 545 ac., both in Nottoway Parish. This totalled 1061 ac. In 1787, 200 ac. of the 545 ac. went from Robert to David; in 1788, 25 ac. of the 545 ac. went from Robert to (? John); and Robert was left holding 320 ac. of the 545 ac. John, who had inherited 105 + 70 + 25 was corrected to 200 ac. And all the while, 1782, 1787, 1788 & 1789 William Tucker Est was shown in Amelia Co. as 47 ac.

In 1788, when William Jr died, 244 ac. went from William Jr to Joel on the land tax records. This seems strange, but see below. In 1789 Nottoway Co. was cut off from Amelia Co.

LAND TAX RECORDS-AMELIA CO.

1785	William Tucker Jr	244 ac.	
1788	Joel Tucker	244 ac.	(1788 alterations say "Wm Tucker 244 by Joel Tucker, Joel Tucker D of William Tucker 244".)

NOTTOWAY CO. VA.

LAND TAX RECORDS

1791-1795	Joel Tucker	244 ac.
1796-1798	Joel Tucker	207 ac.
1799-1819	Joel Tucker est.	147 ac.

There are no deeds recorded for this Joel Tucker. However, when his land tax holding was reduced in 1796 by 37 ac. from 244 ac. to 207 ac., and further reduced in 1799 by 60 ac. from 207 ac. to 147 ac., we find the following deeds recorded:

DB 1-456, 3 Jun 1795, rec 4 Jun 1795, <u>Kennon Tucker & wf Lucy</u> of Nottoway Co. to <u>Daniel Tucker, 37 ac</u>, bo. Peter Jones, Uriah's branch. S/ Kennon x Tucker, Lucy x Tucker. Wit: Peter Jones Senr, Pleasant Bevill, Joshua Hawks Senr.

DB 2-25, 4 Oct 1797. rec 7 Jun 1798. <u>Cannon Tucker & wf Lucy</u>. of Nottoway Co. to <u>Daniel Tucker, 60 ac</u>, bo. on east by Peter Jones & Richard Hawks, on west & south by William Greenhill, & on north by Daniel Tucker. S/ Cannon Tucker, Lucy x Tucker. Wit: Charles Morton, Joshua Hawks Sen, John Hawks, John Spain.

Now who was Kennon (or Cannon) Tucker? And why would he sell 37 + 60 = 97 ac., part of the land being "held" by Joel Tucker? Was he a son of Joel? Was he a son of William Jr? Why did Joel Tucker "estate" of 147 ac. exist from 1799-1818, and cease to exist thereafter? Unfortunately, Nottoway Co. Deed Books 5 and 6 which covered a period between 1816-1825, and Deed Book 9 which covered a period between 1829-1840, and Deed Books 11 and beyond beginning ca 1841, were destroyed.

It may be a coincidence, but 147 ac. on Namozine Cr. shows up in 1839 in the estate of Robert Tucker, brother of Joel. Robert Tucker died intestate ca 1815, and his heirs sold 147 ac., in 1839, being part of their inheritance from their father.

Theory of this compiler:
  (1) The original land purchased by William Tucker Sr included 189 ac. on l.s. Seller fk of Deep Cr. (Amelia Co. DB 1-438, 1742) and 280 ac.. l.s. Seller Fork of Deep Cr. (Amelia Co. DB 2-263, 1745).
  (2) This was the land where William Tucker Sr & his family lived, and totaled 469 ac.
  (3) The Land Tax records in 1782 show this land being "held" by Daniel 125 ac., John 100 ac. & William Jr 244 ac., total 469 ac. (4) It was this 469 ac. that William Tucker Sr willed to sons Daniel, William Jr., & wf Ann (for life, then to Joel).
  (5) When William Jr died in 1786, the 244 ac. which he had held,

passed to the custody of his younger brother Joel. This 244 ac. may have included the inheritance of both William Jr & Joel.

(6) William Jr probably had a son named Kennon (or Cannon) Tucker, who when he came of age and married Lucy, sold to his uncle Daniel Tucker in 1795, 37 ac. and in 1797, 60 ac., total 97 ac.

(7) Thus Joel Tucker was left with his inheritance of 147 ac., which in 1799-1819 was recorded in land tax records as Joel Tucker est.

(8) While this might imply that Joel Tucker died in 1799, it is more probable that he moved from Nottoway Co., leaving an estate there, which was sold ca 1820, the period covered by missing Deed Books 5 & 6.

(9) The 147 ac. shows up in the estate of his brother Robert Tucker in 1839.

(10) Joel Tucker Sr bought land in Halifax Co., Va. beginning in 1795. See following:

HALIFAX CO., VA.

DB 16-403, 2 Apr 1795, rec 27 Jul 1795. Meads Anderson to Joel Tucker for L40., 117 ac. on s.s. Sandy Cr. S/ Meads Anderson. Wit: Joseph Petty, William Irby, William Anderson.

DB 17-175, 25 Mar 1797, rec 26 Jun 1797, George Wood to Joel Tucker, 200 ac. bo. William Childrey, Anderson, Richard Coates, Daniel Easley. S/George Wood, Mary Wood relinq dower right. (See DB 20-162)

DB 17-382, 4 Jan 1798, rec 22 Jan 1798, Jesse Talley to Joel Tucker, for L100., 200 ac. on Banister Ri, bo. Ridley, Adams, Broomstraw Br., Robert Chappel. S/ Jesse Talley. Wit: David Street, John Younger, David Tucker. (See DB 22-110 & DB 26-11)

DB 19-143, 26 Oct 1801, rec 26 Oct 1801, Joel Tucker to Bartlett Graves, for L50., 90 ac. S/ Joel Tucker. Wit: Hudson Farguson, Lemuel Farguson, H. Landrum. (No significant bounds shown).

DB 20-162, 2 Jan 1804, rec 25 Jun 1804, Robert Easley & wf Nancy of Pittsylvania Co., to Joel Tucker Sr of Halifax Co., for $126.00, 31.5 ac. in Halifax Co., being a part of John Easley decd tract, bo. Joel Tucker. S/ Robert Easley, Nancy Easley. Wit: David Tucker, Epa Sydnor, Thomas Davenport Jr. (See DB 17-175 for 200 ac. adj Easley)

DB 22-110, 20 Jan 1809, rec 26 Jun 1809, David Tucker & Joel Tucker to Jesse Talley Sr., for L112.9, 86.5 ac. bo. Chappell's corner, Anderson Rd., a branch. S/ Joel Tucker, David Tucker. Nancy Tucker, wife of sd Joel Tucker, relinq dower right. (See DB 17-382~& DB 26-11)

DB 23-543, 27 Jul 1812, rec 27 Jul 1812, Joel Tucker to Thomas A. Oliver, for L 150, 142 ac. on Sandy Cr., bo Powell, Coleman, Turpin, Cartin spring branch. S/ Joel Tucker. Wf Nancy relinq dower right.

DB 26-11, 25 Mar 1816, rec 25 Mar 1816, Joel Tucker & David Tucker to Jacob Chany, for $500., 225 ac. on s.s. Banister Ri., bo. Powell, Clemmons, Chappell. S/ Joel Tucker, David Tucker. Wit: Joel Tucker Jr., Daniel Clark, Andrew Anderson. (See DB 17-382 & DB 22-110)

NOTE: How Joel Tucker & David Tucker came into joint possession of the 86.5 ac. in DB 22-110 & the 225 ac. in DB 26-11, total of 311.5 ac. is not clear. However, the first land bought in the name of Joel Tucker only, 117 ac. (DB 16-403 in 1795) & 200 ac. (DB 17-175 in 1797), total 317 ac. may be the same as 311.5 ac sold by Joel & David.

DB 34-574, 26 Apr 1827, rec 25 Jun 1827, Joel Tucker Senr to Obed Hendrick for $30., 3 ac. on e.s. Little Polecat Cr. Wit: George W. Wood, Joel Tucker, Andrew Anderson. S/ Joel Tucker. (See DB 34-575)

DB 34-575, 27 Apr 1827, rec 25 Jun 1827, Obediah Hendrick to Joel Tucker Sr, for $30., 3 1/2 ac. on w.s. Little Polecat Cr. . Wit: George W. Wood, Joel Tucker Jr, Andrew Anderson. (See DB 34-574)

DB 55-351, 29 Dec 1807 (or 1311), rec 4 Sep 1812, Thomas Burgess of Campbell Co. to Joel Tucker of. Halifax Co., for L136., 136 ac. on Little Polecat Cr.. bo. Anderson Moore, Obed Hendrick, Obediah Kirby, Wit: Obed Hendrick, Anderson Moore, Edward Stubblefield. Wife Elizabeth Burgess relinq dower.

DB 55-12, 15 Feb 1853, rec 19 Feb 1853, Joel Tucker for affectionate regard for beloved wife Nancy Tucker, all land west of road on-which I now live, above land to remain a part of my estate, and to be used for my benefit free from rent during my natural life. S/ Joel Tucker.

DB 55-13, 15 Feb 1853, Joel Tucker for affectionate regard to wf Nancy Tucker, all household & kitchen furniture, a horse of her choosing, carriage, one-third part of my stock of cattle, sheep & hogs, plus $150.00 in money, crops & provisions on hand at my decease - all to remain in my estate during my natural life. S/ Joel Tucker.

DB 55-14, 15 Feb 1853, Joel Tucker for affectionate regard to wf Nancy Tucker, following negroes: Cornelius, Starling, Daniel, Freeman, Dick, Celia and all future increase of the woman Celia, to be kept in my estate for my natural life.

WB 24-177, wd 25 Nov 1839, wp 23 Jan 1854, will of Joel Tucker Sr. Wife Nancy Tucker - all tract of land lying west of the road and on which I now live with all houses, furniture, 6 negroes of her choice, a horse of her choice, my carryall, 1/3 part of stock.
Residue of negroes divided in 6 parts & equally divided between James O. Tucker, Joel Tucker Jun, John E. Tucker, Robert Tucker, John Tucker & Jane B. Stimpson. (Note: both John E. Tucker & John Tucker appeared as shown)

Land lying east of the road with all stock be sold & money distributed as follows: $150.00 to wife Nancy Tucker, $100.00 to Martha Dickie, $50.00 to Martha Watson, $50.00 equally divided btwn two nieces Nancy Tucker & Martha Tucker; $50.00 to Joel Tucker Jr; $50.00 equally div. btwn Sarah Ford & Mary Ford.

Ex. not to give bond or security & est. not to he appraised.

Ex: James O. Tucker & John Tucker. S/ Joel Tucker.

NOTE: For identification of some of the legatees, refer to: 1850 census cited below; WB 24-561 for Joel's nephew Robert Tucker Jr son of Robert Sr; W3 20-177 for Joel's brother David Tucker; and Nottoway DB 4-544 ref Joel's brother John Tucker Sr. Joel Tucker Jr is most probably not son of Joel Sr. but more probably son of John Sr. James O. Tucker is Joel's nephew, son of David. Jane B. Stimpson is Joel's niece, dau of David. Nancy Tucker is Joel's niece, dau of Robert Sr. Martha Tucker is Joel's niece, dau of Robert Sr. Robert Tucker is probably Joel's nephew Robert Jr, son of Robert Sr. Mary Ford resided in Joel's household in 1850 census. Martha Dickie was formerly Martha Chappell, dau of Robert Chappell Sr. The identities of Martha Watson & Sarah Ford are not clear. John E. Tucker appears to be the 2nd husband of Mary Tucker, who was married 1st to John Tucker Sr, brother of Joel Sr. John Tucker appears to he the orphaned son of William Tucker Jr (brother of Joel Sr), whose guardian was John Tucker Sr (brother of Joel Sr), and who md his 1st cousin Patty (Martha) Tucker dau of John Tucker Sr. (See Nottoway Co. DB 4-544 in chapter on William Tucker Jr for a more details)

DB 55-355, __ Feb 1854, rec 27 Feb 1854, Nancy Tucker to John R. Edmunds, for $1,471.75, 203 ac. on south branch of Polecat Cr., bo. road from Halifax Courthouse to Meadsville, Cole, Edmunds, Chappell, Moore. S/ Nancy Tucker, John R. Edmunds. Wit: George W. Wood, Wm. D. Moore, John W. Chappell.

DB 55-357, Feb 1854, rec 27 Feb 1854, John Tucker Executor of Joel Tucker to John R. Edmunds, 102 ac. for $4.25 per ac. ($428.46), on e.s of road leading from Oak Grove Meeting House to Anderson's Old Mill Site & principally on Chestnut Cr., bo Robert Tucker, Chestnut Cr. Joel Cole decd. (whereas Joel Tucker by his will devised a certain tract of land be sold). S/ John Tucker.

17 Oct 1799 Joel Tucker md Usley Chappell.

MB 1-66, 24 Apr 1807, Joel Tucker md Nancy Moore, Bondsman Anderson Moore.

WB 19-79 , 16 Feb 1839, wp 25 Sep 1839. will of Anderson Moore names <u>dau Nancy Tucker</u>. - $1. , dau Mary Younger - $1., dau Martha Daniel - $1.

WB 1-108, 30 Jan 1921, Robert Tucker md Prudence Chappell, Bondsman <u>Joel Tucker</u>, Wit: Joel Tucker & William Dicker, Signer Robert Chappell father.

<u>1850 CENSUS</u> [4]

<u>Following are families associated with Joel Tucker Sr.</u>
<u>The birthdates are calculated from ages shown in the 1850 Census:</u>

	Name	Age	Calculated Birthdate
Southern District:		--	---
155	William Dickey	69	ca 1791
	Ursley	25	ca 1825
	Ellen Tucker	8	ca 1842
167	Joel Tucker	88	ca 1762
	Nancy	55	ca 1795
	Mary Ford	65	ca 1785
174	John Tucker	67	ca 1783
	Martha	75	ca 1775
	Robert A.	36	ca 1814
	Elizabeth T.	27	ca 1823
	William S.	7	ca 1843
	James F.	5	ca 1845
	Henry	4	ca 1846
	Sarah	2	ca 1848
270	Robert Tucker	59	ca 1791
	Prudence	48	ca 1802
	Nancy	60	ca 1790

STOKES CO. N.C. [5]

"Joel Tucker Sr from Halifax Co. Va - 2 sons Robert A. Tucker & Joel Tucker Jr.

Joel Tucker Jr b 1790 d 1853, will Dec 1844 (1854?) Halifax Co., Va.

Joel was residing with his son Benj. in Stokes Co., N. C.

1850 Census. Children:

Gabriel W. Tucker, b 1813, died post 1880;

Benjamin C. Tucker b 1315, died post 1880.

Benjamin C. Tucker was a farmer & carpenter born in Halifax Co. Va., md 1st Sicily Simmons 2 Jul 1833, Stokes Co, N.C., md 2nd Elizabeth Hill 24 May 1845, Stokes Co, N.C."

The above reference is partially in error. It claims that Robert A. Tucker and Joel Tucker Jr were sons of Joel Tucker Sr But Joel Tucker's will did not name Robert A. and Joel Jr as sons. It is most probable that Joel Jr was his nephew, son of John Tucker & wf Mary (Polly), and was known as Jr only because he was the younger of the two Joels. Robert A. Tucker was named as son of John Tucker & wf Martha (Patsy) in WB 26-510.

SUMMARY: Joel Tucker Sr, youngest son of William Tucker Sr & wf Ann of Amelia Co., b ca 1762 Amelia Co., d 1854 Halifax Co., Va., md 1st 1799 Halifax Co. Ursley Chappell, probably dau of Robert Chappell, md 2nd 1807 Halifax Co., Va. Nancy Moore, dau of Anderson Moore. This compiler has found no evidence that Joel Tucker Sr had any children by either wife.

* * *

4. Chiarito, Marian Dodson,"1850 Census of Halifax County, Virginia"
5. Tuck, Faye R., Notes provided to me in 1984 from book, "Stokes Co., Heritage, N.C."

TJ160000 - JOSEPH TUCKER SR
MD PRUDENCE WOOD
SON OF CAPT ROBERT TUCKER SR
MD MARTHA

BRISTOL PARISH REGISTER [1]

Joseph son of Robt & Martha Tucker born 22th June last bapt 15th Aprill 1723.

AMELIA CO. VA.

WB 1-63, d 26 Sep 1744, p 18 May 1750, will of Robert Tucker. Wit: John Cordle Jr, Henry x Hasten, John Powell. Exr. son Robert. Wife Martha - land & plant. where I live for life, then to son Daniel. Son Joseph, Dau. Sarah Clay. Son Robert. Rest of personal est. to be equally div. btwn my children. No appraisement to be made. Slaves: Negro man Joe to wife then to Joseph. Negro man Dick to wife then to Daniel. Negro girl Sal.

LIST OF TITHABLES

1739 - 43	-	---	Joseph Tucker	listed in household of Robert Tucker
1744	1	---	Joseph Tucker	
1747	1	---	Joseph Tucker	
1749	2	---	Joseph Tucker	Mason, Phillis
1750	1	---	Joseph Tucker	
1751	2	---	Joseph Tucker	David, Williams
1752	1	---	Joseph Tucker	
1753	2	---	Joseph Tucker	Joe
1755	2	---	Joseph Tucker	Joe
1756	2	---	Joseph Tucker	Joe
1762	2	---	Joseph Tucker	Nugeen
1763	2	190	Joseph Tucker	Sugen
1764	2	190	Joseph Tucker	Nugent
1765	2	190	Joseph Tucker	Nugent
1767	2	190	Joseph Tucker	Nugent
1769	4	190	Joseph Tucker Sr, Joseph Tucker Jr	Nugent, Fanny
1770	4	190	Joseph Tucker Sr, Joseph Tucker	Nugent, Fanny

NOTE: Capt Robert Tucker Sr did not deed or will any land in Amelia Co. to his son Joseph. In the Lists of Tithables of Amelia Co., Joseph Tucker is listed as a tithable in the household of his father Robert Tucker from 1739-1743, and beginning in 1744 Joseph Tucker is listed as a separate household. (This conforms with the Bristol Parish Register which records his birth in 1722; thus he was age 16 in 1738 and age 21 in 1743.) Beginning in 1753, the slave Joe is listed in the household of Joseph Tucker, which conforms to the will of his father Capt Robert Tucker Sr above. The list of tithables above indicates this Joseph Tucker (b 1722) had a tithable son named Joseph Tucker Jr. in his household in 1769-70 (b ca 1753).

There was yet another Joseph Tucker (Sr) who patented land from 1712-1755 in the area of Pr. Geo. Co. which became Dinwiddie Co. in 1752, and a Joseph Tucker Jr who patented land from 1745-56 in the same area. See note following.

NOTE: Boddie [2] states that "Joseph Tucker, son of Robert and Martha, was born about 1710 -- his lands fell in Dinwiddie when it was cut off from Amelia -- he married Lucretia, daughter of Maj. Robert Wynne -- they had the following children: Lucretia, b August 15, 1731, -- Robert -- Martha -- Mary -- Joel --."

There are several errors in this account.

(1) Joseph Tucker son of Robert & Martha was not b ca 1710, but b 22 Jun 1722, as per Bristol Parish Register cited at beginning of this chapter.
(2) Dinwiddie Co. was not cut off from Amelia, but from Pr. Geo. Co. in 1752.
(3) Joseph son of Robert & Martha could not have married Lucretia Wynne & they have had a dau. Lucretia b 15 Aug 1731, because Joseph would have been only age 9 in 1731.

This compiler suggests that the Joseph Tucker who md Lucretia, dau of Maj. Robert Wynne, was another Joseph Tucker who, on 28 Sep 1730 (P 14-23), patented 302 ac. l.s. Beaverpond Cr, adj. Robert Wynn.

This compiler further suggests that Joseph Tucker son of Robert & Martha, married Prudence and purchased land l.s. Seller Fork of Deep Cr., adj. to his sister Sarah & her husband John Clay, and near his next older brother William Tucker. See deeds following.

DB 1-436, 19 Nov 1742, rec. 19 Nov 1742, Charles Williamson of Pr. Geo. Co. Va. to Joseph Tucker for L14.5., 190 ac. l.s. Seller Fork of Deep Cr., bo. in part by s.s. Reedy Br. Wit: John Clay, Chas. Clay, & Robert Rowland. (See DB 13-189 for 290 ac.)

DB 13-189, 21 Nov 1774, Joseph Tucker & Prudence Tucker to Abner Osborne for L256.4., 290 ac. in Raleigh Parish, l.s. Seller Fork of Deep Cr., bo. Reedy Cr., Kitt's Horsepen Br., mouth of Reedy Br. Wit: Willliam Tucker, Robert Tucker, Joseph Tucker. S/ Joseph x Tucker, Prudence x Tucker. (See DB 1-436 for 190 ac.)

NOTE: Joseph Tucker bought 190 ac. & sold 290 ac. on l.s. Seller Fork of Deep Cr. This compiler has verified that the 190 ac. & 290 ac. were correctly extracted from the respective deeds. If the acreage figures in both deeds are correct, then it is unclear how he acquired the additional 100 ac. It is most likely that DB 13-189 should be 190 ac. instead of 290 ac., since the list of tithable records above indicate he owned 190 ac. 1763-1770. This area lay along the border where Nottoway Co. was cut off from Amelia Co. in 1789. The Land Tax Records for Amelia Co. beginning in 1782 and for Nottoway Co. beginning in 1789 do not include a Joseph Tucker as holding any land in either county. The Joseph Tucker who held land in 1796 in Nottoway Co. is most likely another Joseph Tucker from Dinwiddie Co.

The subject Joseph Tucker son of Robert & Martha moved from Amelia Co. to Prince Edward Co.

PRINCE EDWARD CO., VA.

DB 5-405, 14 Apr 1775, rec 19 Jun 1775. Thomas Watkins of Amelia Co. to Joseph Tucker of Pr. Edward Co., for L150 plus L50, 341 1/2 ac., in Pr. Edward Co., it being 1/2 of 683 ac. which John Watkins decd devised equally divided to his two sons Thomas Watkins & James Watkins, bo. Abner Watkins, John Watkins, James Townes, Richard Eggleston, James Watkins. S/ Thos Watkins. Wit: Jno Watkins, William Watkins, Fredk x Wills. (See WB 3-123 in which Joseph Tucker willed 141 ac. to son Joseph & 200 ac. to son Wood.)

NOTE: It is most likely that Fredk Wills who witnessed the above deed was married to Joseph Tucker's dau Rachal, and that two of the Watkins brothers married Joseph Tucker's daus. Lucy & Obedience. (See WB 3-123)

WB 3-123 wd 1 Jun 1793, wp 18 Jun 1798 & 17 Sep 1798, will of Joseph Tucker of Prince Edward Co.
Son Joseph Tucker - 141 ac. joining Chris Walthall, Jas. Townes & Abner Watkins, also negro man Peter, one cow & calf.
Son Wood Tucker - 200 ac. whereon I now live, also negro woman Bet & her increase, one feather bed & furniture, two cows & calves, one large chest & 4 hogs.
Dau. Lucy Watkins - negro woman Fanny & her increase, for life, & after her death then to her children, but if she have no lawful children, then equally divided amongst my 4 daughters Rachal Wills, Susannah Tucker, Mary Tucker & Obedience Watkins
Dau. Susannah Tucker - feather bed & furniture, one cow & calf & one womans saddle.
Dau. Mary Tucker - feather bed & furnitrure, one cow & calf, & one chest.

Four Daughters Rachel Wills, Susannah Tucker, Mary Tucker & Obedience Watkins - all remainder of negroes equally divided.

Daughters Lucy Watkins, Rachel Wills & Obedience Watkins remaining cattle equally divided.

To 7 above mentioned children Joseph Tucker, Wood Tucker, Lucy Watkins, Rachel Wills, Susannah Tucker & Obedience Watkins - remainder of my estate equally divided (Note: Only six names appeared in the microfilm copy of this will - the name of dau. Mary Tucker seems to have been inadvertantly omitted.)

Exors: 2 sons Joseph & Wood Tucker, & Dan'l Ellington.

Wit: Dan'l Ellington, Talley Ellington, John Ellington.

WB 3-241, 18 Apr 1798, rec 20 Jul 1801, Inv. of Est of Joseph Tucker, returned by Joseph Tucker & Ellington, Executors.

NOTE: Joseph Tucker's wife Prudence probably died prior to 1793, since she was not mentioned in his will. The deaths of three of his children are indicated in the following wills.

WB 6-240, wd 23 Jun 1825, wp 19 Sep 1825, will of Mary Tucker. To Brother Wood Tucker - negro man Jack with all rest of my property of every description. S/ Mary Tucker. Wit: Owen H. Tucker, Susannah x Tucker, Henry Tucker.

> At court 18 Jul 1825, will of Mary Tucker presented by Wood Tucker for proof, and Abner Watkins opposed the admission of same to record.

> At court 15 Aug 1825, will of Mary Tucker decd again offered by Wood Tucker for proof, and Abner Watkins who opposed, his council being absent, and Owen H. Tucker & Henry Tucker, swore that they were witnesses to will, whereupon the court refused to commit sd will to record. Wood Tucker appeal to next Superior Court granted.

> At court 19 Sep 1825, by consent of Abner Watkins & Wood Tucker, will of Mary Tucker was proved & ordered recorded., & appeal dismissed.

WB 7-346, wd 8 Jul 1825, wp 18 Nov 1833, will of Susannah Tucker, Bro Wood Tucker - two negro men Putrum & Pleasant, & all my other property, during his life, & at his death, to my nephew Owen H. Tucker. S/ Susannah Tucker. Wit: Owen H. Tucker, Daniel M. Tucker, Henry Tucker, Joseph Tucker.

WB 7-395, wd 3 Jul 1825, wp 20 Apr 1835, <u>will of Wood Tucker</u>. To <u>sister Susannah Tucker</u> - after paying debts, loan of rest of my estate during her natural life, & at her death-- To <u>nephew Owen H. Tucker</u>, three of the first choice of negroes & their increase. To <u>brother Joseph Tucker</u> - all remainder of my negroes & their increase, including land whereon I now reside, all stock & all other property, excluding entirely <u>his daughter Martha B   ?</u>, as it is not my wish that she should heir any part of my estate. Ex: Edmund Booker & Owen H. Tucker. S/ Wood Tucker. Wit: Owen H. Tucker, <u>Daniel M. Tucker,</u> Henry Tucker.

WB 7-400, 22 Apr 1835, rec 18 May 1835, I&A <u>Est of Wood Tucker</u> decd. Included 17 slaves. Total value $6,498.51.

WB 7-493, rec. 16 Jan 1937, Acct. Cur. of Owen H. Tucker, Exor. of <u>Wood Tucker, dec</u>.

SUMMARY: Joseph Tucker Sr, son of Capt Robert Tucker Sr & wf Martha, b 1722 in Prince George Co., Va., lived in Amelia Co., Nottoway Co., and Prince Edward Co., d 1798 in Prince Edward Co., Va., md Prudence (probably Wood) prior to 1756, and had issue: (A family chart suggests that his wife was Prudence Wood, and they had a son named Wood Tucker. See below.)

> Joseph Tucker (Jr) b ca 1756 in Amelia Co.
>
> Wood Tucker d 1835 unmarried in Prince Edward Co.
>
> Lucy Tucker md _____ Watkins
>
> Susannah Tucker d 1833 unmarried in Prince Edward Co.
>
> Mary Tucker d 1825 unmarried in Prince Edward Co.
>
> Rachel Tucker md _____ Wills
>
> Obedience Tucker md _____ Watkins

NOTE: The following descendants of Joseph Tucker Sr & wf Prudence were copied from a chart which Martha Tucker Bass received from her aunt Josephine Tucker, who was dean of women at Westhampton College, and which Martha Tucker Bass loaned to this compiler in 1984. Code numbers were inserted to identify the generations, and the surname Tucker was inserted where it was not shown on the chart. This compiler does not attest to the validity of any of this data. bdb.

A1 Capt Robert Tucker Sr

B6 Joseph Tucker (1722-1798) m Prudence Ward? or Wood? d before 1793.

C1 Susannah Tucker left estate to Wood Tucker

C2 Mary Tucker left estate to Wood Tucker

C3 Lucy Tucker m Watkins minister?

C6 Rachael Tucker m Wills

C7 Obedience Tucker m Watkins minister?

C8 Martha (Patsy) Tucker
C4 Wood Tucker
C5 Joseph Tucker (War of 1812) m Christiana Worsham (Brunswick Co.)
  D1 Robin Tucker

  D2 Owen Tucker m 1. Eliz. Neal m 2. Eliz Phillips (settled in Amelia)

    E1 Lucy Tucker m Ed Johnson of Amelia

    E2 Lavina Tucker m ? in Louisiana

    E3 Victoria Tucker died in college

    E4 Henry Tucker (lawyer judge) m Mary Susan Ashbrook (Chesterfield Co.)

      F1 Hester Tucker

      F2 Waverly Tucker

      F3 Ilia Tucker

      F4 Mollie Tucker

      F5 Landon Tucker m Mary Gentry (Richmond)

        G1 Dr. Wavarly Stafford Tucker (Newark, NJ)

        G2 Landon Tucker

    E5 Joel Tucker (Physician - died during war)

    E6 Josephine Tucker

    E7 Rose Tucker (died before war)

    E8 Lucie Tucker m Billy Dayne

      F1 John Tucker Dayne

      F2 Nattie Dayne died in Tenn

      F3 Marie Dayne m Hoge

        G1 Dr. Haven Hoge (Sandston)

    E9 Betty Tucker m Robinson (Nottoway)

    E10 Alpheus Tucker (Giles Co.)

      F1 Robert Tucker

      F2 Henry Tucker

      F3 James Tucker

F4 Victoria Tucker

F5 Monica Tucker

E11 Olivia Tucker (Prisoner of War)

E12 Alexander Campbell Tucker m 1st-cousin Ophelia Tucker dau of Daniel Tucker & wf Polly (Mary) Ward

    F1 Floyd Woodruff Tucker m Mary Ellis (Ashland)

        G1 Margaret Tucker

        G2 Wm. Gregory Tucker

        G3 Floyd Woodruff Tucker Jr d 1954, mayor of Ashland, m Emma Lee Priddy

            H1 (dau) Mrs. Gerhardt Larson

            H2 Floyd Woodruff Tucker III

        G4 Mary Tucker (Mrs.Anderson Bland)

        G5 A. Campbell Tucker and Sarah Cardwell

        G6 Katherine Tucker m Ben Smith (Ashland)

            H1 Ben H Smith

D3 Joel Tucker died young

D4 Daniel Tucker m Polly (Mary) Ward (Ballsville, Powhatan Co.)

    E1 Ophelia Tucker m 1st cousin Alexander Campbell Tucker, son of Owen Tucker & 2nd wf Eliz. Phillips. (See Alexander Campbell Tucker above)

    E2 Rose Tucker

D5 George Tucker (died young)

D6 Rebecca W. Tucker (3 slaves) (b?-d 3 Sep 1866)

D7 Henry Tucker (or Joseph Henry Tucker)(b 10 Sep 1797, d 7 May 1859) (25 slaves) md 1st, 11 Dec 1834 Elizabeth Farley (b 22 Aug 1818-d 31 Mar 1837) & had one son.

    E1 Cornelius Tucker (b 13 Feb 1836-d 4 Jun 1862) m 17 Jul 1861 Molly Buster & had one child (not named).

D7 Henry Tucker (or Joseph Henry Tucker) md 2nd, 21 Dec 1843 Louise Agnes McGehee (b 1825-d 19 Jul 1865) dau of Jacob McGehee & wf Mildred Clark, & had issue:

    E2 Walter Jacob Tucker (b 20 Nov 1844, d 23 Jan 1914)

        F1 Joel Henry Tucker

        F2 Walter Tucker

F3 Mary (Mildred) Tucker

F4 George Tucker

F5 Thomas Tucker

E3 Eliza Mildred Christian Tucker b 12 Nov 1846, d 10 Sep 1863

E4 Elvira (Ella) Louise Tucker (1 Dec 1848-1936) m 26 Dec 1871 Ashton File

E5 Henry Tucker (or Henry Joseph Tucker) b 19 Dec 1849, d 2 Dec 1913, m 18 Mar 1902 Josephine (or Josie D.) Lucy

F1 Henry Tucker m Kate Edmunds

G1 Henry Tucker III

G2 Josephine Tucker

E6 Antonia M. Tucker (b 24 Dec 1891) m 18 Dec 1878 Thomas Patterson

E7 Joel Tucker (or Joel Thomas Tucker) (b 18 Jun 1854-d 29 Sep 1927) in 30 May 1888 Martha Ellen Miller (b 4 Jun 1868-d 14 May 1961) dau of Christy Miller & wf Mary Quissenberry.

F1 Susan Louise Tucker (1889-1932) m 8 Feb 1919 James Oscar Kirk

G1 James Oscar Kirk Jr (1920-) m Carolyn Goode

H1 Randolph Tucker Kirk (1945-) m 1st Mary Lou Hughes

H2 Susan Kirk (1953-)

H3 Archer Kirk (1955-) twin

H4 Read Kirk (1955-) twin

F2 Jesse Miller Tucker (1892-1973) m 27 Dec 1919 Florence Edith Smith

G1 Anne Byrd Tucker (1921-19__) m William Donald Moore

H1 William Donald Moore (Jr) (1944-)

H2 Linda Anne Moore (1948-)

G2 Jesse Miller Tucker Jr (1922-1977) m Nancy Hite

H1 Jesse Miller Tucker III

H2 James Tucker

H3 Katherine Tucker

H4 Janette Tucker

G3 Martha Jane Tucker (1924-) Vincent Kenneth Bass (1920-1979) (Note: This is the Martha Bass who provided this compiler with all this data on the Joseph

Tucker Sr line.bdb)

> H1 Judith Lee Bass b 21 Mar 1956, m Dwight Graham
>
> H2 Stuart Kenneth Bass b 7 May 1957
>
> H3 Thomas Lyn Bass b 14 Sep 1961
>
> G4 Florence Virginia Tucker (1927-1967) m Levi Gillikin
>
> > H1 Martha Lorraine Gillikin (1950-) m James Chapman
> >
> > H2 Thomas Lyle Gillikin (1952-)
>
> F3 James T. Tucker 1896-?) m 15 Jun 1938 Katherine Huff
>
> F4 Josephine Tucker (1902-1972) (Note: This is the Josephine Tucker who prepared the charts from which this data was taken. bdb)

E8 Martha Anne Tucker (14 Jun 1856-10 Jul 1862)

E9 George Washington Tucker (17 Jun 1359-3 Aug 1862)

D8 Biddle Tucker died young

D9 Sally Tucker died young

D10 Patsy Tucker m 1804 Borman (Baptist minsister) went south Tennessee

D11 Betsy Tucker m Pinkington (Pinkerton) went south Tennessee.

* * *

1. Boddie, John B., "Births 1720-1792 from the Bristol Parish Register of Henrico, Prince George and Dinwiddie."

2. Boddie, John B., "Historical Southern Families", Vol 5, pp 296

TJ161000 - WOOD TUCKER
SON OF JOSEPH TUCKER
MD PRUDENCE WOOD

PRINCE EDWARD CO., VA

WB 3-123 wd 1 Jun 1793, wp 18 Jun 1798 & 17 Sep 1798, will of Joseph Tucker of Prince Edward Co.- names: - Son Joseph Tucker - Son Wood Tucker - 200 ac. whereon I now live, also negro woman Bet & her increase, one feather bed & furniture, two cows & calves, one large chest & 4 hogs. - Dau. Lucy Watkins - 4 daughters Rachal Wills; Susannah Tucker, Mary Tucker & Obedience Watkins - Exors: 2 sons Joseph & Wood Tucker, & Dan'l Ellington.

WB 6-240, wd 23 Jun 1825, wp 19 Sep 1825, will of Mary Tucker. To Brother Wood Tucker - negro man Jack with all rest of my property of every description. S/ Mary Tucker. Wit: Owen H. Tucker, Susannah x Tucker, Henry Tucker.

> At court 18 Jul 1825, will of Mary Tucker presented by Wood Tucker for proof, and Abner Watkins opposed the admission of same to record.

> At court 15 Aug 1825, will of Mary Tucker decd again offered by Wood Tucker for proof, and Abner Watkins who opposed, his council being absent, and Owen H. Tucker & Henry Tucker, swore that they were witnesses to will, whereupon the court refused to commit sd will to record. Wood Tucker appeal to next Superior Court granted.

> At court 19 Sep 1825, by consent of Abner Watkins & Wood Tucker, will of Mary Tucker was proved & ordered recorded., & appeal dismissed.

WB 7-346, wd 8 Jul 1825, wp 18 Nov 1833, will of Susannah Tucker. To Bro Wood Tucker - two negro men Putrum & Pleasant, & all my other property, during his life, & at his death, to my nephew Owen H. Tucker. S/ Susannah Tucker. Wit: Owen H. Tucker, Daniel. M. Tucker, Henry Tucker, Joseph Tucker.

WB 7-395, wd 8 Jul 1825, wp 20 Apr 1835, will of Wood Tucker.
To sister Susannah Tucker - after paying debts, loan of rest of my estate during her natural life, & at her death--
To nephew Owen H. Tucker, three of the first choice of negroes & their increase.
To brother Joseph Tucker - all remainder of my negroes & their increase, including land whereon I now reside, all stock & all other property, excluding entirely his daughter Martha B   ?, as it is not my wish that she should heir any part of my estate.

Ex: Edmund Booker & Owen H. Tucker. S/ Wood Tucker.
Wit: Owen H. Tucker, <u>Daniel M. Tucker, Henry Tucker</u>.

WB 7-400, 22 Apr 1835, rec 18 May 1835, I&A <u>Est of Wood Tucker</u> decd. Included 17 slaves. Total value $6,498.51.

WB 7-493, rec. 16 Jan 1837, Acct. Cur. of Owen H. Tucker, Exor. of <u>Wood Tucker, dec.</u>

<u>1810 CENSUS</u> [1]

	Males					Females					Free Negro & Slave
	Under 10	10 to 16	16 to 26	26 to 45	45 & up	Under 10	10 to 16	16 to 26	26 to 45	45 & up	
Tucker, Wood	--	--	--	--	1	0	0	0	1	1	13
Tucker, Joseph	2	1	3	0	1	2	0	2	0	1	2

NOTE: Wood Tucker was age 45-up in the 1810 census, so he was born ca 1765 or earlier. Two females, ages 45-up and 26-45 living in his household would indicate that, in 1810, he may have been married and had a daughter. However, in his will written in 1825 and probated in 1835, he left his estate to his sister Susannah, his brother Joseph and his nephew Owen H. Tucker.

NOTE: The following descendants of Joseph Tucker Sr & wf Prudence were copied from a chart which Martha Tucker Bass received from her aunt Josephine Tucker, who was dean of women at Westhampton College, and which Martha Tucker Bass loaned to this compiler in 1984. Code numbers were inserted to identify the generations, and the surnname Tucker was inserted where it was not shown on the chart. BDB.

B6 Joseph Tucker (1722-1798) m Prudence Ward? or Wood? d before 1793.

    C1 Susannah Tucker left estate to Wood Tucker

    C2 Mary Tucker left estate to Wood Tucker

    C3 Lucy Tucker m Watkins minister?

    C4 Wood Tucker

    C6 Rachael Tucker m Wills

C7 Obedience Tucker m Watkins minister?

C8 Martha (Patsy) Tucker

C5 Joseph Tucker (War of 1812) m Christiana Worsham (Brunswick Co.)

(See complete chart in the chapter for Joseph Tucker Sr, to which the above names were indexed.)

SUMMARY: Wood Tucker, son of Joseph Tucker & wf Prudence Wood, b ca or before 1765 probably in Amelia Co., d 1835 in Prince Edward Co., may have had a wife and daughter who died prior to 1825.

* * *

1. "U.S. Census of Prince Edward County, Va., 1810" Compiled by Lucy K. McGhee.

TJ162000 - JOSEPH TUCKER JR

MD CHRISTIANA WORSHAM
SON OF JOSEPH TUCKER SR
MD PRUDENCE WOOD

PRINCE EDWARD CO. VA.

WB 3-123 wd 1 Jun 1793, wp 18 Jun 1798 & 17 Sep 1798, will of Joseph Tucker of Prince Edward Co. - names: - Son Joseph Tucker - 141 ac. joining. Chris Walthall, Jas. Townes & Abner Watkins, also negro man Peter, one cow & calf. - Son Wood Tucker - Dau. Lucy Watkins – 4 daughters Rachal Wills, Susannah Tucker, Mary Tucker & Obedience Watkins - Exors: 2 sons Joseph & Wood Tucker, & Dan'l Ellington.

WB 3-241, 18 Apr 1798, rec 20 Jul 1801, Inv. of Est of Joseph Tucker, returned by Joseph Tucker & Daniel Ellington, Executors.

MARRIAGE [2] 19 Dec 1804. James Borum married Patsy Tucker, dau. of Joseph Tucker who is surety. Married 22 Dec.

DB 14-440, rec 13 Oct 1810, Wood Tucker, Joseph Tucker & wf Chrischancy(?), of Pr. Edward Co. to Sterling Smith, of James Town in same county, for L62.7.3., 20 3/4 ac., bo. Joseph Tucker, Wood Tucker, Branch Walthall, William T. Smith, Joel Tucker. S/ Wood x Tucker, Joseph Tucker, Chrischancy x Tucker. Wit: Pleasant Ellington, Edmund Booker, John Walthall. Memo: Be it remembered that the within mentioned land is a part of the tract willed to us by our father and be it further mentioned that Wood Tucker has sold 6 ac. & 65/160 and Joseph Tucker has sold 14 and 61/160 both of which parcels make up the within quantity say 20 3/4 ac. S/ Wood Tucker, Joseph Tucker. Wit: Thomas Rice, Pleasant Ellington, John Walthall.

1810 CENSUS [3]

	Males					Females					Free
	Under 10	10 to 16	16 to 26	26 to 45	45 & up	Under 10	10 to 16	16 to 26	26 to 45	45 & up	Negro & Slave
Tucker, Wood	--	--	--	--	1	0	0	0	1	1	13
Tucker, Joseph	2	1	3	0	1	2	0	2	0	1	2

NOTE: If Joseph Tucker Jr and his wife were age 45-up in the 1810 census, they were born ca or before 1765. In the same household were 3 males & 2 females age 16-26 (b 1784-94), 1 male age 10-16 (b 1794-1800) 1 male & 2 females under 10 (b 1800 -10). He was married ca 1783.

DB 16-243, 28 Sep 1814, Joseph Tucker to Sterling Smith, 20 3/4 ac. Churchaney(?) Tucker, wf of Joseph Tucker acknowledged.

DB 18-335, 7 Apr 1824, rec 19 Apr 1824, Joseph Tucker & wf Christiana to Henry Tucker, for $989.16, 125 ac. bo. Wood Tucker, Jeremiah Farley, Benajah Marshall, James Jackson Sr & Branch Waltham, with the further understanding that sd Joseph Tucker & wf to remain on the sd land during their natural life uninterrupted, but to be subject to control of sd Henry Tucker, and at their death the said personal property & increase to be disposed of as Joseph & wf may see cause. Wit: Owen H. Tucker, Pat H. Noble, Winson Noble. (See WB 3-123 for 141 ac. less DB 14-440 for 14+ ac. = 127 ac.)

WB 7-346, wd 8 Jul 1825, wp 18 Nov 1833, will of Susannah Tucker. Bro Wood Tucker - two negro men Putrum & Pleasant, & all my other property, during his life, & at his death, to my nephew Owen H. Tucker. Wit: Owen H. Tucker, Daniel M. Tucker, Henry Tucker, Joseph Tucker.

WB 7-395, wd 8 Jul 1825, wp 20 Apr 1835, will of Wood Tucker. To sister Susannah Tucker - after paying debts, loan of rest of any estate during her natural life, & at her death-- To nephew Owen H. Tucker, three of the first choice of negroes & their increase. To brother Joseph Tucker - all remainder of my negroes & their increase, including land whereon I now reside, all stock & all other property, excluding entirely his daughter Martha Borum(?) as it is not my wish that she should heir any part of my. estate. Ex: Edmund Booker & Owen H. Tucker. S/ Wood Tucker. Wit: Owen H. Tucker, Daniel M. Tucker, Henry Tucker.

NOTE: At this point in time, Joseph Tucker Jr had sold the 141 ac. inherited from his father Joseph Sr, 126 ac. of it to his son Henry. There are no other deeds for Joseph Jr in Pr. Edward Co. However, Wood Tucker willed to his sister Susannah for life & then to his brother. Joseph Jr, land whereon he (Wood) resided. (See WB 7-395). This most likely was the 200 ac. (- 4+ ac. = 196 ac.) which Wood inherited. Joseph Tucker Jr apparently died intestate after 1835.

SUMMARY: Joseph Tucker Jr, son of Joseph Tucker Sr & wf Prudence, b before 1765 in Amelia Co., d after 1835 in Pr. Edward Co., and ca 1783 Christiana Worsham, and had issue (See below).

NOTE: The following descendants of Joseph Tucker Sr & wf Prudence were copied from a chart which Martha Tucker Bass received from her aunt Josephine Tucker, who was dean of women at Westhampton College, and which Martha Tucker Bass loaned to this compiler in 1984. Code numbers were inserted to identify the generations, and the surname Tucker was inserted where it was not shown on the chart. BDB.

B6 Joseph Tucker (1722-1798) m Prudence Ward? or Wood? d before 1793.

C5 <u>Joseph Tucker (War of 1812) m Christiana Worsham (Brunswick Co.)</u>

   D1 Robin Tucker

   D2 Owen Tucker m 1. Eliz. Neal m 2. Eliz Phillips (settled in Amelia)

   D3 Joel Tucker died young

   D4 Daniel Tucker m Polly (Mary) Ward (Ballsville, Powhatan Co.)

   D5 George Tucker (died young)

   D6 Rebecca W. Tucker (3 slaves) (b? -d 3 Sep 1866)

   D7 Henry Tucker (or Joseph Henry Tucker) (b 10 Sep 1797-d 7 May 1859) (25 slaves) md 1st 11 Dec 1834 Elizabeth Farley (b 22 Aug 1818-d 31 Mar 1837) Henry Tucker (or Joseph Henry Tucker) md 2nd 21 Dec 1843 Louise Agnes McGehee (b 1825-d 19 Jul 1865)

   (See complete chart in the chapter for Joseph Tucker Sr,
   to which the above names were indexed.)
   * * *

2. "Prince Edward Co. Va. Marriages, 1754-1810," Compiled & published by Catherine Lindsay Knorr, 1950.

3. "U.S. Census of Prince Edward County, Va., 1810" Compiled by Lucy K. McGhee.

TJ162100 - OWEN H. TUCKER
MD 1ST ELIZ. NEAL
MD 2ND ELIZ. PHILLIPS
SON OF JOSEPH TUCKER JR
MD CHRISTIANA WORSHAM

NOTTOWAY CO., VA

WE 5-73, wd 24 Apr 1823, wp 5 Jun 1823, <u>will of Joel Tucker</u>. To <u>brother Henry Tucker</u> - bal of est both real & personal, after paying debts. <u>Exors: brother Henry Tucker & Owen Tucker</u>. Signed by Williama Buford at request of Joel Tucker. Acknowledged by John H. Cooke, Robert Jones, Thomas Jones, Wm. R. Fontaine.

PRINCE EDWARD CO., VA.

WB 6-240, wd 23 Jun 1825, wp 19 Sep 1825. <u>will of Mary Tucker</u>. To Brother Wood Tucker - negro man Jack with all rest of my property of every description. S/ Mary Tucker. <u>Wit: Owen H. Tucker</u>, Susannah x Tucker, Henry Tucker.

> At court 18 Jul 1825, will of Mary Tucker presented by Wood Tucker for proof, and Abner Watkins opposed the admission of same to record.

> At court 15 Aug 1825, will of Mary Tucker decd again offered by Wood Tucker for proof, and Abner Watkins who opposed, his council being absent, and <u>Owen H. Tucker & Henry Tucker, swore that they were witnesses to will</u>, whereupon the court refused to commit sd will to record. Wood Tucker appeal to next Superior Court granted.

> At court 19 Sep 1825, by consent of Abner Watkins & Wood Tucker, will of Mary Tucker was proved & ordered recorded, & appeal dismissed.

WB 7-346, wd 8 Jul 1825, wp 18 Nov 1833, <u>will of Susannah Tucker</u>. Bro Wood Tucker - two negro men Putrum & Pleasant, & all my other property, during his life, & at his death, to my <u>nephew Owen H. Tucker</u>. S/ Susannah Tucker. <u>Wit: Owen H. Tucker</u>, Daniel M. Tucker, Henry Tucker, Joseph Tucker.

WB 7-395, wd 8 Jul 1825, wp 20 Apr 1835, <u>will of Wood Tucker</u>. To sister Susannah Tucker - after paying debts, loan of rest of my estate during hernatural life, & at her death-- To <u>nephew Owen H. Tucker</u>, three of the first choice of negroes & their increase. To brother Joseph Tucker - all remainder of my negroes & their increase, including land whereon I now reside, all stock & all other property, excluding entirely his daughter Martha B_____?, as it is not my wish that she should heir any part of my estate. Ex: Edmund Booker & Owen H. Tucker. S/ Wood Tucker. Wit: Owen H. Tucker, Daniel M. Tucker, Henry Tucker.

WB 7-400, 22 Apr 1835, rec 18 May 1835, I&A Est of Wood Tucker decd. Included 17 slaves. Total value $6,498.51.

WB 7-493, rec. 16 Jan 1837, Acct. Cur. of Owen H. Tucker, Exor. of Wood Tucker, dec.

AMELIA CO., VA.

NOTE: See WB 18-51 (1857-1864) for the will of Owen H. Tucker, and the following will book references pertaining to him: 17-510, 18-97, 18-281, 18-325, 18-375, 19-77, & 19-81, which were not analyzed by this compiler.

SUMMARY:

NOTE: The following descendants of Joseph Tucker Sr & wf Prudence were copied from a chart which Martha Tucker Bass received from her aunt Josephine Tucker, who was dean of women at Westhampton College, and which Martha Tucker Bass loaned to this compiler in 1984. Code numbers were inserted to identify the generations, and the surname Tucker was inserted where it was not shown on the chart. BDB.

B3 Joseph Tucker (1722-1798) m Prudence Ward? or Wood? d before 1793.

C5 Joseph Tucker (War of 1812) m Christiana Worsham (Brunswick Co.)

D2 Owen Tucker m 1. Eliz. Neal m 2. Eliz Phillips (settled in Amelia)

    E1 Lucy Tucker m Ed Johnson of Amelia

    E2 Lavina Tucker m ? in Louisiana

    E3 Victoria Tucker died in college

    E4 Henry Tucker (lawyer judge) m Mary Susan Ashhrook (Chesterfield Co.)

    E5 Joel Tucker (Physician - died during war)

    E6 Josephine Tucker

    E7 Rose Tucker (died before war)

    E8 Lucie Tucker m Billy Dayne

    E9 Betty Tucker m Robinson (Nottoway)

E10 Alpheus Tucker (Giles Co.)

E11 Olivia Tucker (Prisoner of War)

E12 Alexander Campbell Tucker m 1st-cousin Aphelia Tucker dau of Daniel Tucker & wf Polly (Mary) Ward

(See complete chart in the chapter for Joseph Tucker Sr, to which the above names were indexed.)

TJ162200 - JOEL TUCKER
SON OF JOSEPH TUCKER JR
MD CHRISTIANA WORSHAM

NOTTOWAY CO., VA

WB 5-73, wd 24 Apr 1823, wp 5 Jun 1823, <u>will of Joel Tucker</u>. To <u>brother Henry Tucker</u> - bal of est both real & personal after paying debts. <u>Exors: brother Henry Tucker & Owen Tucker</u>. Signed by William Buford at request of Joel Tucker. Acknowledged by John H. Cooke, Robert Jones, Thomas Jones, Wm. R. Fontaine.

NOTE: Joel Tucker must have been at least age 21 when he made his will in 1823, so he was born before 1802.

NOTE: The following descendants of Joseph Tucker Sr & wf Prudence were copied from a chart which Martha Tucker Bass received from her aunt Josephine Tucker, who was dean of women at Westhampton College, and which Martha Tucker Bass loaned to this compiler in 1984. Code numbers were inserted to identify the generations, and the surname Tucker was inserted where it was not shown on the chart. BDB.

B6 Joseph Tucker (1722-1798) m Prudence Ward? or Wood? d before 1793.

C5 Joseph Tucker (War of 1812) m Christiana Worsham (Brunswick Co.)

> D1 Robin Tucker
>
> D2 Owen Tucker m 1. Eliz. Neal m 2. Eliz Phillips (settled in Amelia)
>
> D3 <u>Joel Tucker died Young</u>
>
> D4 Daniel Tucker m Polly (Mary) Ward (Ballsville, Powhatan Co.)
>
> D5 George Tucker (died young)
>
> D6 Rebecca W. Tucker (3 slaves) (b?-d 3 Sep 1866)
>
> D7 Henry Tucker (or Joseph Henry Tucker) (b 10 Sep 1797-d 7 May 1859) (25 slaves) md 1st 11 Dec 1834 Elizabeth Farley (b 22 Aug 1818-d 31 Mar 1837), md 2nd 21 Dec 1843 Louise Agness McGehee (b 1825-d 19 Jul 1865)

D8 Biddie Tucker died young

D9 Sally Tucker died young

D10 Patsy Tucker m 1804 Borman (Baptist minsister) went south Tennessee

D11 Betsy Tucker m Pinkington (Pinkerton) went south Tennessee

(See complete chart in the chapter for Joseph Tucker Sr,
to which the above names were indexed.)

SUMMARY: Joel Tucker, son of Joseph Tucker Jr & wf Christiana Worsham, b before 1802, d 1823 in Nottoway Co. without issue.

TJ162300 - HENRY TUCKER

(OR JOSEPH HENRY TUCKER)
MD 1ST ELIZABETH FARLEY
MD 2ND LOUISE AGNESS MCGEHEE
SON OF JOSEPH TUCKER JR
MD CHRISTIANA WORSHAM

PRINCE EDWARD CO., VA.

NOTE: The subject Henry Tucker (or Joseph Henry Tucker) (1797-1859) was, in 1825, a witness to the wills of his aunts Mary Tucker (-1825) & Susannah Tucker (-1833) & his uncle Wood Tucker (-1835), who were sisters and brother of his father Joseph Tucker Jr. See the following wills.

WB 6-240, wd 23 Jun 1825, wp 19 Sep 1825. will of Mary Tucker. To Brother Wood Tucker - negro man Jack with all rest of my property of every description. S/ Mary Tucker. Wit: Owen H. Tucker, Susannah x Tucker, Henry Tucker.

> At court 18 Jul 1825, will of Mary Tucker presented by Wood Tucker for proof, and Abner Watkins opposed the admission of same to record.

> At court 15 Aug 1825, will of Mary Tucker decd again offered by Wood Tucker for proof, and Abner Watkins who opposed, his council being absent, and Owen H. Tucker & Henry Tucker, swore that they were witnesses to will, whereupon the court refused to commit sd will to record. Wood Tucker appeal to next Superior Court granted.

> At court 19 Sep 1825, by consent of Abner Watkins & Wood Tucker, will of Mary Tucker was proved & ordered recorded., & appeal dismissed.

WB 7-346, wd 8 Jul 1825, wp 18 Nov 1833, will of Susannah Tucker. Bro Wood Tucker - two negro men Putrum & Pleasant, & all my other property, during his life, & at his death, to my nephew Owen H. Tucker. S/ Susannah Tucker. Wit: Owen H. Tucker, Daniel M. Tucker, Henry Tucker, Joseph Tucker.

WB 7-395, wd 8 Jul 1825, wp 20 Apr 1835, will of Wood Tucker. To sister Susannah Tucker - after paying debts, loan of rest of my estate during her natural life, & at her death -- To nephew Owen H. Tucker, three of the first choice of negroes & their increase. To brother Joseph Tucker - all remainder of my negroes & their increase, including land whereon I now reside, all stock & all other property, excluding entirely his daughter Martha B____?, as it is not my wish that she should heir any part of my estate. Ex: Edmund Booker & Owen H. Tucker. S/ Wood Tucker. Wit: Owen H. Tucker, Daniel M. Tucker, Henry Tucker.

NOTE: The subject Henry Tucker (1797-1859) md 1st 1834 Elizabeth Farley (1818-1837), dau of Stith Farley (-1857) & they had one son Cornelius Tucker (1836-1862). See wills following.

WB 10-357, wd 29 Dec 1846, wp 16 Feb 1857, will of Stith Farley. Names sons Albert Farley, Stith T. Farley, dau. Eliza W.A. Farley, dau. Nancy M. Farley, To wife Maria Farley, the plantation whereon I live for life, & at her death, then to be equally divided btwn Nancy M. Farley & my grandson Cornelius Tucker. ---. Executrix: wife Maria Farley. S/- Stith Farley. No witnesses.

NOTE: Maria Farley may be the second wife of Stith Farley for an earlier marriage is recorded.

10 Aug 1804. Stith Farley md Frances Goode, dau of Robert Goode who consents. Sur. Joseph Goode.

WB 11-285, wd 22 Mar 1862, wp 21 Jul 1862, will of Cornelius Tucker. 2/3 of my est, with 2/3 of my interest in est. of my grandfather Stith Farley, to the child heir of my body who is to be born in the course of two months. Remaining 1/3 of my estate to wife Mollie L. Tucker, together with 1/3 of my interest in est. of my grandfather Stith Farley. Ex: Friend George W. Vaughan. S/ C. Tucker. Wit: A. C. Tucker, J. R. Jeter, W. B. Farley, Thomas S. Scott.

WB 11-465, 5 Sep 1862, rec 18 Jan 1864, I&A Est Cornelius Tucker, Total value $4,266.00. Did not include any slaves.

WB 11-520, rec 20 Jun 1854, Est. of Cornelius Tucker in account with G. W. Vaughan Adm.

NOTE: The subject Henry Tucker (1797-1859) md 2nd 1843 Louise Agness McGehee (1825-1865), dau of Jacob McGehee. See will following.

WB 10-161, wd 16 Dec 1854, wp 15 Jan 1855, will of Thomas C. McGehee. To mother (not named) all my estate, including interest that may accrue to me from the legacies of my two sisters Elvira McGehee & Moriah McGehee (now decd) from est. of my father Jacob McGehee; & at her death, est. to he sold & divided 1/2 to my sister Elizabeth A. McGehee, and 1/2 equally divided btwn children of my brother William McGehee and my sister Louise Tucker's children.
S/ Thomas C. McGehee.

Note: 12 Dec 1781. Jacob McGehee md Anne Weaver. Sur. Moore Weaver.

17 Sep 1792. Larkin Anderson md Elizabeth McGehee, dau of Jacob McGehee who consents. Sur. Benjamin Hodnett.

NOTE: The following descendants of Joseph Tucker Sr & wf Prudence were copied from a chart which Martha Tucker Bass received from her aunt Josephine Tucker, who was dean of women at Westhampton College, and which Martha Tucker Bass loaned to this compiler in 1984. Code numbers were inserted to identify the generations, and the surnname Tucker was inserted where it was not shown on the chart. BDB.

B6 Joseph Tucker (1722-1798) m Prudence Ward? or Wood? d before 1793.

C5 Joseph Tucker (War of 1812) m Christiana Worsham (Brunswick Co.)

D7 <u>Henry Tucker (or Joseph Henry Tucker) (b 10 Sep 1797-d 7 May 1859) (25 slaves) md 1st 11 Dec 1834 Elizabeth Farley (b 22 Aug 1818-d 31 Mar 1837)</u>

    E1 Cornelius Tucker (b 13 Feb 1836-d 4 Jun 1862) m 17 Jul 1861 Molly Buster & had one child

D7 <u>Henry Tucker (or Joseph Henry Tucker) md 2nd 21 Dec 1843 Louise Agnes McGehee (b 1825-d 19 Jul 1865)</u>

    E2 Walter Jacob Tucker (b 20 Nov 1844, d 23 Jan 1914)

    E3 Eliza Mildred Christian Tucker (b 12 Nov 1846, d 10 Sep 1868)

    E4 Elvira (Ella) Louise Tucker (1 Dec 1848-1936) m 26 Dec 1871 Ashton File

    E5 Henry Tucker (or Henry Joseph Tucker) b 19 Dec 1849, d 2 Dec 1913, m 18 Mar 1902 Josephine (or Josie D.) Lucy

    E6 Antonia M. Tucker (b 24 Dec 1851) m 18 Dec 1878 Thomas Patterson

    E7 Joel Tucker (or Joel Thomas Tucker (b 18 Jun 1854-d 29 Sep 1927) in 30 May 1888 Martha Ellen Miller (b 4 Jun 1868-d 14 May 1961)

    E8 Martha Anne Tucker (14 Jun 1856-10 Jul 1862)

    E9 George Washington Tucker (17 Jun 1859-3 Aug 1862)

      (See complete chart in the chapter for Joseph Tucker Sr,
        to which the above names were indexed.)

TD170000 - DANIEL TUCKER SR

MD ELIZABETH
SON OF CAPT ROBERT TUCKER SR
MD MARTHA

BRISTOL PARISH REGISTER [1]

Dan: of Robt & Martha Tucker born Janr last bapt May 10th 1725.

Daniel Son of William and Eliza Tucker born 29th Janr 1725.

NOTE: The subject Daniel Tucker is the son of Robert and Martha born Jan 1725, and baptized 10 May 1725.

AMELIA CO. VA.

WB 1-63, d 26 Sep 1744, p 18 May 1750, will of Robert Tucker. Wit: John Cordle Jr, Henry x Hasten, John Powell. Exr. son Robert. Wife Martha - land & plant. where I live for life, then to son Daniel. Son Joseph. Dau. Sarah Clay. Son Robert. Rest of personal est. to be equally div. btwn my children. No appraisement to be made. Slaves: Negro man Joe to wife then to Joseph. Negro man Dick to wife then to Daniel. Negro girl Sal.

LIST OF TITHABLES

1741 - 1744	-	---	Daniel Tucker
1747	1	---	Danill Tucker
1749	1	---	Daniel Tucker
1750	2	---	Daniel Tucker
1751	3	---	Daniel Tucker
1752	3	---	Daniel Tucker
1753	2	---	Daniel Tucker
1755	3	---	Daniel Tucke
1756	3	---	Daniel Tucker
1762	3	---	Daniel Tucker
1763	3	__	Daniel Tucker
1765	3	_76	Daniel Tucker Sen
1767	4	176	Daniel Tucker, Robert Tucker
1769	4	200	Daniel Tucker, Robert Tucker
1770	3	200	Daniel Tucker Sen, Robert Tucker

NOTE: Daniel Tucker was listed as a tithable in the household of his father Capt Robert Tucker Sr from 1741-1744. Beginning in 1747, this Daniel Tucker was listed as a separate household. This conforms with the Bristol Parish Register which records his birth in 1725, and he was age 16 in 1741 and age 21 in 1746. Beginning in 1751, a slave Dick was listed in the household of Daniel Tucker, which conforms with the will of his father Capt Robert Tucker Sr above.

NOTE: In 1765 & 1770, he was shown as Daniel Tucker Sr, indicating that, either he had a son named Daniel Jr, or there was another younger (junior) Daniel Tucker in the same area. He may have been one of his several nephews named Daniel.

NOTE: The Robert Tucker listed as a 16-yr-up tithable in the household of Daniel Tucker, 1767-70 may have been his son, or may have been one of his several nephews named Robert. No reference was found for a Robert Tucker son of Daniel.

NOTE: The Lists of Tithables for 1771-1781 are incomplete or missing, and this Daniel Tucker had sold his land and left the county before the land tax records and personal tax records were started in 1782.

DB 10-67, 27 Oct 1768, <u>Daniel Tucker of Raleigh Parish</u> to Robert Bolling of Bristol Parish in Dinwiddie Co., for L375., <u>176 ac. in fork of Tucker's Br. of Namozene Cr.</u>, bo. beg. at sd Bolling's (formerly Munn's) cor. on Tucker's Br., Brooking's (formerly Bland's) line to north fork of sd br., up south fork of main br. Wit: David Adams, James Old, Daniel Tucker. <u>Wf Eliza</u> relinq. dower. S/ Daniel Tucker.

NOTE: The above deed was probably the same 176 ac. which Robert Tucker Sr acquired by Patent 23-775, 30 Aug 1744, and the same land and plantation which he willed to his wife Martha for life, then to son Daniel by WB 1-63 in 1750.

NOTE: The above deed also established Elizabeth as the wife of Daniel. And another Daniel Tucker was witness to that deed. Could this be his son Daniel Jr, or another younger Daniel?

NOTE: After selling his inheritance, the subject Daniel then bought from his brother-in-law and sister, John & Sarah Clay, 200 ac. which was part of an original patent in 1747 to his brother William. See patent and deeds following.

Patent 28-276, 1 Oct 1747, William Tucker, Amelia Co., <u>400 ac.</u> btwn the Swethouse & Seller Creeks. (See DB 3-219)

DB 3-219, rec. 4 Mar 1748, William Tucker for love & affection I have & care unto William Gallemore and for his better advancement in the world, <u>400 ac.</u>, btwn Swethouse & Seller Creeks, bo. Charles Clay, Abraham Jones, Abraham Hanks, Jo Hanks, Rich'd Jones. Wit: John Clay, Henry Jones, William Jones. (See DB 8-232)

DB 8-232, 10 Oct 1763, Rec 24 Nov 1763, William Gallemore & wf Mary to John Cordle for L61., 200 ac. btwn Swethouse & Cellar Creeks, being part of 400 ac. granted to William Tucker by patent 1 Oct 1747. S/ William x Gallemore, Mary x Gallemore. Wit: John Broadway, John Hawks. (See DB 9-267)

DB 9-267, 7 Aug 1767, John Cordle & wf Ann to John Clay, for L74.13.3, 200 ac. btwn Swethouse & Cellar Creeks, being part of 400 ac. granted to William Tucker by Patent 1 Oct 1747. (See DB 10-76)

DB 10-76, 23 Mar 1768, rec. 27 Oct 1768, John Clay & wf Sarah to Daniel Tucker for L61., 200 ac. btwn the Sweathouse & Cellar Creeks, being part of 400 ac. granted to William Tucker by patent 1 Oct 1747. Wit: Robert Stanfield, John Clay Jun, Sarah Clay. (Sarah Clay is sister of Daniel Tucker). (See DB 14-216)

DB 14-216, 28 Jul 1777, Daniel Tucker of Dinwiddie Co. to Daniel Pitchford of Amelia Co., for L80., 200 ac. in Amelia Co., on br. of Swethouse Cr., bo. Joshua Spain, Henry Jones, Peter Jones, Richard Hawks. Wit: Joshua Spain, Newman Spain, Mary Spain. S/ Daniel Tucker. (See DB 10-76).

NOTE: In the above deed, the subject Daniel Tucker sold in 1777 the 200 ac. bought from John Clay, and was referred to as "Daniel Tucker of Dinwiddie Co." Only fragmented records remain for Dinwiddie Co, so we have no record of Daniel there. However, Mecklenburg Co. DB 6-465 (1784) referred to "Daniel Tucker of Dinwiddie Co.", and DB 6-510 (1785) referred to "Daniel Tucker of Mecklenburg Co." The subject Daniel Tucker's oldest brother James and his descendants, also lived in Prince George, Dinwiddie, Lunenburg & in Mecklenburg Co. after 1765.

BODDIE[2]

But before we look at Mecklenburg Co, VA, let us consider the writings of Boddie. In referring to Daniel Tucker son of Robert & Martha, and to DB 14-216 above, he said "on account of the name "SPAIN", it is believed that these deeds were those of Daniel Tucker who moved to Wake County, N.C. and died there with a will - dated 1790, probated 1792 - wife not named - Children: Mary Spain, Martha Ellington, Elizabeth Guerrant, William Tucker, Sally Ellington, Daniel Tucker, Pascal Tucker, Nancy Tucker, Lucy Maxey, Joseph Tucker, Rebecca Russell, Mason Fowler, Pleasant Tucker; grandchildren: Spain, Eppes, Sally, Pascal".

320

Now the subject Daniel Tucker (b 1725, son of Robert Sr & Martha) had a nephew, Daniel Tucker (1740-1818, son of Robert Jr & Frances) who, according to Boddie, also lived for a time in Wake Co., NC before moving to Georgia. See separate chapter for that Daniel Tucker son of Robert Jr.

The subject Daniel Tucker (b 1725 son of Robert Sr & Martha) also had another nephew Daniel (b ca 1740 son of William & Ann). That Daniel was listed as a separate household beginning in 1767 and specifically identified as "Daniel Tucker son of William". He lived in Amelia and Nottoway Co. until he sold his land in 1808 and left Nottoway. See separate chapter for that Daniel Tucker son of William.

There was yet another Daniel Tucker, b 29 Jan 1725, son of William and Eliza, according to Boddie's Bristol Parish Register.

Also, the subject Daniel Tucker (b 1725 and his brother Joseph b 1722, sons of Robert Sr & Martha) are not to be confused with earlier brothers Daniel & Joseph Tucker who patented land in 1724 in Pr. Geo. Co. (now Dinwiddie) and would have been born prior to 1703. Daniel Tucker, Patent 12-299 (1724) 129 ac btwn his brother Jos. Tucker & Maj. Robert Munford.

In Surry Co, a Daniel Tucker Patent 12-447 (1725) 215 ac.

In Amhearst Co, a Daniel Tucker, Patent 41-443 (1773) 6 ac. & Patent 54-361 (1805) 100 ac.

In Mecklenburg Co DB 6-34 (1780), a Daniel Tucker & wf Jane sold 55 ac, and WB 10-96 (1824) Daniel Tucker Sr's will named wife Jane & son Daniel Jr. In 1787, a Daniel Tucker md Jincy Cardin; in 1808, a Daniel Tucker Jr md Mary Parrish.

In Prince Edward Co, a Daniel Tucker, Patent 39-485 (1797) 98 ac.

Because there were so many Daniel Tuckers living in the same areas during the same time periods, it is almost impossible to sort them out. But because of the sequence of dates, it appears the Daniel Tucker Sr (b 1725 son of Robert Sr & Martha) is the same "Daniel Tucker of Dinwiddie" who sold his land in Amelia in 1777. But he does not appear to be the same "Daniel Tucker of Dinwiddie" who bought land in Mecklenburg beginning in 1766, and he does not appear to be the same Daniel Tucker Sr who died in Mecklenburg in 1824.

In the absence of any more definitive data, we have only Boddie's account of Daniel Tucker in Wake Co., NC, which is summarized here without verification:

SUMMARY: Daniel Tucker b 1725 in Prince George Co. Va., son of Capt Robert Tucker Sr & wf Martha, married Elizabeth ____, inherited 176 ac. in Amelia Co. from his father in 1750, sold that inheritance and bought 200 ac. in Amelia Co. from his brother-in-law & sister in 1768, sold the 200 ac. in 1777 as "Daniel Tucker of Dinwiddie" Co. According to Boddie, the subject Daniel Tucker died 1792 in Wake Co., NC, leaving issue (not verified by this compiler):

Mary Tucker md ____ Spain

Martha Tucker md ____ Ellington

Elizabeth Tucker md ____ Guerrant

William Tucker

Sally Tucker md ____ Ellington

Daniel Tucker

Pascal Tucker

Nancy Tucker

Lucy Tucker md ____ Maxey

Joseph Tucker

Rebecca Tucker md ____ Russell

Mason Fowler (?)

Pleasant Tucker

* * *

1. Boddie, John B., "Births 1720-1792 From The Bristol Parish Register of Henrico, Prince George and Dinwiddie"

2. Boddie, John B., "Historical Southern Families", Vol II, pp 259-60

INDEX

325

330

S

T

333

335

www.ingramcontent.com/pod-product-compliance
Lightning Source LLC
Chambersburg PA
CBHW060000100426
42740CB00010B/1349